WAGE SLAVES

Translation made in arrangement with AM-Book (www.am-book.com)

Translated by Hanna Strömberg.
International imprint edited by Andy Brown
Production assistance by Noah Van Nostrand

First English North American Edition

Library and Archives Canada Cataloguing in Publication

Bogdanska, Daria, 1988-
[Wage Slaves. English]
    Wage Slaves / written and illustrated by Daria Bogdanska ; translated by
Hanna Strömberg.

Translation of: Wage Slaves.
ISBN 978-1-77262-036-8 (softcover)

    1. Bogdanska, Daria, 1988- --Comic books, strips, etc. 2. Wages--Foreign
workers--Sweden--Malmö--Comic books, strips, etc. 3. Foreign workers--Legal
status, laws, etc.--Sweden--Malmö--Comic books, strips, etc. 4. Immigrants--
Employment--Sweden--Malmö--Comic books, strips, etc. 5. Autobiographical
comics. 6. Nonfiction comics. I. Strömberg, Hanna, 1974-, translator II. Title.
III. Title: Wage Slaves. English.

HD8580.M35B6413 2019   331.6'209485022   C2018-905608-8

Part of the international imprint from Conundrum Press
Conundrum Press
Wolfville, Nova Scotia, Canada
www.conundrumpress.com

Conundrum Press acknowledges the financial assistance of the Canada Council for
the Arts, the Government of Canada, and the Nova Scotia Creative Industries
Fund toward this publication.

The cost of this translation was defrayed by a subsidy from the Swedish Arts
Council, gratefully acknowledged.

Canada Council   Conseil des Arts
for the Arts   du Canada

Canada   NOVA SCOTIA

FOR MY MOM, ALDONA, AND MY GRANDMOTHER IRENA

THANK YOU: MENDI, KRISSE, JOHANNA, DYLAN, SEBASTIAN, HAENNES,
SAM, MISCHA AND ALL OF SMEDSTORP, LIV MAREND, JOHANNA
KARLSSON, DANIEL, HENRIK BROMANDER, HANNA PETTERSSON, ALL
THE TEACHERS AT THE COMIC ART SCHOOL, DOTTERBOLAGET,
KÄLLAREKOLLEKTIVET, HANNA LT, HENRIK JOHANSSON, DANIEL AGU-
IRRE, MALMÖ LS, DAVID E, FREDRIK, MARKUS, MAC, AUGUST, AMY,
SCOUT, LINNEA, MATTIAS E, MALMÖ PUNX, MARIE, AJ,
JOSEFINE EDENVIK, JOHANNES KLENELL, KAROLINA BANG
AND ALL OF MY FRIENDS WHO HAVE HELPED ME BUT WHOM I'VE
FORGOTTEN TO MENTION.

DARIA BOGDANSKA

WAGE SLAVES

TRANSLATION BY
HANNA STRÖMBERG

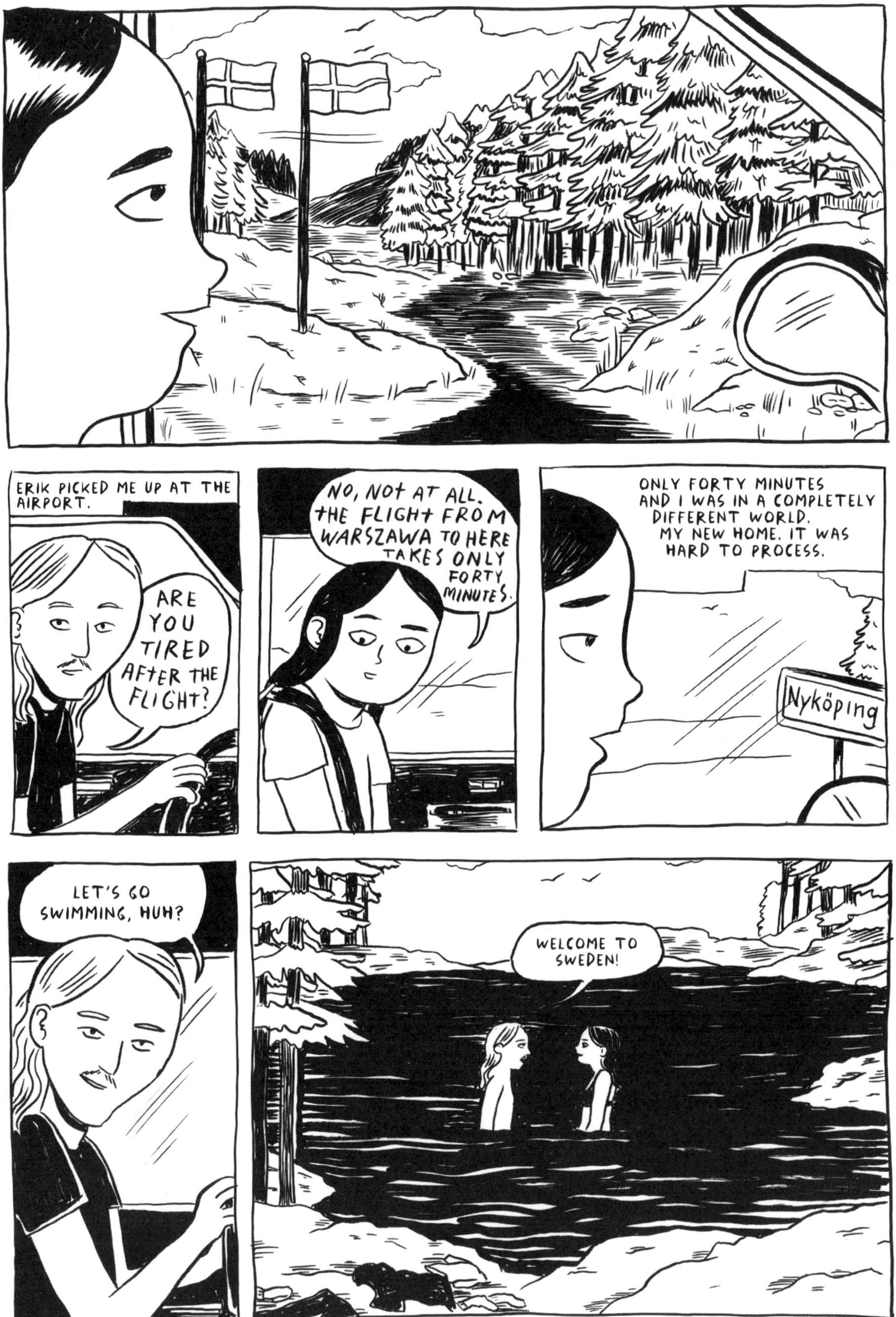
ERIK PICKED ME UP AT THE AIRPORT.
ARE YOU TIRED AFTER THE FLIGHT?
NO, NOT AT ALL. THE FLIGHT FROM WARSZAWA TO HERE TAKES ONLY FORTY MINUTES.
ONLY FORTY MINUTES AND I WAS IN A COMPLETELY DIFFERENT WORLD. MY NEW HOME. IT WAS HARD TO PROCESS.
Nyköping
LET'S GO SWIMMING, HUH?
WELCOME TO SWEDEN!

FINALLY, MALMO!

I HITCHED A RIDE FROM NYKOPING WITH SOME PUNKS IN A VOLKSWAGEN VAN. BOTH ME AND MY CLOTHES REEKED OF SMOKE AND DOG HAIR AFTER THAT RIDE. I STEPPED OUT OF THE OLD VAN AND WENT DIRECTLY TO BE INTERVIEWED FOR A ROOM.

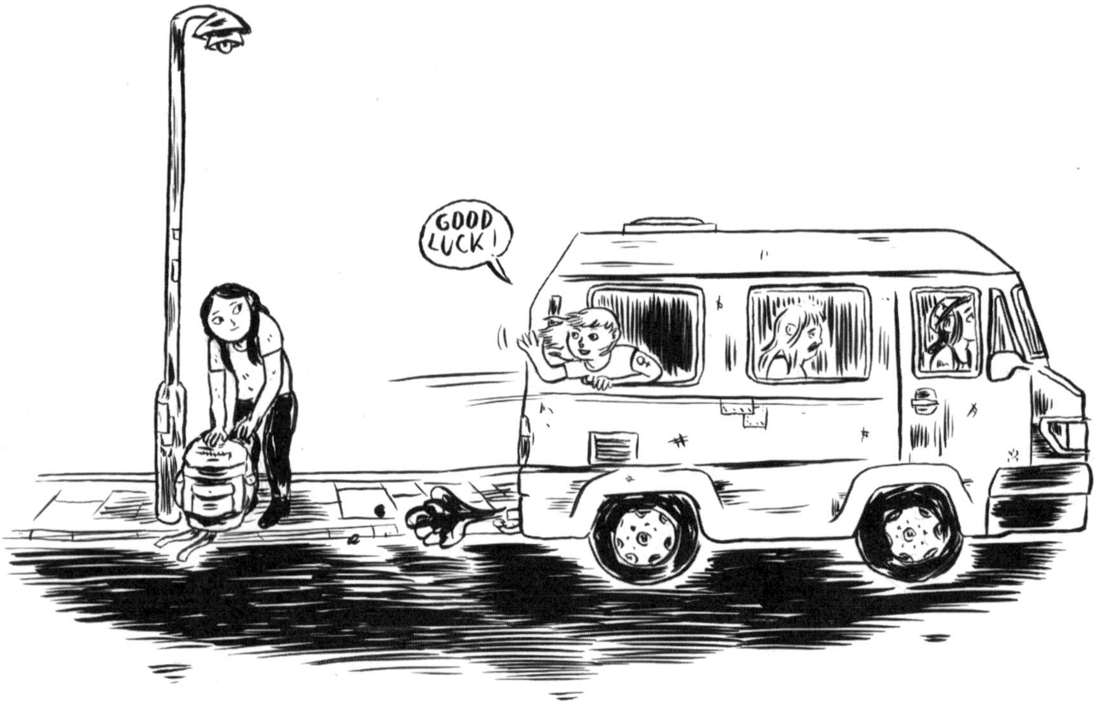
GOOD LUCK!

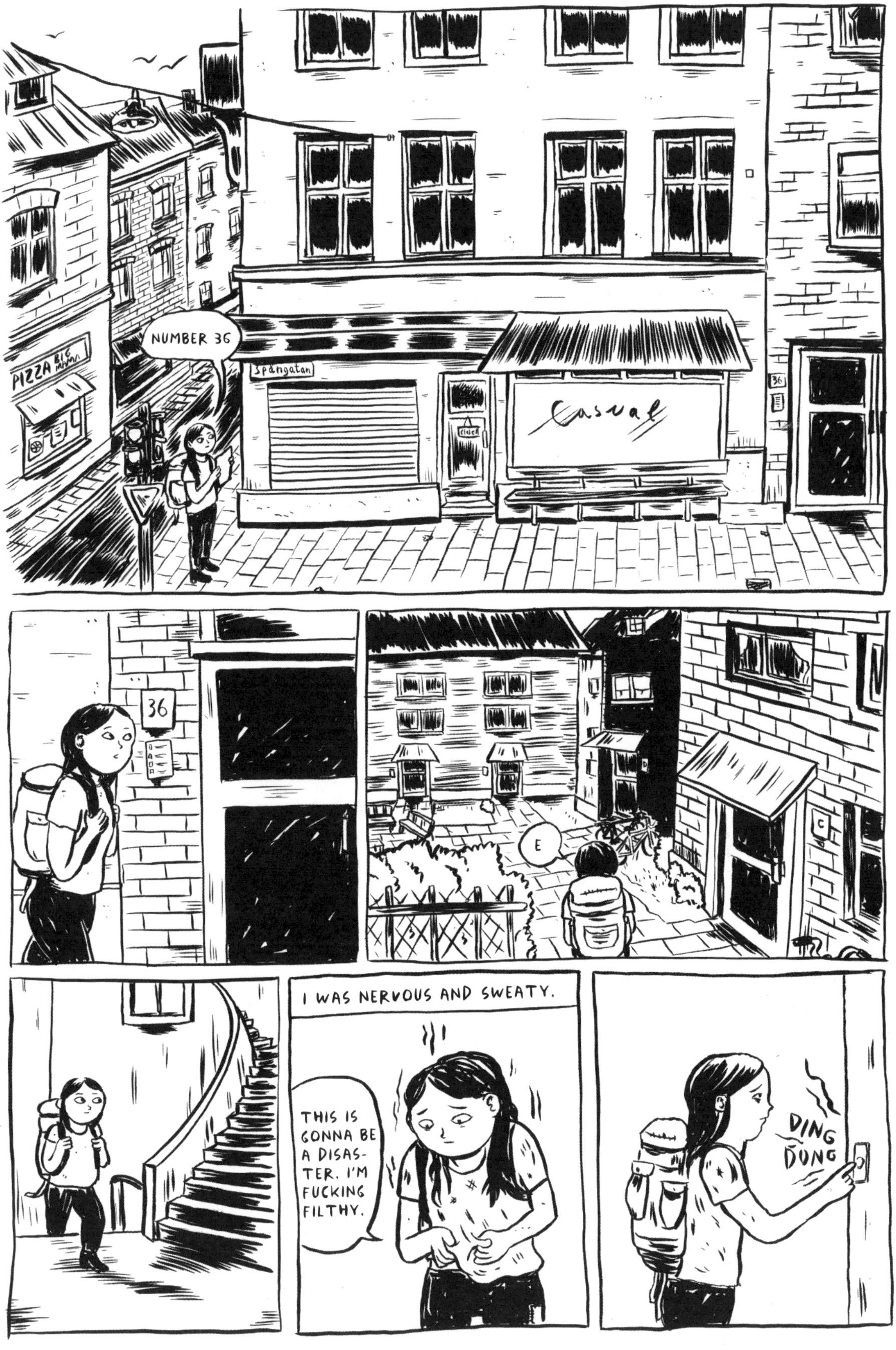
NUMBER 36
PIZZA BIG MAMA
Spångatan
36
E
I WAS NERVOUS AND SWEATY.
THIS IS GONNA BE A DISASTER. I'M FUCKING FILTHY.
DING DONG

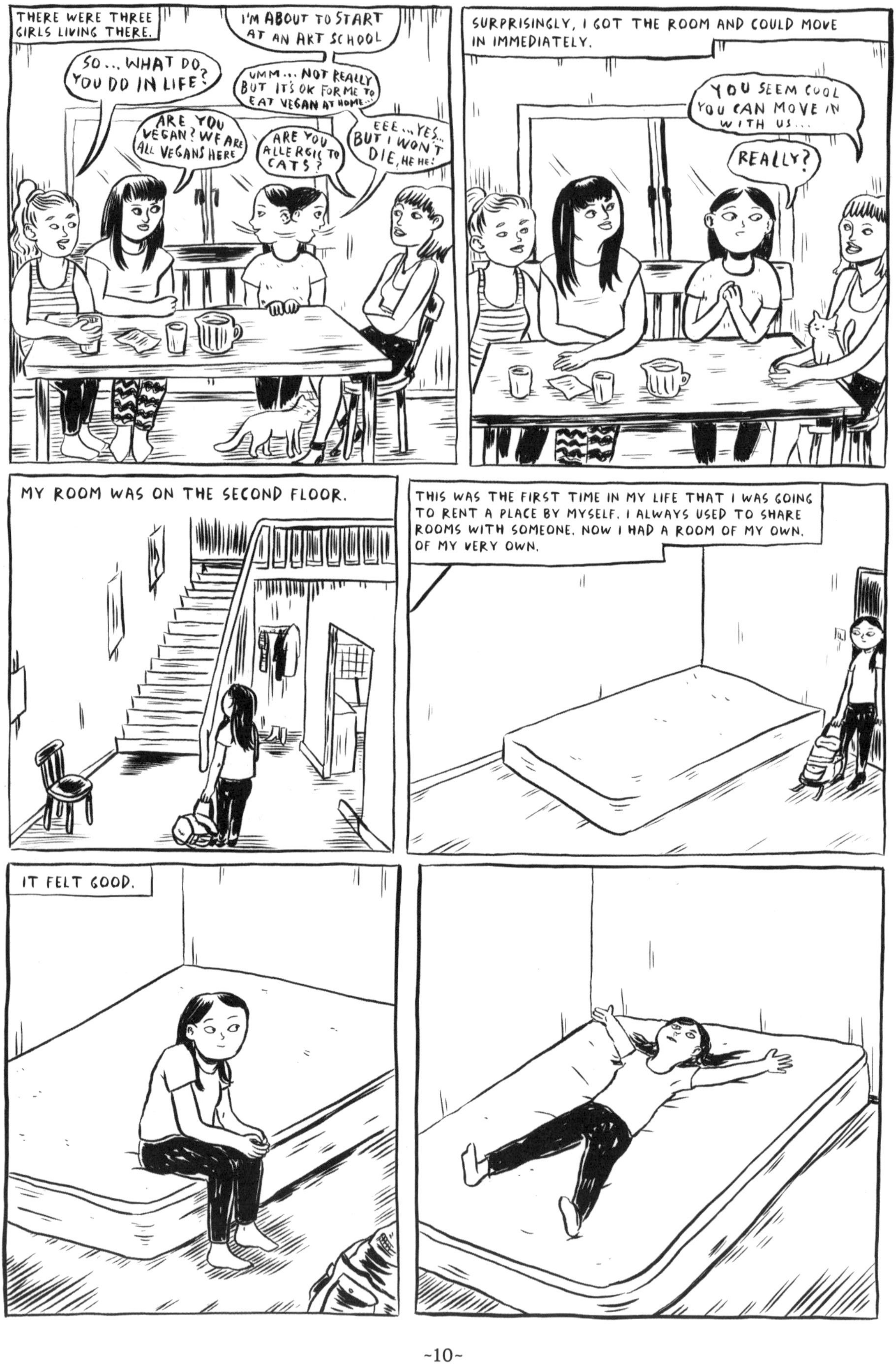
THERE WERE THREE GIRLS LIVING THERE.
SO... WHAT DO YOU DO IN LIFE?
I'M ABOUT TO START AT AN ART SCHOOL
ARE YOU VEGAN? WE ARE ALL VEGANS HERE
UMM... NOT REALLY BUT IT'S OK FOR ME TO EAT VEGAN AT HOME...
ARE YOU ALLERGIC TO CATS?
EEE... YES... BUT I WON'T DIE, HE HE!
SURPRISINGLY, I GOT THE ROOM AND COULD MOVE IN IMMEDIATELY.
YOU SEEM COOL YOU CAN MOVE IN WITH US...
REALLY?
MY ROOM WAS ON THE SECOND FLOOR.
THIS WAS THE FIRST TIME IN MY LIFE THAT I WAS GOING TO RENT A PLACE BY MYSELF. I ALWAYS USED TO SHARE ROOMS WITH SOMEONE. NOW I HAD A ROOM OF MY OWN. OF MY VERY OWN.
IT FELT GOOD.

GOOD MORNING MALMO.

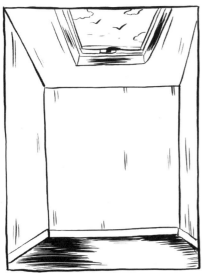

IT WAS MAYBE SIX IN THE MORNING, BUT I COULDN'T GET BACK TO SLEEP. I WENT FOR A WALK.

YAAWN

THE STREETS WERE STILL QUIET. IT WAS MY FIRST WALK IN THE CITY THAT WAS GOING TO BE MY HOME. IT FELT BIG. A NEW BEGINNING. INTO THE UNKNOWN. TABULA RASA...

I DIDN'T EVEN KNOW WHERE I WAS. IT JUST FELT GOOD TO WALK, WITHOUT A DESTINATION. "JUST STRAIGHT AHEAD"

"IT'S SO HARD HERE
LIVING ON THE RUN
CAN'T REMEMBER WHERE I BEGUN.
JUST NEED TO ANCHOR
SOLID LIKE A STONE.
PLEASE DON'T REMIND ME
I'LL BE GETTING
HOME"*

MORMORS BAGERI

BUT SOON I WAS HUNGRY, AND I REALIZED I DIDN'T HAVE ANY FOOD AT HOME.

HELP

* GREG SAGE "ON THE RUN"

PANHANDLER'S SIGN = HELP

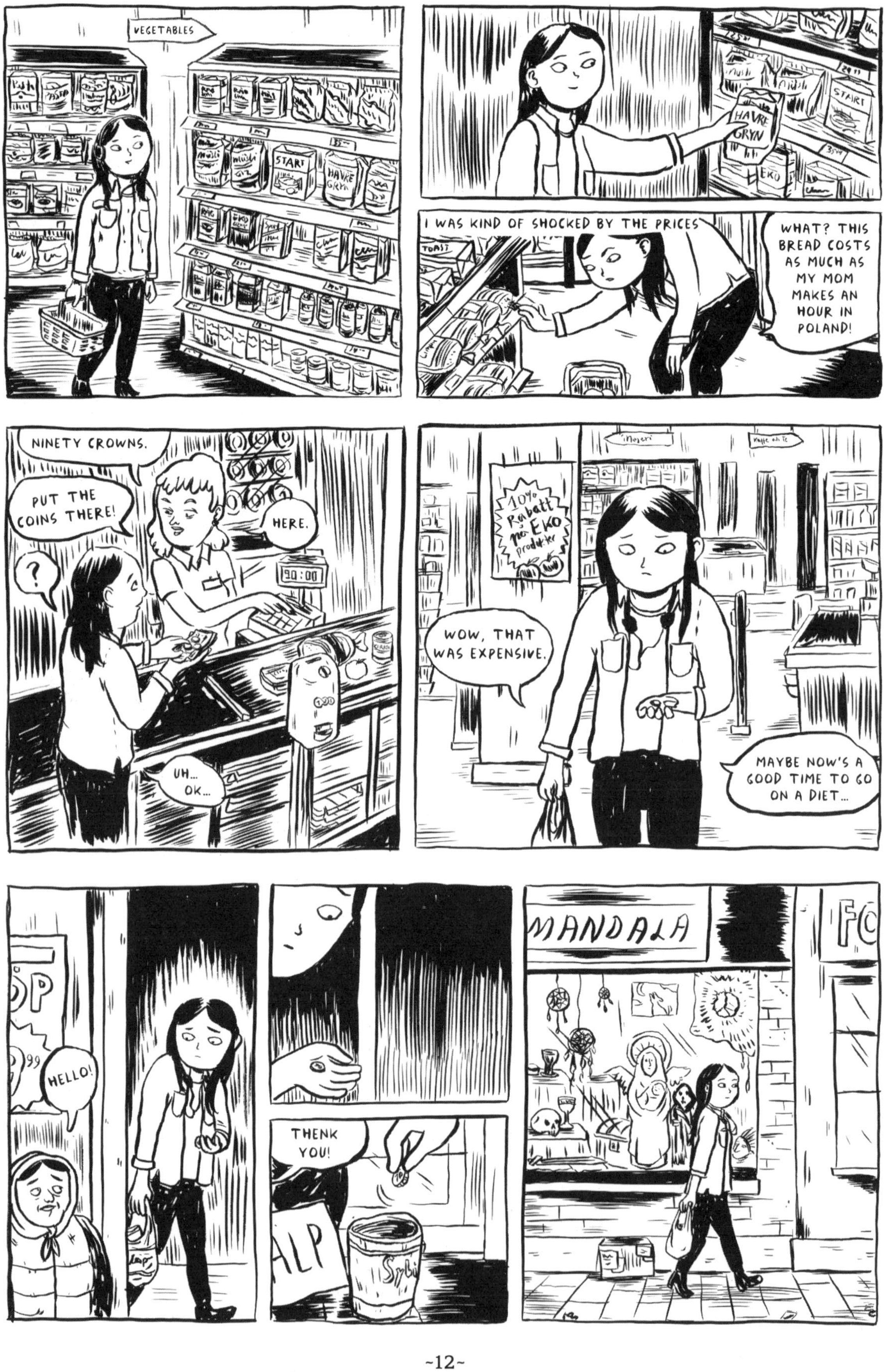
VEGETABLES
START
HAVRE GRYN
I WAS KIND OF SHOCKED BY THE PRICES
TOAST
WHAT? THIS BREAD COSTS AS MUCH AS MY MOM MAKES AN HOUR IN POLAND!
NINETY CROWNS.
PUT THE COINS THERE!
HERE.
?
90:00
UH... OK...
10% Rabatt på EKO produkter
WOW, THAT WAS EXPENSIVE.
MAYBE NOW'S A GOOD TIME TO GO ON A DIET...
HELLO!
THENK YOU!
MANDALA

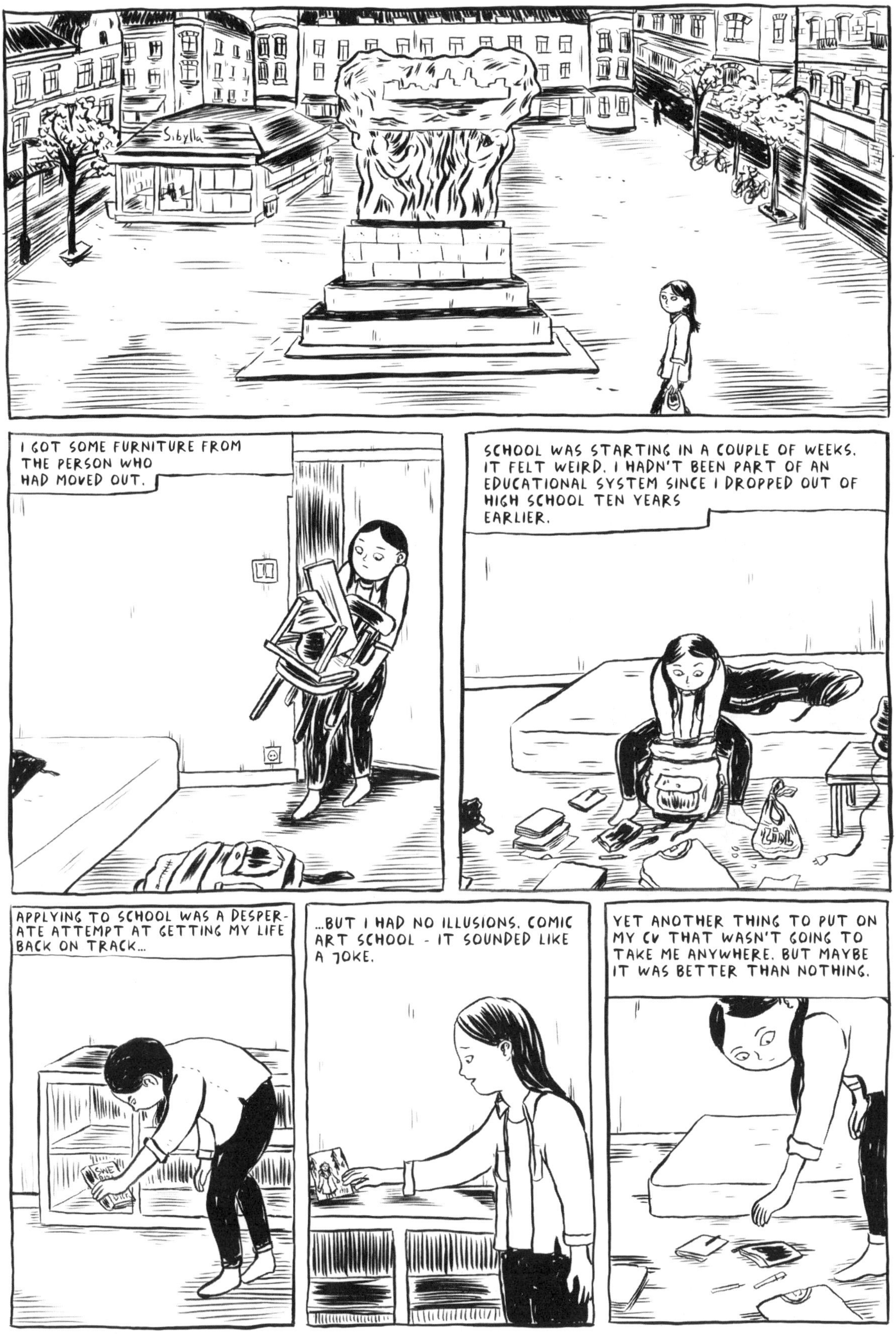
Sibylla
I GOT SOME FURNITURE FROM THE PERSON WHO HAD MOVED OUT.
SCHOOL WAS STARTING IN A COUPLE OF WEEKS. IT FELT WEIRD. I HADN'T BEEN PART OF AN EDUCATIONAL SYSTEM SINCE I DROPPED OUT OF HIGH SCHOOL TEN YEARS EARLIER.
APPLYING TO SCHOOL WAS A DESPERATE ATTEMPT AT GETTING MY LIFE BACK ON TRACK...
...BUT I HAD NO ILLUSIONS. COMIC ART SCHOOL - IT SOUNDED LIKE A JOKE.
YET ANOTHER THING TO PUT ON MY CV THAT WASN'T GOING TO TAKE ME ANYWHERE. BUT MAYBE IT WAS BETTER THAN NOTHING.

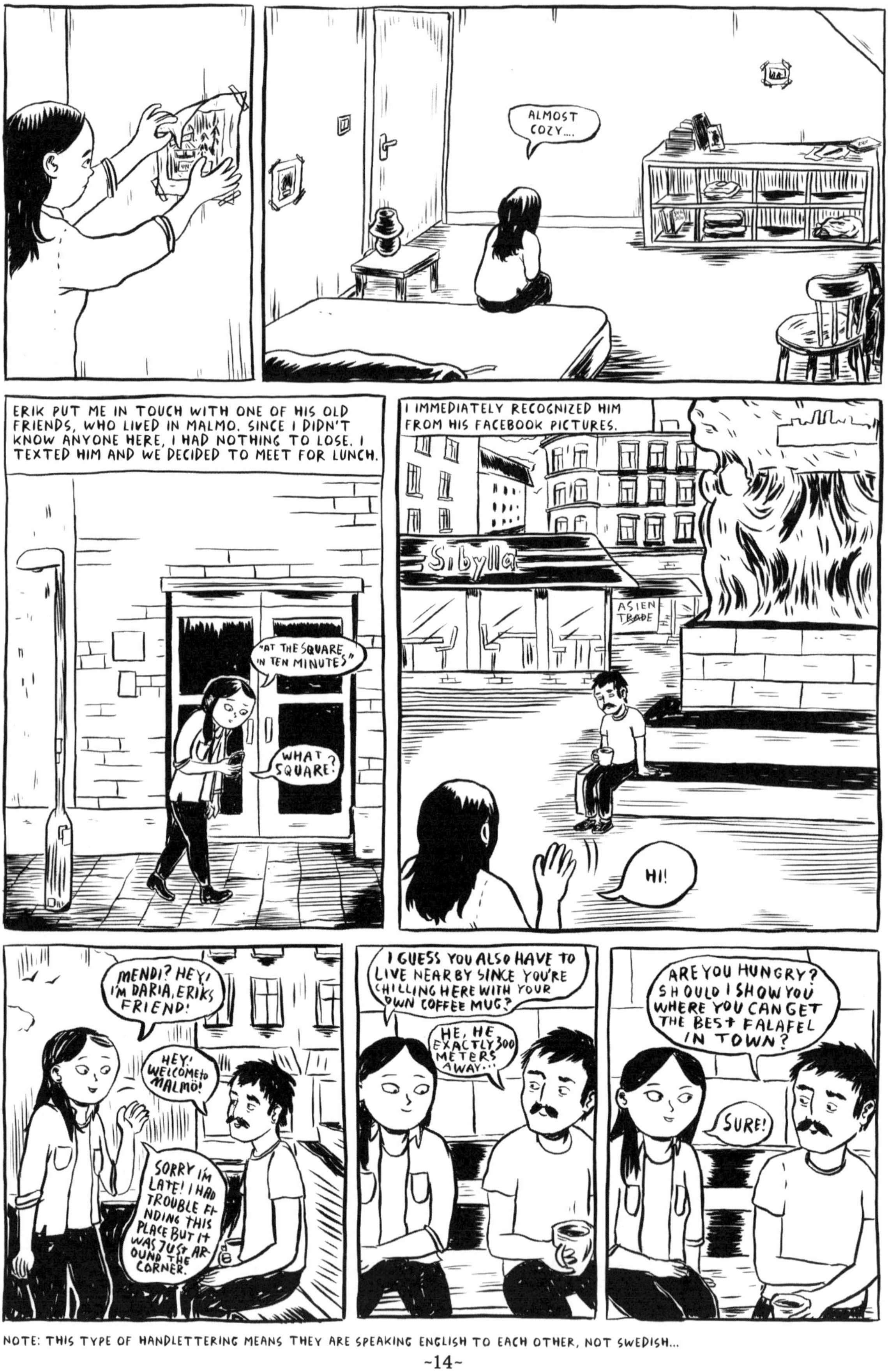
ALMOST COZY....
ERIK PUT ME IN TOUCH WITH ONE OF HIS OLD FRIENDS, WHO LIVED IN MALMO. SINCE I DIDN'T KNOW ANYONE HERE, I HAD NOTHING TO LOSE. I TEXTED HIM AND WE DECIDED TO MEET FOR LUNCH.
"AT THE SQUARE, IN TEN MINUTES"
WHAT SQUARE?
I IMMEDIATELY RECOGNIZED HIM FROM HIS FACEBOOK PICTURES.
Sibylla
ASIEN TRADE
HI!
MENDI? HEY, I'M DARIA, ERIK'S FRIEND!
HEY! WELCOME to MALMÖ!
SORRY I'M LATE! I HAD TROUBLE FINDING THIS PLACE BUT IT WAS JUST AROUND THE CORNER.
I GUESS YOU ALSO HAVE TO LIVE NEARBY SINCE YOU'RE CHILLING HERE WITH YOUR OWN COFFEE MUG?
HE, HE EXACTLY 300 METERS AWAY...
ARE YOU HUNGRY? SHOULD I SHOW YOU WHERE YOU CAN GET THE BEST FALAFEL IN TOWN?
SURE!

NOTE: THIS TYPE OF HANDLETTERING MEANS THEY ARE SPEAKING ENGLISH TO EACH OTHER, NOT SWEDISH...

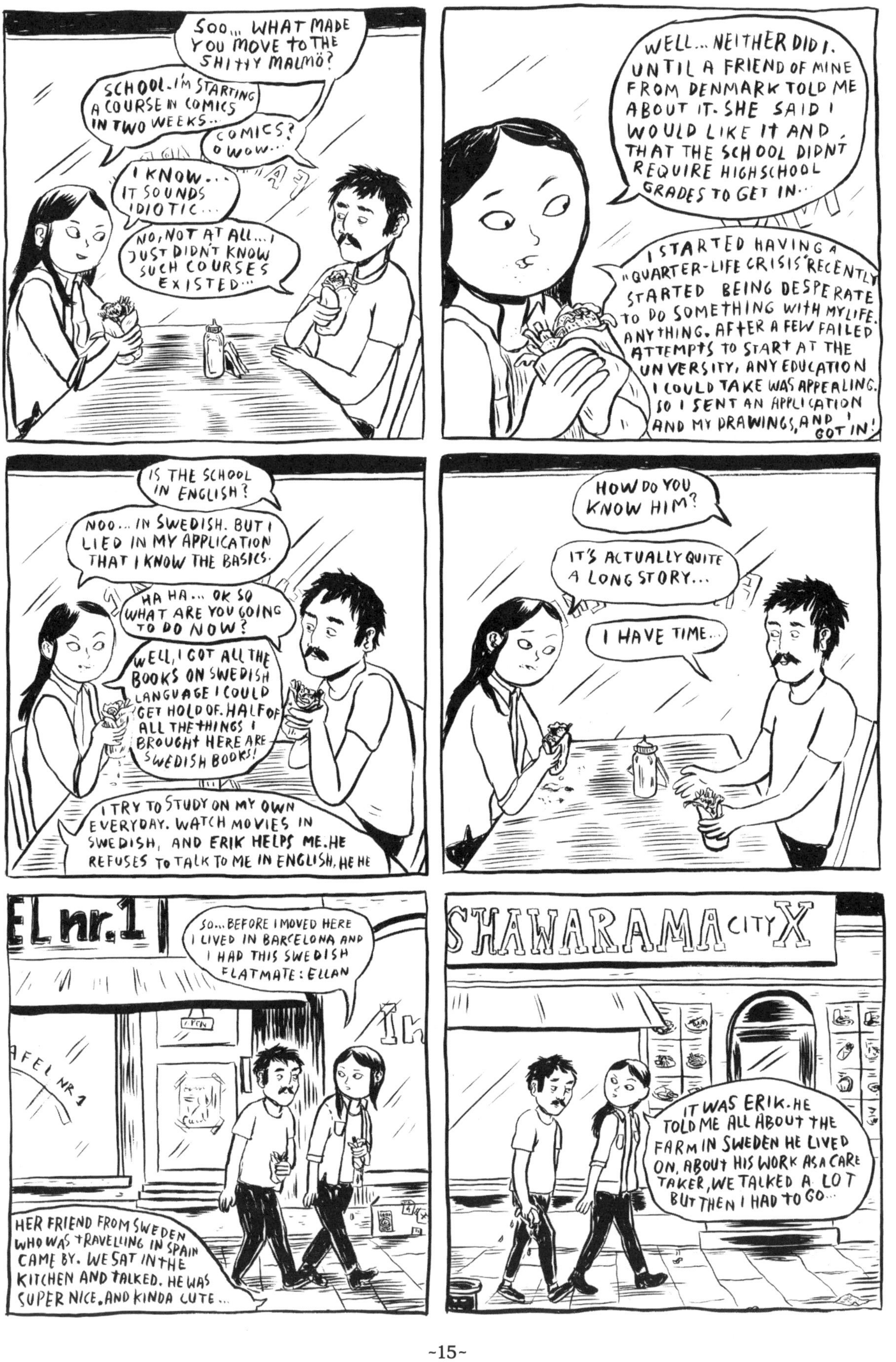
SOO... WHAT MADE YOU MOVE TO THE SHITTY MALMÖ?
SCHOOL. I'M STARTING A COURSE IN COMICS IN TWO WEEKS...
COMICS? O WOW...
I KNOW... IT SOUNDS IDIOTIC...
NO, NOT AT ALL... I JUST DIDN'T KNOW SUCH COURSES EXISTED...
WELL... NEITHER DID I. UNTIL A FRIEND OF MINE FROM DENMARK TOLD ME ABOUT IT. SHE SAID I WOULD LIKE IT AND THAT THE SCHOOL DIDN'T REQUIRE HIGHSCHOOL GRADES TO GET IN...
I STARTED HAVING A "QUARTER-LIFE CRISIS" RECENTLY. STARTED BEING DESPERATE TO DO SOMETHING WITH MY LIFE. ANYTHING. AFTER A FEW FAILED ATTEMPTS TO START AT THE UNVERSITY, ANY EDUCATION I COULD TAKE WAS APPEALING. SO I SENT AN APPLICATION AND MY DRAWINGS, AND I GOT IN!
IS THE SCHOOL IN ENGLISH?
NOO... IN SWEDISH. BUT I LIED IN MY APPLICATION THAT I KNOW THE BASICS.
HA HA... OK SO WHAT ARE YOU GOING TO DO NOW?
WELL, I GOT ALL THE BOOKS ON SWEDISH LANGUAGE I COULD GET HOLD OF. HALF OF ALL THE THINGS I BROUGHT HERE ARE SWEDISH BOOKS!
I TRY TO STUDY ON MY OWN EVERYDAY. WATCH MOVIES IN SWEDISH, AND ERIK HELPS ME. HE REFUSES TO TALK TO ME IN ENGLISH, HE HE
HOW DO YOU KNOW HIM?
IT'S ACTUALLY QUITE A LONG STORY...
I HAVE TIME...
EL nr.1
SO... BEFORE I MOVED HERE I LIVED IN BARCELONA AND I HAD THIS SWEDISH FLATMATE: ELLAN
HER FRIEND FROM SWEDEN WHO WAS TRAVELLING IN SPAIN CAME BY. WE SAT IN THE KITCHEN AND TALKED. HE WAS SUPER NICE. AND KINDA CUTE...
SHAWARAMA CITY X
IT WAS ERIK. HE TOLD ME ALL ABOUT THE FARM IN SWEDEN HE LIVED ON, ABOUT HIS WORK AS A CARE TAKER, WE TALKED A LOT BUT THEN I HAD TO GO...

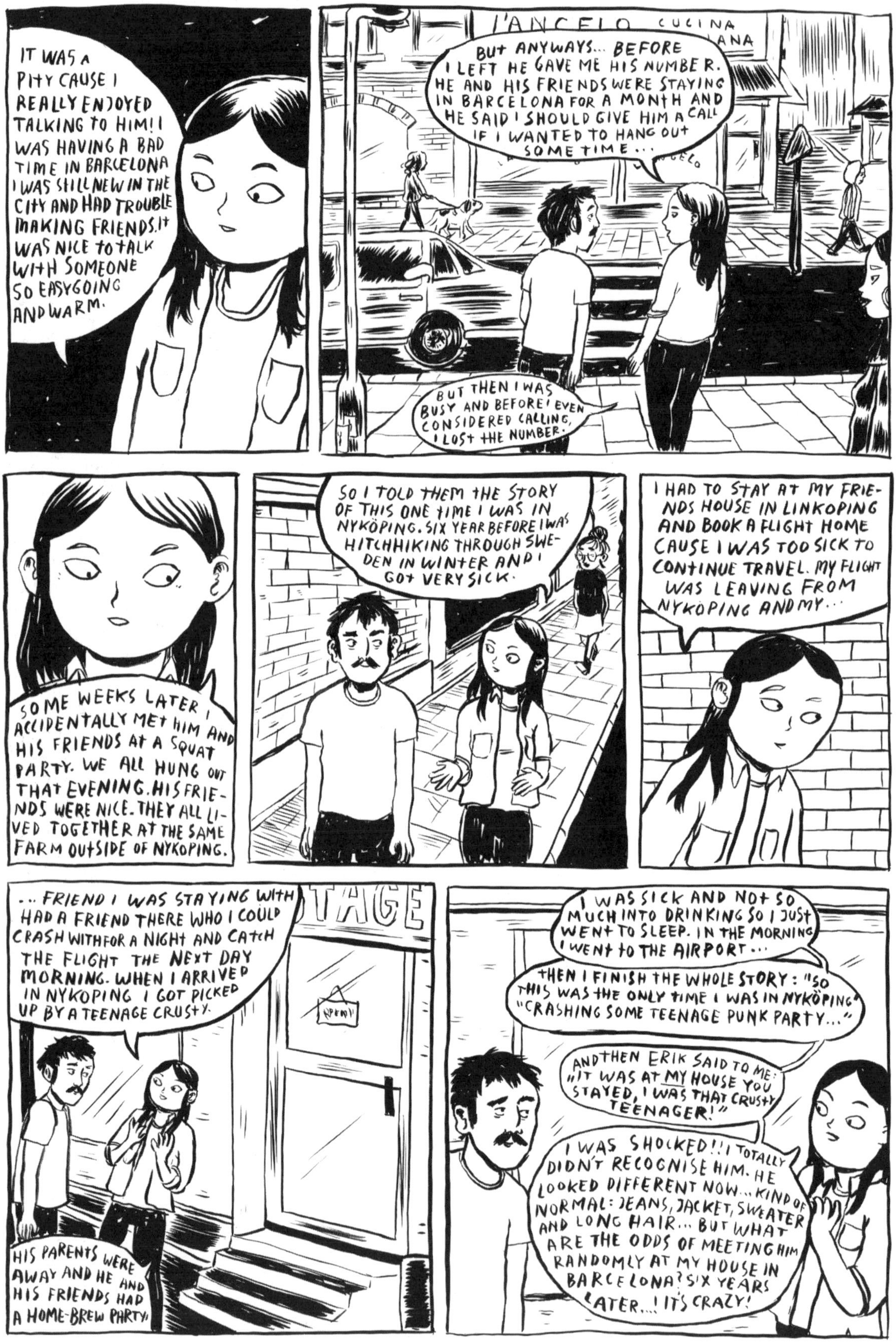
IT WAS A PITY CAUSE I REALLY ENJOYED TALKING TO HIM! I WAS HAVING A BAD TIME IN BARCELONA I WAS STILL NEW IN THE CITY AND HAD TROUBLE MAKING FRIENDS. IT WAS NICE TO TALK WITH SOMEONE SO EASYGOING AND WARM.
BUT ANYWAYS... BEFORE I LEFT HE GAVE ME HIS NUMBER. HE AND HIS FRIENDS WERE STAYING IN BARCELONA FOR A MONTH AND HE SAID I SHOULD GIVE HIM A CALL IF I WANTED TO HANG OUT SOME TIME...
BUT THEN I WAS BUSY AND BEFORE I EVEN CONSIDERED CALLING, I LOST THE NUMBER.
SOME WEEKS LATER I ACCIDENTALLY MET HIM AND HIS FRIENDS AT A SQUAT PARTY. WE ALL HUNG OUT THAT EVENING. HIS FRIENDS WERE NICE. THEY ALL LIVED TOGETHER AT THE SAME FARM OUTSIDE OF NYKOPING.
SO I TOLD THEM THE STORY OF THIS ONE TIME I WAS IN NYKÖPING. SIX YEAR BEFORE I WAS HITCHHIKING THROUGH SWEDEN IN WINTER AND I GOT VERY SICK.
I HAD TO STAY AT MY FRIENDS HOUSE IN LINKOPING AND BOOK A FLIGHT HOME CAUSE I WAS TOO SICK TO CONTINUE TRAVEL. MY FLIGHT WAS LEAVING FROM NYKOPING AND MY...
...FRIEND I WAS STAYING WITH HAD A FRIEND THERE WHO I COULD CRASH WITH FOR A NIGHT AND CATCH THE FLIGHT THE NEXT DAY MORNING. WHEN I ARRIVED IN NYKOPING I GOT PICKED UP BY A TEENAGE CRUSTY.
HIS PARENTS WERE AWAY AND HE AND HIS FRIENDS HAD A HOME-BREW PARTY.
I WAS SICK AND NOT SO MUCH INTO DRINKING SO I JUST WENT TO SLEEP. IN THE MORNING I WENT TO THE AIRPORT...
THEN I FINISH THE WHOLE STORY: "SO THIS WAS THE ONLY TIME I WAS IN NYKÖPING" "CRASHING SOME TEENAGE PUNK PARTY..."
AND THEN ERIK SAID TO ME: "IT WAS AT MY HOUSE YOU STAYED, I WAS THAT CRUSTY TEENAGER!"
I WAS SHOCKED!! I TOTALLY DIDN'T RECOGNISE HIM. HE LOOKED DIFFERENT NOW... KIND OF NORMAL: JEANS, JACKET, SWEATER AND LONG HAIR... BUT WHAT ARE THE ODDS OF MEETING HIM RANDOMLY AT MY HOUSE IN BARCELONA? SIX YEARS LATER...! IT'S CRAZY!

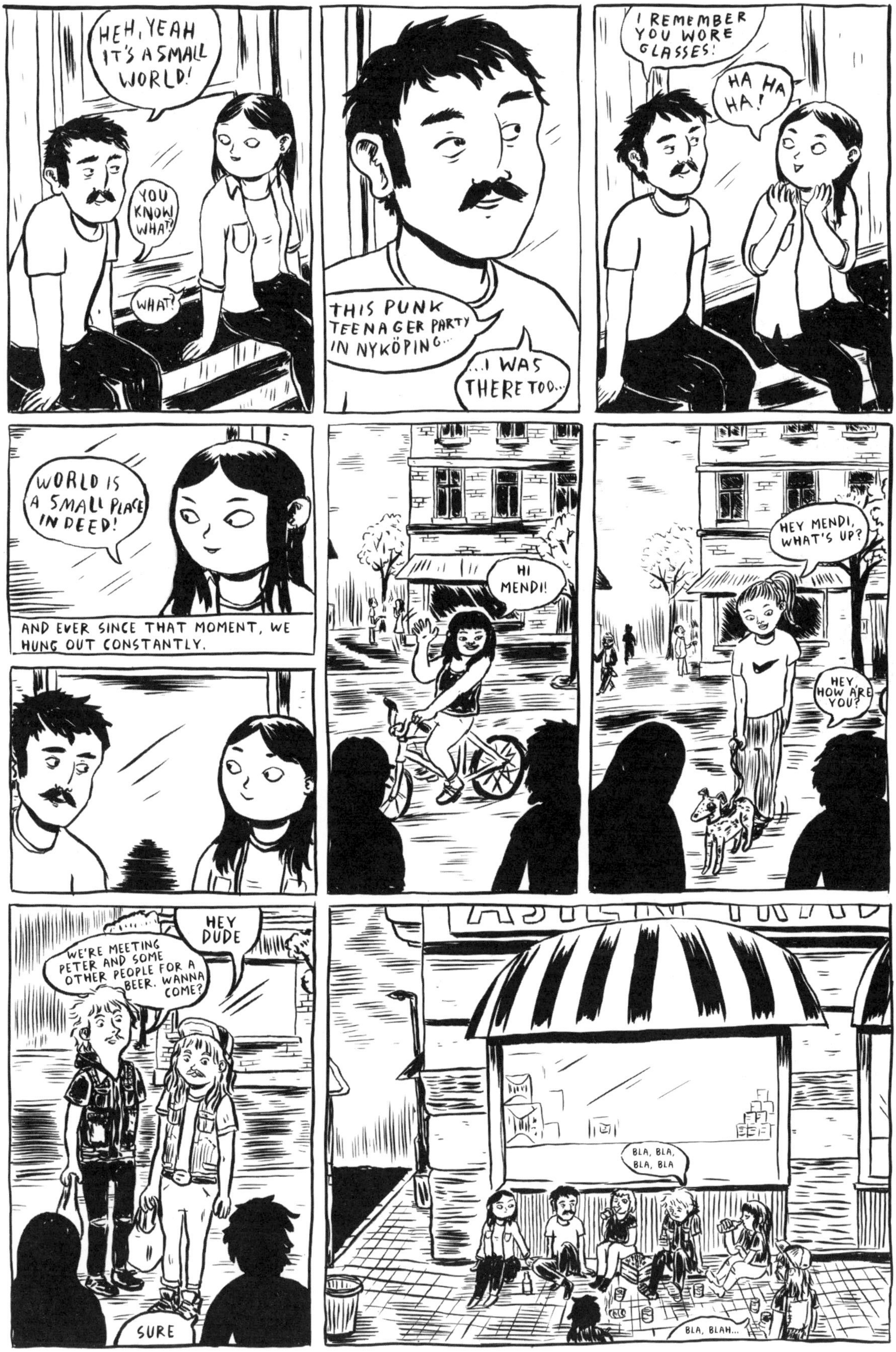
HEH, YEAH IT'S A SMALL WORLD!
YOU KNOW WHAT?
WHAT?
THIS PUNK TEENAGER PARTY IN NYKÖPING...
...I WAS THERE TOO...
I REMEMBER YOU WORE GLASSES!
HA HA HA!
WORLD IS A SMALL PLACE INDEED!
AND EVER SINCE THAT MOMENT, WE HUNG OUT CONSTANTLY.
HI MENDI!
HEY MENDI, WHAT'S UP?
HEY, HOW ARE YOU?
HEY DUDE
WE'RE MEETING PETER AND SOME OTHER PEOPLE FOR A BEER. WANNA COME?
SURE
BLA, BLA, BLA, BLA
BLA, BLAH...

I ONLY HAD ENOUGH MONEY FOR ONE MONTH'S RENT. I NEEDED A JOB. MENDI LENT ME HIS OLD COMPUTER SO I COULD SEARCH ONLINE.

JOBBSAFARI, METROJOBS AND BLOCKET BECAME MY FAVOURITE WEBSITES.

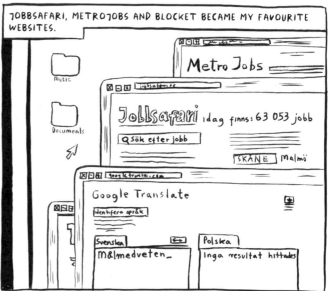

Music

Documents

Metro Jobs

Jobbsafari Idag finns: 63 053 jobb

Sök efter jobb

SKÅNE Malmö

Google Translate

Identifera språk

Svenska   Polska
M&lmedveten_   Inga resultat hittades

SO, WHAT JOBS AWAIT ME TODAY?

PRODUCT MANAGER   SERVICE ADVISOR
EVENT FINANCE ASSISTANT
JUNIOR BRAND MANAGER
            SENIOR PRODUCT COORDINATOR
ACCOUNT MANAGER
SALES MANAGER   CRM ANALITYKER
                        RESOURCE MANAGER
BUSINESS   INTERN-
MANAGER   SERVIS-
                           MEDARBETARE
                        PRODUCTIONS
BUSI...   COACH

WHAT DOES THAT EVEN MEAN?

AREN'T THERE ANY JOBS FOR NORMAL PEOPLE ANYMORE?

I HAD NO EDUCATION, NO USEFUL SKILLS, AND I DIDN'T SPEAK SWEDISH. I FOUND A FORUM FOR THE POLISH COMMUNITY IN SWEDEN.

THIS IS HOPELESS.

SCROLL SCROLL

MOST OF THE ADS WERE FOR TYPICALLY "MALE" JOBS: CONSTRUCTION, PLUMBING, AND PAVING.

Polonia Info

THE ADS DIRECTED AT WOMEN WERE ONLY: CLEANING AND "HOSTESSES". EVERYONE KNEW WHAT THAT MEANT.

CLEANING? WHY NOT?

AND WALK IN MY MOTHER'S FOOTSTEPS...

BUT FOR ALL THE CLEANING JOBS, I HAD TO HAVE A SOCIAL SECURITY NUMBER AND A DRIVER'S LICENSE. I HAD NEITHER.

"HOSTESS"?

HMMM...

NO, DEFINITELY NOT.

SIGN: SKATTEVERKET = TAX AUTHORITY

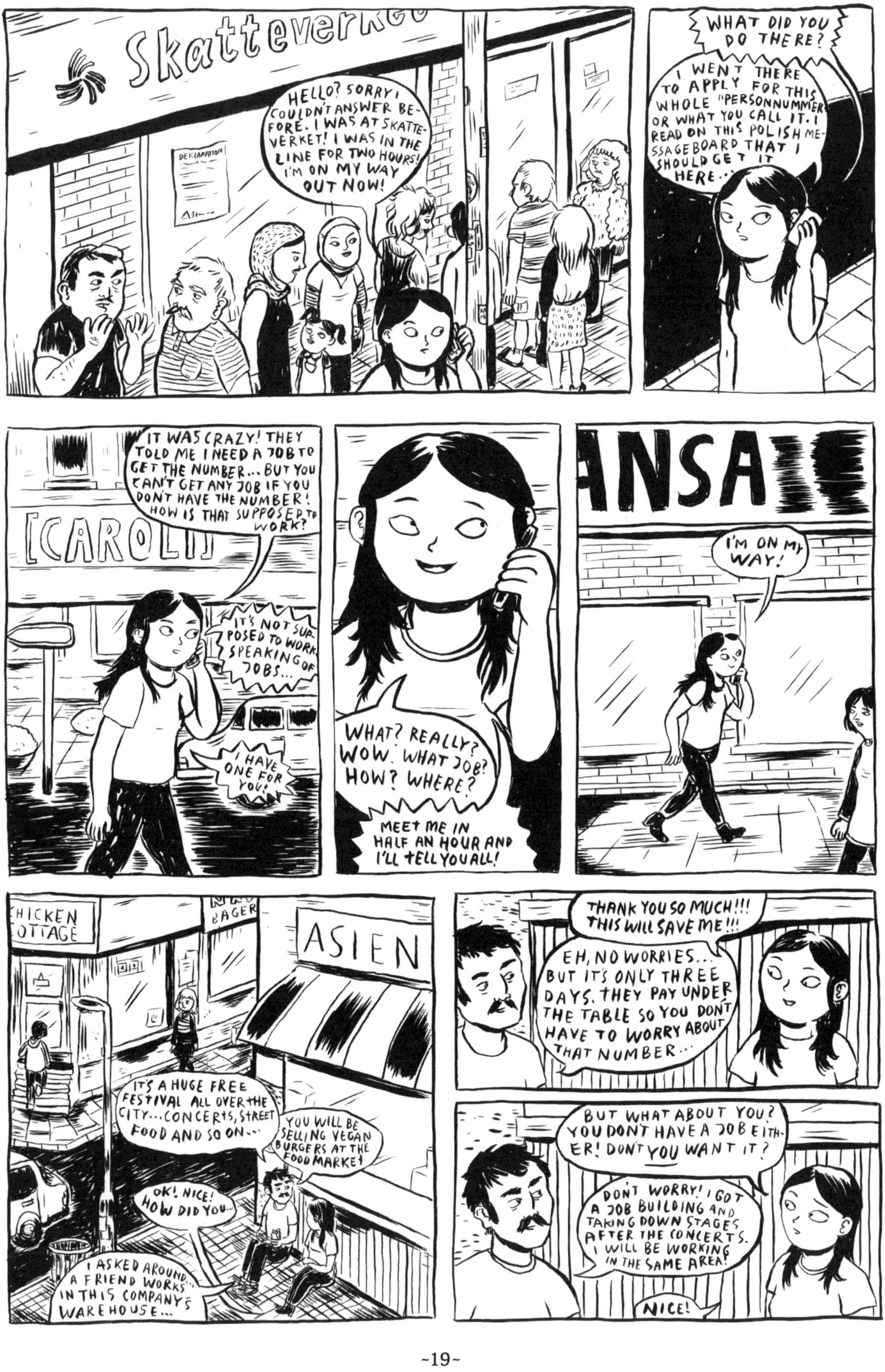
HELLO? SORRY I COULDN'T ANSWER BEFORE. I WAS AT SKATTEVERKET! I WAS IN THE LINE FOR TWO HOURS! I'M ON MY WAY OUT NOW!
WHAT DID YOU DO THERE?
I WENT THERE TO APPLY FOR THIS WHOLE "PERSONNUMMER" OR WHAT YOU CALL IT. I READ ON THIS POLISH MESSAGEBOARD THAT I SHOULD GET IT HERE...
IT WAS CRAZY! THEY TOLD ME I NEED A JOB TO GET THE NUMBER... BUT YOU CAN'T GET ANY JOB IF YOU DON'T HAVE THE NUMBER! HOW IS THAT SUPPOSED TO WORK?
[CAROLI]
IT'S NOT SUPPOSED TO WORK. SPEAKING OF JOBS...
I HAVE ONE FOR YOU!
WHAT? REALLY? WOW. WHAT JOB? HOW? WHERE?
MEET ME IN HALF AN HOUR AND I'LL TELL YOU ALL!
ANSA
I'M ON MY WAY!
BAGER
ASIEN
IT'S A HUGE FREE FESTIVAL ALL OVER THE CITY... CONCERTS, STREET FOOD AND SO ON...
YOU WILL BE SELLING VEGAN BURGERS AT THE FOOD MARKET
OK! NICE! HOW DID YOU...
I ASKED AROUND... A FRIEND WORKS IN THIS COMPANY'S WAREHOUSE...
THANK YOU SO MUCH!!! THIS WILL SAVE ME!!!
EH, NO WORRIES... BUT IT'S ONLY THREE DAYS. THEY PAY UNDER THE TABLE SO YOU DON'T HAVE TO WORRY ABOUT THAT NUMBER...
BUT WHAT ABOUT YOU? YOU DON'T HAVE A JOB EITHER! DON'T YOU WANT IT?
DON'T WORRY! I GOT A JOB BUILDING AND TAKING DOWN STAGES AFTER THE CONCERTS. I WILL BE WORKING IN THE SAME AREA!
NICE!

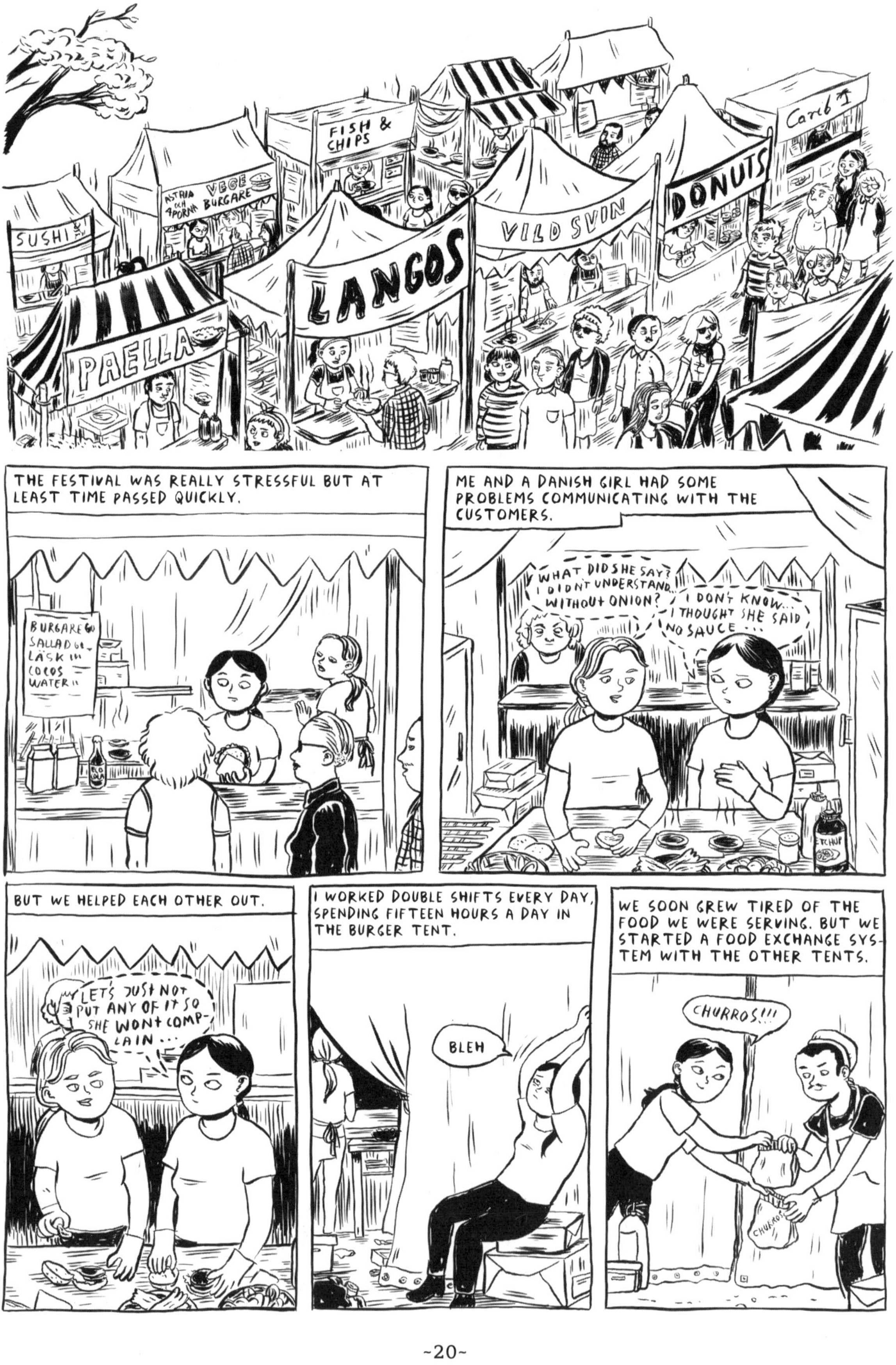

SUSHI
ASTRID OCH APORNA
VEGE BURGARE
FISH & CHIPS
Carib
LANGOS
VILD SVIN
DONUTS
PAELLA
THE FESTIVAL WAS REALLY STRESSFUL BUT AT LEAST TIME PASSED QUICKLY.
BURGARE
SALLAD
LÄSK
COCOS WATER
ME AND A DANISH GIRL HAD SOME PROBLEMS COMMUNICATING WITH THE CUSTOMERS.
WHAT DID SHE SAY? I DIDN'T UNDERSTAND... WITHOUT ONION?
I DON'T KNOW... I THOUGHT SHE SAID NO SAUCE...
BUT WE HELPED EACH OTHER OUT.
LET'S JUST NOT PUT ANY OF IT SO SHE WON'T COMPLAIN...
I WORKED DOUBLE SHIFTS EVERY DAY, SPENDING FIFTEEN HOURS A DAY IN THE BURGER TENT.
BLEH
WE SOON GREW TIRED OF THE FOOD WE WERE SERVING. BUT WE STARTED A FOOD EXCHANGE SYSTEM WITH THE OTHER TENTS.
CHURROS!!!
CHURROS

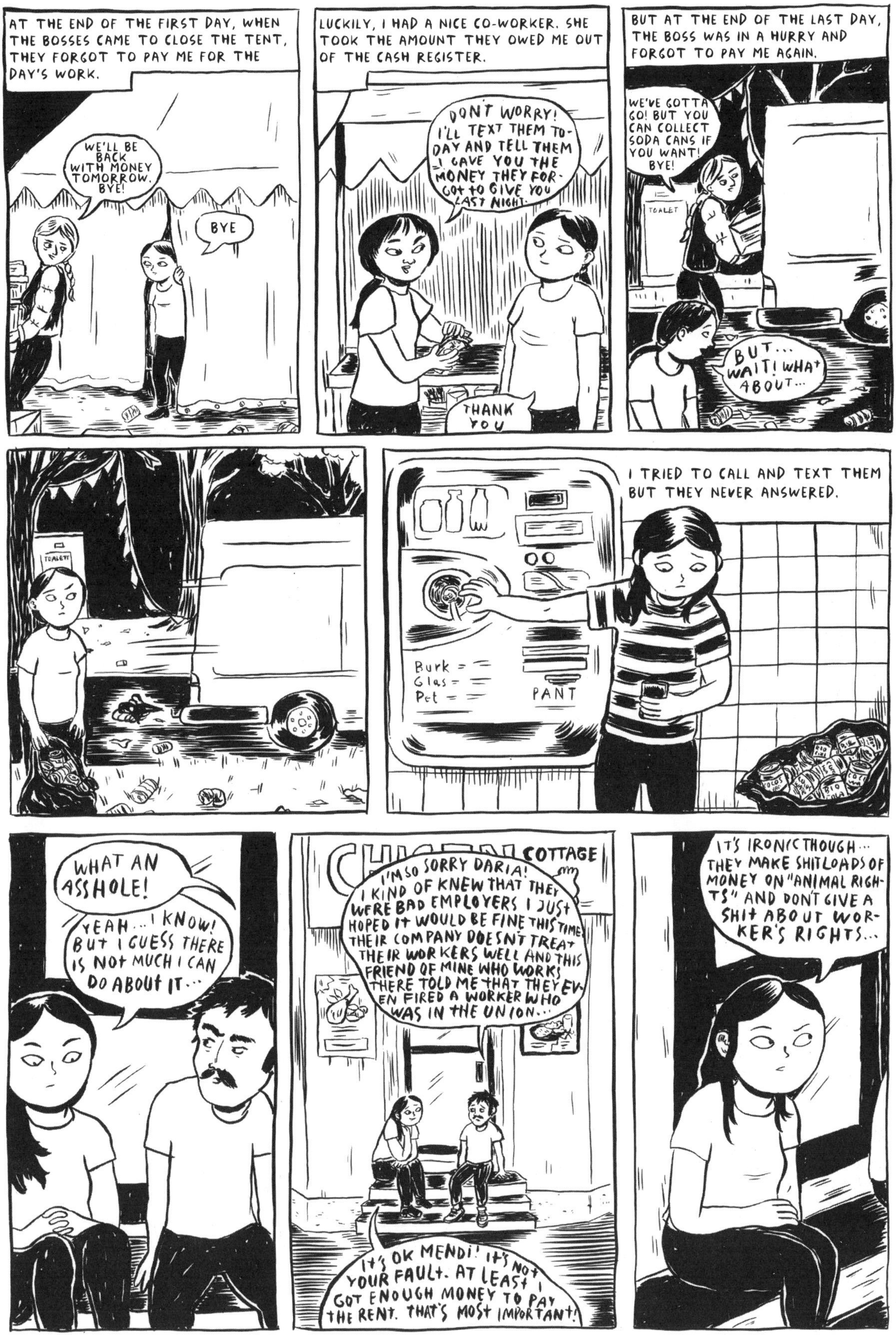
AT THE END OF THE FIRST DAY, WHEN THE BOSSES CAME TO CLOSE THE TENT, THEY FORGOT TO PAY ME FOR THE DAY'S WORK.
WE'LL BE BACK WITH MONEY TOMORROW. BYE!
BYE
LUCKILY, I HAD A NICE CO-WORKER. SHE TOOK THE AMOUNT THEY OWED ME OUT OF THE CASH REGISTER.
DON'T WORRY! I'LL TEXT THEM TODAY AND TELL THEM I GAVE YOU THE MONEY THEY FORGOT TO GIVE YOU LAST NIGHT.
THANK YOU
BUT AT THE END OF THE LAST DAY, THE BOSS WAS IN A HURRY AND FORGOT TO PAY ME AGAIN.
WE'VE GOTTA GO! BUT YOU CAN COLLECT SODA CANS IF YOU WANT! BYE!
TOALET
BUT... WAIT! WHAT ABOUT...
TOALETT
I TRIED TO CALL AND TEXT THEM BUT THEY NEVER ANSWERED.
Burk
Glas
Pet
PANT
WHAT AN ASSHOLE!
YEAH... I KNOW! BUT I GUESS THERE IS NOT MUCH I CAN DO ABOUT IT...
COTTAGE
I'M SO SORRY DARIA! I KIND OF KNEW THAT THEY WERE BAD EMPLOYERS I JUST HOPED IT WOULD BE FINE THIS TIME. THEIR COMPANY DOESN'T TREAT THEIR WORKERS WELL AND THIS FRIEND OF MINE WHO WORKS THERE TOLD ME THAT THEY EVEN FIRED A WORKER WHO WAS IN THE UNION...
IT'S OK MENDI! IT'S NOT YOUR FAULT. AT LEAST I GOT ENOUGH MONEY TO PAY THE RENT. THAT'S MOST IMPORTANT!
IT'S IRONIC THOUGH... THEY MAKE SHITLOADS OF MONEY ON "ANIMAL RIGHTS" AND DON'T GIVE A SHIT ABOUT WORKER'S RIGHTS...

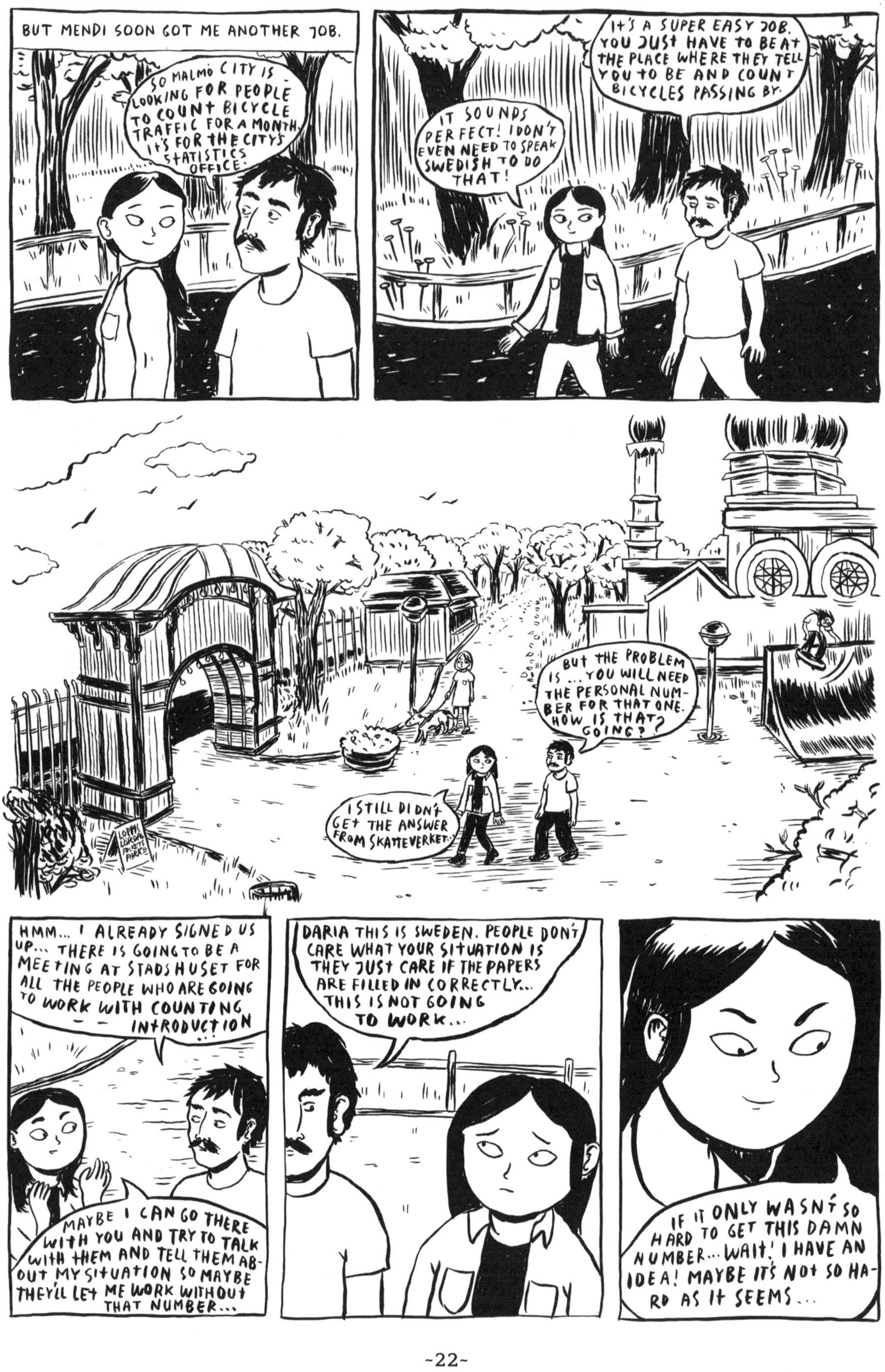
BUT MENDI SOON GOT ME ANOTHER JOB.
SO MALMÖ CITY IS LOOKING FOR PEOPLE TO COUNT BICYCLE TRAFFIC FOR A MONTH. IT'S FOR THE CITY'S STATISTICS OFFICE.
IT'S A SUPER EASY JOB. YOU JUST HAVE TO BE AT THE PLACE WHERE THEY TELL YOU TO BE AND COUNT BICYCLES PASSING BY.
IT SOUNDS PERFECT! I DON'T EVEN NEED TO SPEAK SWEDISH TO DO THAT!
BUT THE PROBLEM IS ... YOU WILL NEED THE PERSONAL NUMBER FOR THAT ONE. HOW IS THAT GOING?
I STILL DIDN'T GET THE ANSWER FROM SKATTEVERKET...
HMM... I ALREADY SIGNED US UP... THERE IS GOING TO BE A MEETING AT STADSHUSET FOR ALL THE PEOPLE WHO ARE GOING TO WORK WITH COUNTING -- INTRODUCTION...
MAYBE I CAN GO THERE WITH YOU AND TRY TO TALK WITH THEM AND TELL THEM ABOUT MY SITUATION SO MAYBE THEY'LL LET ME WORK WITHOUT THAT NUMBER...
DARIA THIS IS SWEDEN. PEOPLE DON'T CARE WHAT YOUR SITUATION IS THEY JUST CARE IF THE PAPERS ARE FILLED IN CORRECTLY... THIS IS NOT GOING TO WORK...
IF IT ONLY WASN'T SO HARD TO GET THIS DAMN NUMBER... WAIT! I HAVE AN IDEA! MAYBE IT'S NOT SO HARD AS IT SEEMS...

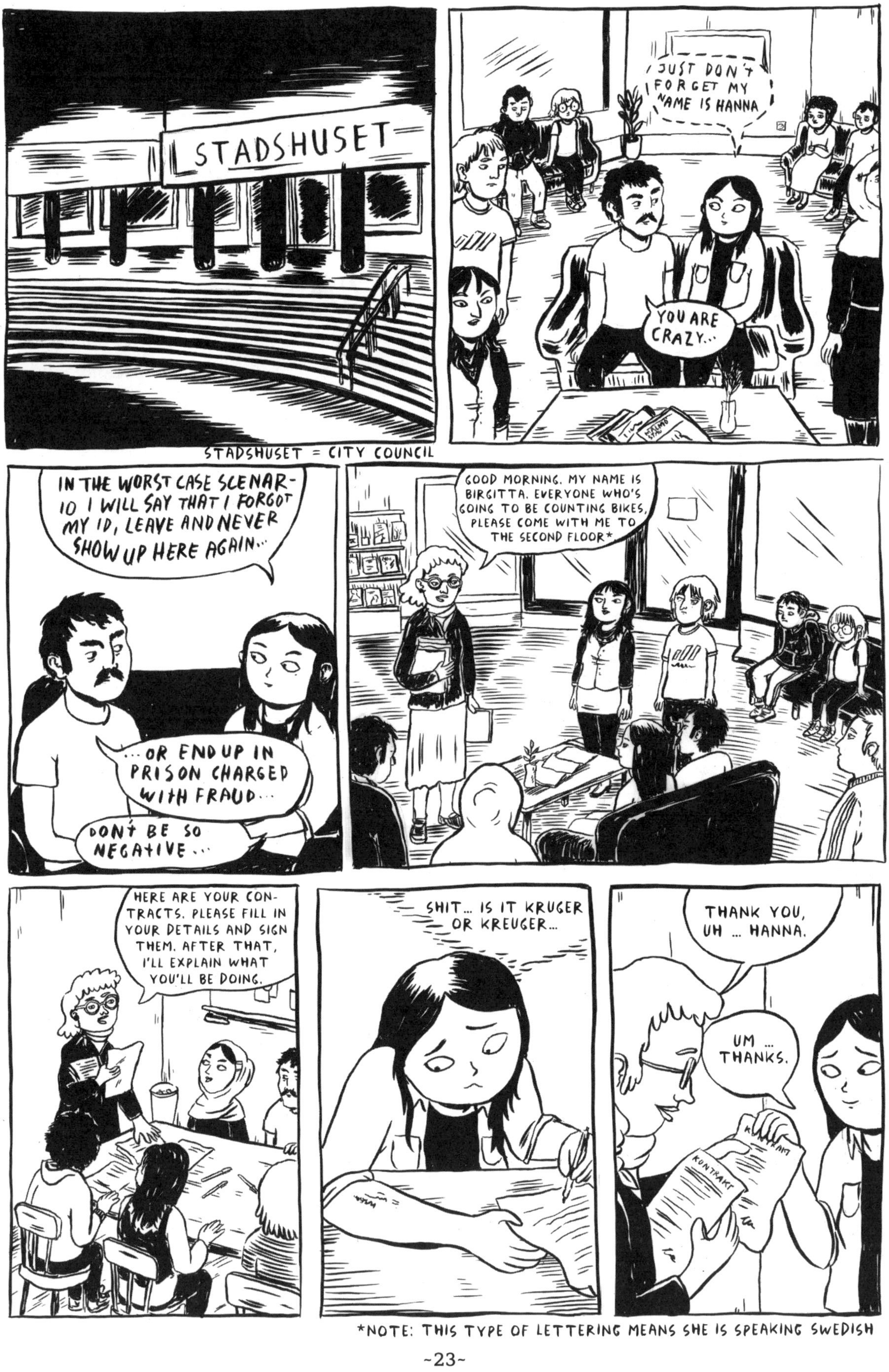
STADSHUSET
STADSHUSET = CITY COUNCIL
JUST DON'T FORGET MY NAME IS HANNA
YOU ARE CRAZY...
IN THE WORST CASE SCENARIO I WILL SAY THAT I FORGOT MY ID, LEAVE AND NEVER SHOW UP HERE AGAIN...
...OR END UP IN PRISON CHARGED WITH FRAUD...
DON'T BE SO NEGATIVE...
GOOD MORNING. MY NAME IS BIRGITTA. EVERYONE WHO'S GOING TO BE COUNTING BIKES, PLEASE COME WITH ME TO THE SECOND FLOOR*
HERE ARE YOUR CONTRACTS. PLEASE FILL IN YOUR DETAILS AND SIGN THEM. AFTER THAT, I'LL EXPLAIN WHAT YOU'LL BE DOING.
SHIT... IS IT KRUGER OR KREUGER...
THANK YOU, UH ... HANNA.
UM ... THANKS.
KONTRAKT

*NOTE: THIS TYPE OF LETTERING MEANS SHE IS SPEAKING SWEDISH

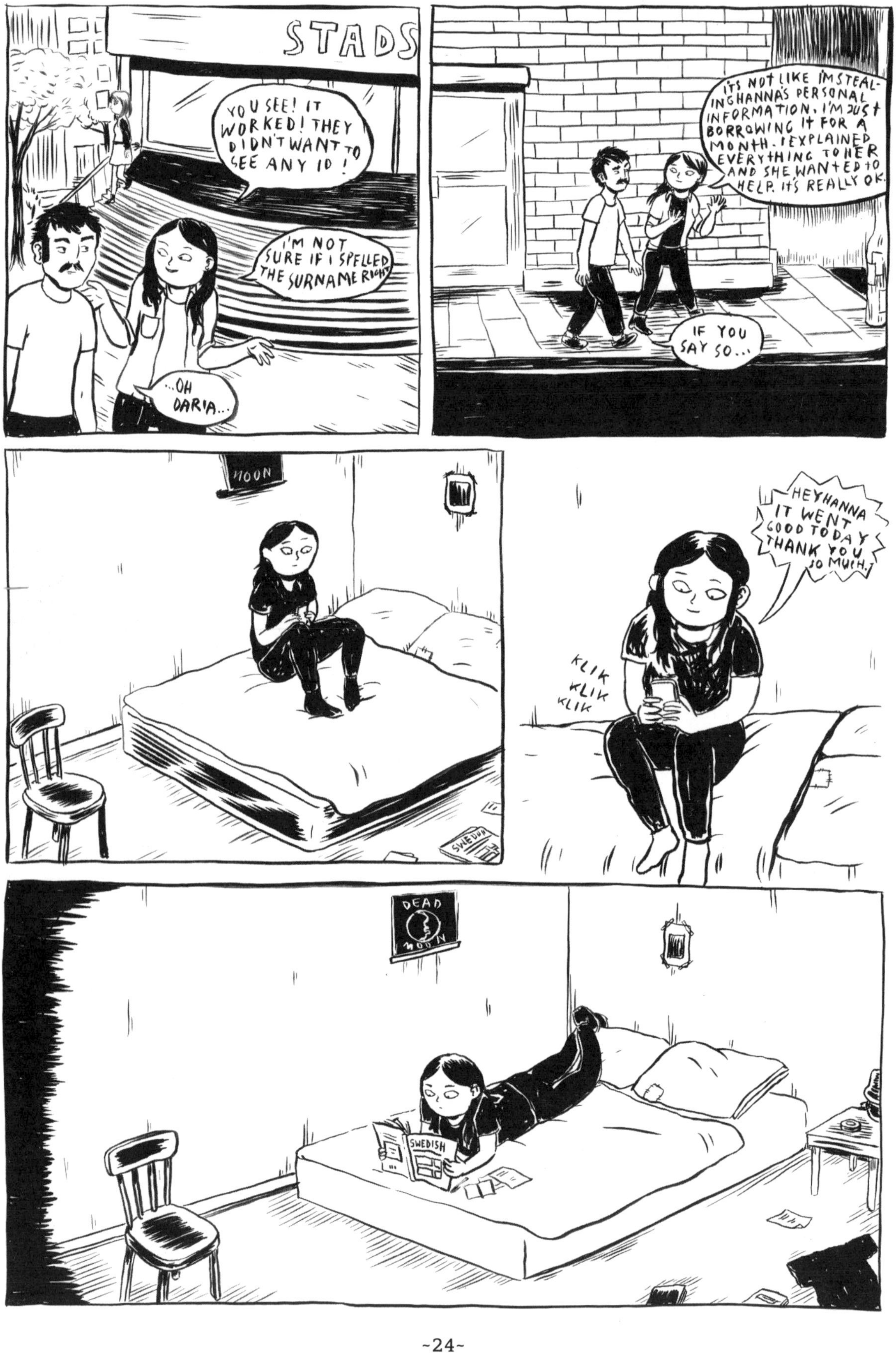
STADS
YOU SEE! IT WORKED! THEY DIDN'T WANT TO SEE ANY ID!
I'M NOT SURE IF I SPELLED THE SURNAME RIGHT
...OH DARIA...
IT'S NOT LIKE I'M STEALING HANNA'S PERSONAL INFORMATION, I'M JUST BORROWING IT FOR A MONTH. I EXPLAINED EVERYTHING TO HER AND SHE WANTED TO HELP. IT'S REALLY OK.
IF YOU SAY SO...
MOON
SWEDISH
KLIK
KLIK
KLIK
HEY HANNA IT WENT GOOD TODAY THANK YOU SO MUCH.
DEAD MOON
SWEDISH

A LETTER?
FOR ME?

FINALLY! AN ANSWER!

WHAT DO THEY MEAN
BY "FINANCIALLY
ACTIVE"?

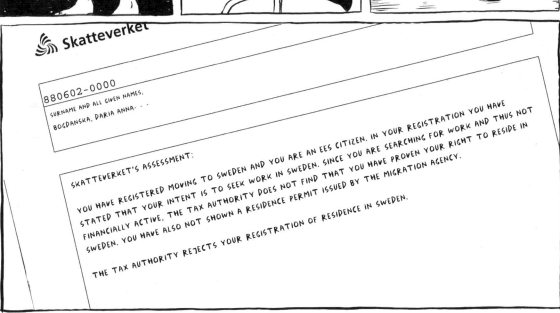

Skatteverket

880602-0000
SURNAME AND ALL GIVEN NAMES,
BOGDANSKA, DARIA ANNA---

SKATTEVERKET'S ASSESSMENT:

YOU HAVE REGISTERED MOVING TO SWEDEN AND YOU ARE AN EES CITIZEN. IN YOUR REGISTRATION YOU HAVE
STATED THAT YOUR INTENT IS TO SEEK WORK IN SWEDEN. SINCE YOU ARE SEARCHING FOR WORK AND THUS NOT
FINANCIALLY ACTIVE, THE TAX AUTHORITY DOES NOT FIND THAT YOU HAVE PROVEN YOUR RIGHT TO RESIDE IN
SWEDEN. YOU HAVE ALSO NOT SHOWN A RESIDENCE PERMIT ISSUED BY THE MIGRATION AGENCY.

THE TAX AUTHORITY REJECTS YOUR REGISTRATION OF RESIDENCE IN SWEDEN.

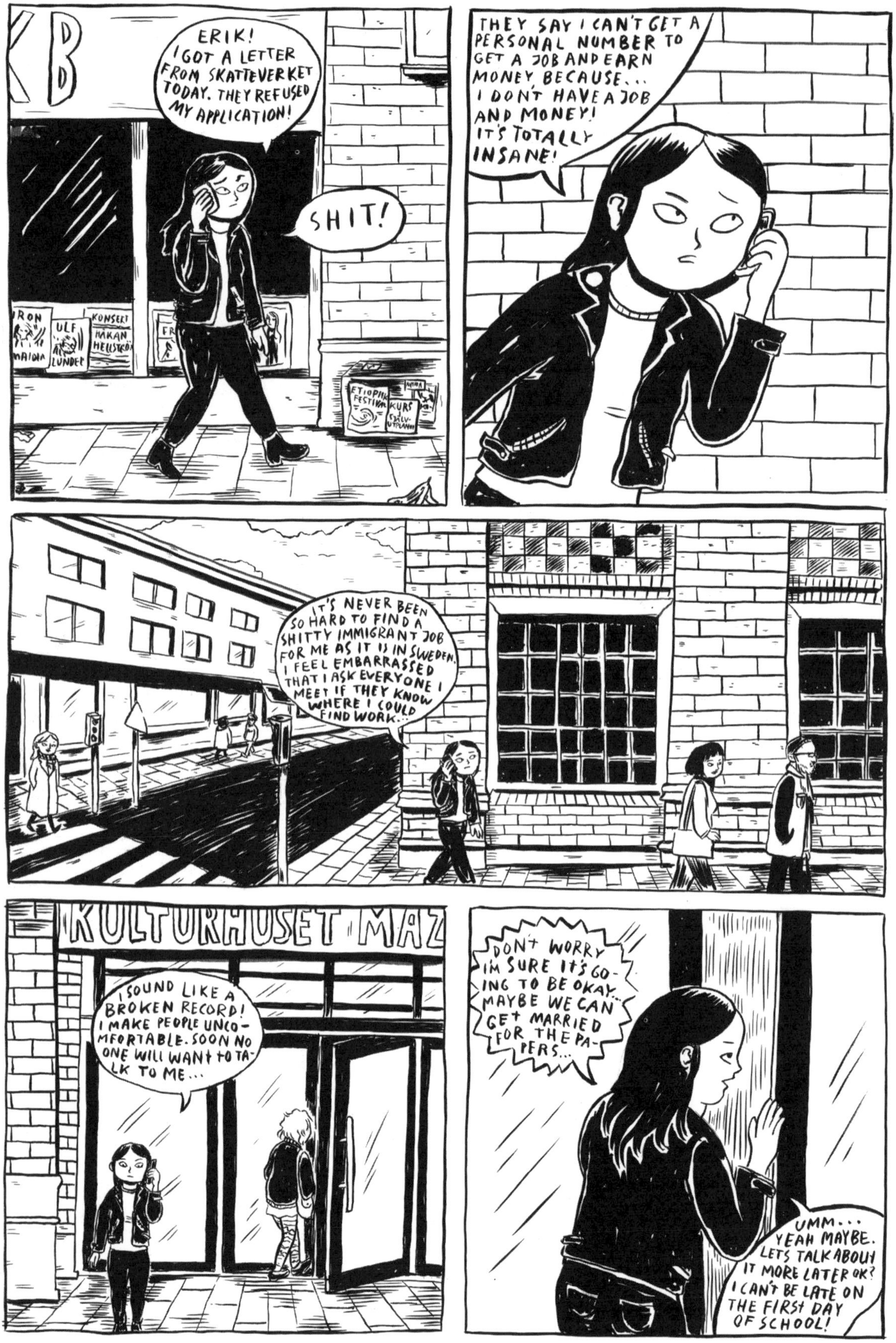
KB
ERIK! I GOT A LETTER FROM SKATTEVERKET TODAY. THEY REFUSED MY APPLICATION!
SHIT!
THEY SAY I CAN'T GET A PERSONAL NUMBER TO GET A JOB AND EARN MONEY BECAUSE... I DON'T HAVE A JOB AND MONEY! IT'S TOTALLY INSANE!
IT'S NEVER BEEN SO HARD TO FIND A SHITTY IMMIGRANT JOB FOR ME AS IT IS IN SWEDEN. I FEEL EMBARRASSED THAT I ASK EVERYONE I MEET IF THEY KNOW WHERE I COULD FIND WORK...
KULTURHUSET MAZ
I SOUND LIKE A BROKEN RECORD! I MAKE PEOPLE UNCO-MFORTABLE. SOON NO ONE WILL WANT TO TA-LK TO ME...
DON'T WORRY I'M SURE IT'S GO-ING TO BE OKAY... MAYBE WE CAN GET MARRIED FOR THE PA-PERS...
UMM... YEAH MAYBE. LETS TALK ABOUT IT MORE LATER OK? I CAN'T BE LATE ON THE FIRST DAY OF SCHOOL!

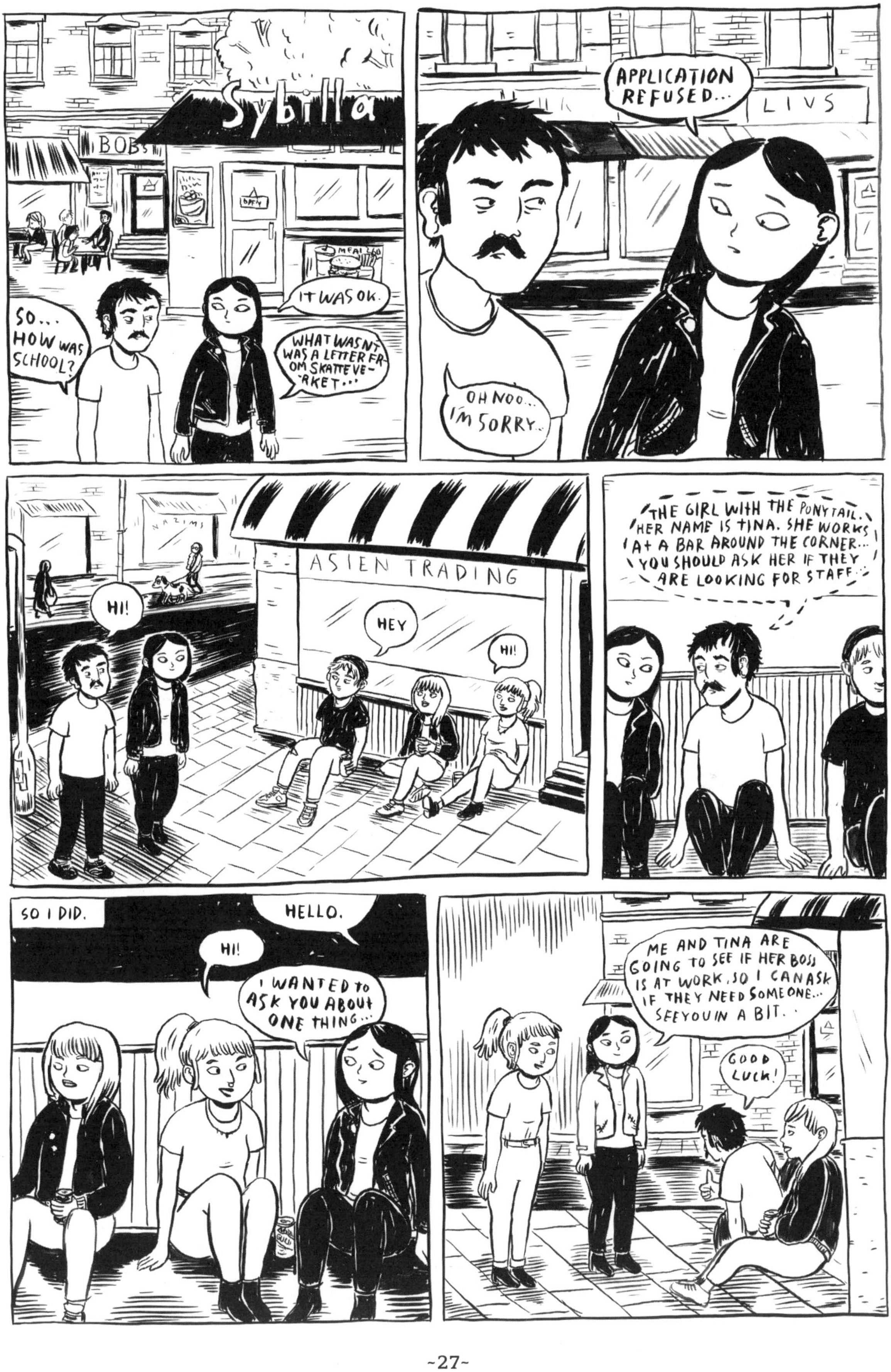
Sybilla
BOBS
SO... HOW WAS SCHOOL?
IT WAS OK.
WHAT WASN'T WAS A LETTER FROM SKATTEVERKET...
LIVS
APPLICATION REFUSED...
OH NOO... I'M SORRY..
ASIEN TRADING
HI!
HEY
HI!
THE GIRL WITH THE PONYTAIL. HER NAME IS TINA. SHE WORKS AT A BAR AROUND THE CORNER... YOU SHOULD ASK HER IF THEY ARE LOOKING FOR STAFF..
SO I DID.
HELLO.
HI!
I WANTED TO ASK YOU ABOUT ONE THING...
ME AND TINA ARE GOING TO SEE IF HER BOSS IS AT WORK, SO I CAN ASK IF THEY NEED SOMEONE... SEE YOU IN A BIT..
GOOD LUCK!

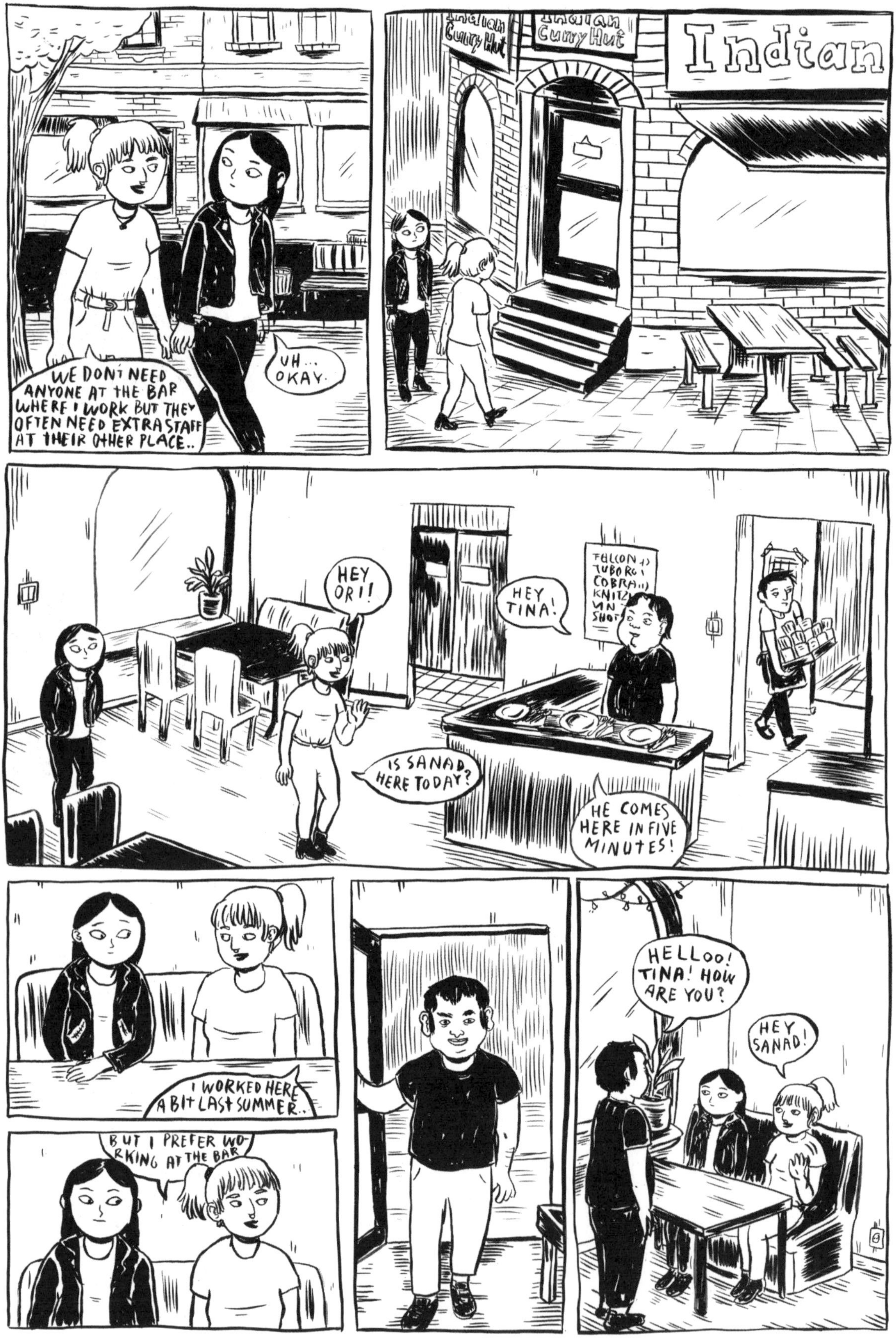

WE DON'T NEED ANYONE AT THE BAR WHERE I WORK BUT THEY OFTEN NEED EXTRA STAFF AT THEIR OTHER PLACE..
UH... OKAY.
Indian Curry Hut
Indian Curry Hut
Indian
HEY ORI!
HEY TINA!
IS SANAD HERE TODAY?
HE COMES HERE IN FIVE MINUTES!
I WORKED HERE A BIT LAST SUMMER..
BUT I PREFER WORKING AT THE BAR
HELLOo! TINA! HOW ARE YOU?
HEY SANAD!

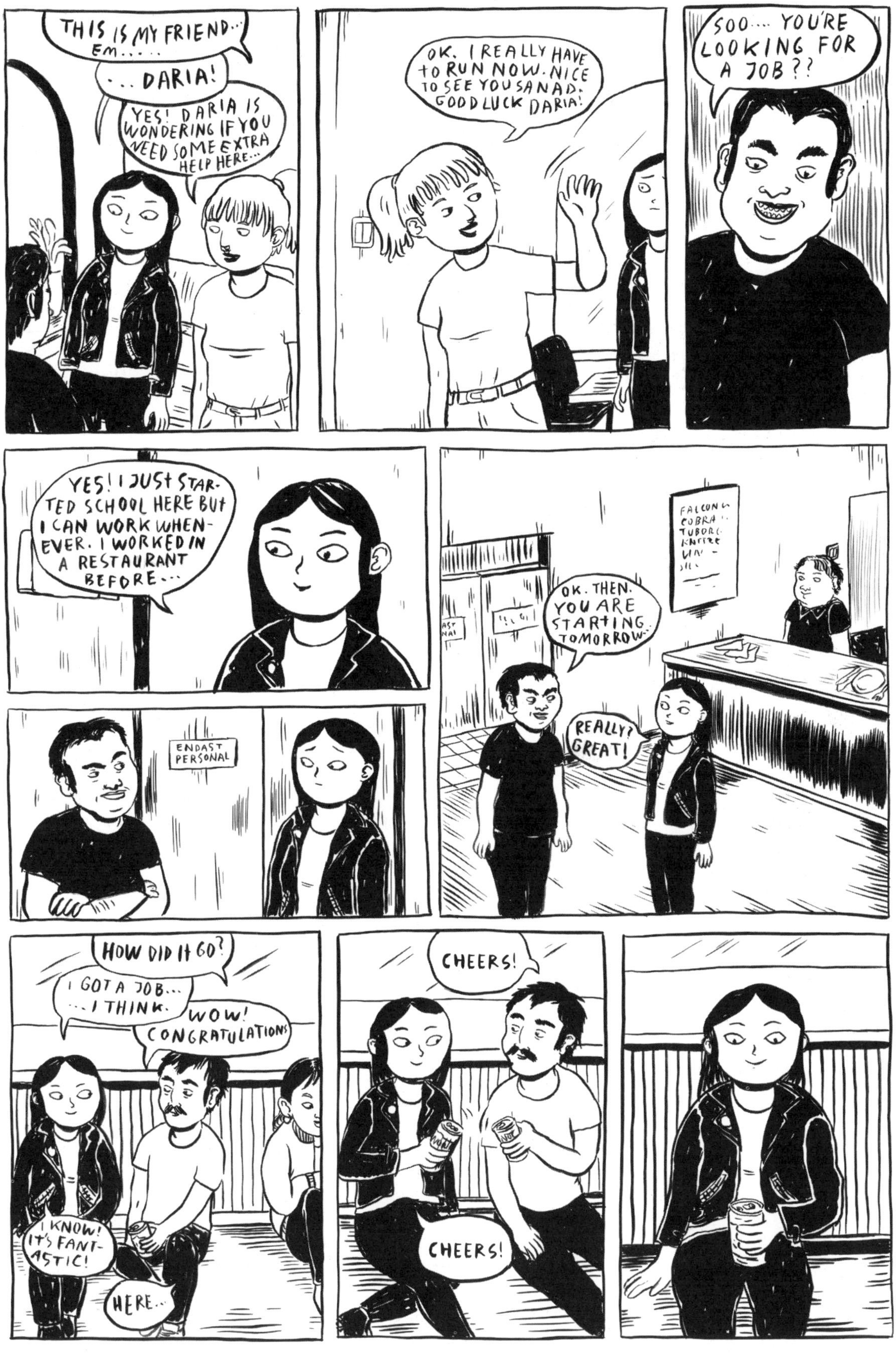
THIS IS MY FRIEND... EM.....
...DARIA!
YES! DARIA IS WONDERING IF YOU NEED SOME EXTRA HELP HERE...
OK. I REALLY HAVE TO RUN NOW. NICE TO SEE YOU SANAD. GOOD LUCK DARIA!
SOO.... YOU'RE LOOKING FOR A JOB??
YES! I JUST STARTED SCHOOL HERE BUT I CAN WORK WHENEVER. I WORKED IN A RESTAURANT BEFORE...
ENDAST PERSONAL
OK. THEN. YOU ARE STARTING TOMORROW..
REALLY? GREAT!
HOW DID IT GO?
I GOT A JOB... ...I THINK.
WOW! CONGRATULATIONS
I KNOW! IT'S FANTASTIC!
HERE...
CHEERS!
CHEERS!

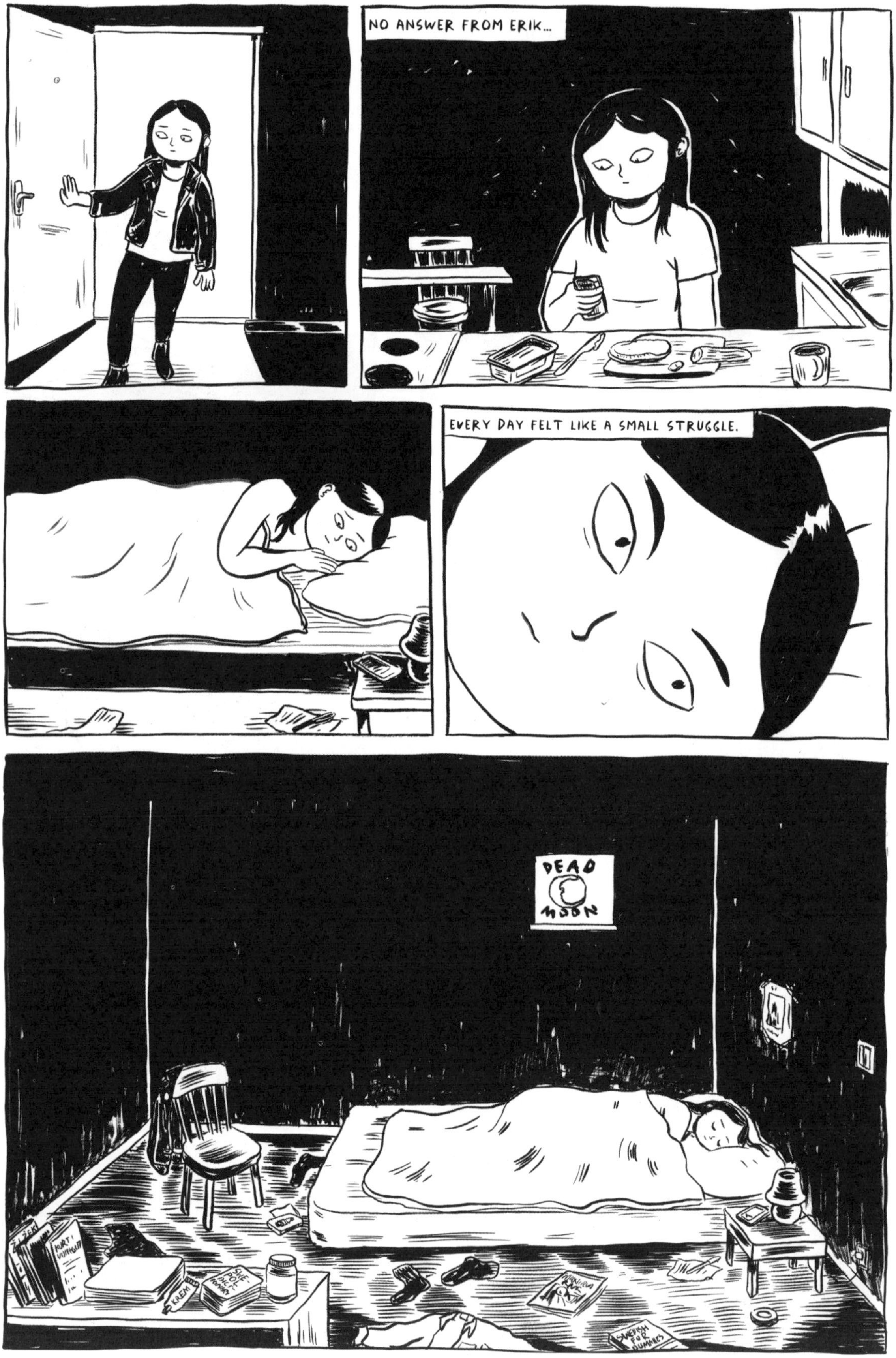
NO ANSWER FROM ERIK...
EVERY DAY FELT LIKE A SMALL STRUGGLE.
DEAD MOON
SWEDISH FOR DUMMIES

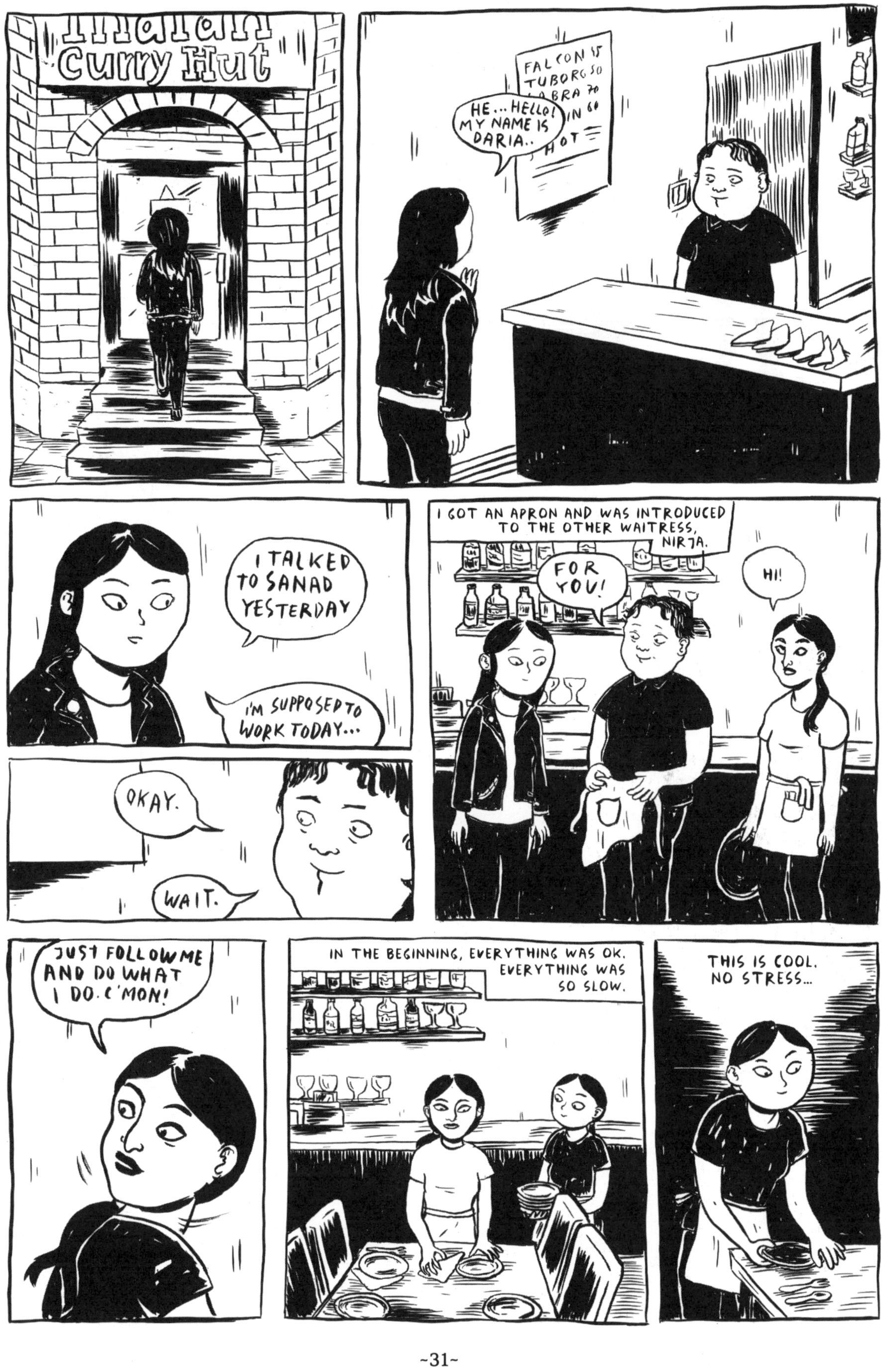
Curry Hut
FALCON 55
TUBORG 50
HE... HELLO! MY NAME IS DARIA..
I TALKED TO SANAD YESTERDAY
I'M SUPPOSED TO WORK TODAY...
OKAY.
WAIT.
I GOT AN APRON AND WAS INTRODUCED TO THE OTHER WAITRESS, NIRJA.
FOR YOU!
HI!
JUST FOLLOW ME AND DO WHAT I DO. C'MON!
IN THE BEGINNING, EVERYTHING WAS OK. EVERYTHING WAS SO SLOW.
THIS IS COOL. NO STRESS...

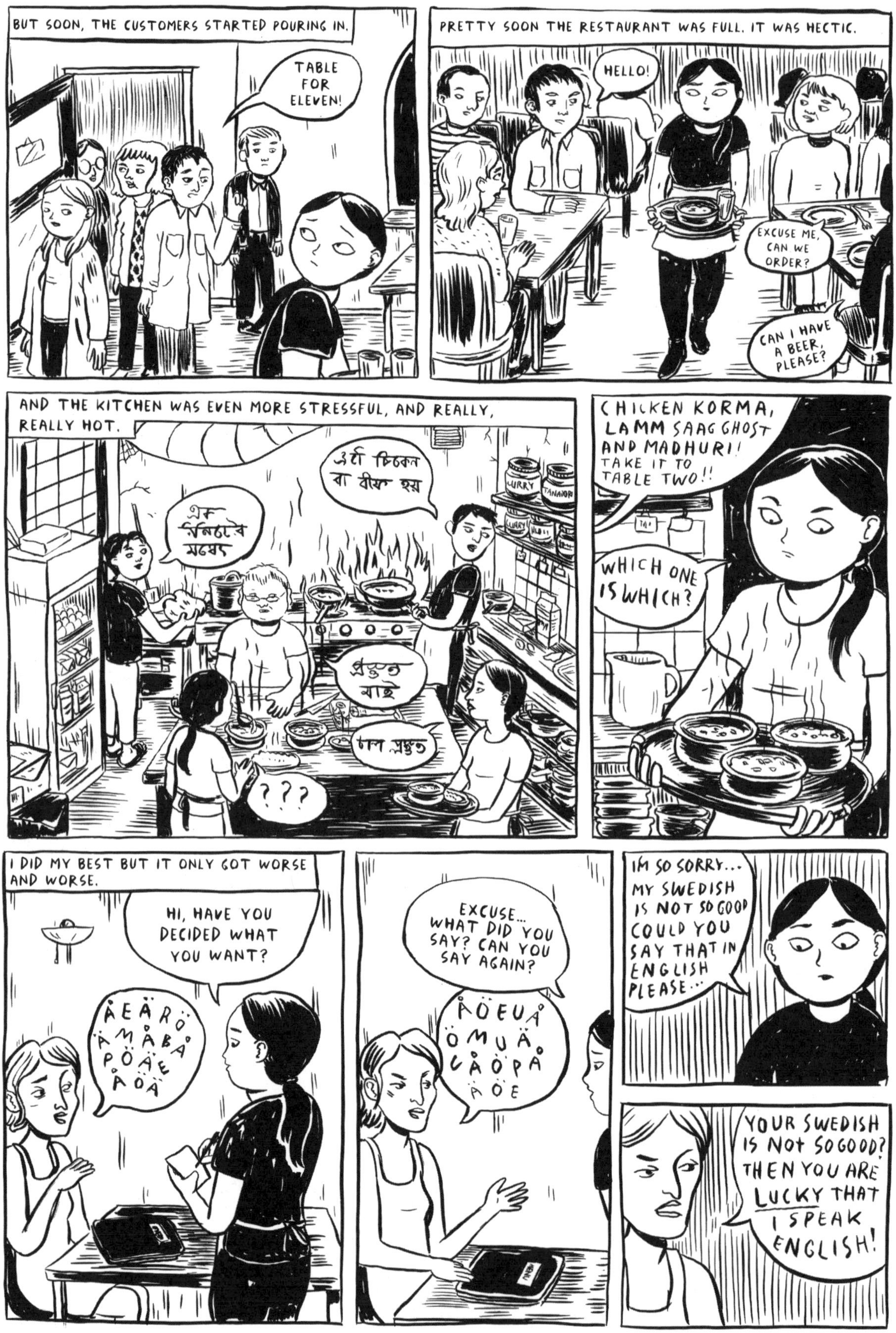
BUT SOON, THE CUSTOMERS STARTED POURING IN.
TABLE FOR ELEVEN!
PRETTY SOON THE RESTAURANT WAS FULL. IT WAS HECTIC.
HELLO!
EXCUSE ME, CAN WE ORDER?
CAN I HAVE A BEER, PLEASE?
AND THE KITCHEN WAS EVEN MORE STRESSFUL, AND REALLY, REALLY HOT.
CURRY
TANDOORI
???
CHICKEN KORMA, LAMM SAAG GHOST AND MADHURI! TAKE IT TO TABLE TWO!!
WHICH ONE IS WHICH?
I DID MY BEST BUT IT ONLY GOT WORSE AND WORSE.
HI, HAVE YOU DECIDED WHAT YOU WANT?
EXCUSE... WHAT DID YOU SAY? CAN YOU SAY AGAIN?
I'M SO SORRY... MY SWEDISH IS NOT SO GOOD COULD YOU SAY THAT IN ENGLISH PLEASE...
YOUR SWEDISH IS NOT SO GOOD? THEN YOU ARE LUCKY THAT I SPEAK ENGLISH!

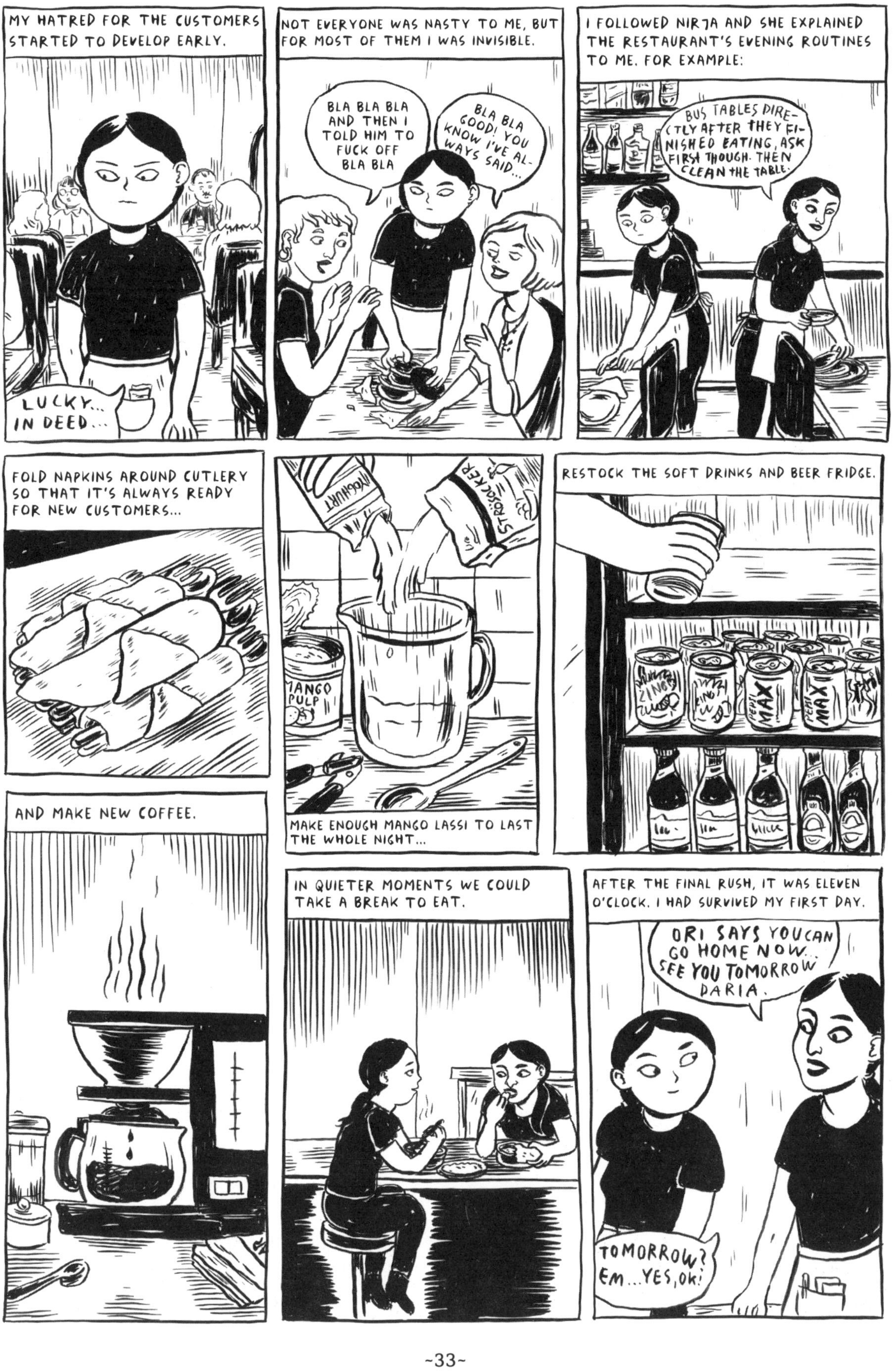
MY HATRED FOR THE CUSTOMERS STARTED TO DEVELOP EARLY.
LUCKY... IN DEED...
NOT EVERYONE WAS NASTY TO ME, BUT FOR MOST OF THEM I WAS INVISIBLE.
BLA BLA BLA AND THEN I TOLD HIM TO FUCK OFF BLA BLA
BLA BLA GOOD! YOU KNOW I'VE ALWAYS SAID...
I FOLLOWED NIRJA AND SHE EXPLAINED THE RESTAURANT'S EVENING ROUTINES TO ME. FOR EXAMPLE:
BUS TABLES DIRECTLY AFTER THEY FINISHED EATING, ASK FIRST THOUGH. THEN CLEAN THE TABLE.
FOLD NAPKINS AROUND CUTLERY SO THAT IT'S ALWAYS READY FOR NEW CUSTOMERS...
YOGHURT
STRÖSOCKER
MANGO PULP
MAKE ENOUGH MANGO LASSI TO LAST THE WHOLE NIGHT...
RESTOCK THE SOFT DRINKS AND BEER FRIDGE.
PEPSI MAX
PEPSI MAX
AND MAKE NEW COFFEE.
IN QUIETER MOMENTS WE COULD TAKE A BREAK TO EAT.
AFTER THE FINAL RUSH, IT WAS ELEVEN O'CLOCK. I HAD SURVIVED MY FIRST DAY.
ORI SAYS YOU CAN GO HOME NOW... SEE YOU TOMORROW DARIA.
TOMORROW? EM... YES, OK!

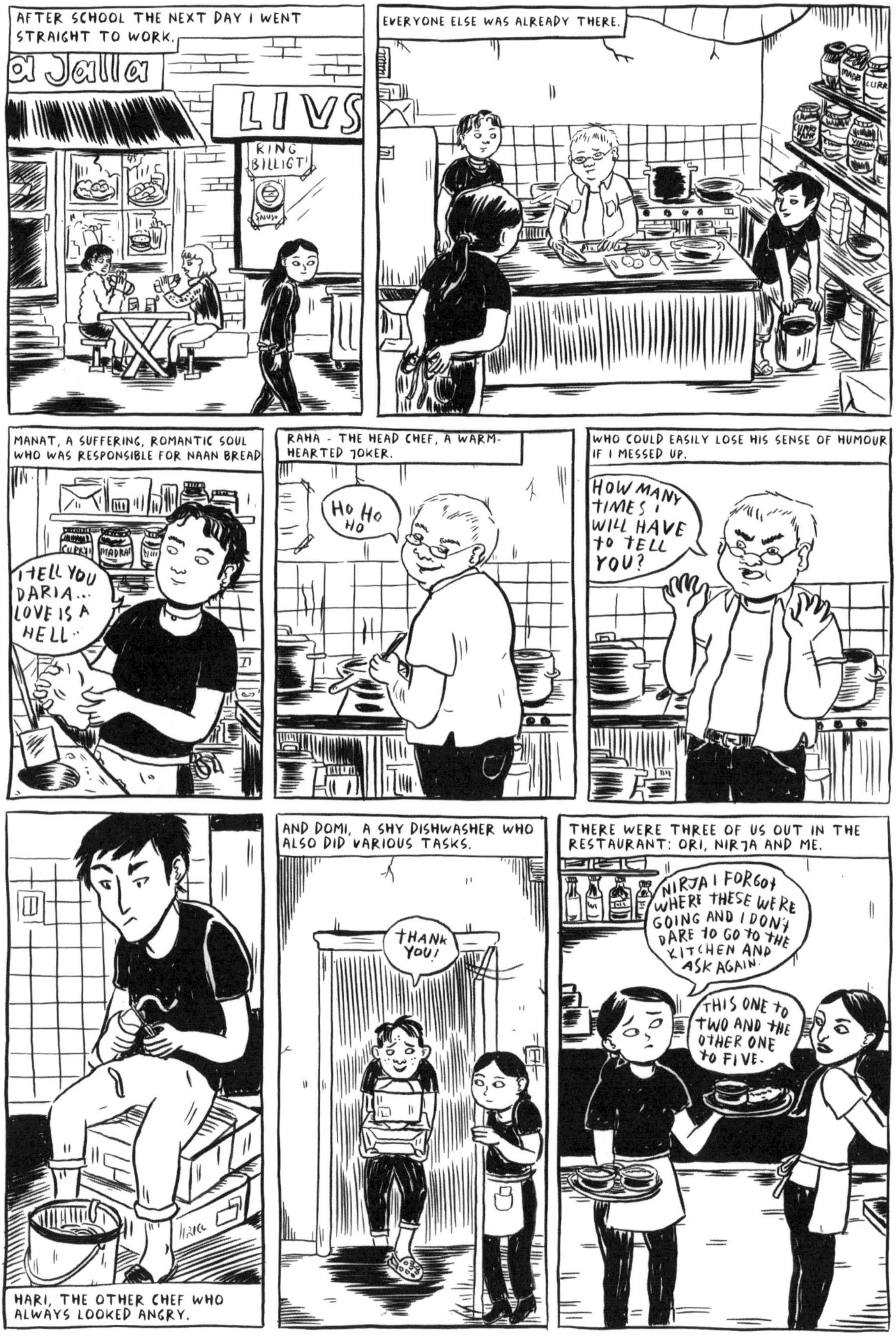
AFTER SCHOOL THE NEXT DAY I WENT STRAIGHT TO WORK.
a Jalla
LIVS
RING BILLIGT
EVERYONE ELSE WAS ALREADY THERE.
MANAT, A SUFFERING, ROMANTIC SOUL WHO WAS RESPONSIBLE FOR NAAN BREAD
I TELL YOU DARIA... LOVE IS A HELL..
RAHA - THE HEAD CHEF, A WARM-HEARTED JOKER.
HO HO HO
WHO COULD EASILY LOSE HIS SENSE OF HUMOUR IF I MESSED UP.
HOW MANY TIMES I WILL HAVE TO TELL YOU?
HARI, THE OTHER CHEF WHO ALWAYS LOOKED ANGRY.
AND DOMI, A SHY DISHWASHER WHO ALSO DID VARIOUS TASKS.
THANK YOU!
THERE WERE THREE OF US OUT IN THE RESTAURANT: ORI, NIRJA AND ME.
NIRJA I FORGOT WHERE THESE WERE GOING AND I DON'T DARE TO GO TO THE KITCHEN AND ASK AGAIN.
THIS ONE TO TWO AND THE OTHER ONE TO FIVE.

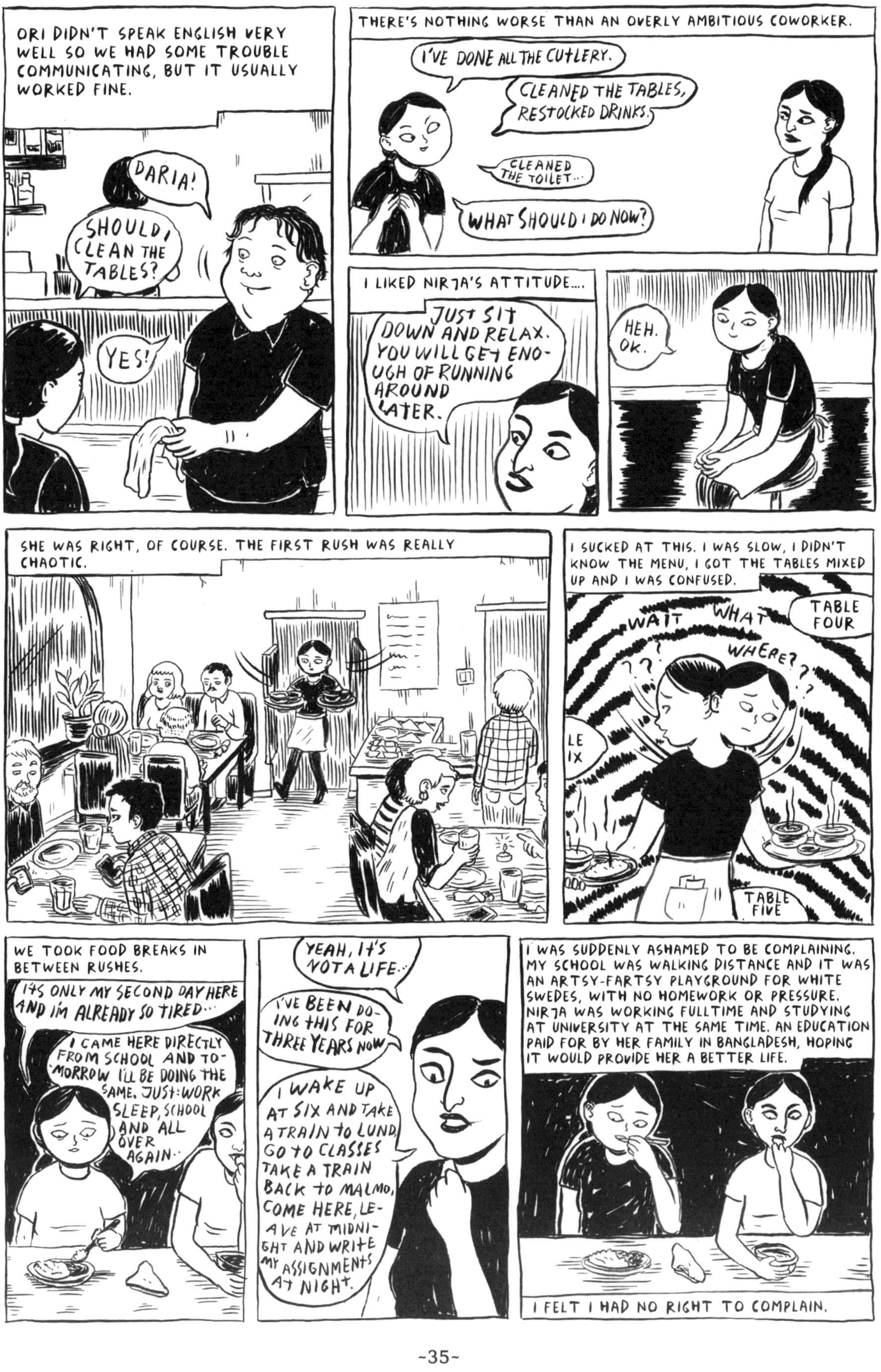
ORI DIDN'T SPEAK ENGLISH VERY WELL SO WE HAD SOME TROUBLE COMMUNICATING, BUT IT USUALLY WORKED FINE.
DARIA!
SHOULD I CLEAN THE TABLES?
YES!
THERE'S NOTHING WORSE THAN AN OVERLY AMBITIOUS COWORKER.
I'VE DONE ALL THE CUTLERY.
CLEANED THE TABLES, RESTOCKED DRINKS.
CLEANED THE TOILET...
WHAT SHOULD I DO NOW?
I LIKED NIRJA'S ATTITUDE....
JUST SIT DOWN AND RELAX. YOU WILL GET ENO-UGH OF RUNNING AROUND LATER.
HEH. OK.
SHE WAS RIGHT, OF COURSE. THE FIRST RUSH WAS REALLY CHAOTIC.
I SUCKED AT THIS. I WAS SLOW, I DIDN'T KNOW THE MENU, I GOT THE TABLES MIXED UP AND I WAS CONFUSED.
WAIT
WHAT
TABLE FOUR
WHERE??
??
LE IX
TABLE FIVE
WE TOOK FOOD BREAKS IN BETWEEN RUSHES.
IT'S ONLY MY SECOND DAY HERE AND I'M ALREADY SO TIRED...
I CAME HERE DIRECTLY FROM SCHOOL AND TO-MORROW I'LL BE DOING THE SAME. JUST: WORK SLEEP, SCHOOL AND ALL OVER AGAIN..
YEAH, IT'S NOT A LIFE...
I'VE BEEN DO-ING THIS FOR THREE YEARS NOW
I WAKE UP AT SIX AND TAKE A TRAIN TO LUND, GO TO CLASSES TAKE A TRAIN BACK TO MALMO, COME HERE, LE-AVE AT MIDNI-GHT AND WRITE MY ASSIGNMENTS AT NIGHT.
I WAS SUDDENLY ASHAMED TO BE COMPLAINING. MY SCHOOL WAS WALKING DISTANCE AND IT WAS AN ARTSY-FARTSY PLAYGROUND FOR WHITE SWEDES, WITH NO HOMEWORK OR PRESSURE. NIRJA WAS WORKING FULLTIME AND STUDYING AT UNIVERSITY AT THE SAME TIME. AN EDUCATION PAID FOR BY HER FAMILY IN BANGLADESH, HOPING IT WOULD PROVIDE HER A BETTER LIFE.
I FELT I HAD NO RIGHT TO COMPLAIN.

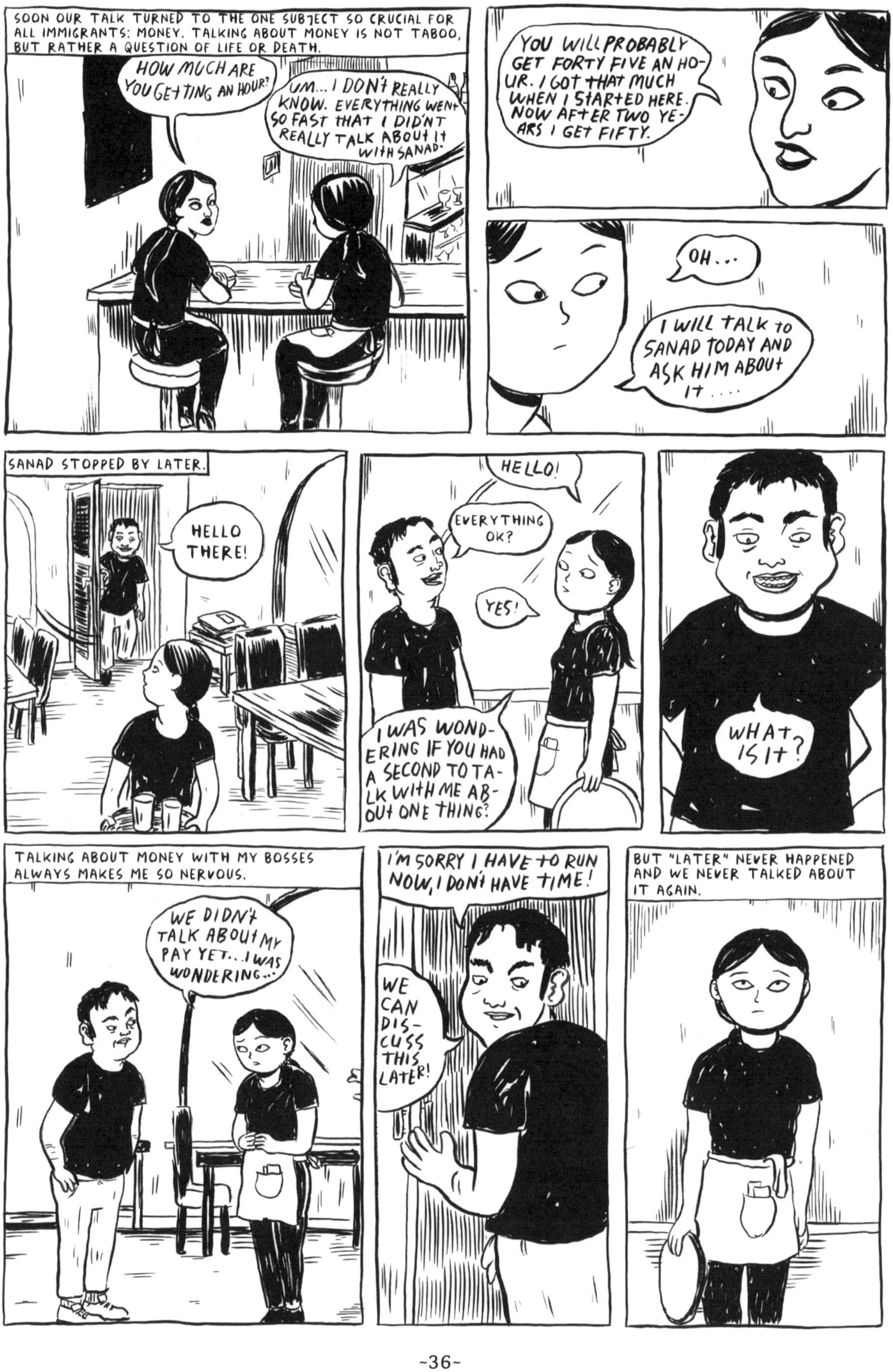
SOON OUR TALK TURNED TO THE ONE SUBJECT SO CRUCIAL FOR ALL IMMIGRANTS: MONEY. TALKING ABOUT MONEY IS NOT TABOO, BUT RATHER A QUESTION OF LIFE OR DEATH.
HOW MUCH ARE YOU GETTING AN HOUR?
UM... I DON'T REALLY KNOW. EVERYTHING WENT SO FAST THAT I DIDN'T REALLY TALK ABOUT IT WITH SANAD.
YOU WILL PROBABLY GET FORTY FIVE AN HOUR. I GOT THAT MUCH WHEN I STARTED HERE. NOW AFTER TWO YEARS I GET FIFTY.
OH...
I WILL TALK TO SANAD TODAY AND ASK HIM ABOUT IT....
SANAD STOPPED BY LATER.
HELLO THERE!
HELLO!
EVERYTHING OK?
YES!
I WAS WONDERING IF YOU HAD A SECOND TO TALK WITH ME ABOUT ONE THING?
WHAT IS IT?
TALKING ABOUT MONEY WITH MY BOSSES ALWAYS MAKES ME SO NERVOUS.
WE DIDN'T TALK ABOUT MY PAY YET...I WAS WONDERING...
I'M SORRY I HAVE TO RUN NOW, I DON'T HAVE TIME!
WE CAN DISCUSS THIS LATER!
BUT "LATER" NEVER HAPPENED AND WE NEVER TALKED ABOUT IT AGAIN.

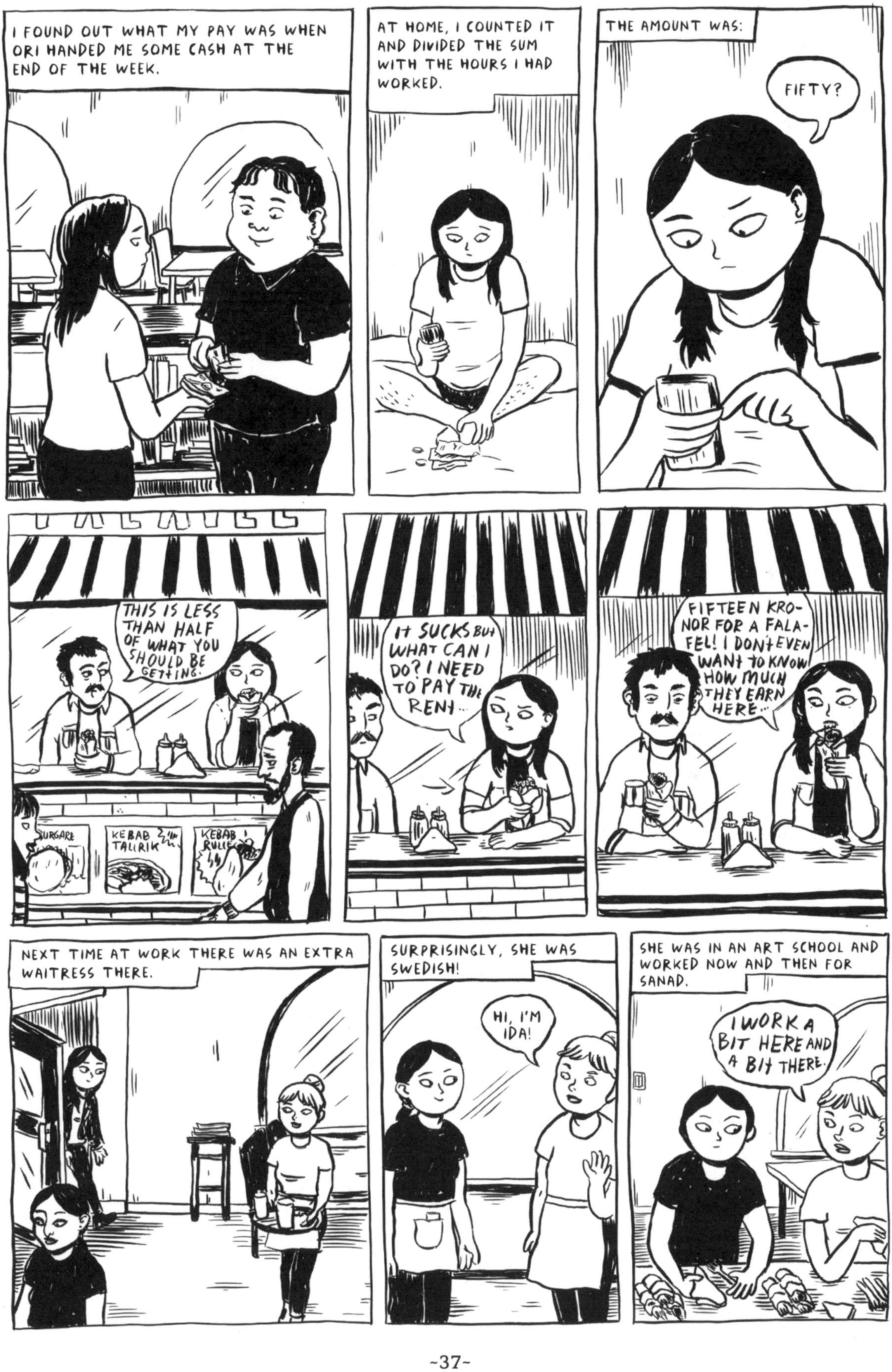
I FOUND OUT WHAT MY PAY WAS WHEN ORI HANDED ME SOME CASH AT THE END OF THE WEEK.
AT HOME, I COUNTED IT AND DIVIDED THE SUM WITH THE HOURS I HAD WORKED.
THE AMOUNT WAS:
FIFTY?
THIS IS LESS THAN HALF OF WHAT YOU SHOULD BE GETTING.
KEBAB TALLRIK
KEBAB RULLE
IT SUCKS BUT WHAT CAN I DO? I NEED TO PAY THE RENT...
FIFTEEN KRONOR FOR A FALAFEL! I DON'T EVEN WANT TO KNOW HOW MUCH THEY EARN HERE...
NEXT TIME AT WORK THERE WAS AN EXTRA WAITRESS THERE.
SURPRISINGLY, SHE WAS SWEDISH!
HI, I'M IDA!
SHE WAS IN AN ART SCHOOL AND WORKED NOW AND THEN FOR SANAD.
I WORK A BIT HERE AND A BIT THERE.

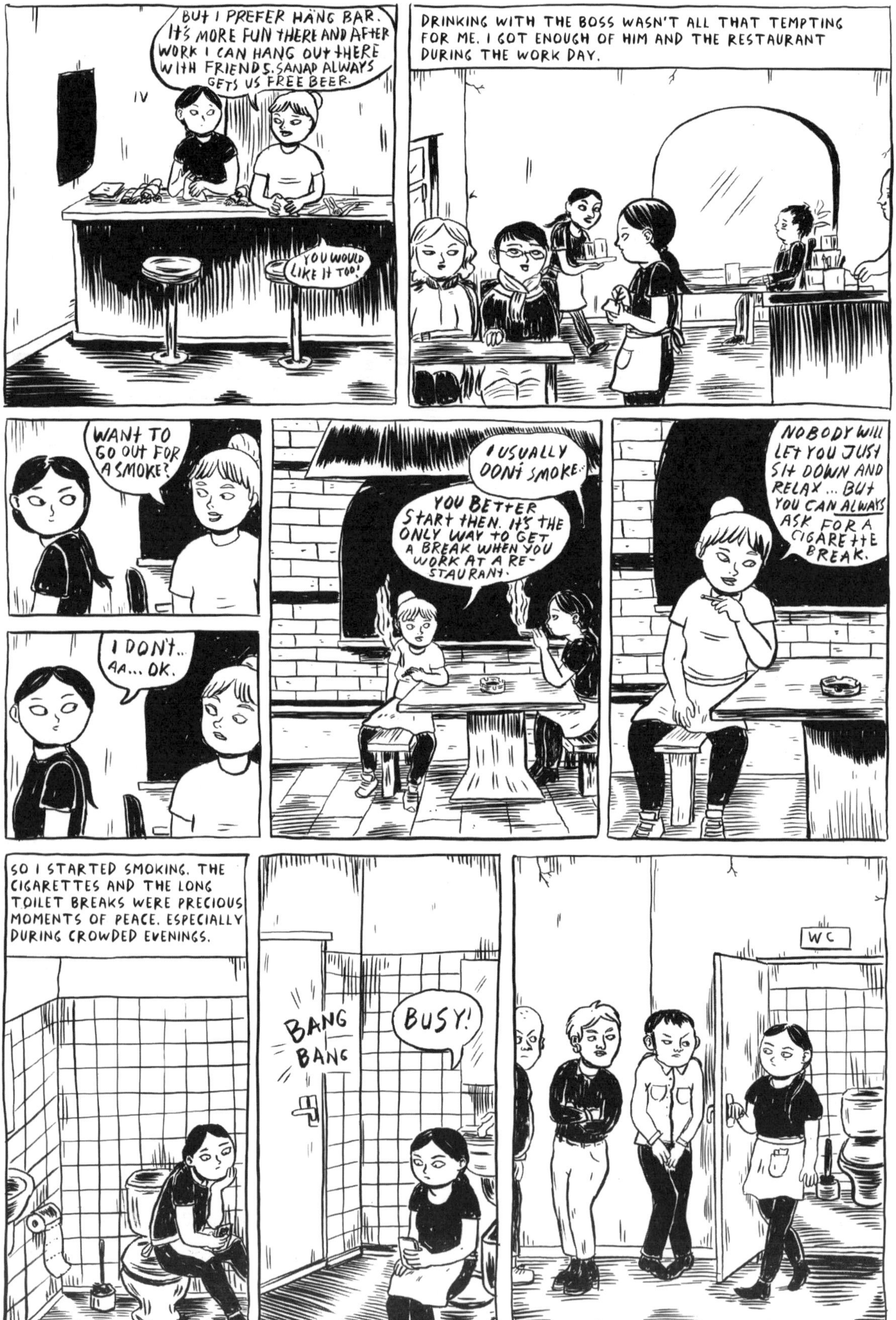
BUT I PREFER HÄNG BAR. IT'S MORE FUN THERE AND AFTER WORK I CAN HANG OUT THERE WITH FRIENDS. SANAD ALWAYS GETS US FREE BEER.
IV
YOU WOULD LIKE IT TOO!
DRINKING WITH THE BOSS WASN'T ALL THAT TEMPTING FOR ME. I GOT ENOUGH OF HIM AND THE RESTAURANT DURING THE WORK DAY.
WANT TO GO OUT FOR A SMOKE?
I DON'T.. AA... OK.
I USUALLY DON'T SMOKE...
YOU BETTER START THEN. IT'S THE ONLY WAY TO GET A BREAK WHEN YOU WORK AT A RESTAURANT.
NOBODY WILL LET YOU JUST SIT DOWN AND RELAX ... BUT YOU CAN ALWAYS ASK FOR A CIGARETTE BREAK.
SO I STARTED SMOKING. THE CIGARETTES AND THE LONG TOILET BREAKS WERE PRECIOUS MOMENTS OF PEACE. ESPECIALLY DURING CROWDED EVENINGS.
BANG BANG
BUSY!
WC

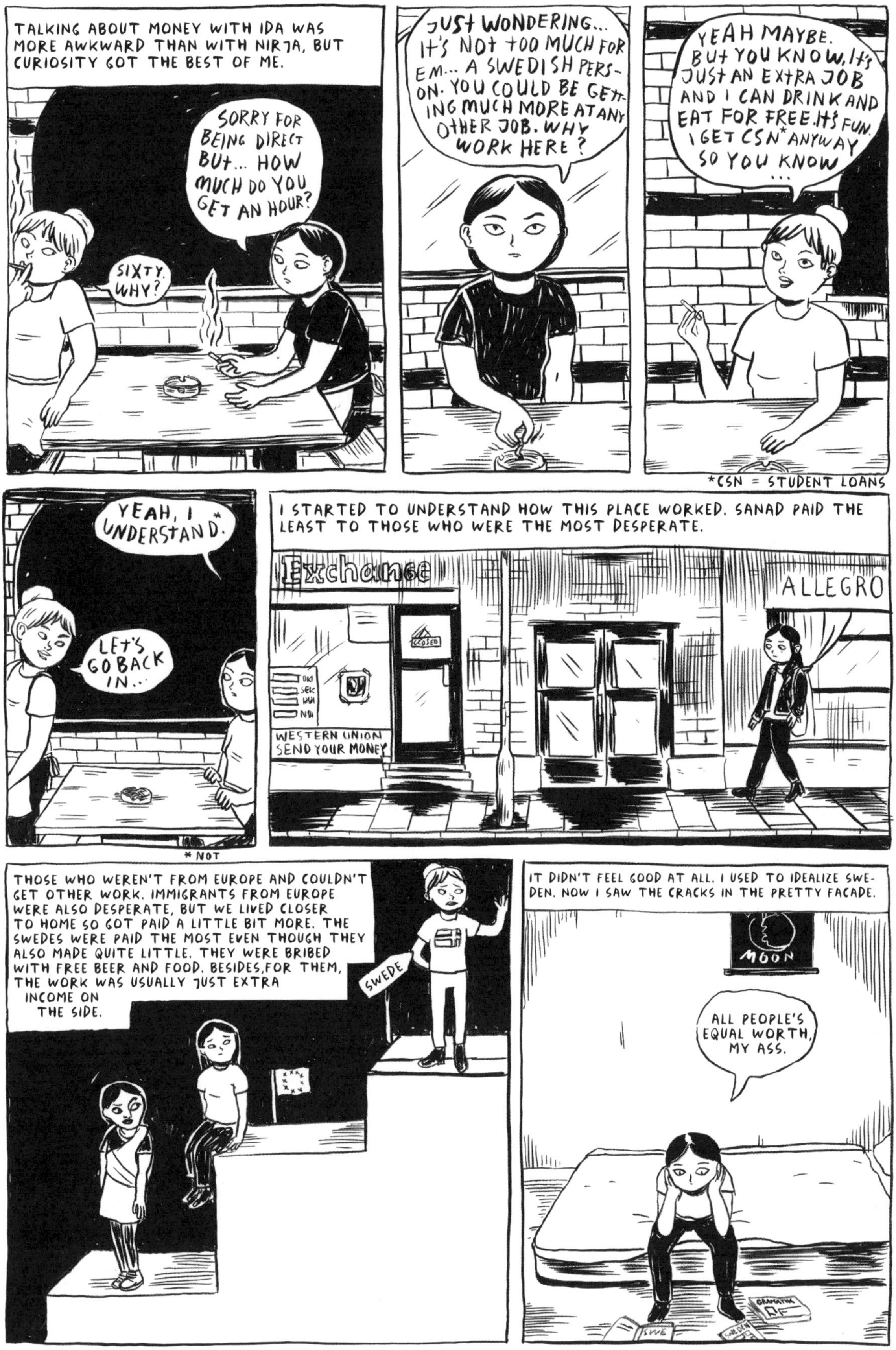
TALKING ABOUT MONEY WITH IDA WAS MORE AWKWARD THAN WITH NIRJA, BUT CURIOSITY GOT THE BEST OF ME.
SORRY FOR BEING DIRECT BUT... HOW MUCH DO YOU GET AN HOUR?
SIXTY. WHY?
JUST WONDERING... IT'S NOT TOO MUCH FOR EM... A SWEDISH PERSON. YOU COULD BE GETTING MUCH MORE AT ANY OTHER JOB. WHY WORK HERE?
YEAH MAYBE. BUT YOU KNOW, IT'S JUST AN EXTRA JOB AND I CAN DRINK AND EAT FOR FREE. IT'S FUN. I GET CSN* ANYWAY SO YOU KNOW ...
*CSN = STUDENT LOANS
YEAH, I UNDERSTAND.*
LET'S GO BACK IN...
* NOT
I STARTED TO UNDERSTAND HOW THIS PLACE WORKED. SANAD PAID THE LEAST TO THOSE WHO WERE THE MOST DESPERATE.
Exchange
CLOSED
WESTERN UNION SEND YOUR MONEY
ALLEGRO
THOSE WHO WEREN'T FROM EUROPE AND COULDN'T GET OTHER WORK. IMMIGRANTS FROM EUROPE WERE ALSO DESPERATE, BUT WE LIVED CLOSER TO HOME SO GOT PAID A LITTLE BIT MORE. THE SWEDES WERE PAID THE MOST EVEN THOUGH THEY ALSO MADE QUITE LITTLE. THEY WERE BRIBED WITH FREE BEER AND FOOD. BESIDES, FOR THEM, THE WORK WAS USUALLY JUST EXTRA INCOME ON THE SIDE.
SWEDE
IT DIDN'T FEEL GOOD AT ALL. I USED TO IDEALIZE SWEDEN. NOW I SAW THE CRACKS IN THE PRETTY FACADE.
MOON
ALL PEOPLE'S EQUAL WORTH, MY ASS.

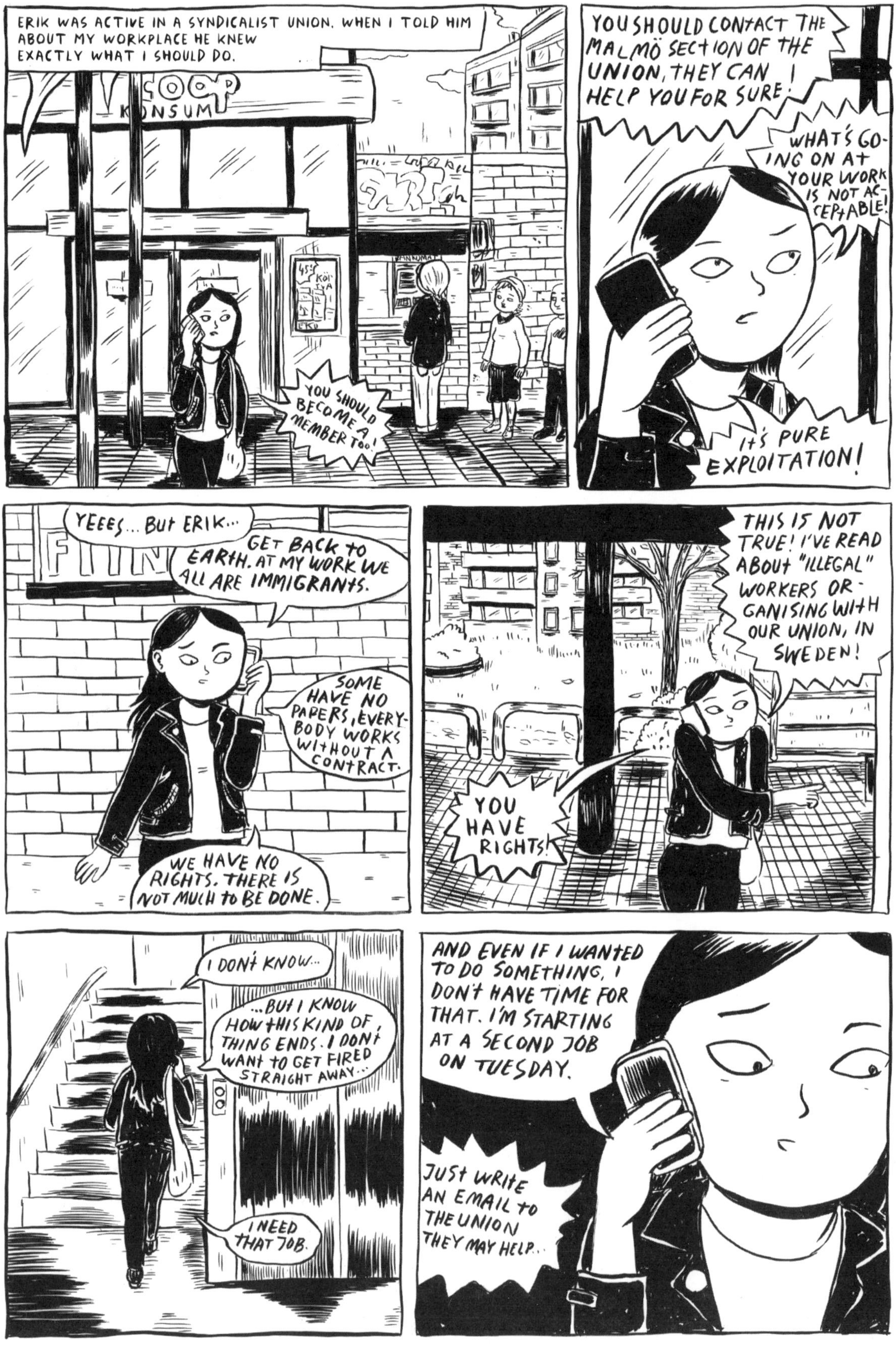
ERIK WAS ACTIVE IN A SYNDICALIST UNION. WHEN I TOLD HIM ABOUT MY WORKPLACE HE KNEW EXACTLY WHAT I SHOULD DO.
COOP
KONSUM
YOU SHOULD BECOME A MEMBER TOO!
YOU SHOULD CONTACT THE MALMÖ SECTION OF THE UNION, THEY CAN HELP YOU FOR SURE!
WHAT'S GOING ON AT YOUR WORK IS NOT ACCEPTABLE!
IT'S PURE EXPLOITATION!
YEEES... BUT ERIK...
GET BACK TO EARTH. AT MY WORK WE ALL ARE IMMIGRANTS.
SOME HAVE NO PAPERS, EVERYBODY WORKS WITHOUT A CONTRACT.
WE HAVE NO RIGHTS. THERE IS NOT MUCH TO BE DONE.
THIS IS NOT TRUE! I'VE READ ABOUT "ILLEGAL" WORKERS ORGANISING WITH OUR UNION, IN SWEDEN!
YOU HAVE RIGHTS!
I DON'T KNOW...
...BUT I KNOW HOW THIS KIND OF THING ENDS. I DON'T WANT TO GET FIRED STRAIGHT AWAY...
I NEED THAT JOB.
AND EVEN IF I WANTED TO DO SOMETHING, I DON'T HAVE TIME FOR THAT. I'M STARTING AT A SECOND JOB ON TUESDAY.
JUST WRITE AN EMAIL TO THE UNION THEY MAY HELP...

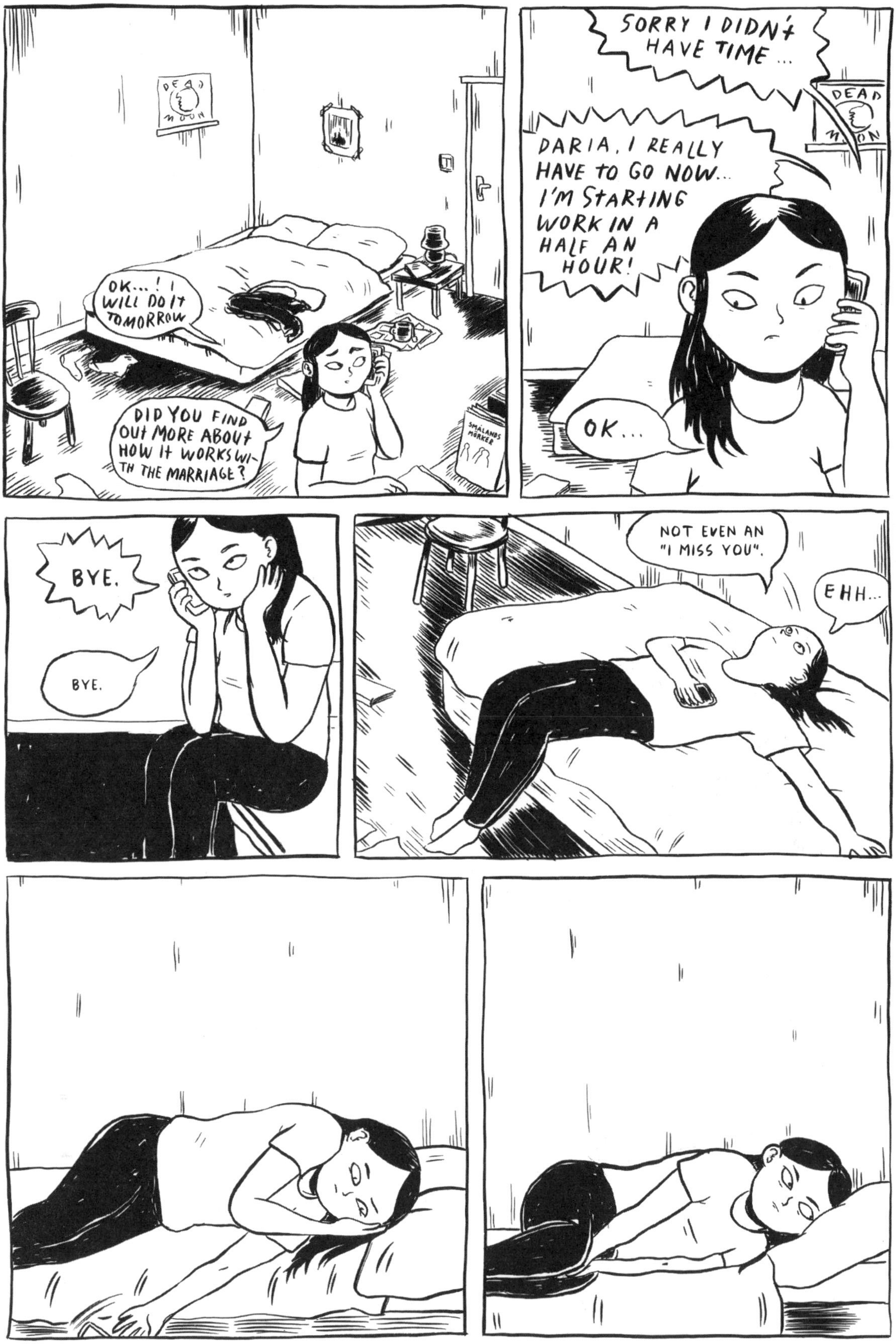
DID YOU FIND OUT MORE ABOUT HOW IT WORKS WITH THE MARRIAGE?
OK...! I WILL DO IT TOMORROW
SMÅLANDS MÖRKER
SORRY I DIDN'T HAVE TIME...
DARIA, I REALLY HAVE TO GO NOW... I'M STARTING WORK IN A HALF AN HOUR!
OK...
BYE.
BYE.
NOT EVEN AN "I MISS YOU".
EHH...

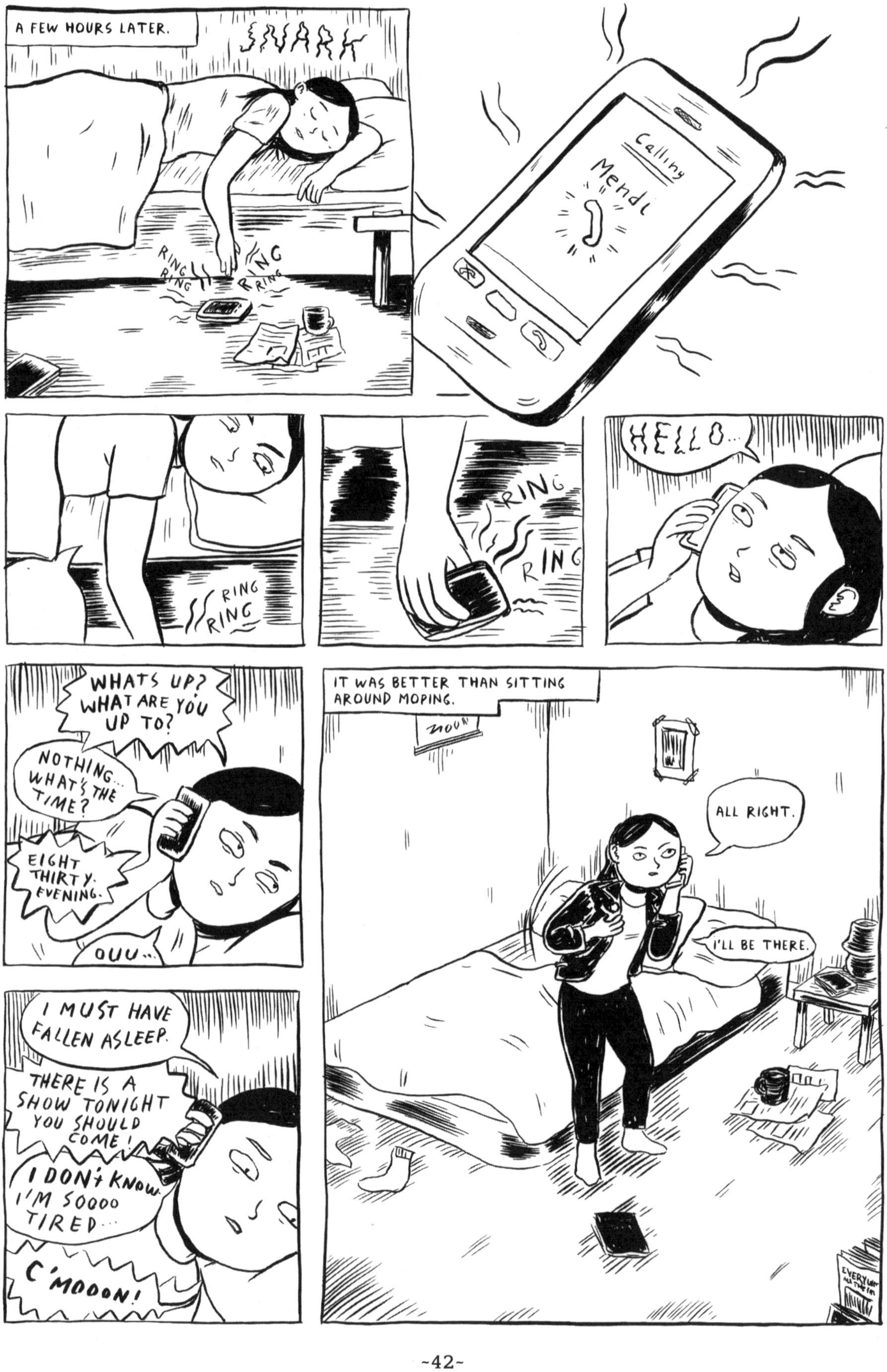
A FEW HOURS LATER.
SNARK
RING RING
RING RING
Calling
Mendi
RING
RING
RING
RING
HELLO...
WHATS UP? WHAT ARE YOU UP TO?
NOTHING... WHAT'S THE TIME?
EIGHT THIRTY. EVENING.
OUU...
I MUST HAVE FALLEN ASLEEP.
THERE IS A SHOW TONIGHT YOU SHOULD COME!
I DON'T KNOW. I'M SOOOO TIRED...
C'MOOON!
IT WAS BETTER THAN SITTING AROUND MOPING.
ALL RIGHT.
I'LL BE THERE.

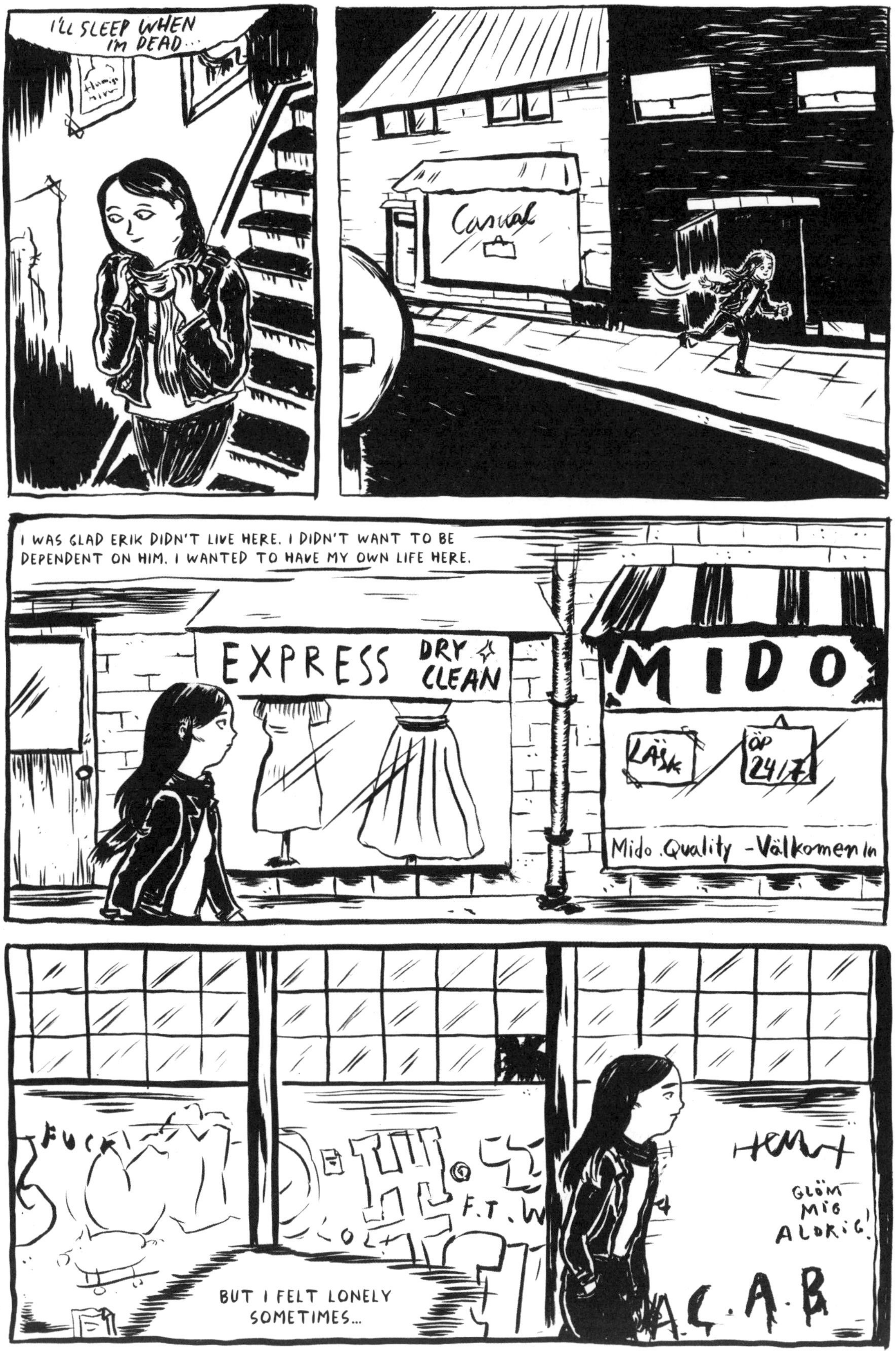
I'LL SLEEP WHEN I'M DEAD...
Casual
I WAS GLAD ERIK DIDN'T LIVE HERE. I DIDN'T WANT TO BE DEPENDENT ON HIM. I WANTED TO HAVE MY OWN LIFE HERE.
EXPRESS
DRY CLEAN
MIDO
LÄSK
ÖP 24/7
Mido Quality -Välkomen In
FUCK
F.T.W
GLÖM MIG ALDRIG!
A.C.A.B
BUT I FELT LONELY SOMETIMES...

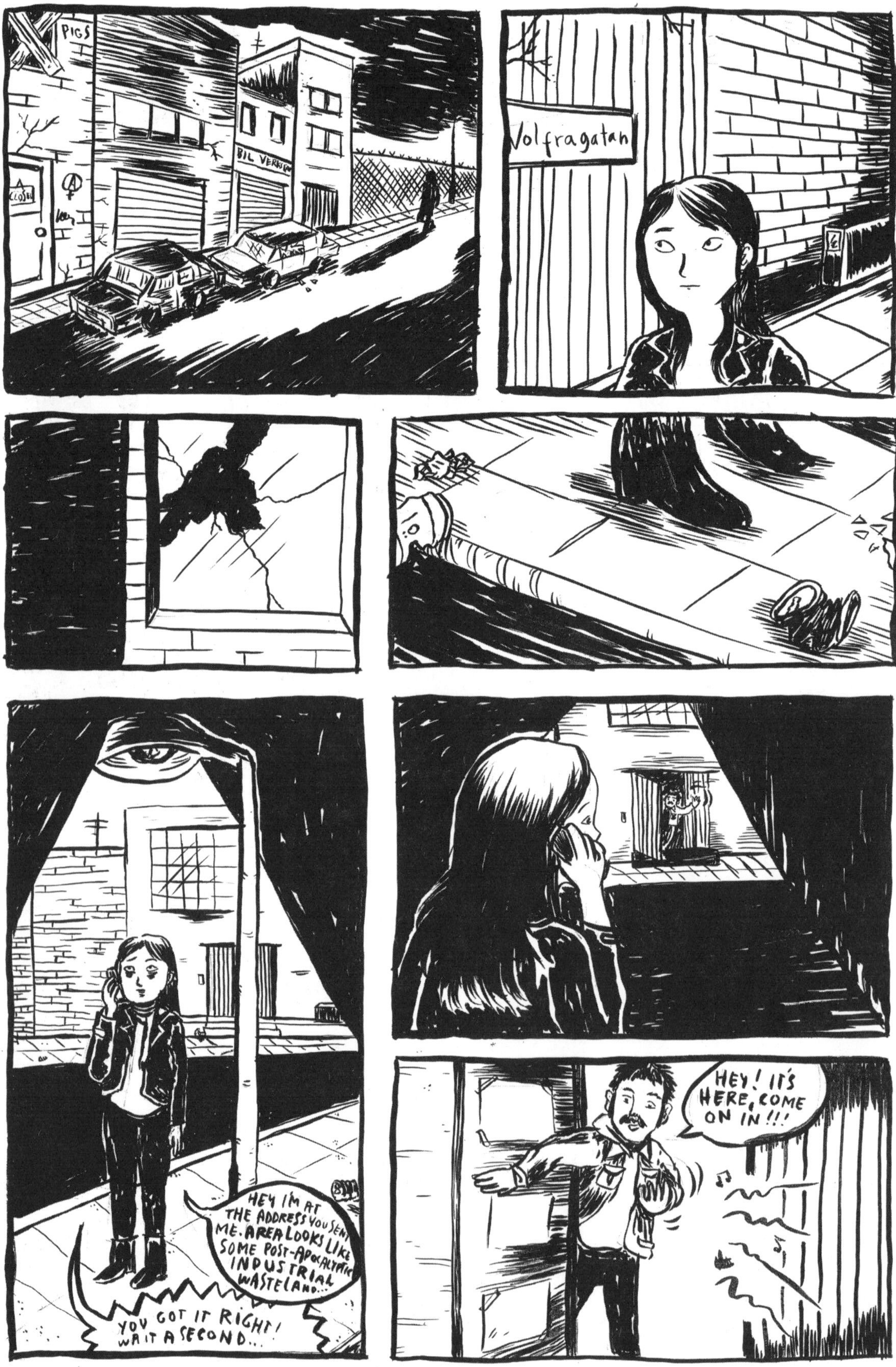
PIGS
Volfragatan
HEY I'M AT THE ADDRESS YOU SENT ME. AREA LOOKS LIKE SOME POST-APOCALYPTIC INDUSTRIAL WASTELAND...
YOU GOT IT RIGHT! WAIT A SECOND...
HEY! IT'S HERE, COME ON IN!!!

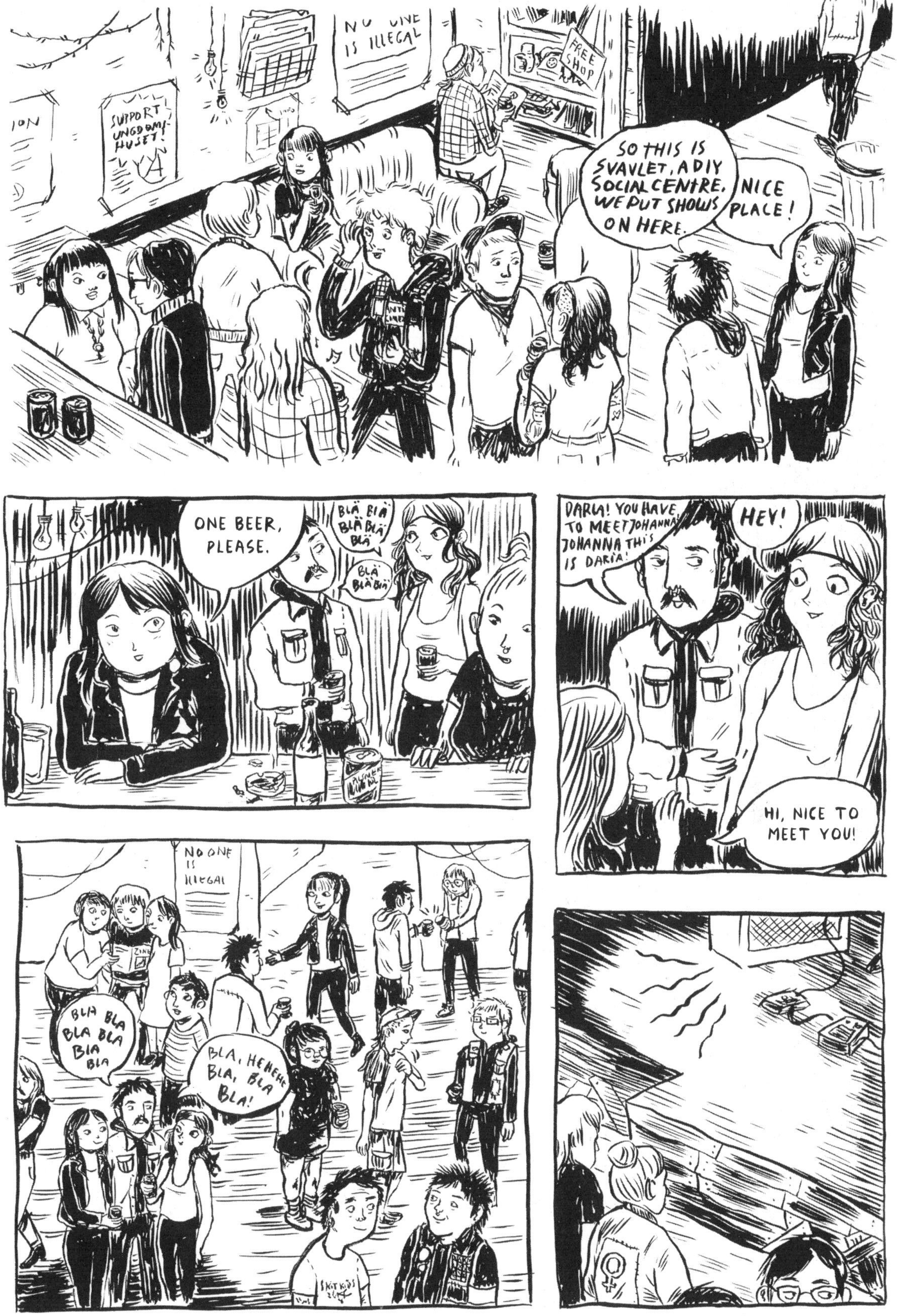

SUPPORT UNGDOMSHUSET!
NO ONE IS ILLEGAL
FREE SHOP
SO THIS IS SVAVLET, A DIY SOCIAL CENTRE, WE PUT SHOWS ON HERE.
NICE PLACE!
ONE BEER, PLEASE.
BLÄ BLÄ BLÄ BLÄ BLÄ
BLÄ BLÄ BLÄ
DARIA! YOU HAVE TO MEET JOHANNA! JOHANNA THIS IS DARIA!
HEY!
HI, NICE TO MEET YOU!
NO ONE IS ILLEGAL
ZINE
BLA BLA BLA BLA BLA BLA
BLA, HEHEHE BLA, BLA BLA!

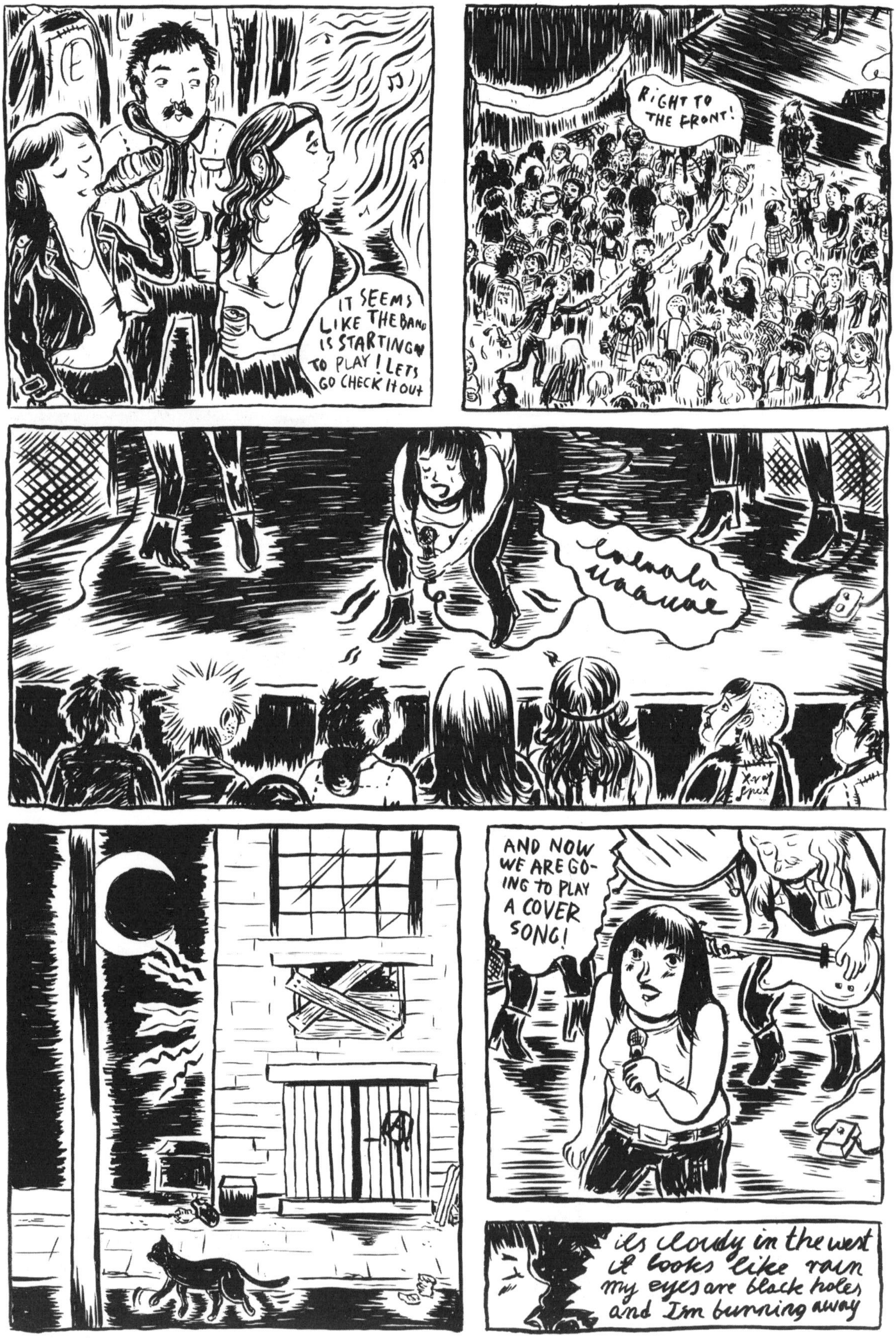
IT SEEMS LIKE THE BAND IS STARTING TO PLAY! LETS GO CHECK IT OUT
RIGHT TO THE FRONT!
X-ray Spex
AND NOW WE ARE GOING TO PLAY A COVER SONG!
its cloudy in the west
it looks like rain
my eyes are black holes
and Im burning away

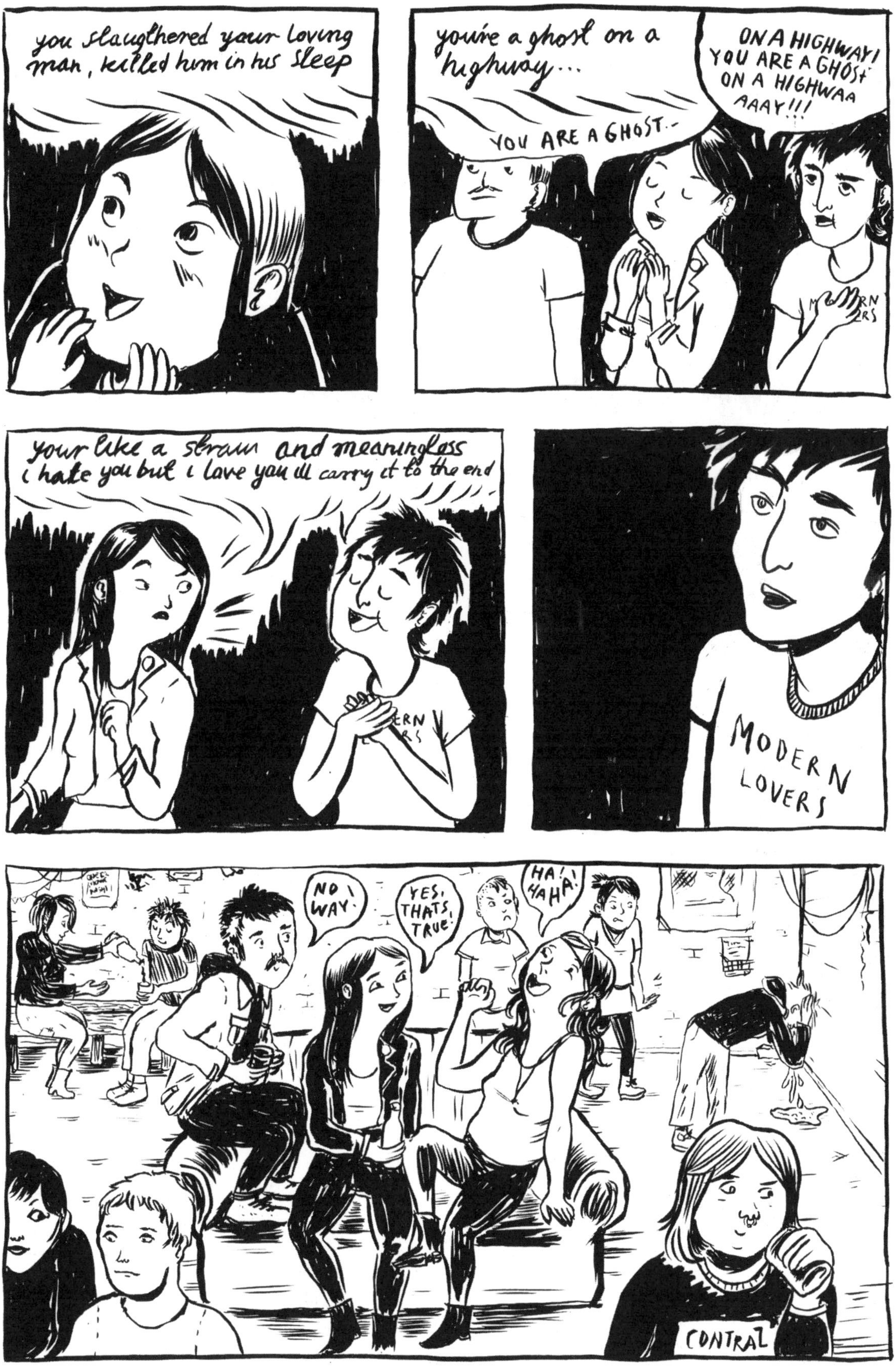
you slaughtered your loving man, killed him in his sleep
you're a ghost on a highway...
ON A HIGHWAY! YOU ARE A GHOST ON A HIGHWAA AAAY!!!
YOU ARE A GHOST..
MODERN LOVERS
your like a stream and meaningless i hate you but i love you ill carry it to the end
MODERN LOVERS
NO WAY.
YES, THATS TRUE!
HA! HAHA!
CONTRAZ

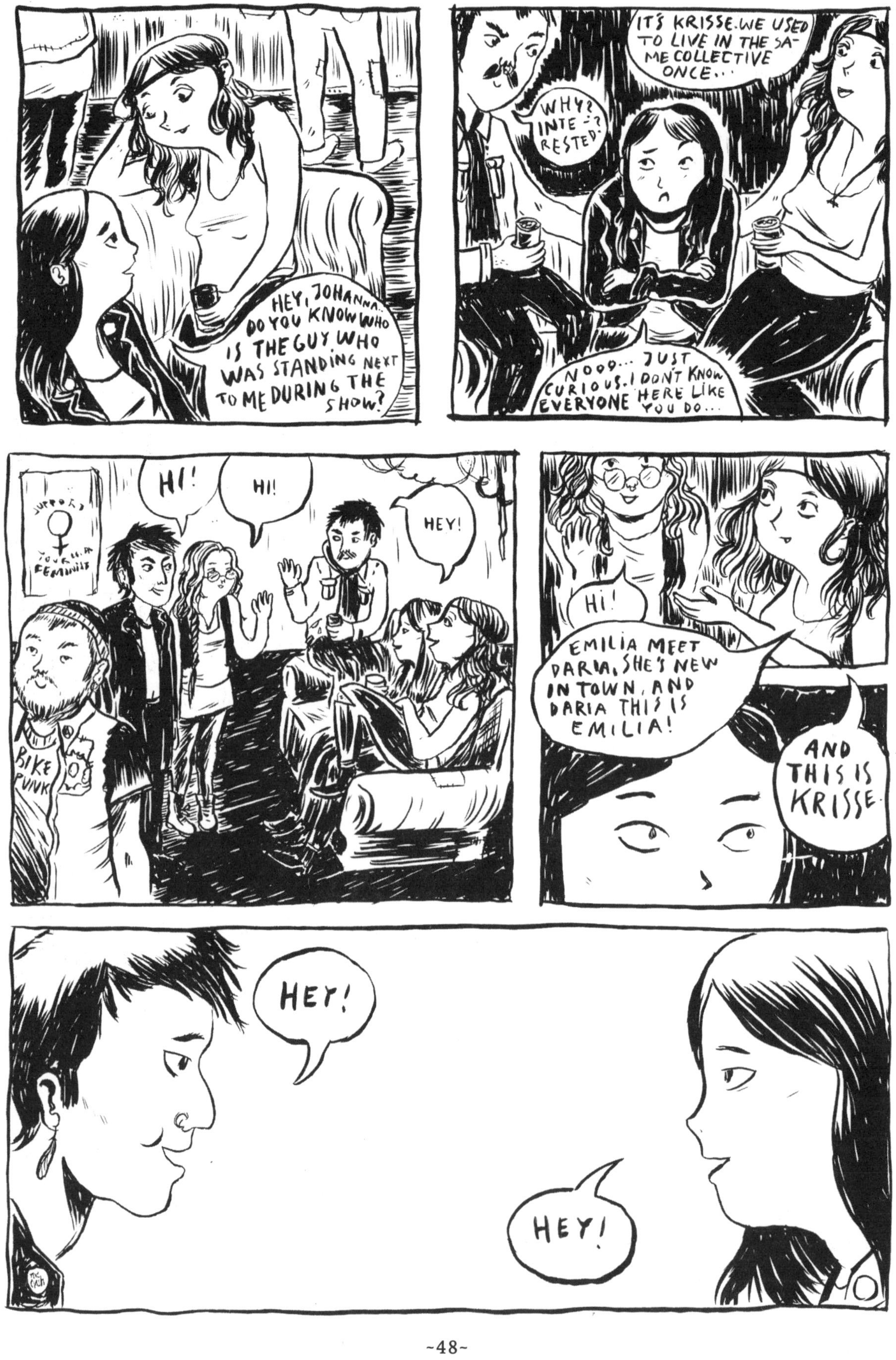
HEY, JOHANNA.. DO YOU KNOW WHO IS THE GUY WHO WAS STANDING NEXT TO ME DURING THE SHOW?
IT'S KRISSE. WE USED TO LIVE IN THE SAME COLLECTIVE ONCE...
WHY? INTE-? RESTED?
NOOO... JUST CURIOUS. I DON'T KNOW EVERYONE HERE LIKE YOU DO...
HI!
HI!
HEY!
BIKE PUNK
HI!
EMILIA MEET DARIA, SHE'S NEW IN TOWN, AND DARIA THIS IS EMILIA!
AND THIS IS KRISSE.
HEY!
HEY!

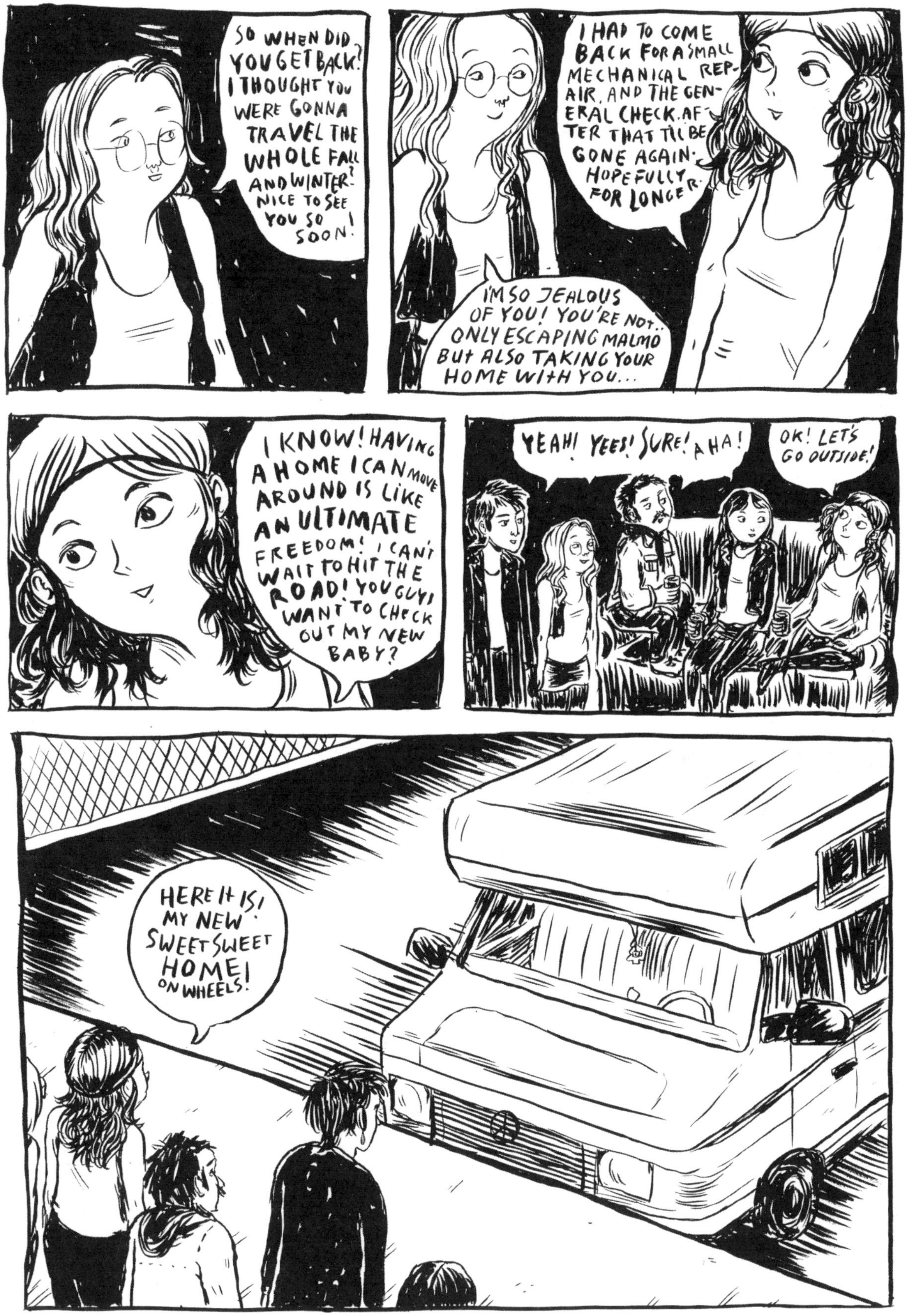
SO WHEN DID YOU GET BACK? I THOUGHT YOU WERE GONNA TRAVEL THE WHOLE FALL AND WINTER? NICE TO SEE YOU SO SOON!
I HAD TO COME BACK FOR A SMALL MECHANICAL REPAIR, AND THE GENERAL CHECK. AFTER THAT I'LL BE GONE AGAIN. HOPEFULLY FOR LONGER.
I'M SO JEALOUS OF YOU! YOU'RE NOT ONLY ESCAPING MALMÖ BUT ALSO TAKING YOUR HOME WITH YOU...
I KNOW! HAVING A HOME I CAN MOVE AROUND IS LIKE AN ULTIMATE FREEDOM! I CAN'T WAIT TO HIT THE ROAD! YOU GUYS WANT TO CHECK OUT MY NEW BABY?
YEAH! YEES! SURE! AHA!
OK! LET'S GO OUTSIDE!
HERE IT IS! MY NEW SWEET SWEET HOME! ON WHEELS!

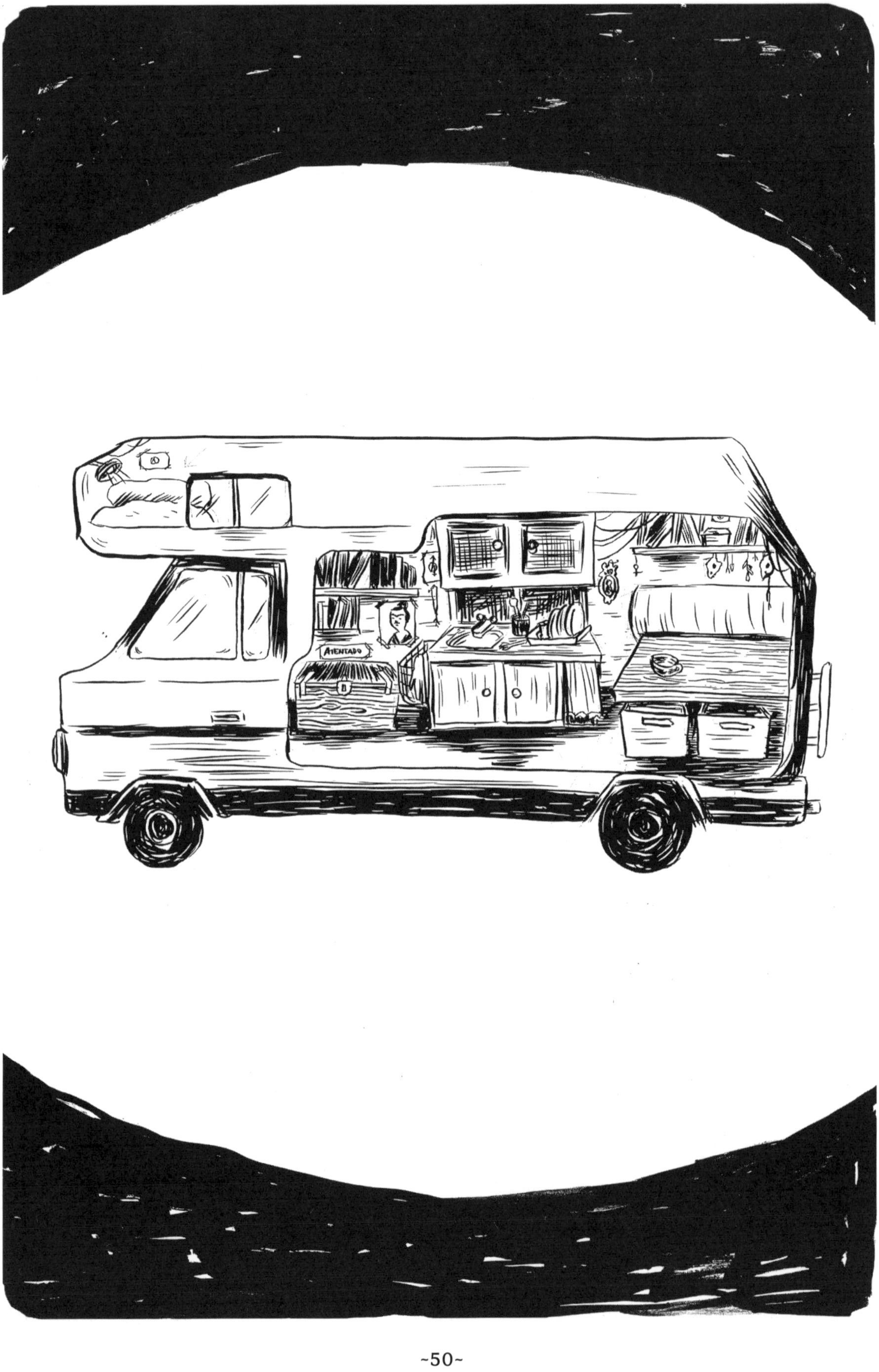
ATENTADO

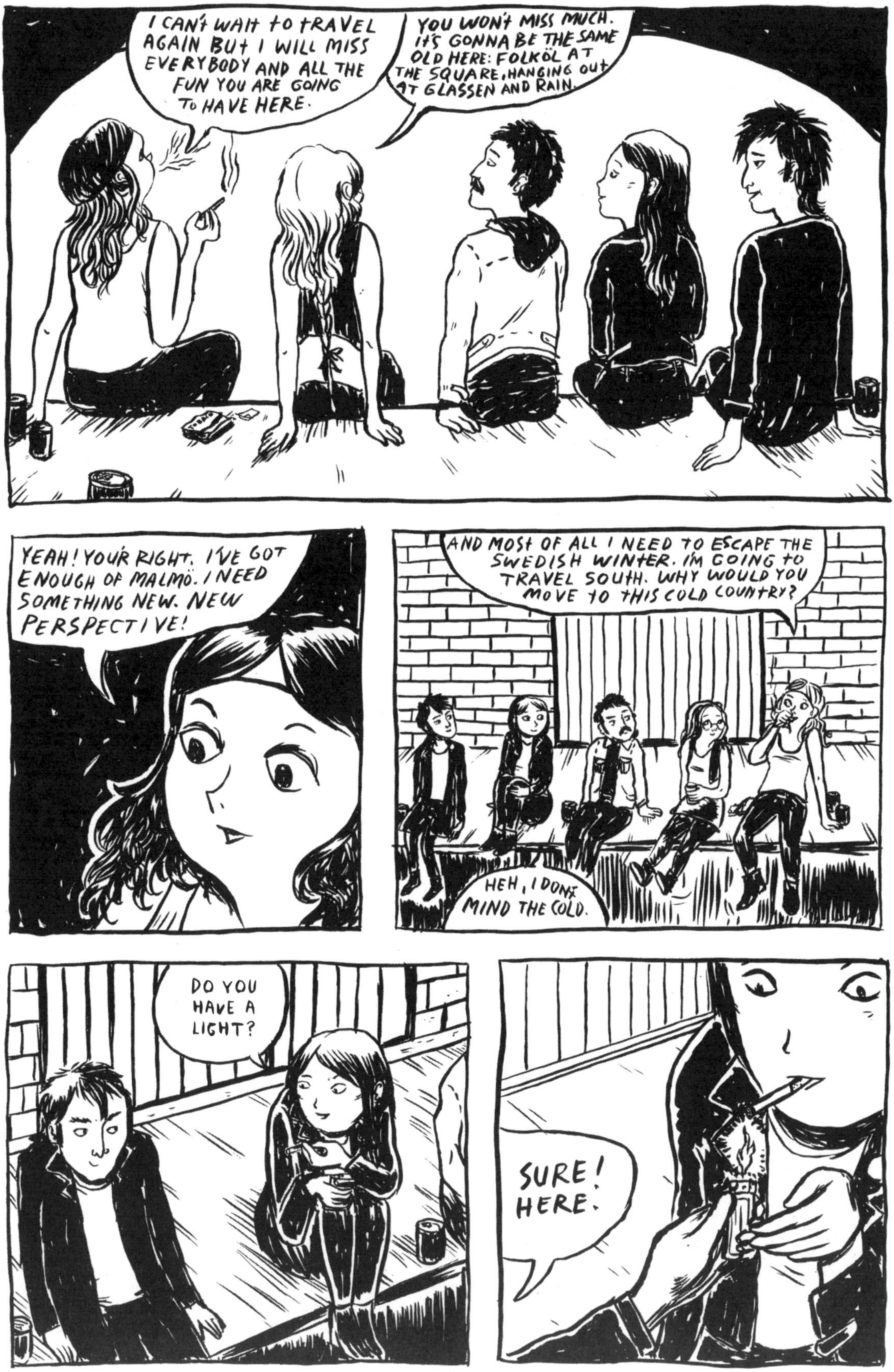
I CAN'T WAIT TO TRAVEL AGAIN BUT I WILL MISS EVERYBODY AND ALL THE FUN YOU ARE GOING TO HAVE HERE.
YOU WON'T MISS MUCH. IT'S GONNA BE THE SAME OLD HERE: FOLKÖL AT THE SQUARE, HANGING OUT AT GLASSEN AND RAIN.
YEAH! YOU'R RIGHT. I'VE GOT ENOUGH OF MALMÖ. I NEED SOMETHING NEW. NEW PERSPECTIVE!
AND MOST OF ALL I NEED TO ESCAPE THE SWEDISH WINTER. I'M GOING TO TRAVEL SOUTH. WHY WOULD YOU MOVE TO THIS COLD COUNTRY?
HEH, I DON'T MIND THE COLD.
DO YOU HAVE A LIGHT?
SURE! HERE.

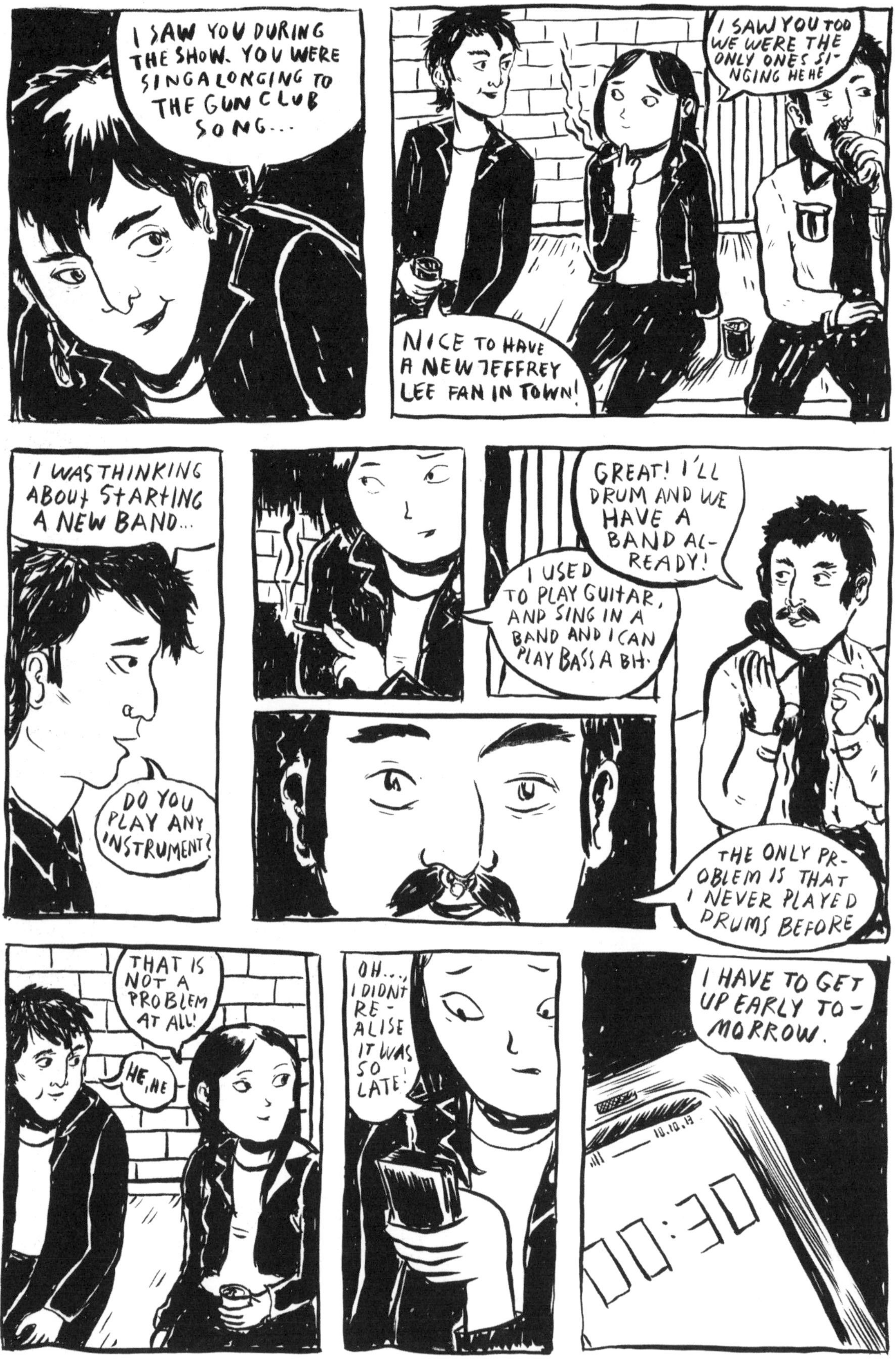
I SAW YOU DURING THE SHOW. YOU WERE SINGALONGING TO THE GUN CLUB SONG...
I SAW YOU TOO WE WERE THE ONLY ONES SINGING HEHE
NICE TO HAVE A NEW JEFFREY LEE FAN IN TOWN!
I WAS THINKING ABOUT STARTING A NEW BAND...
DO YOU PLAY ANY INSTRUMENT?
I USED TO PLAY GUITAR, AND SING IN A BAND AND I CAN PLAY BASS A BIT.
GREAT! I'LL DRUM AND WE HAVE A BAND ALREADY!
THE ONLY PROBLEM IS THAT I NEVER PLAYED DRUMS BEFORE
THAT IS NOT A PROBLEM AT ALL!
HE, HE
OH..., I DIDNT REALISE IT WAS SO LATE!
I HAVE TO GET UP EARLY TOMORROW.
10.10.13
03:00

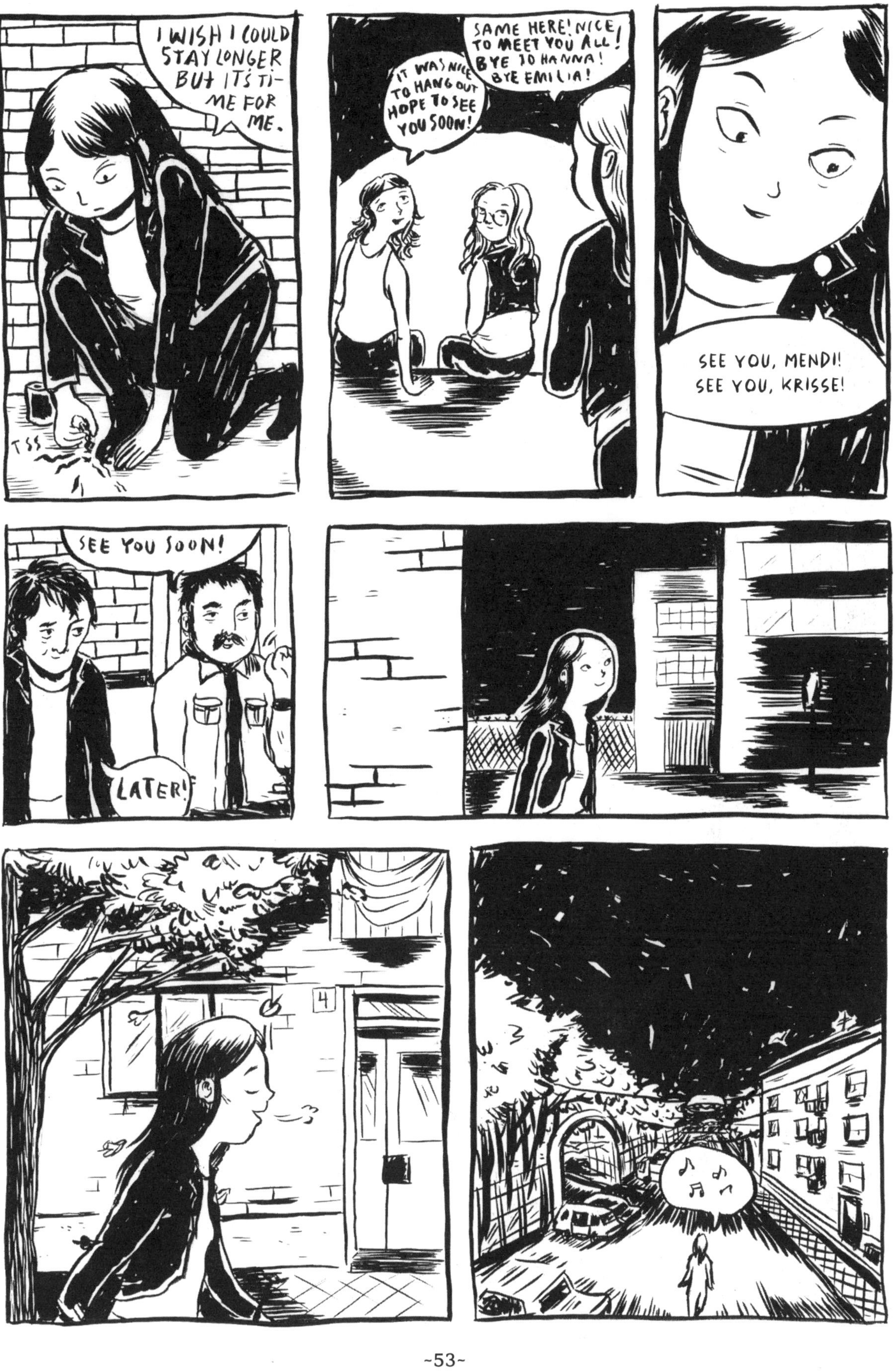
I WISH I COULD STAY LONGER BUT IT'S TI-ME FOR ME.
TSS
IT WAS NICE TO HANG OUT HOPE TO SEE YOU SOON!
SAME HERE! NICE TO MEET YOU ALL! BYE TO HANNA! BYE EMILIA!
SEE YOU, MENDI! SEE YOU, KRISSE!
SEE YOU SOON!
LATER!
4

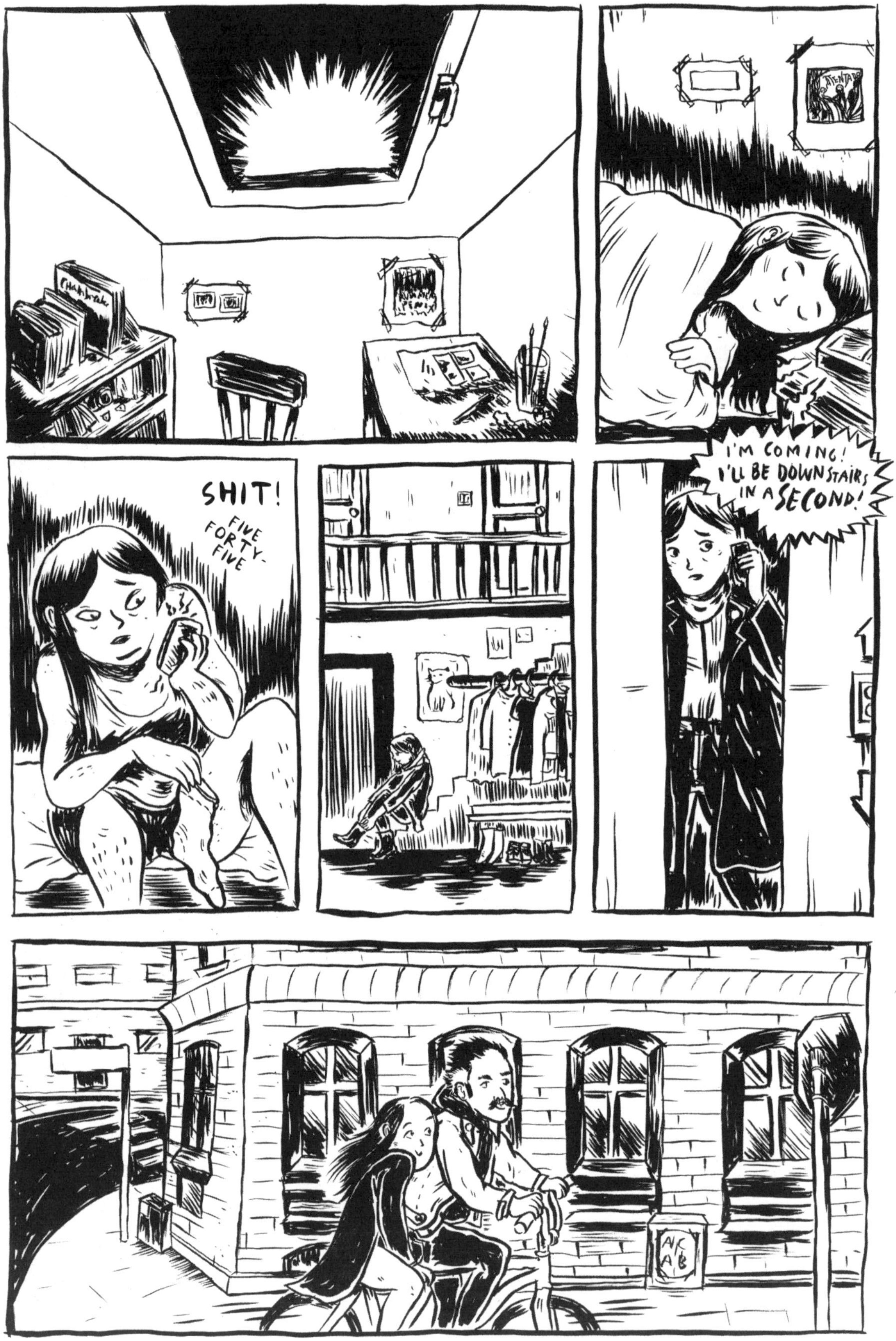
SHIT!
FIVE FORTY-FIVE
I'M COMING! I'LL BE DOWNSTAIRS IN A SECOND!

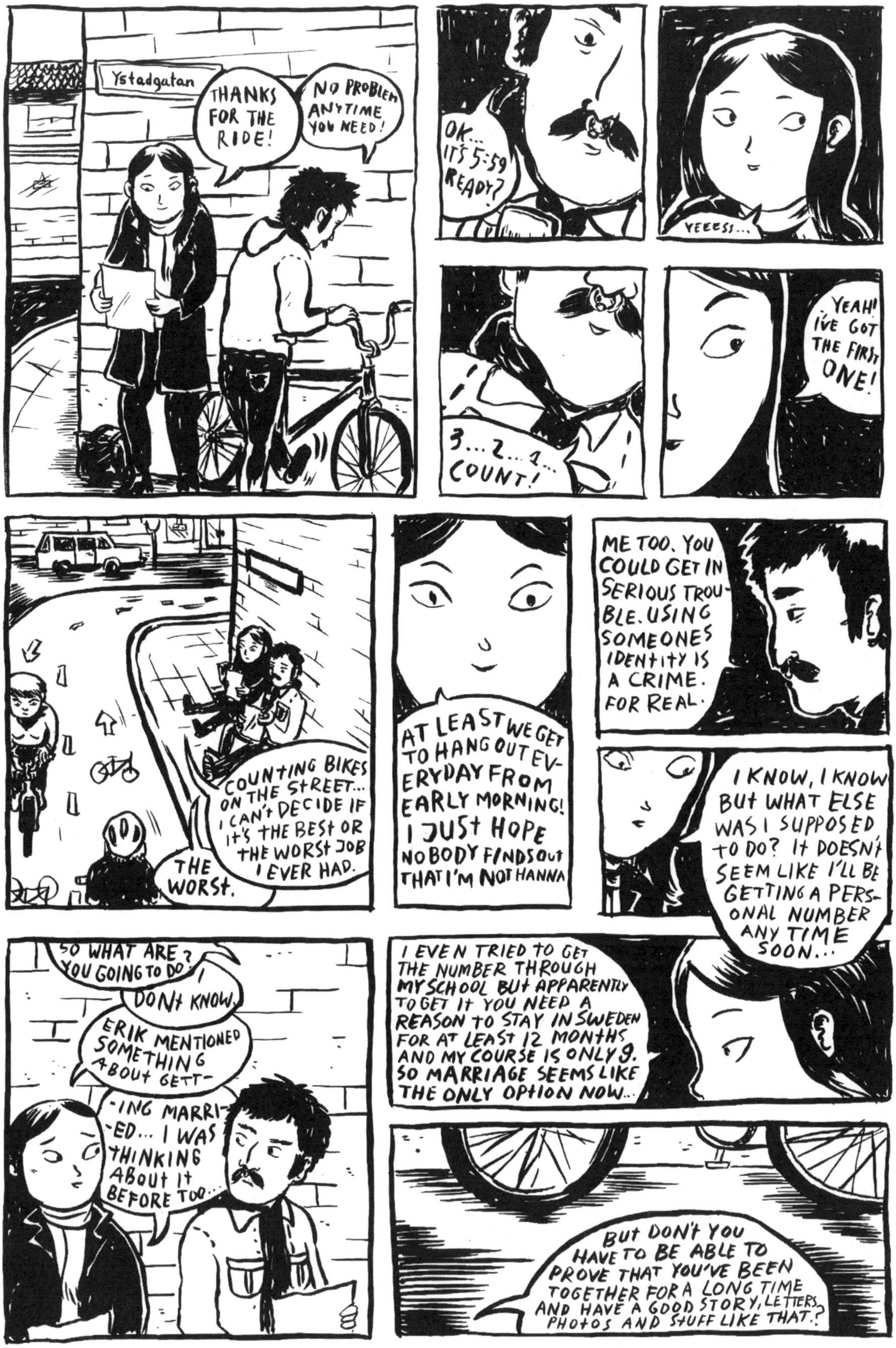
Ystadgatan
THANKS FOR THE RIDE!
NO PROBLEM ANYTIME YOU NEED!
OK... IT'S 5:59 READY?
YEEESS...
3... 2... 1... COUNT!
YEAH! I'VE GOT THE FIRST ONE!
COUNTING BIKES ON THE STREET... I CAN'T DECIDE IF IT'S THE BEST OR THE WORST JOB I EVER HAD.
THE WORST.
AT LEAST WE GET TO HANG OUT EVERYDAY FROM EARLY MORNING! I JUST HOPE NOBODY FINDS OUT THAT I'M NOT HANNA
ME TOO. YOU COULD GET IN SERIOUS TROUBLE. USING SOMEONES IDENTITY IS A CRIME. FOR REAL.
I KNOW, I KNOW BUT WHAT ELSE WAS I SUPPOSED TO DO? IT DOESN'T SEEM LIKE I'LL BE GETTING A PERSONAL NUMBER ANY TIME SOON...
SO WHAT ARE YOU GOING TO DO?
I DON'T KNOW.
ERIK MENTIONED SOMETHING ABOUT GETT-
-ING MARRIED... I WAS THINKING ABOUT IT BEFORE TOO...
I EVEN TRIED TO GET THE NUMBER THROUGH MY SCHOOL BUT APPARENTLY TO GET IT YOU NEED A REASON TO STAY IN SWEDEN FOR AT LEAST 12 MONTHS AND MY COURSE IS ONLY 9. SO MARRIAGE SEEMS LIKE THE ONLY OPTION NOW...
BUT DON'T YOU HAVE TO BE ABLE TO PROVE THAT YOU'VE BEEN TOGETHER FOR A LONG TIME AND HAVE A GOOD STORY, LETTERS, PHOTOS AND STUFF LIKE THAT?

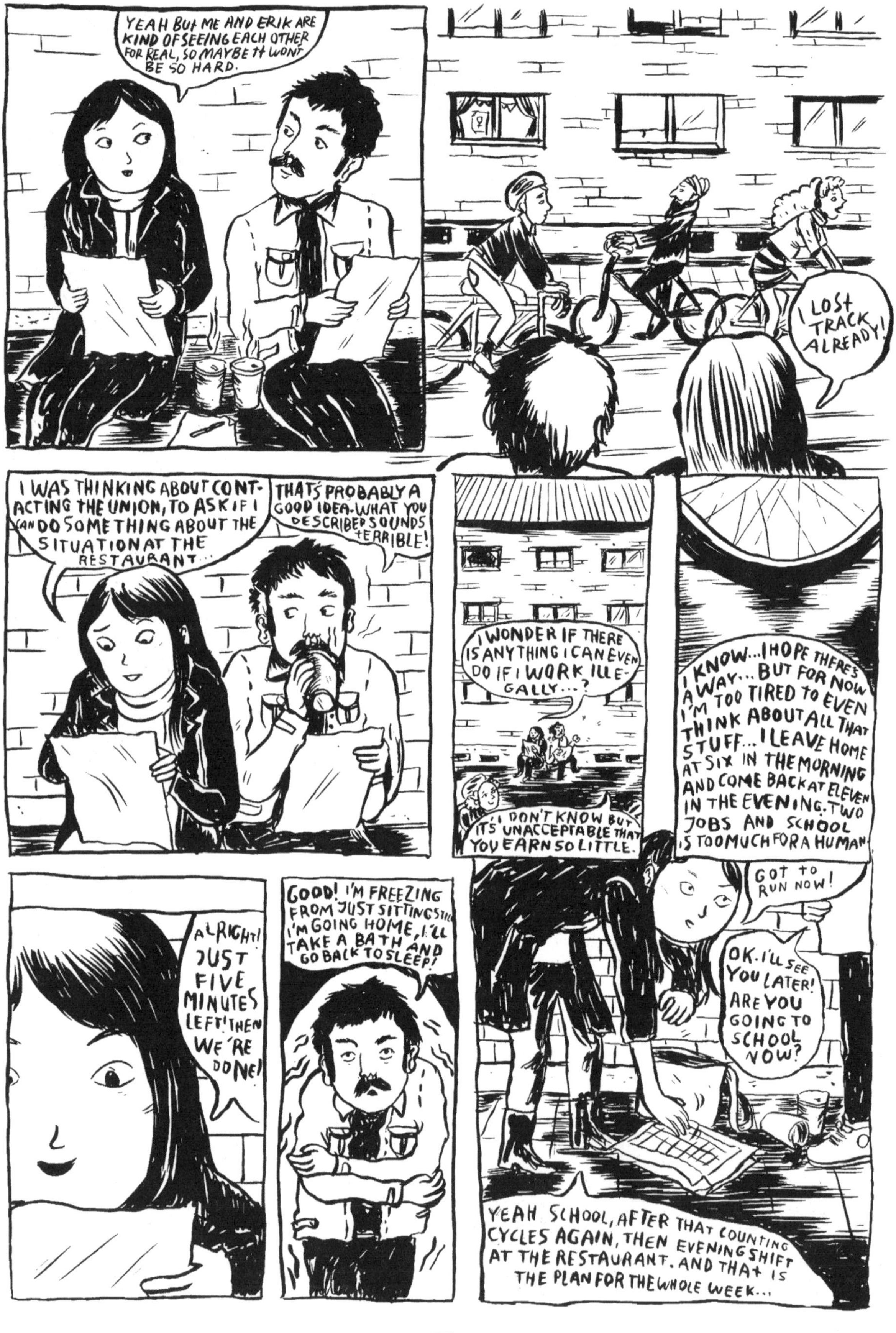
YEAH BUT ME AND ERIK ARE KIND OF SEEING EACH OTHER FOR REAL, SO MAYBE IT WONT BE SO HARD.
I LOST TRACK ALREADY!
I WAS THINKING ABOUT CONTACTING THE UNION, TO ASK IF I CAN DO SOMETHING ABOUT THE SITUATION AT THE RESTAURANT...
THAT'S PROBABLY A GOOD IDEA. WHAT YOU DESCRIBED SOUNDS TERRIBLE!
I WONDER IF THERE IS ANYTHING I CAN EVEN DO IF I WORK ILLEGALLY...?
I DON'T KNOW BUT IT'S UNACCEPTABLE THAT YOU EARN SO LITTLE.
I KNOW... I HOPE THERE'S A WAY... BUT FOR NOW I'M TOO TIRED TO EVEN THINK ABOUT ALL THAT STUFF... I LEAVE HOME AT SIX IN THE MORNING AND COME BACK AT ELEVEN IN THE EVENING. TWO JOBS AND SCHOOL IS TOO MUCH FOR A HUMAN.
ALRIGHT! JUST FIVE MINUTES LEFT! THEN WE'RE DONE!
GOOD! I'M FREEZING FROM JUST SITTING STILL. I'M GOING HOME, I'LL TAKE A BATH AND GO BACK TO SLEEP!
GOT TO RUN NOW!
OK. I'LL SEE YOU LATER! ARE YOU GOING TO SCHOOL NOW?
YEAH SCHOOL, AFTER THAT COUNTING CYCLES AGAIN, THEN EVENING SHIFT AT THE RESTAURANT. AND THAT IS THE PLAN FOR THE WHOLE WEEK...

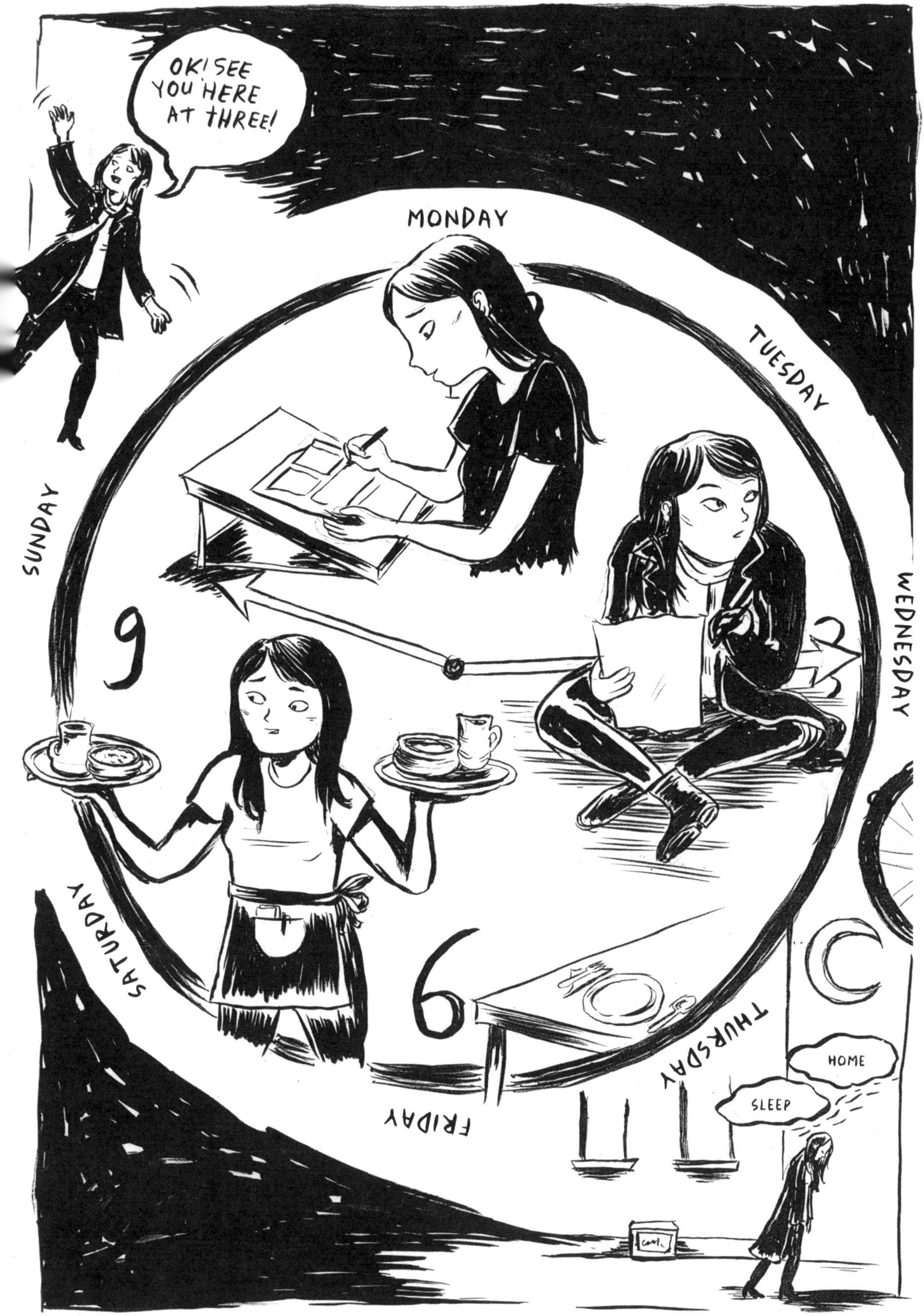
OK! SEE YOU HERE AT THREE!
MONDAY
TUESDAY
WEDNESDAY
THURSDAY
FRIDAY
SATURDAY
SUNDAY
9
3
6
HOME
SLEEP

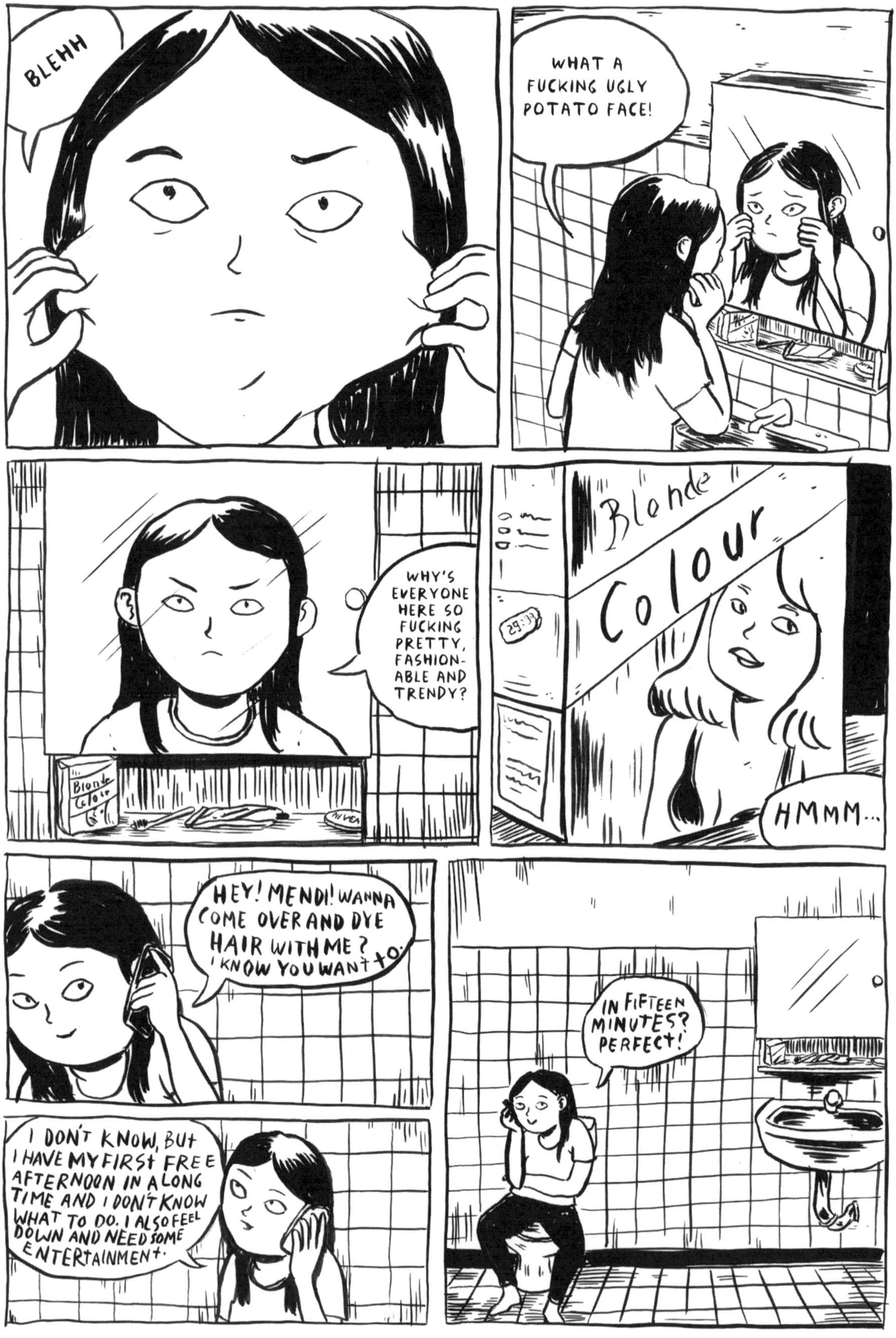
BLEHH
WHAT A FUCKING UGLY POTATO FACE!
WHY'S EVERYONE HERE SO FUCKING PRETTY, FASHION-ABLE AND TRENDY?
Blonde Colour
HMMM...
HEY! MENDI! WANNA COME OVER AND DYE HAIR WITH ME? I KNOW YOU WANT TO.
I DON'T KNOW, BUT I HAVE MY FIRST FREE AFTERNOON IN A LONG TIME AND I DON'T KNOW WHAT TO DO. I ALSO FEEL DOWN AND NEED SOME ENTERTAINMENT.
IN FIFTEEN MINUTES? PERFECT!

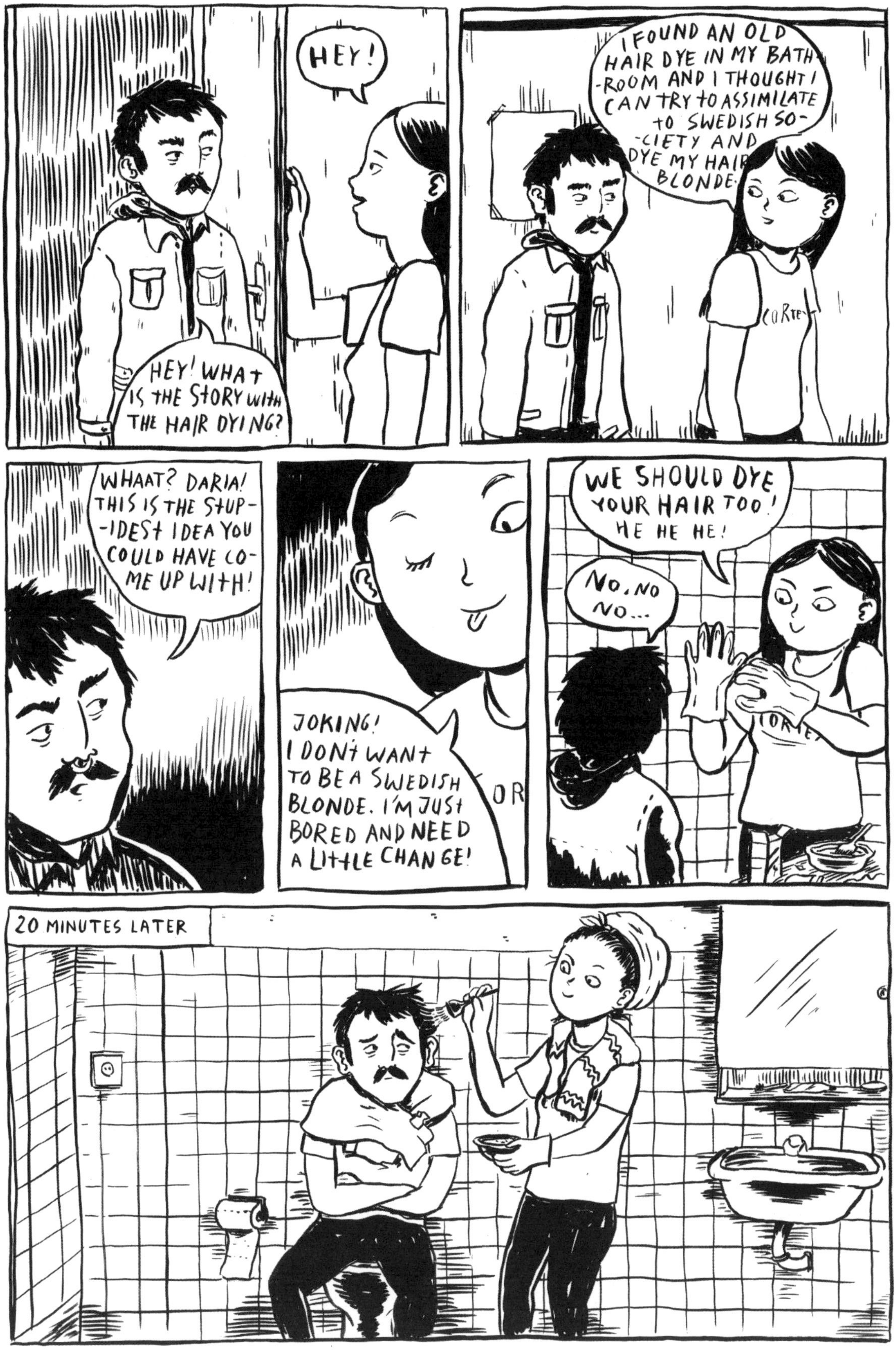
HEY!
HEY! WHAT IS THE STORY WITH THE HAIR DYING?
I FOUND AN OLD HAIR DYE IN MY BATH-ROOM AND I THOUGHT I CAN TRY TO ASSIMILATE TO SWEDISH SO-CIETY AND DYE MY HAIR BLONDE.
WHAAT? DARIA! THIS IS THE STUP-IDEST IDEA YOU COULD HAVE CO-ME UP WITH!
JOKING! I DON'T WANT TO BE A SWEDISH BLONDE. I'M JUST BORED AND NEED A LITTLE CHANGE!
WE SHOULD DYE YOUR HAIR TOO! HE HE HE!
NO, NO NO...
20 MINUTES LATER

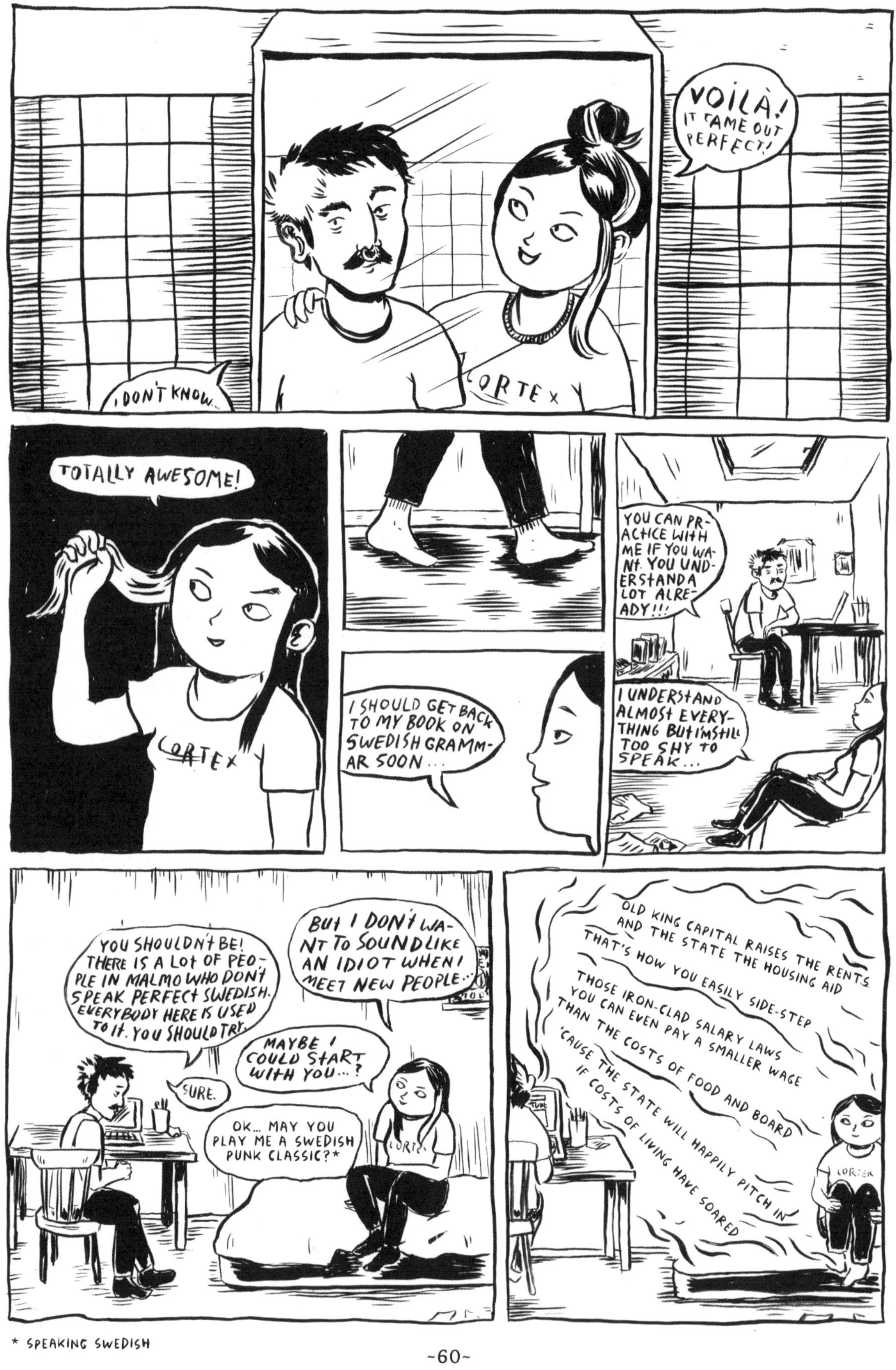
VOILÀ! IT CAME OUT PERFECT!
I DON'T KNOW...
CORTEX
TOTALLY AWESOME!
CORTEX
I SHOULD GET BACK TO MY BOOK ON SWEDISH GRAMMAR SOON...
YOU CAN PRACTICE WITH ME IF YOU WANT. YOU UNDERSTAND A LOT ALREADY!!!
I UNDERSTAND ALMOST EVERYTHING BUT I'M STILL TOO SHY TO SPEAK...
YOU SHOULDN'T BE! THERE IS A LOT OF PEOPLE IN MALMO WHO DON'T SPEAK PERFECT SWEDISH. EVERYBODY HERE IS USED TO IT. YOU SHOULD TRY.
BUT I DON'T WANT TO SOUND LIKE AN IDIOT WHEN I MEET NEW PEOPLE...
MAYBE I COULD START WITH YOU...?
SURE.
OK... MAY YOU PLAY ME A SWEDISH PUNK CLASSIC?*
OLD KING CAPITAL RAISES THE RENTS
AND THE STATE THE HOUSING AID
THAT'S HOW YOU EASILY SIDE-STEP
THOSE IRON-CLAD SALARY LAWS
YOU CAN EVEN PAY A SMALLER WAGE
THAN THE COSTS OF FOOD AND BOARD
'CAUSE THE STATE WILL HAPPILY PITCH IN
IF COSTS OF LIVING HAVE SOARED

* SPEAKING SWEDISH

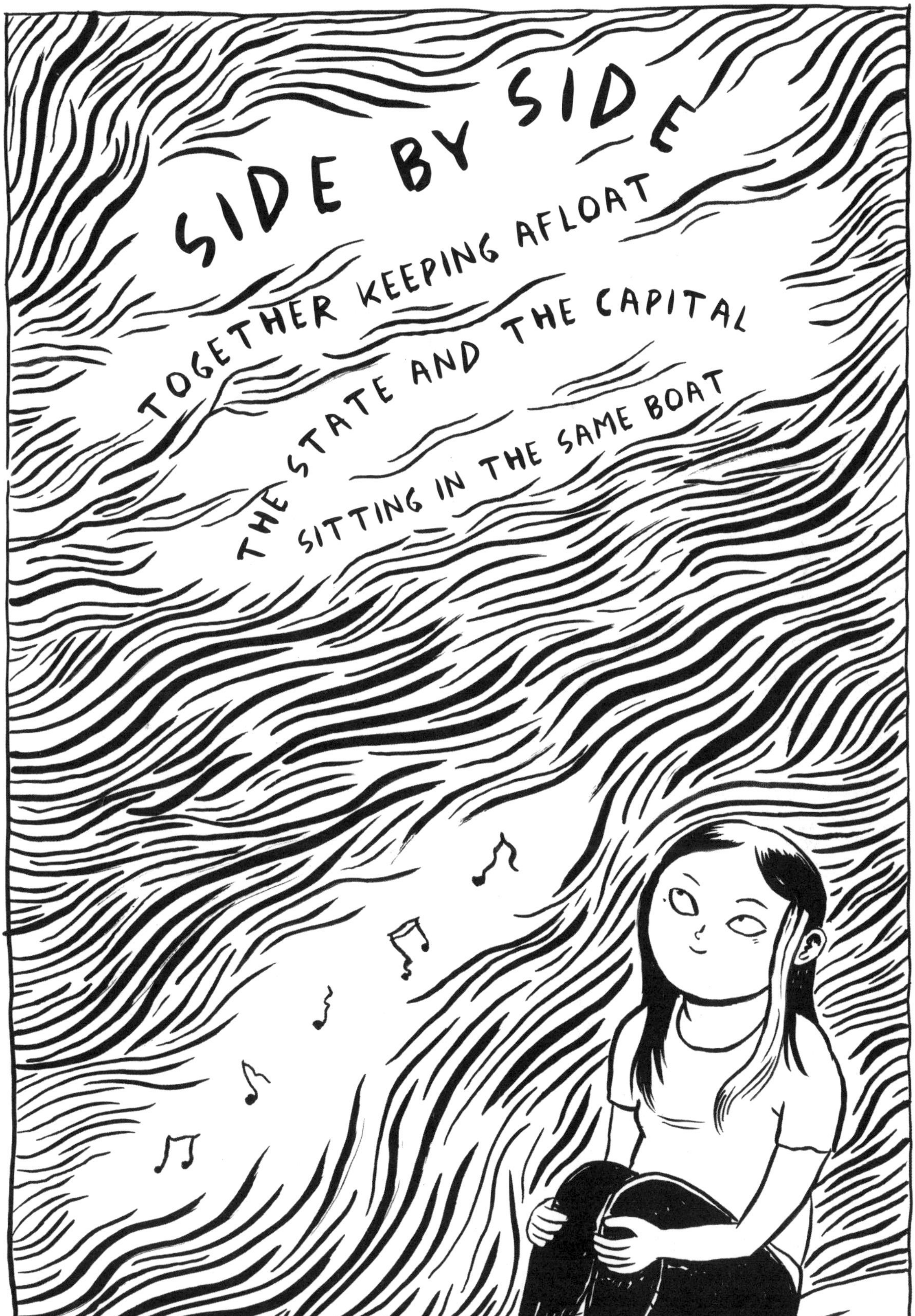
SIDE BY SIDE
TOGETHER KEEPING AFLOAT
THE STATE AND THE CAPITAL
SITTING IN THE SAME BOAT

"STATEN OCH KAPITALET" BY EBBA GRÖN

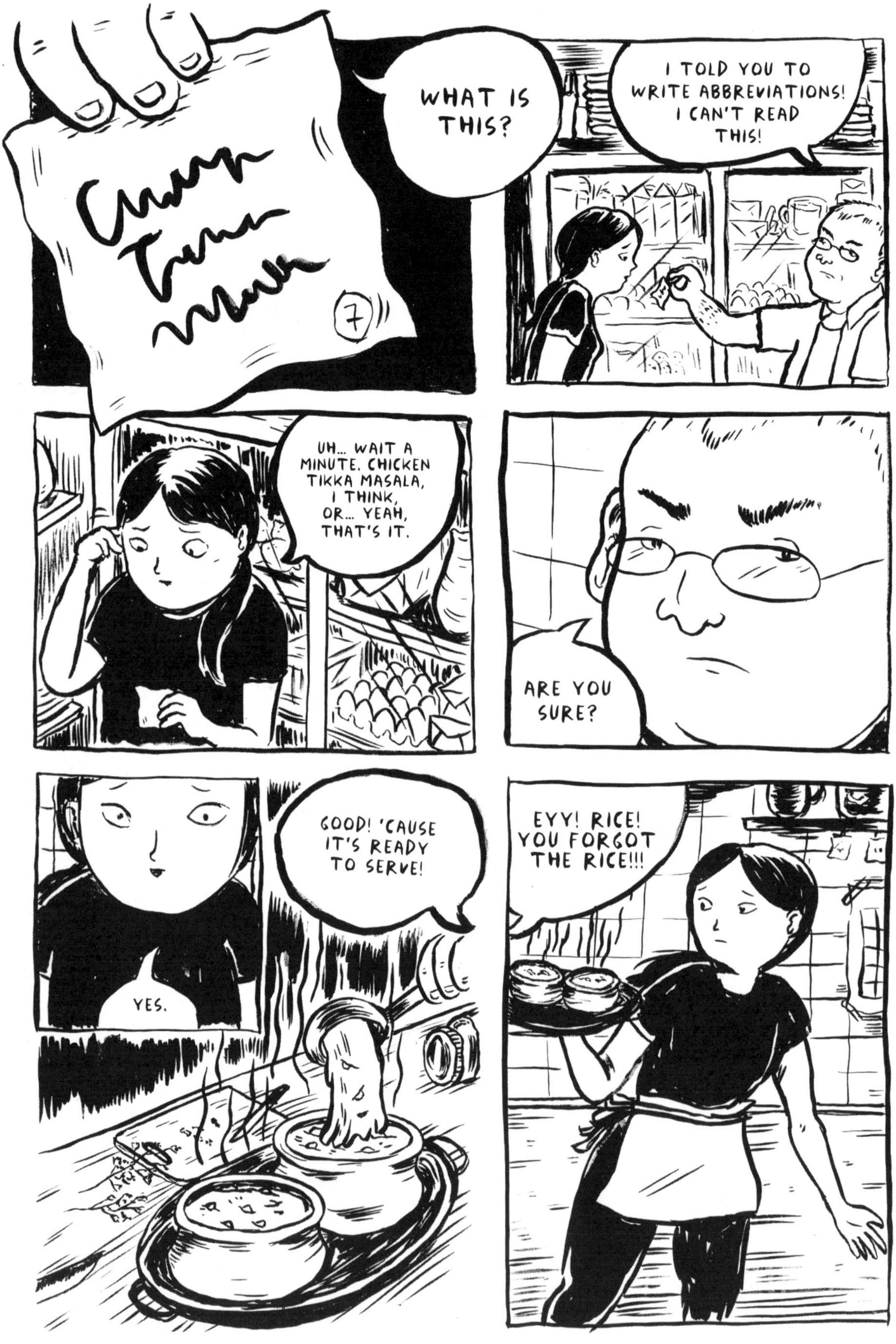
WHAT IS THIS?
I TOLD YOU TO WRITE ABBREVIATIONS! I CAN'T READ THIS!
UH... WAIT A MINUTE. CHICKEN TIKKA MASALA, I THINK, OR... YEAH, THAT'S IT.
ARE YOU SURE?
YES.
GOOD! 'CAUSE IT'S READY TO SERVE!
EYY! RICE! YOU FORGOT THE RICE!!!

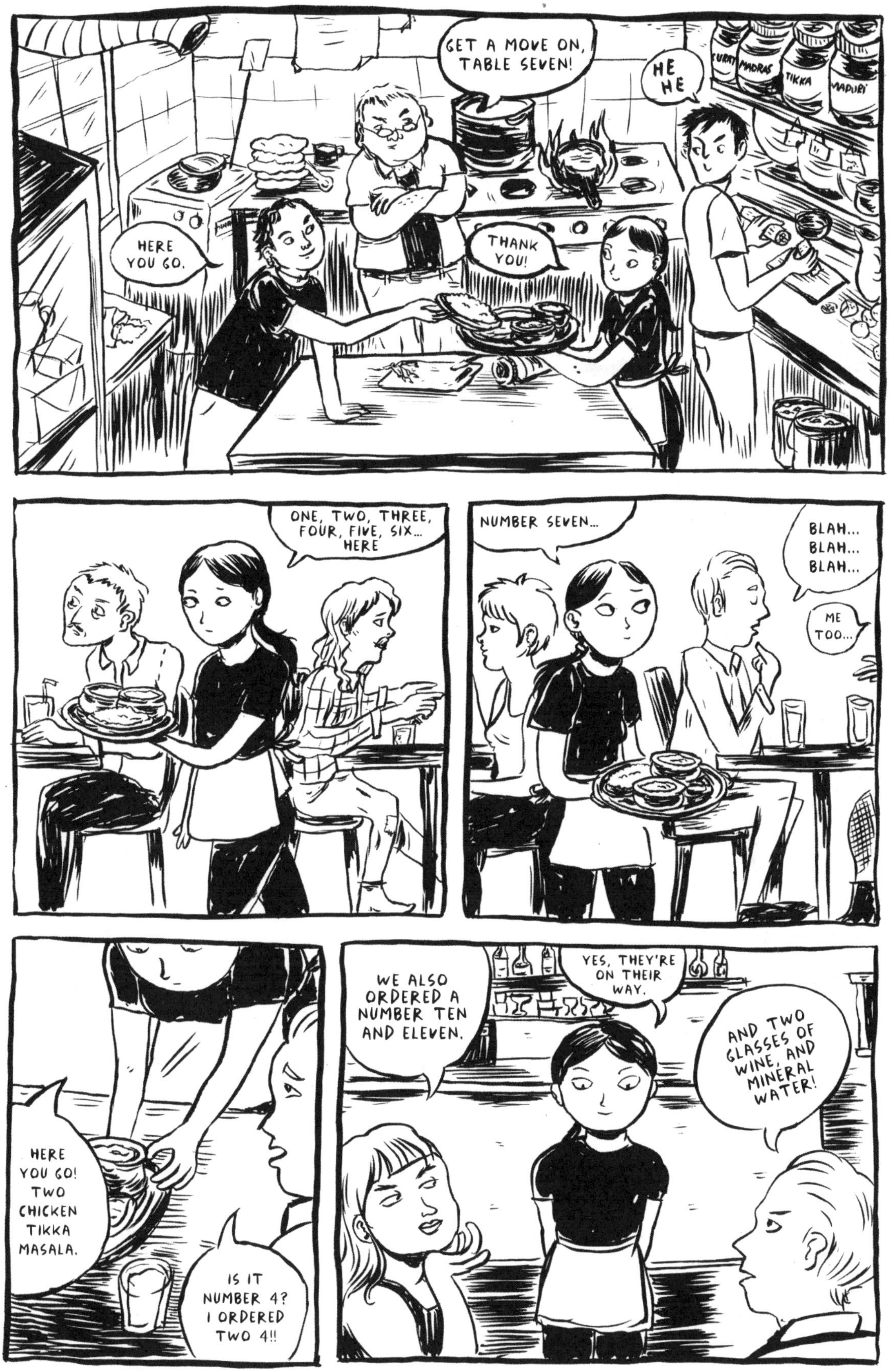
GET A MOVE ON, TABLE SEVEN!
HE HE
CURRY
MADRAS
TIKKA
MADURI
HERE YOU GO.
THANK YOU!
ONE, TWO, THREE, FOUR, FIVE, SIX... HERE
NUMBER SEVEN...
BLAH... BLAH... BLAH...
ME TOO...
HERE YOU GO! TWO CHICKEN TIKKA MASALA.
IS IT NUMBER 4? I ORDERED TWO 4!!
WE ALSO ORDERED A NUMBER TEN AND ELEVEN.
YES, THEY'RE ON THEIR WAY.
AND TWO GLASSES OF WINE, AND MINERAL WATER!

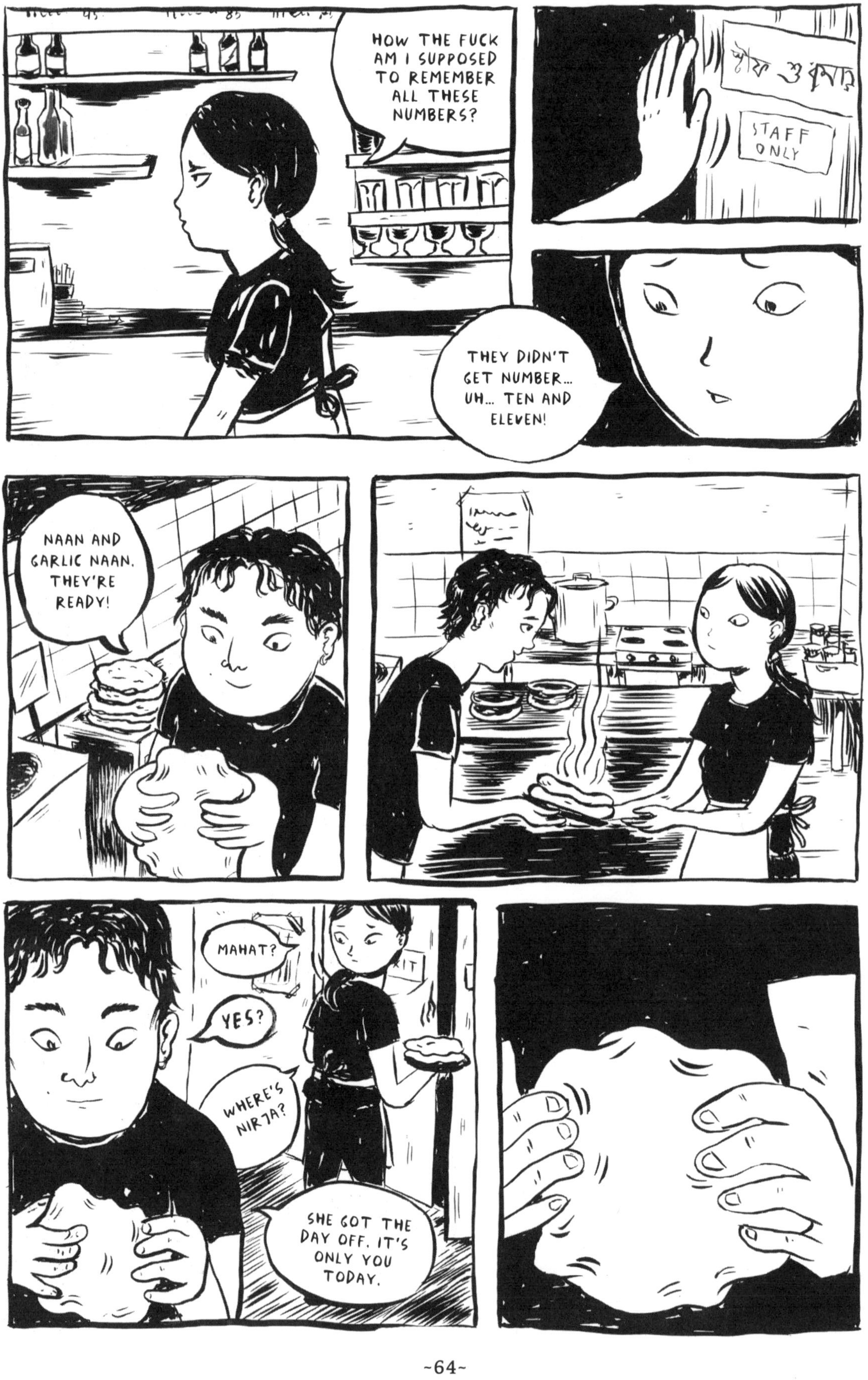
HOW THE FUCK AM I SUPPOSED TO REMEMBER ALL THESE NUMBERS?
STAFF ONLY
THEY DIDN'T GET NUMBER... UH... TEN AND ELEVEN!
NAAN AND GARLIC NAAN. THEY'RE READY!
MAHAT?
YES?
WHERE'S NIRJA?
SHE GOT THE DAY OFF. IT'S ONLY YOU TODAY.

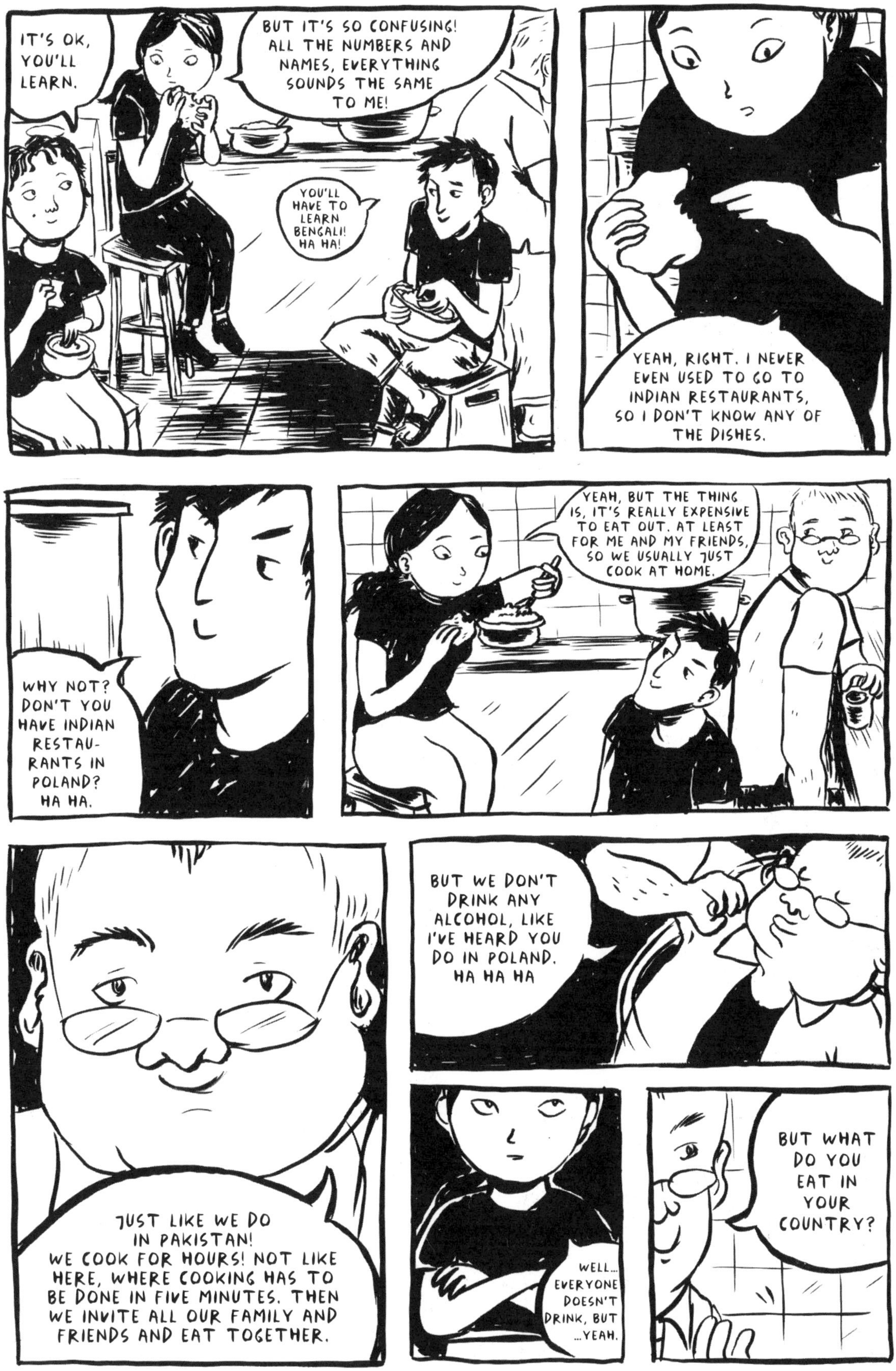
IT'S OK, YOU'LL LEARN.
BUT IT'S SO CONFUSING! ALL THE NUMBERS AND NAMES, EVERYTHING SOUNDS THE SAME TO ME!
YOU'LL HAVE TO LEARN BENGALI! HA HA!
YEAH, RIGHT. I NEVER EVEN USED TO GO TO INDIAN RESTAURANTS, SO I DON'T KNOW ANY OF THE DISHES.
WHY NOT? DON'T YOU HAVE INDIAN RESTAU-RANTS IN POLAND? HA HA.
YEAH, BUT THE THING IS, IT'S REALLY EXPENSIVE TO EAT OUT. AT LEAST FOR ME AND MY FRIENDS, SO WE USUALLY JUST COOK AT HOME.
JUST LIKE WE DO IN PAKISTAN! WE COOK FOR HOURS! NOT LIKE HERE, WHERE COOKING HAS TO BE DONE IN FIVE MINUTES. THEN WE INVITE ALL OUR FAMILY AND FRIENDS AND EAT TOGETHER.
BUT WE DON'T DRINK ANY ALCOHOL, LIKE I'VE HEARD YOU DO IN POLAND. HA HA HA
WELL... EVERYONE DOESN'T DRINK, BUT ...YEAH.
BUT WHAT DO YOU EAT IN YOUR COUNTRY?

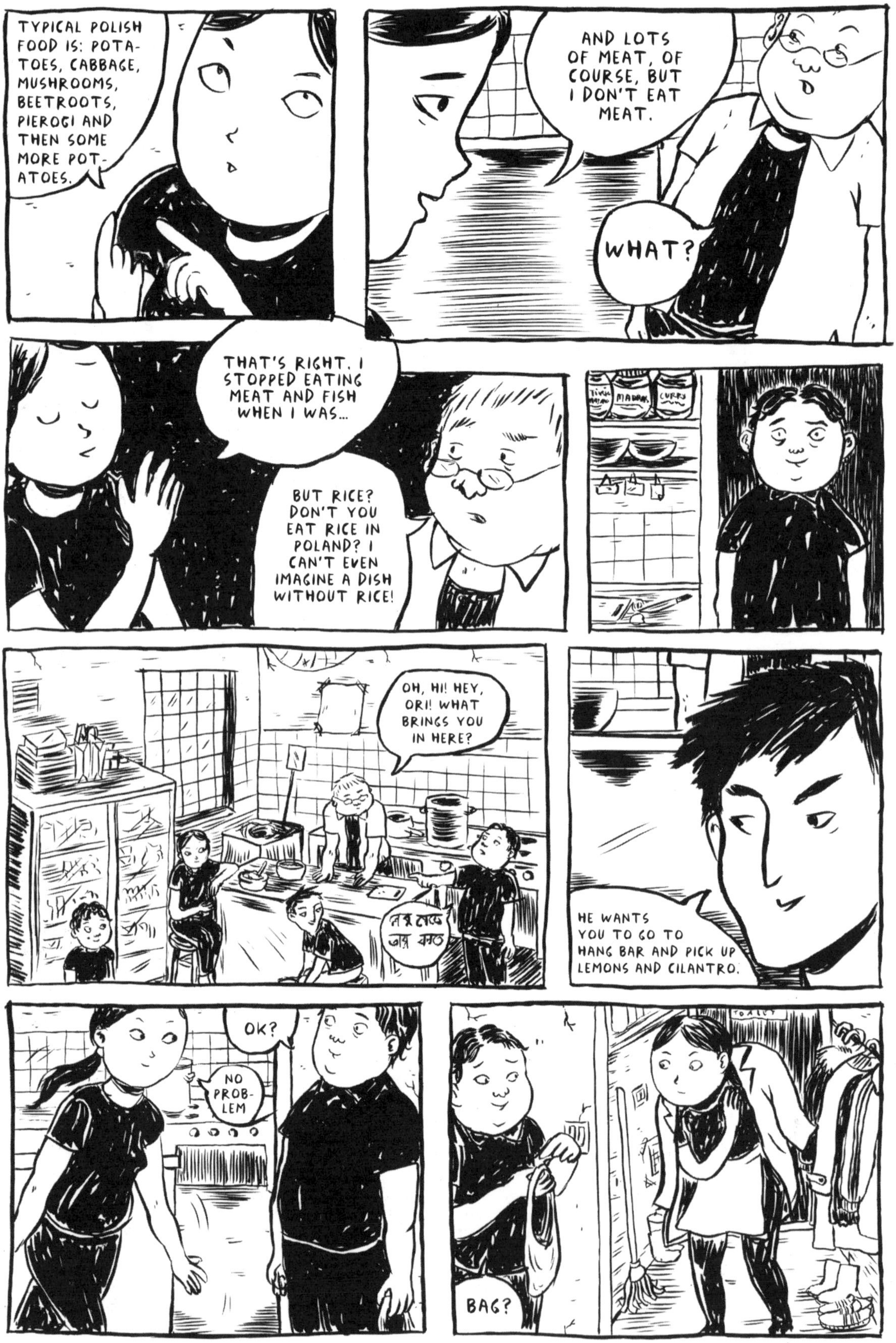
TYPICAL POLISH FOOD IS: POTATOES, CABBAGE, MUSHROOMS, BEETROOTS, PIEROGI AND THEN SOME MORE POTATOES.
AND LOTS OF MEAT, OF COURSE, BUT I DON'T EAT MEAT.
WHAT?
THAT'S RIGHT. I STOPPED EATING MEAT AND FISH WHEN I WAS...
BUT RICE? DON'T YOU EAT RICE IN POLAND? I CAN'T EVEN IMAGINE A DISH WITHOUT RICE!
MADRAS
CURRY
OH, HI! HEY, ORI! WHAT BRINGS YOU IN HERE?
HE WANTS YOU TO GO TO HANG BAR AND PICK UP LEMONS AND CILANTRO.
OK?
NO PROBLEM
BAG?

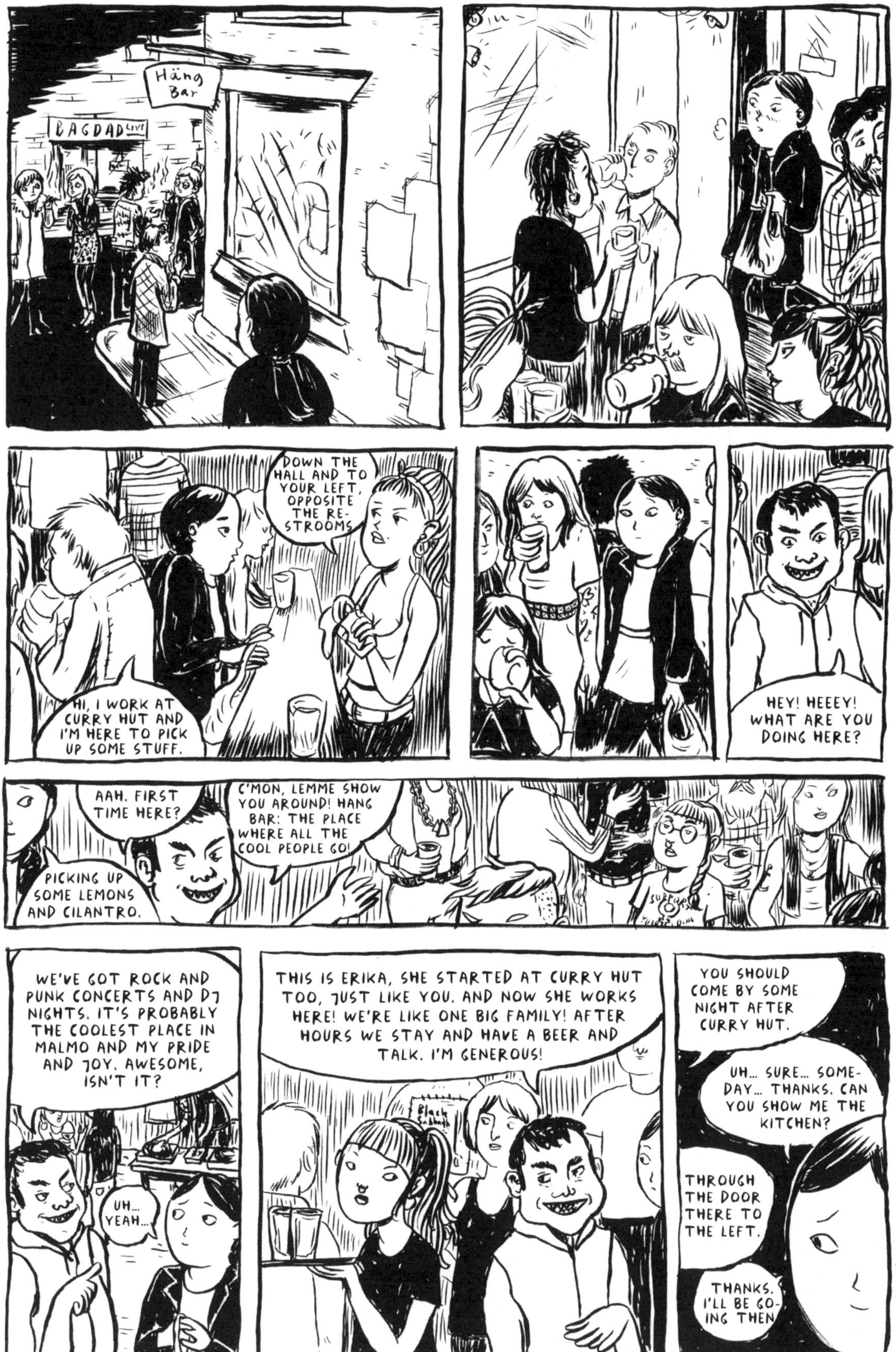
Häng Bar
BAGDAD LIVE
DOWN THE HALL AND TO YOUR LEFT, OPPOSITE THE RE-STROOMS
HI, I WORK AT CURRY HUT AND I'M HERE TO PICK UP SOME STUFF.
HEY! HEEEY! WHAT ARE YOU DOING HERE?
AAH. FIRST TIME HERE?
PICKING UP SOME LEMONS AND CILANTRO.
C'MON, LEMME SHOW YOU AROUND! HANG BAR: THE PLACE WHERE ALL THE COOL PEOPLE GO!
WE'VE GOT ROCK AND PUNK CONCERTS AND DJ NIGHTS. IT'S PROBABLY THE COOLEST PLACE IN MALMO AND MY PRIDE AND JOY. AWESOME, ISN'T IT?
UH... YEAH...
THIS IS ERIKA, SHE STARTED AT CURRY HUT TOO, JUST LIKE YOU. AND NOW SHE WORKS HERE! WE'RE LIKE ONE BIG FAMILY! AFTER HOURS WE STAY AND HAVE A BEER AND TALK. I'M GENEROUS!
Black Sabbath
YOU SHOULD COME BY SOME NIGHT AFTER CURRY HUT.
UH... SURE... SOME-DAY... THANKS. CAN YOU SHOW ME THE KITCHEN?
THROUGH THE DOOR THERE TO THE LEFT.
THANKS. I'LL BE GO-ING THEN

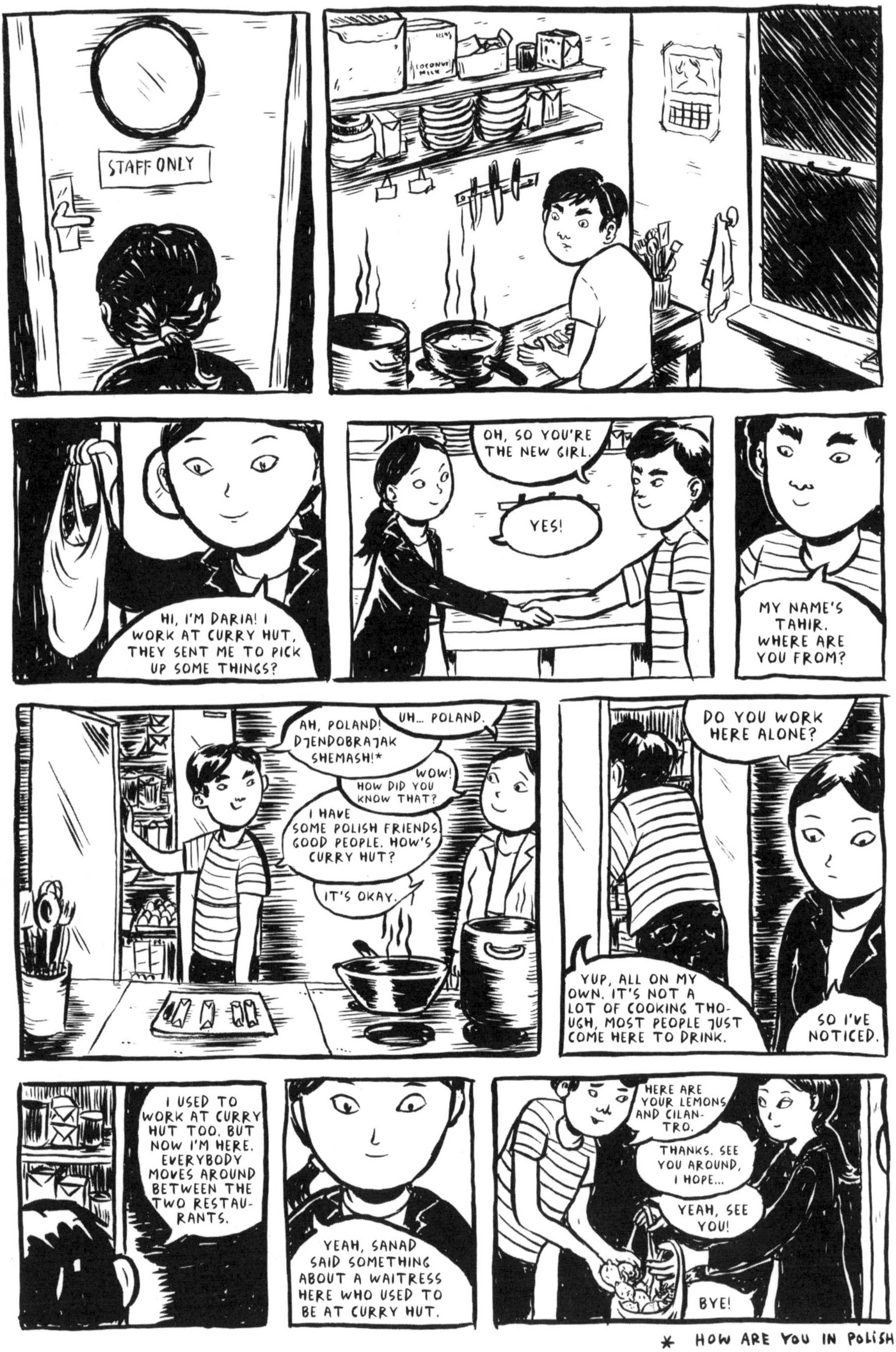
STAFF ONLY
HI, I'M DARIA! I WORK AT CURRY HUT, THEY SENT ME TO PICK UP SOME THINGS?
OH, SO YOU'RE THE NEW GIRL.
YES!
MY NAME'S TAHIR. WHERE ARE YOU FROM?
UH... POLAND.
AH, POLAND! DJENDOBRAJAK SHEMASH!*
WOW! HOW DID YOU KNOW THAT?
I HAVE SOME POLISH FRIENDS. GOOD PEOPLE. HOW'S CURRY HUT?
IT'S OKAY.
DO YOU WORK HERE ALONE?
YUP, ALL ON MY OWN. IT'S NOT A LOT OF COOKING THOUGH, MOST PEOPLE JUST COME HERE TO DRINK.
SO I'VE NOTICED.
I USED TO WORK AT CURRY HUT TOO. BUT NOW I'M HERE. EVERYBODY MOVES AROUND BETWEEN THE TWO RESTAURANTS.
YEAH, SANAD SAID SOMETHING ABOUT A WAITRESS HERE WHO USED TO BE AT CURRY HUT.
HERE ARE YOUR LEMONS AND CILANTRO.
THANKS. SEE YOU AROUND, I HOPE...
YEAH, SEE YOU!
BYE!

* HOW ARE YOU IN POLISH

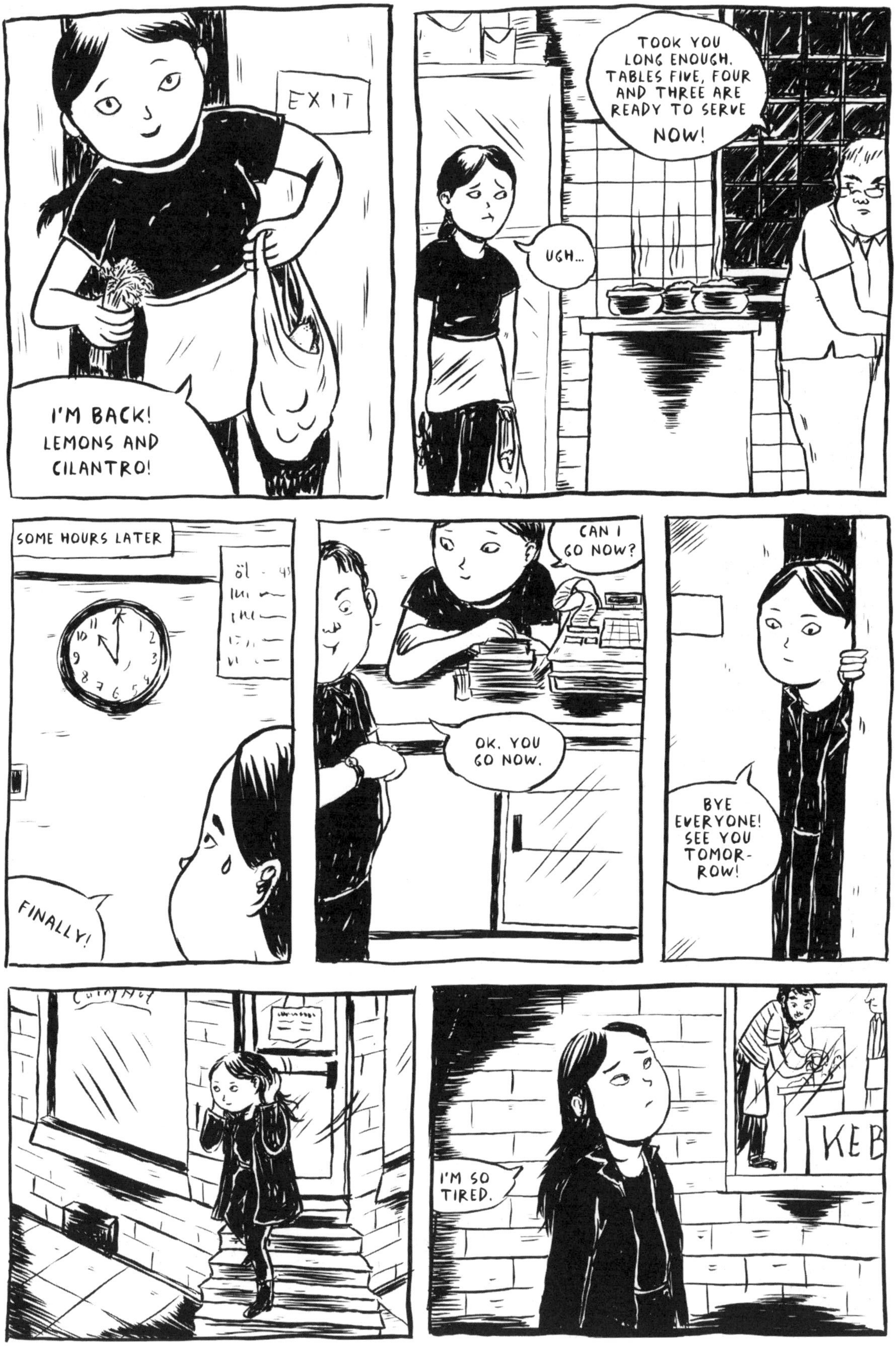
I'M BACK! LEMONS AND CILANTRO!
EXIT
TOOK YOU LONG ENOUGH. TABLES FIVE, FOUR AND THREE ARE READY TO SERVE NOW!
UGH...
SOME HOURS LATER
FINALLY!
CAN I GO NOW?
OK. YOU GO NOW.
BYE EVERYONE! SEE YOU TOMOR-ROW!
I'M SO TIRED.
KEB

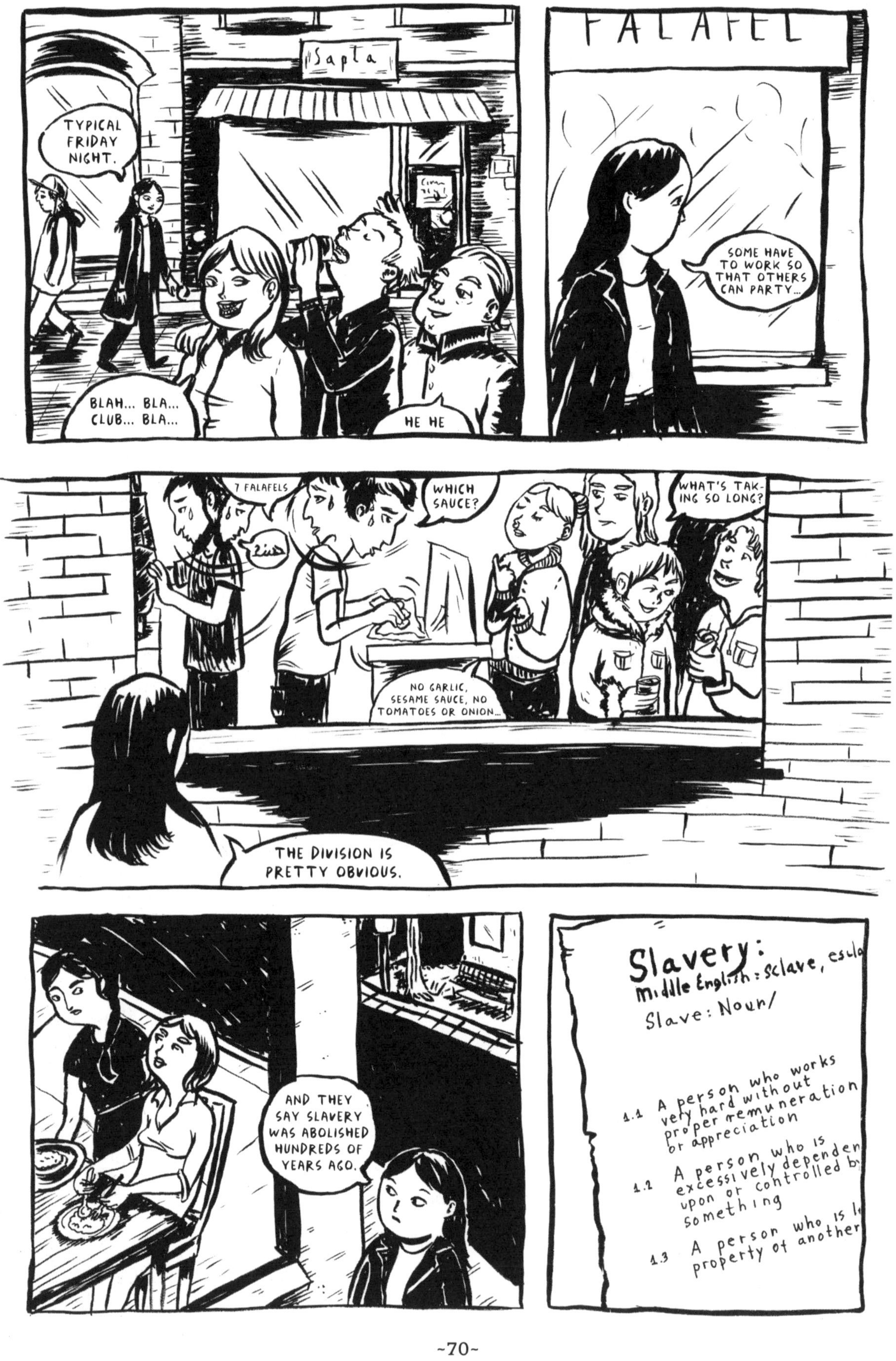
Sapta
TYPICAL FRIDAY NIGHT.
BLAH... BLA... CLUB... BLA...
HE HE
FALAFEL
SOME HAVE TO WORK SO THAT OTHERS CAN PARTY...
7 FALAFELS
WHICH SAUCE?
WHAT'S TAKING SO LONG?
NO GARLIC, SESAME SAUCE, NO TOMATOES OR ONION...
THE DIVISION IS PRETTY OBVIOUS.
AND THEY SAY SLAVERY WAS ABOLISHED HUNDREDS OF YEARS AGO.
Slavery:
Middle English: sclave, escla
Slave: Noun/
1.1 A person who works very hard without proper remuneration or appreciation
1.2 A person who is excessively dependen upon or controlled by something
1.3 A person who is l property of another

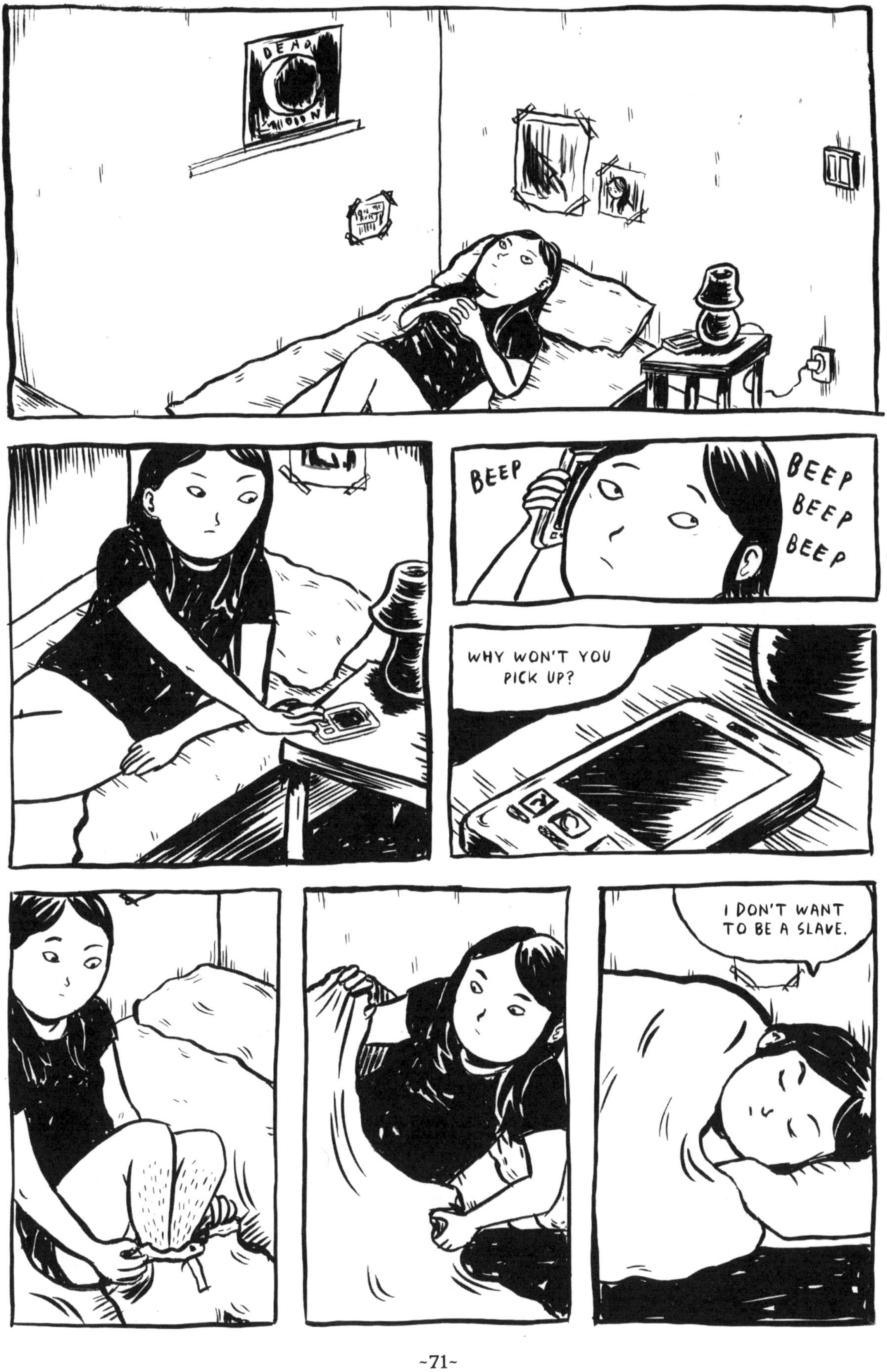
DEAD MOON
BEEP
BEEP
BEEP
BEEP
WHY WON'T YOU PICK UP?
I DON'T WANT TO BE A SLAVE.

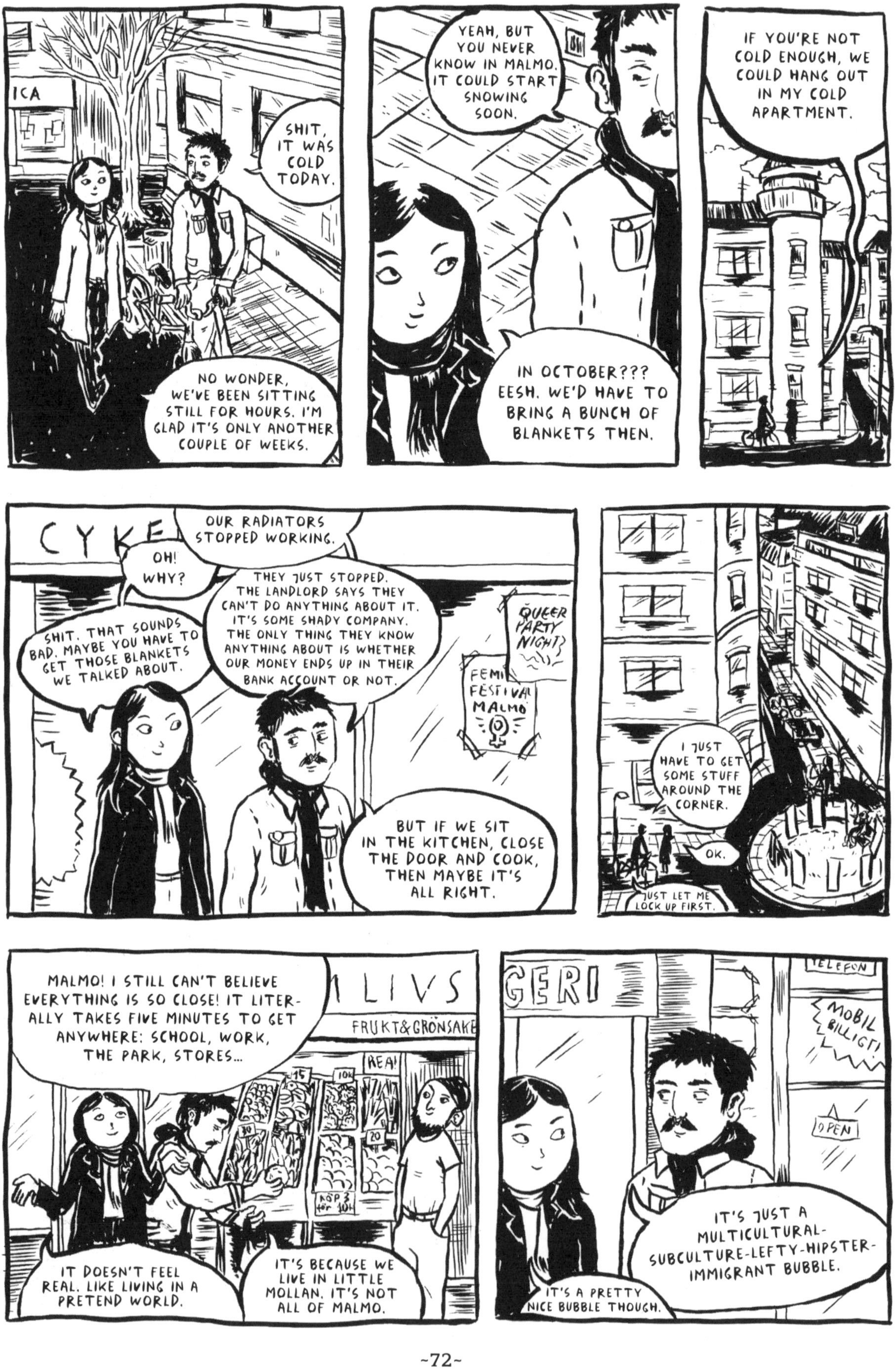
ICA
SHIT, IT WAS COLD TODAY.
NO WONDER, WE'VE BEEN SITTING STILL FOR HOURS. I'M GLAD IT'S ONLY ANOTHER COUPLE OF WEEKS.
YEAH, BUT YOU NEVER KNOW IN MALMO. IT COULD START SNOWING SOON.
IN OCTOBER??? EESH. WE'D HAVE TO BRING A BUNCH OF BLANKETS THEN.
IF YOU'RE NOT COLD ENOUGH, WE COULD HANG OUT IN MY COLD APARTMENT.
CYKE
OUR RADIATORS STOPPED WORKING.
OH! WHY?
THEY JUST STOPPED. THE LANDLORD SAYS THEY CAN'T DO ANYTHING ABOUT IT. IT'S SOME SHADY COMPANY. THE ONLY THING THEY KNOW ANYTHING ABOUT IS WHETHER OUR MONEY ENDS UP IN THEIR BANK ACCOUNT OR NOT.
SHIT. THAT SOUNDS BAD. MAYBE YOU HAVE TO GET THOSE BLANKETS WE TALKED ABOUT.
QUEER PARTY NIGHT?
FEMI FESTIVAL MALMÖ
BUT IF WE SIT IN THE KITCHEN, CLOSE THE DOOR AND COOK, THEN MAYBE IT'S ALL RIGHT.
I JUST HAVE TO GET SOME STUFF AROUND THE CORNER.
OK.
JUST LET ME LOCK UP FIRST.
LIVS
FRUKT&GRÖNSAKE
REA!
MALMO! I STILL CAN'T BELIEVE EVERYTHING IS SO CLOSE! IT LITERALLY TAKES FIVE MINUTES TO GET ANYWHERE: SCHOOL, WORK, THE PARK, STORES...
IT DOESN'T FEEL REAL. LIKE LIVING IN A PRETEND WORLD.
IT'S BECAUSE WE LIVE IN LITTLE MOLLAN. IT'S NOT ALL OF MALMO.
GERI
TELEFON
MOBIL BILLIGT!
OPEN
IT'S JUST A MULTICULTURAL-SUBCULTURE-LEFTY-HIPSTER-IMMIGRANT BUBBLE.
IT'S A PRETTY NICE BUBBLE THOUGH.

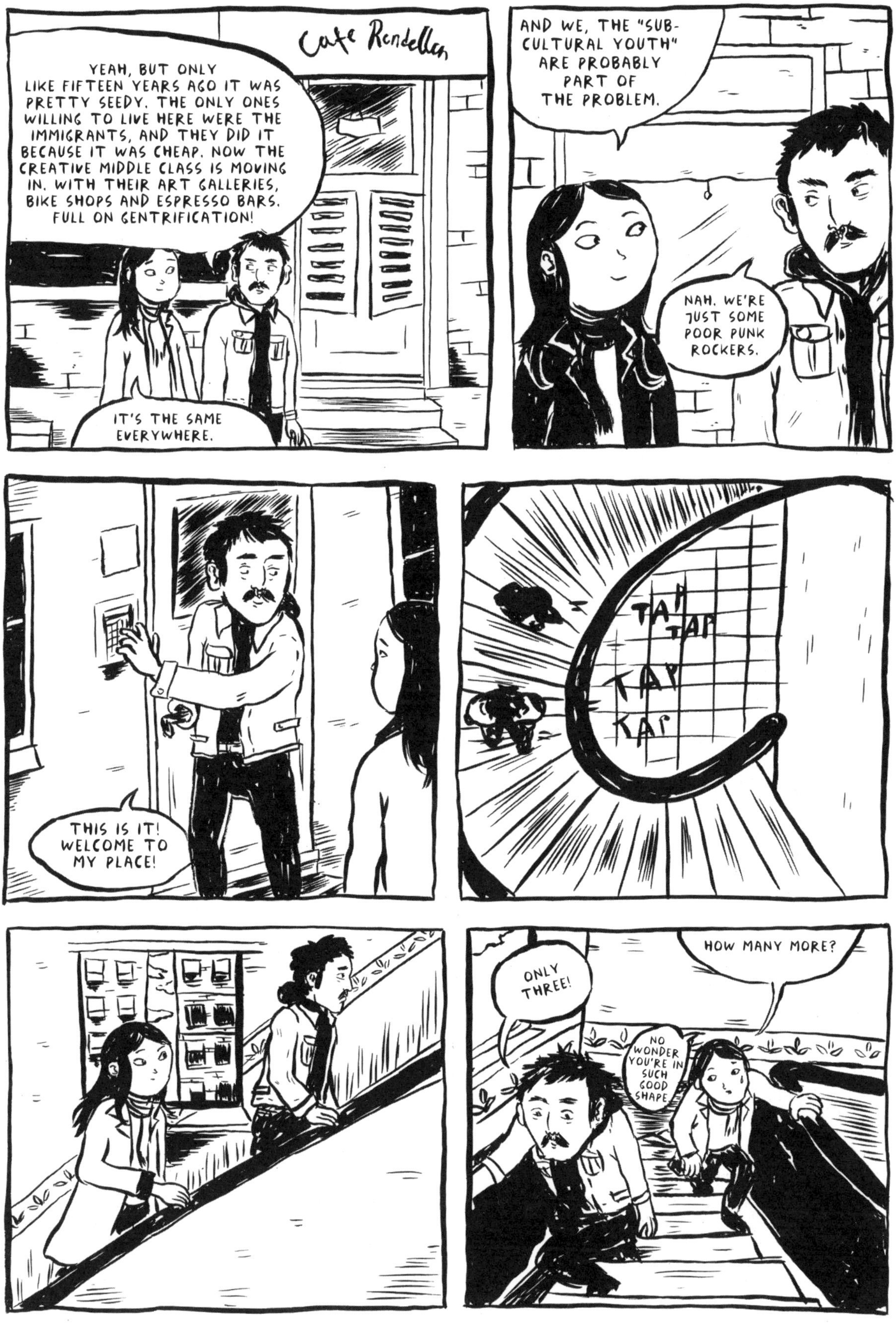
Cafe Rendellen
YEAH, BUT ONLY LIKE FIFTEEN YEARS AGO IT WAS PRETTY SEEDY. THE ONLY ONES WILLING TO LIVE HERE WERE THE IMMIGRANTS, AND THEY DID IT BECAUSE IT WAS CHEAP. NOW THE CREATIVE MIDDLE CLASS IS MOVING IN. WITH THEIR ART GALLERIES, BIKE SHOPS AND ESPRESSO BARS. FULL ON GENTRIFICATION!
IT'S THE SAME EVERYWHERE.
AND WE, THE "SUB-CULTURAL YOUTH" ARE PROBABLY PART OF THE PROBLEM.
NAH. WE'RE JUST SOME POOR PUNK ROCKERS.
THIS IS IT! WELCOME TO MY PLACE!
TAP TAP
TAP
TAP
ONLY THREE!
HOW MANY MORE?
NO WONDER YOU'RE IN SUCH GOOD SHAPE.

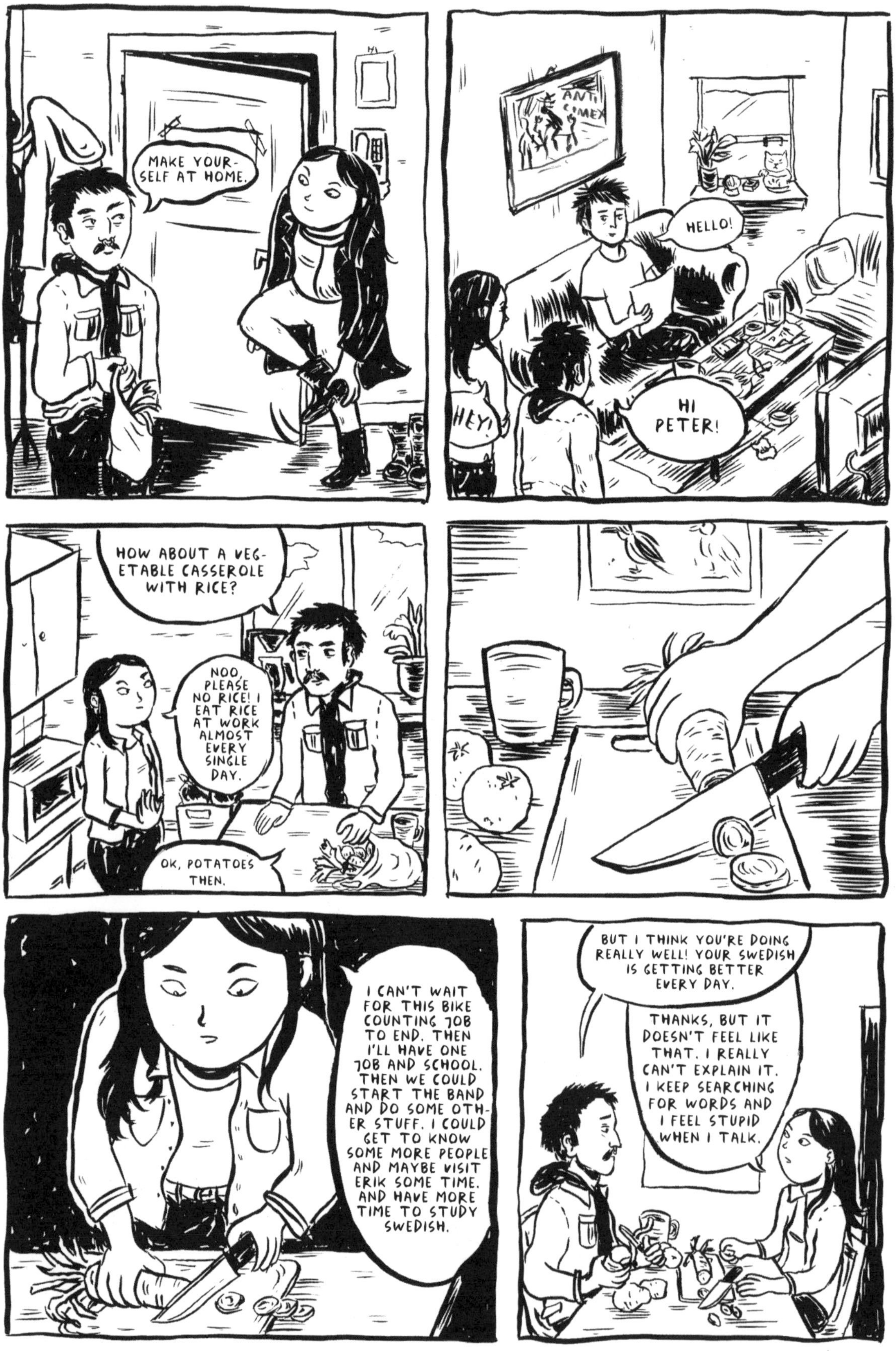
MAKE YOUR-SELF AT HOME.
ANTI COMEX
HELLO!
HEY!
HI PETER!
HOW ABOUT A VEG-ETABLE CASSEROLE WITH RICE?
NOO, PLEASE NO RICE! I EAT RICE AT WORK ALMOST EVERY SINGLE DAY.
OK, POTATOES THEN.
I CAN'T WAIT FOR THIS BIKE COUNTING JOB TO END. THEN I'LL HAVE ONE JOB AND SCHOOL. THEN WE COULD START THE BAND AND DO SOME OTH-ER STUFF. I COULD GET TO KNOW SOME MORE PEOPLE AND MAYBE VISIT ERIK SOME TIME. AND HAVE MORE TIME TO STUDY SWEDISH.
BUT I THINK YOU'RE DOING REALLY WELL! YOUR SWEDISH IS GETTING BETTER EVERY DAY.
THANKS, BUT IT DOESN'T FEEL LIKE THAT. I REALLY CAN'T EXPLAIN IT. I KEEP SEARCHING FOR WORDS AND I FEEL STUPID WHEN I TALK.

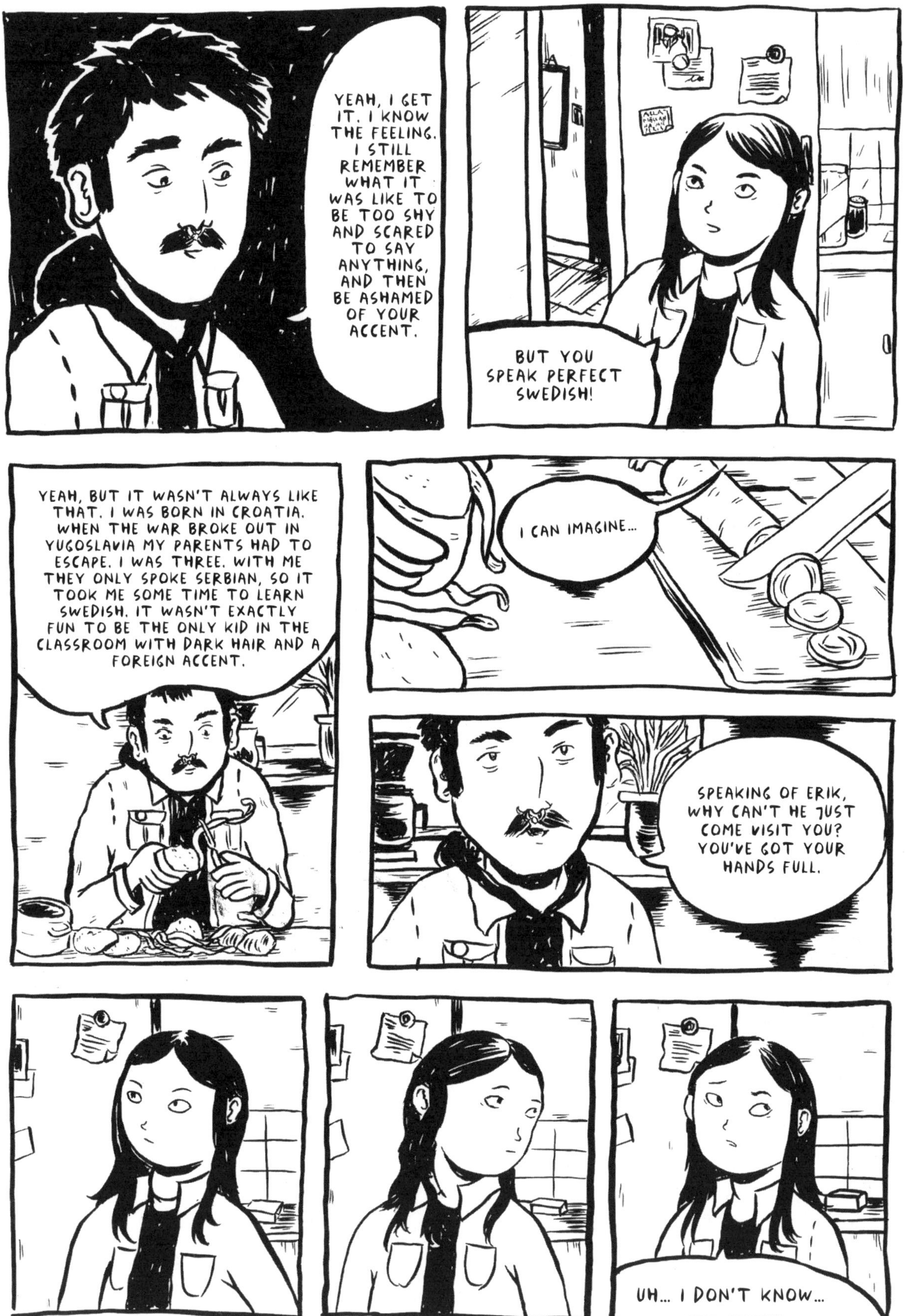
YEAH, I GET IT. I KNOW THE FEELING. I STILL REMEMBER WHAT IT WAS LIKE TO BE TOO SHY AND SCARED TO SAY ANYTHING, AND THEN BE ASHAMED OF YOUR ACCENT.
BUT YOU SPEAK PERFECT SWEDISH!
YEAH, BUT IT WASN'T ALWAYS LIKE THAT. I WAS BORN IN CROATIA. WHEN THE WAR BROKE OUT IN YUGOSLAVIA MY PARENTS HAD TO ESCAPE. I WAS THREE. WITH ME THEY ONLY SPOKE SERBIAN, SO IT TOOK ME SOME TIME TO LEARN SWEDISH. IT WASN'T EXACTLY FUN TO BE THE ONLY KID IN THE CLASSROOM WITH DARK HAIR AND A FOREIGN ACCENT.
I CAN IMAGINE...
SPEAKING OF ERIK, WHY CAN'T HE JUST COME VISIT YOU? YOU'VE GOT YOUR HANDS FULL.
UH... I DON'T KNOW...

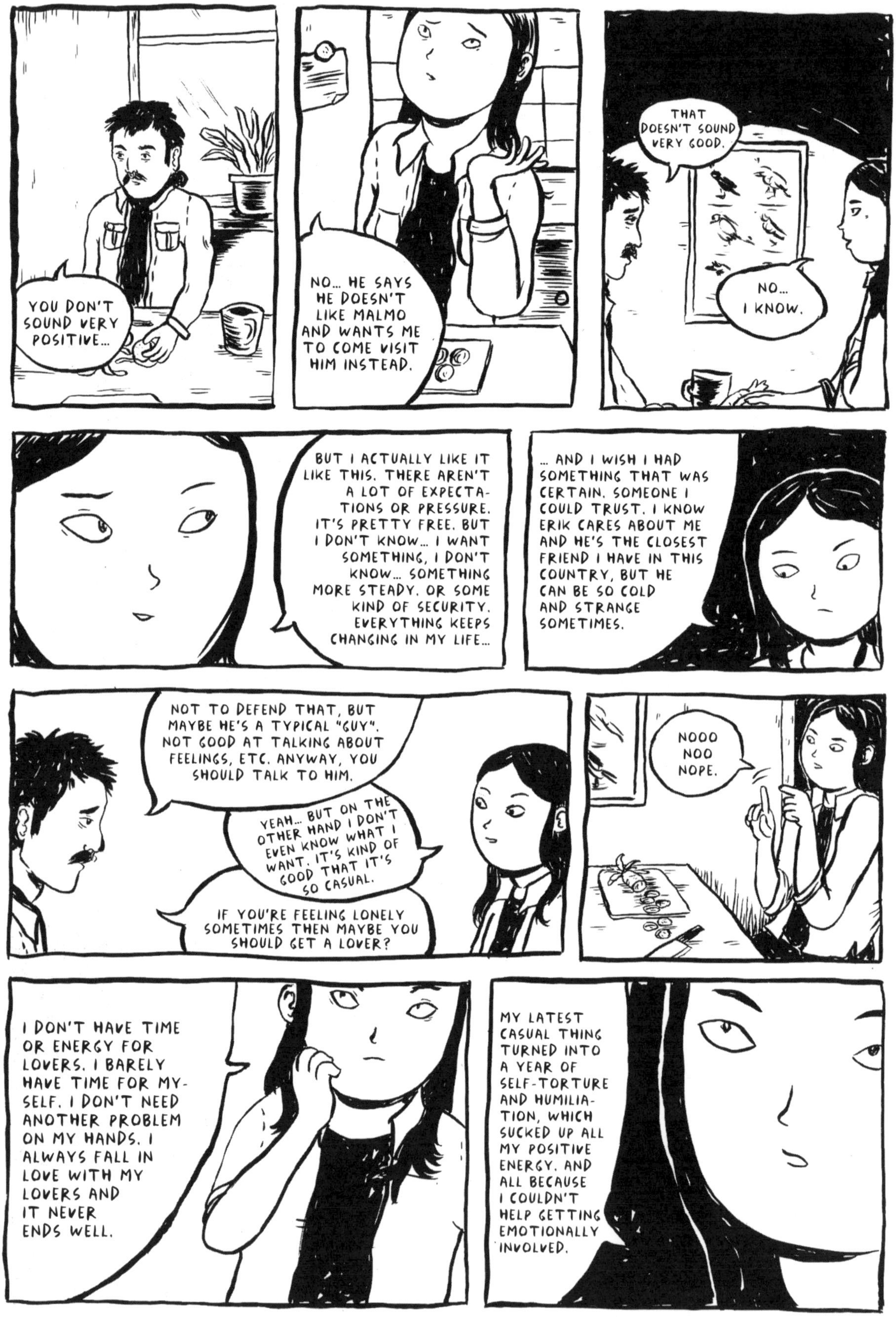
YOU DON'T SOUND VERY POSITIVE...
NO... HE SAYS HE DOESN'T LIKE MALMO AND WANTS ME TO COME VISIT HIM INSTEAD.
THAT DOESN'T SOUND VERY GOOD.
NO... I KNOW.
BUT I ACTUALLY LIKE IT LIKE THIS. THERE AREN'T A LOT OF EXPECTATIONS OR PRESSURE. IT'S PRETTY FREE. BUT I DON'T KNOW... I WANT SOMETHING, I DON'T KNOW... SOMETHING MORE STEADY. OR SOME KIND OF SECURITY. EVERYTHING KEEPS CHANGING IN MY LIFE...
... AND I WISH I HAD SOMETHING THAT WAS CERTAIN. SOMEONE I COULD TRUST. I KNOW ERIK CARES ABOUT ME AND HE'S THE CLOSEST FRIEND I HAVE IN THIS COUNTRY, BUT HE CAN BE SO COLD AND STRANGE SOMETIMES.
NOT TO DEFEND THAT, BUT MAYBE HE'S A TYPICAL "GUY". NOT GOOD AT TALKING ABOUT FEELINGS, ETC. ANYWAY, YOU SHOULD TALK TO HIM.
YEAH... BUT ON THE OTHER HAND I DON'T EVEN KNOW WHAT I WANT. IT'S KIND OF GOOD THAT IT'S SO CASUAL.
IF YOU'RE FEELING LONELY SOMETIMES THEN MAYBE YOU SHOULD GET A LOVER?
NOOO NOO NOPE.
I DON'T HAVE TIME OR ENERGY FOR LOVERS. I BARELY HAVE TIME FOR MYSELF. I DON'T NEED ANOTHER PROBLEM ON MY HANDS. I ALWAYS FALL IN LOVE WITH MY LOVERS AND IT NEVER ENDS WELL.
MY LATEST CASUAL THING TURNED INTO A YEAR OF SELF-TORTURE AND HUMILIATION, WHICH SUCKED UP ALL MY POSITIVE ENERGY. AND ALL BECAUSE I COULDN'T HELP GETTING EMOTIONALLY INVOLVED.

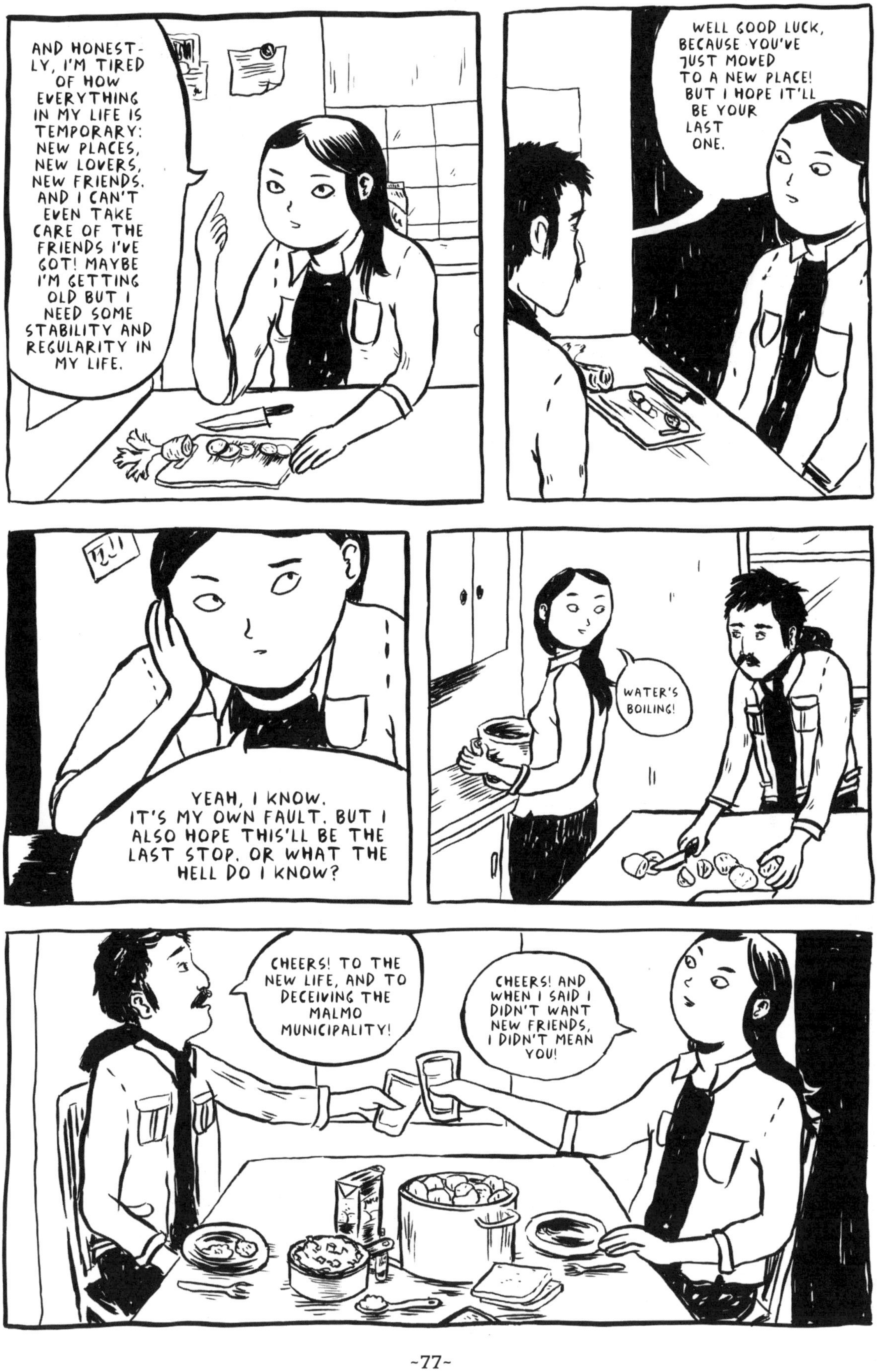
AND HONEST-LY, I'M TIRED OF HOW EVERYTHING IN MY LIFE IS TEMPORARY: NEW PLACES, NEW LOVERS, NEW FRIENDS. AND I CAN'T EVEN TAKE CARE OF THE FRIENDS I'VE GOT! MAYBE I'M GETTING OLD BUT I NEED SOME STABILITY AND REGULARITY IN MY LIFE.
WELL GOOD LUCK, BECAUSE YOU'VE JUST MOVED TO A NEW PLACE! BUT I HOPE IT'LL BE YOUR LAST ONE.
YEAH, I KNOW. IT'S MY OWN FAULT. BUT I ALSO HOPE THIS'LL BE THE LAST STOP. OR WHAT THE HELL DO I KNOW?
WATER'S BOILING!
CHEERS! TO THE NEW LIFE, AND TO DECEIVING THE MALMO MUNICIPALITY!
CHEERS! AND WHEN I SAID I DIDN'T WANT NEW FRIENDS, I DIDN'T MEAN YOU!

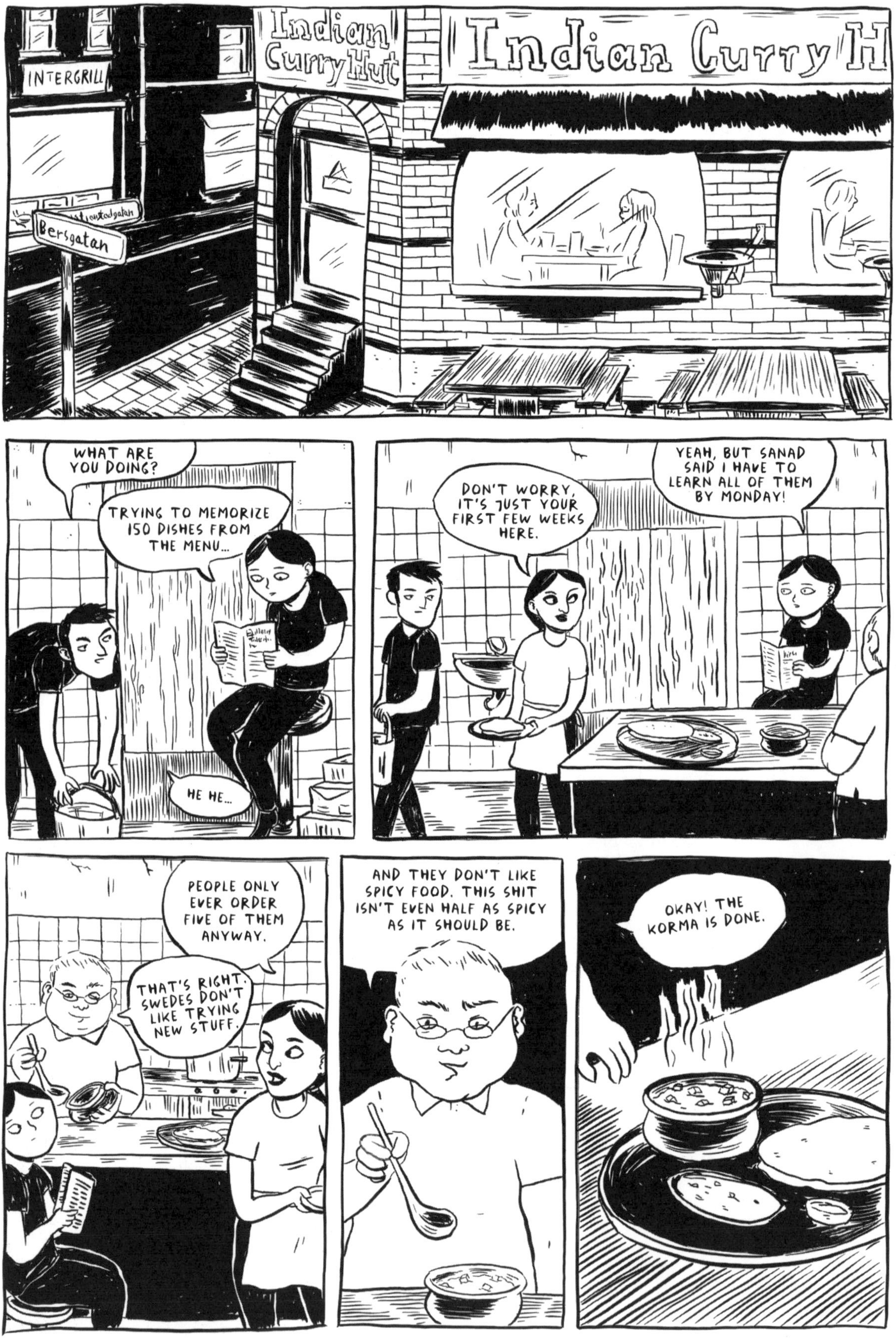
Indian Curry Hut
Indian Curry H
INTERGRILL
Bersgatan
WHAT ARE YOU DOING?
TRYING TO MEMORIZE 150 DISHES FROM THE MENU...
HE HE...
DON'T WORRY, IT'S JUST YOUR FIRST FEW WEEKS HERE.
YEAH, BUT SANAD SAID I HAVE TO LEARN ALL OF THEM BY MONDAY!
PEOPLE ONLY EVER ORDER FIVE OF THEM ANYWAY.
THAT'S RIGHT. SWEDES DON'T LIKE TRYING NEW STUFF.
AND THEY DON'T LIKE SPICY FOOD. THIS SHIT ISN'T EVEN HALF AS SPICY AS IT SHOULD BE.
OKAY! THE KORMA IS DONE.

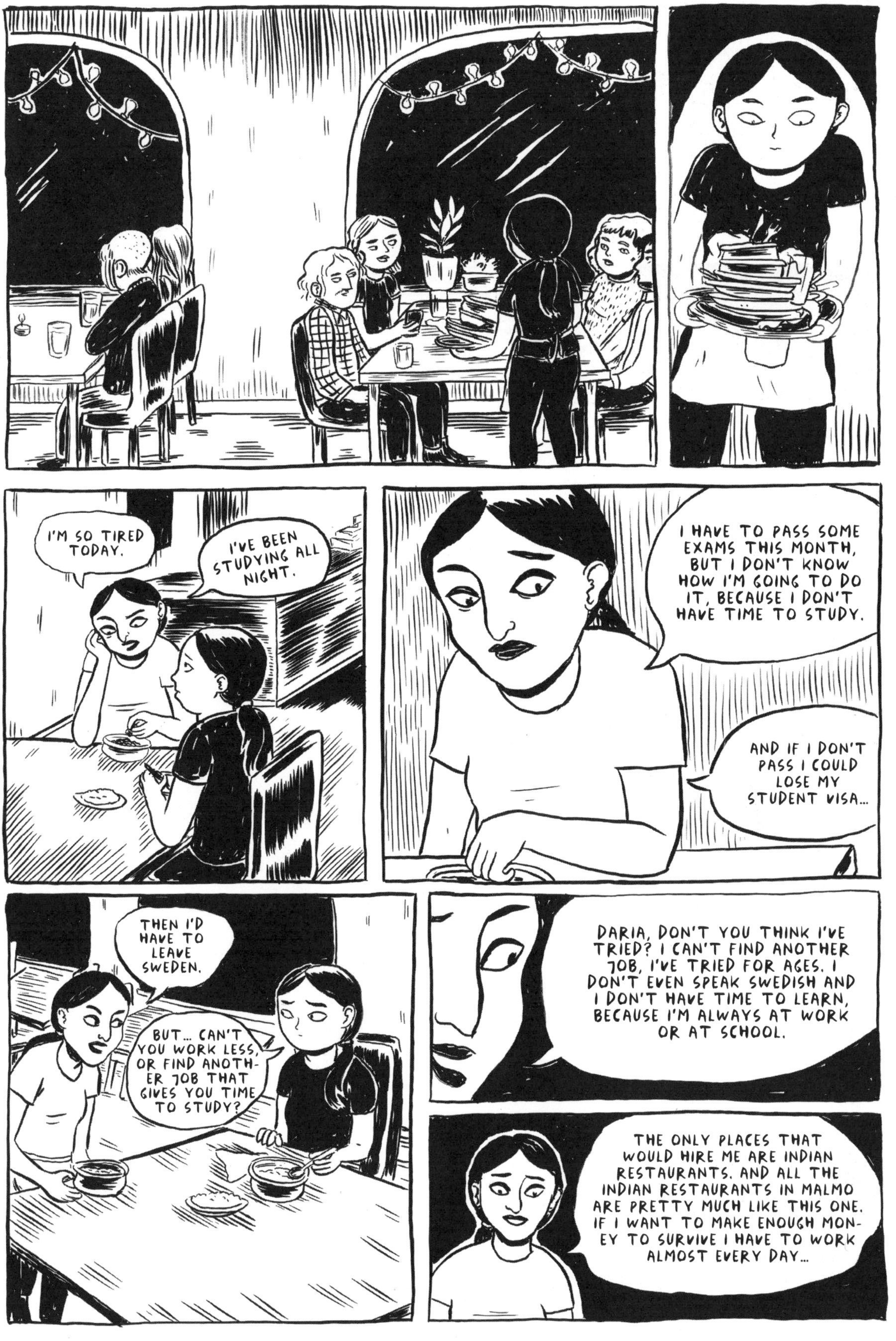
I'M SO TIRED TODAY.
I'VE BEEN STUDYING ALL NIGHT.
I HAVE TO PASS SOME EXAMS THIS MONTH, BUT I DON'T KNOW HOW I'M GOING TO DO IT, BECAUSE I DON'T HAVE TIME TO STUDY.
AND IF I DON'T PASS I COULD LOSE MY STUDENT VISA...
THEN I'D HAVE TO LEAVE SWEDEN.
BUT... CAN'T YOU WORK LESS, OR FIND ANOTHER JOB THAT GIVES YOU TIME TO STUDY?
DARIA, DON'T YOU THINK I'VE TRIED? I CAN'T FIND ANOTHER JOB, I'VE TRIED FOR AGES. I DON'T EVEN SPEAK SWEDISH AND I DON'T HAVE TIME TO LEARN, BECAUSE I'M ALWAYS AT WORK OR AT SCHOOL.
THE ONLY PLACES THAT WOULD HIRE ME ARE INDIAN RESTAURANTS. AND ALL THE INDIAN RESTAURANTS IN MALMO ARE PRETTY MUCH LIKE THIS ONE. IF I WANT TO MAKE ENOUGH MONEY TO SURVIVE I HAVE TO WORK ALMOST EVERY DAY...

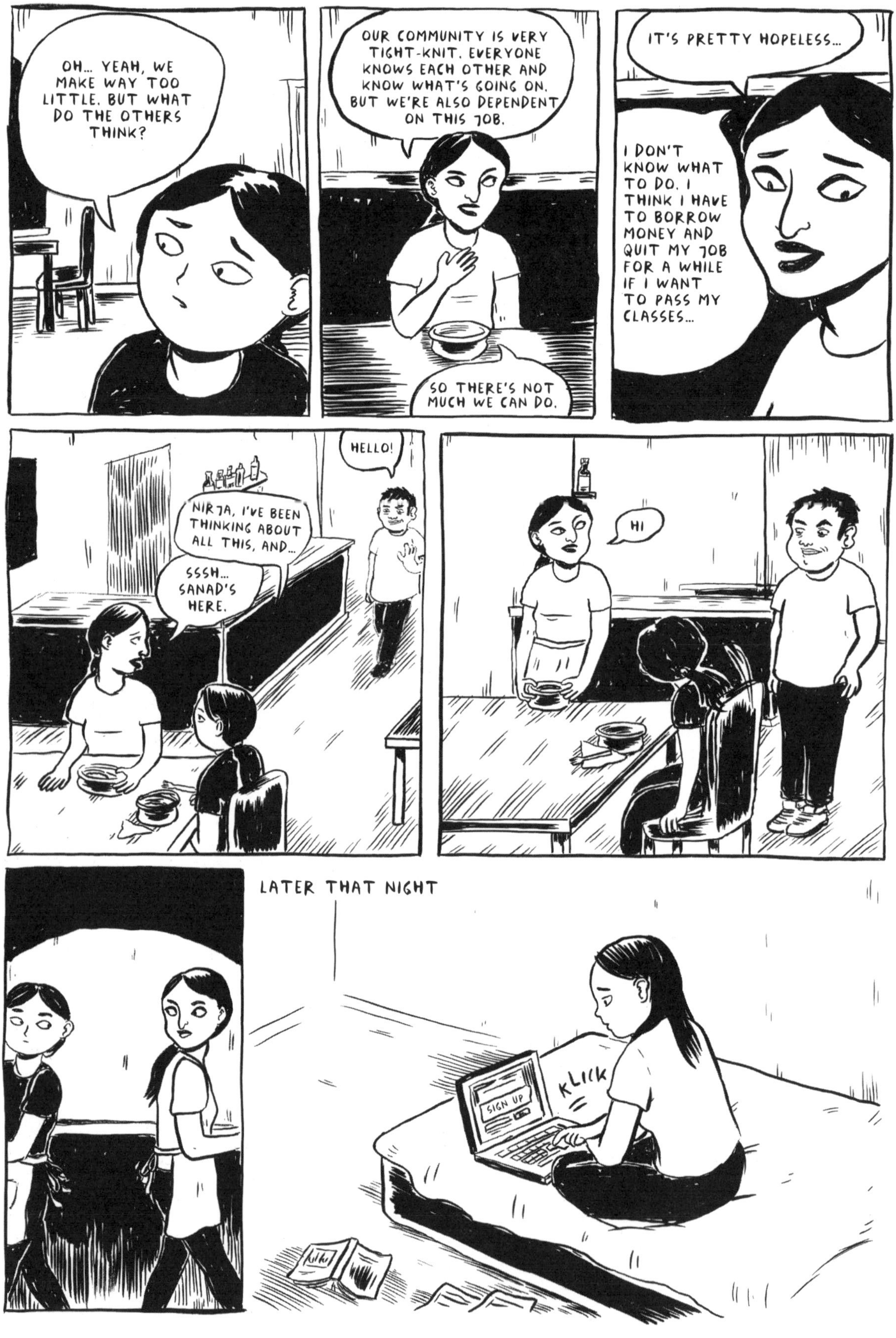
OH... YEAH, WE MAKE WAY TOO LITTLE. BUT WHAT DO THE OTHERS THINK?
OUR COMMUNITY IS VERY TIGHT-KNIT. EVERYONE KNOWS EACH OTHER AND KNOW WHAT'S GOING ON. BUT WE'RE ALSO DEPENDENT ON THIS JOB.
SO THERE'S NOT MUCH WE CAN DO.
IT'S PRETTY HOPELESS...
I DON'T KNOW WHAT TO DO. I THINK I HAVE TO BORROW MONEY AND QUIT MY JOB FOR A WHILE IF I WANT TO PASS MY CLASSES...
NIRJA, I'VE BEEN THINKING ABOUT ALL THIS, AND...
HELLO!
SSSH... SANAD'S HERE.
HI
LATER THAT NIGHT
SIGN UP
KLICK

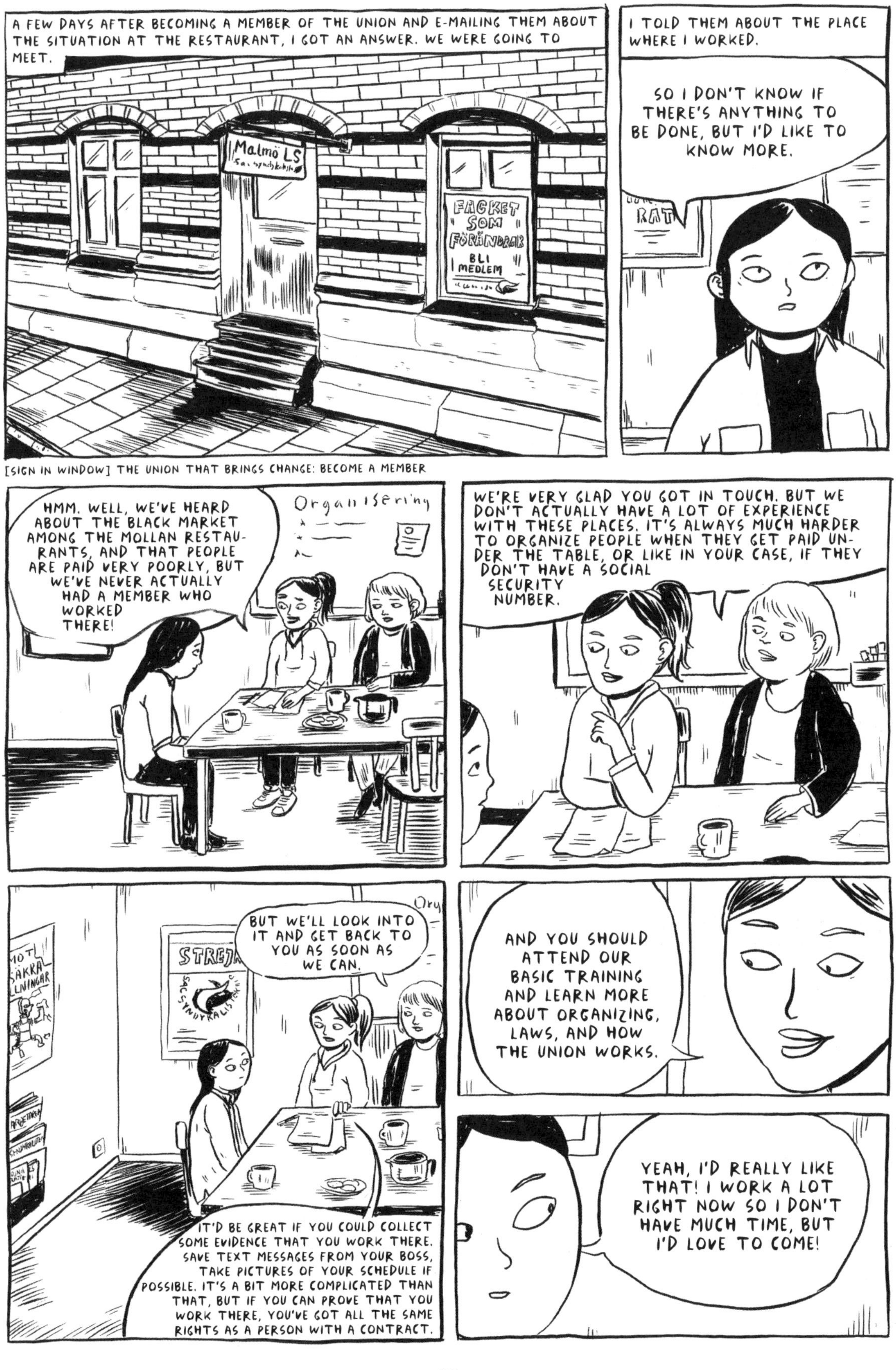
A FEW DAYS AFTER BECOMING A MEMBER OF THE UNION AND E-MAILING THEM ABOUT THE SITUATION AT THE RESTAURANT, I GOT AN ANSWER. WE WERE GOING TO MEET.
Malmö LS
FACKET SOM FÖRÄNDRAR
BLI MEDLEM
I TOLD THEM ABOUT THE PLACE WHERE I WORKED.
SO I DON'T KNOW IF THERE'S ANYTHING TO BE DONE, BUT I'D LIKE TO KNOW MORE.
[SIGN IN WINDOW] THE UNION THAT BRINGS CHANGE: BECOME A MEMBER
HMM. WELL, WE'VE HEARD ABOUT THE BLACK MARKET AMONG THE MOLLAN RESTAURANTS, AND THAT PEOPLE ARE PAID VERY POORLY, BUT WE'VE NEVER ACTUALLY HAD A MEMBER WHO WORKED THERE!
Organisering
WE'RE VERY GLAD YOU GOT IN TOUCH. BUT WE DON'T ACTUALLY HAVE A LOT OF EXPERIENCE WITH THESE PLACES. IT'S ALWAYS MUCH HARDER TO ORGANIZE PEOPLE WHEN THEY GET PAID UNDER THE TABLE, OR LIKE IN YOUR CASE, IF THEY DON'T HAVE A SOCIAL SECURITY NUMBER.
BUT WE'LL LOOK INTO IT AND GET BACK TO YOU AS SOON AS WE CAN.
IT'D BE GREAT IF YOU COULD COLLECT SOME EVIDENCE THAT YOU WORK THERE. SAVE TEXT MESSAGES FROM YOUR BOSS, TAKE PICTURES OF YOUR SCHEDULE IF POSSIBLE. IT'S A BIT MORE COMPLICATED THAN THAT, BUT IF YOU CAN PROVE THAT YOU WORK THERE, YOU'VE GOT ALL THE SAME RIGHTS AS A PERSON WITH A CONTRACT.
AND YOU SHOULD ATTEND OUR BASIC TRAINING AND LEARN MORE ABOUT ORGANIZING, LAWS, AND HOW THE UNION WORKS.
YEAH, I'D REALLY LIKE THAT! I WORK A LOT RIGHT NOW SO I DON'T HAVE MUCH TIME, BUT I'D LOVE TO COME!

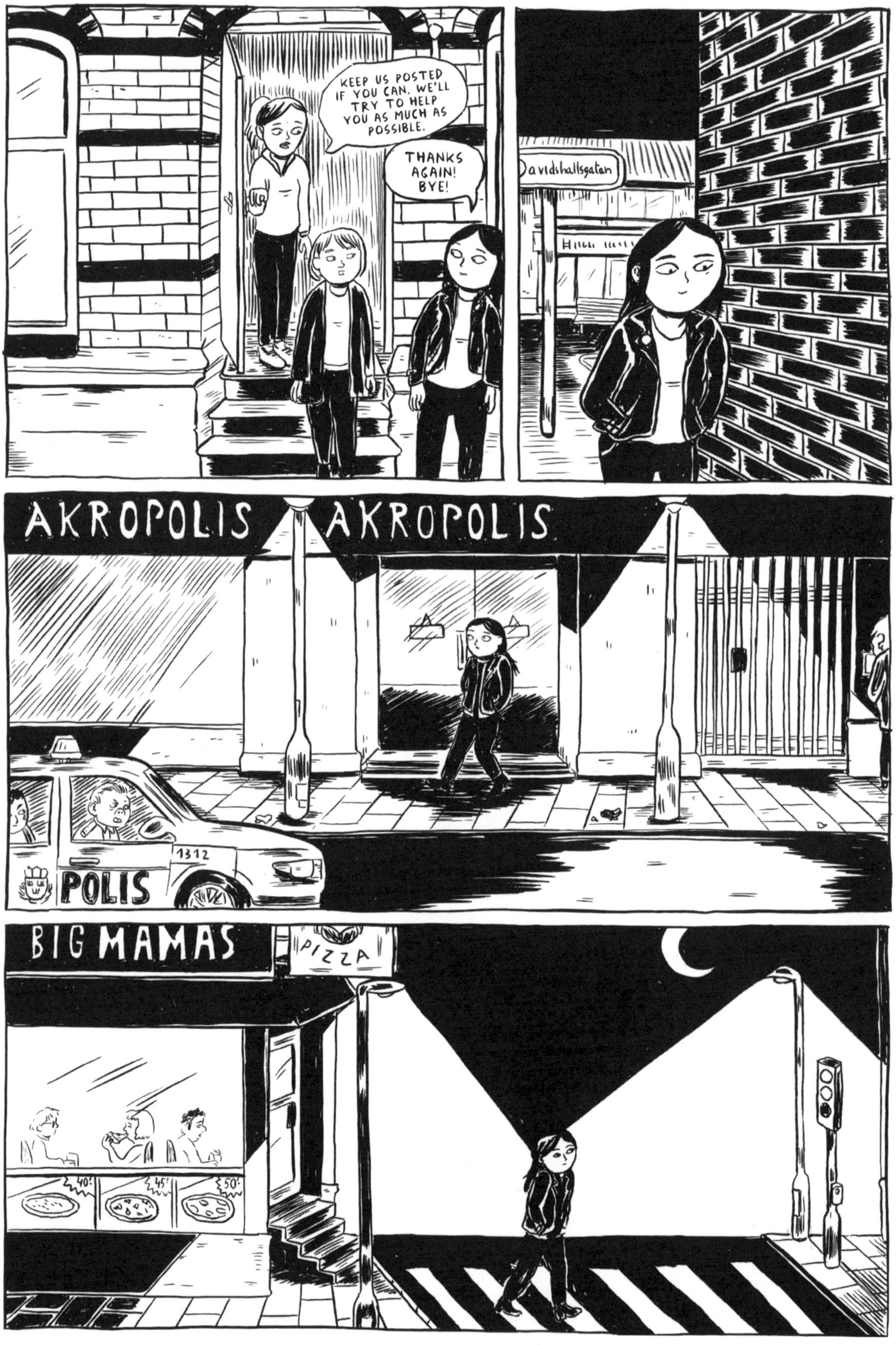
KEEP US POSTED IF YOU CAN. WE'LL TRY TO HELP YOU AS MUCH AS POSSIBLE.
THANKS AGAIN! BYE!
Davidshallsgatan
AKROPOLIS AKROPOLIS
1312
POLIS
BIG MAMAS
PIZZA
40:-
45:-
50:-

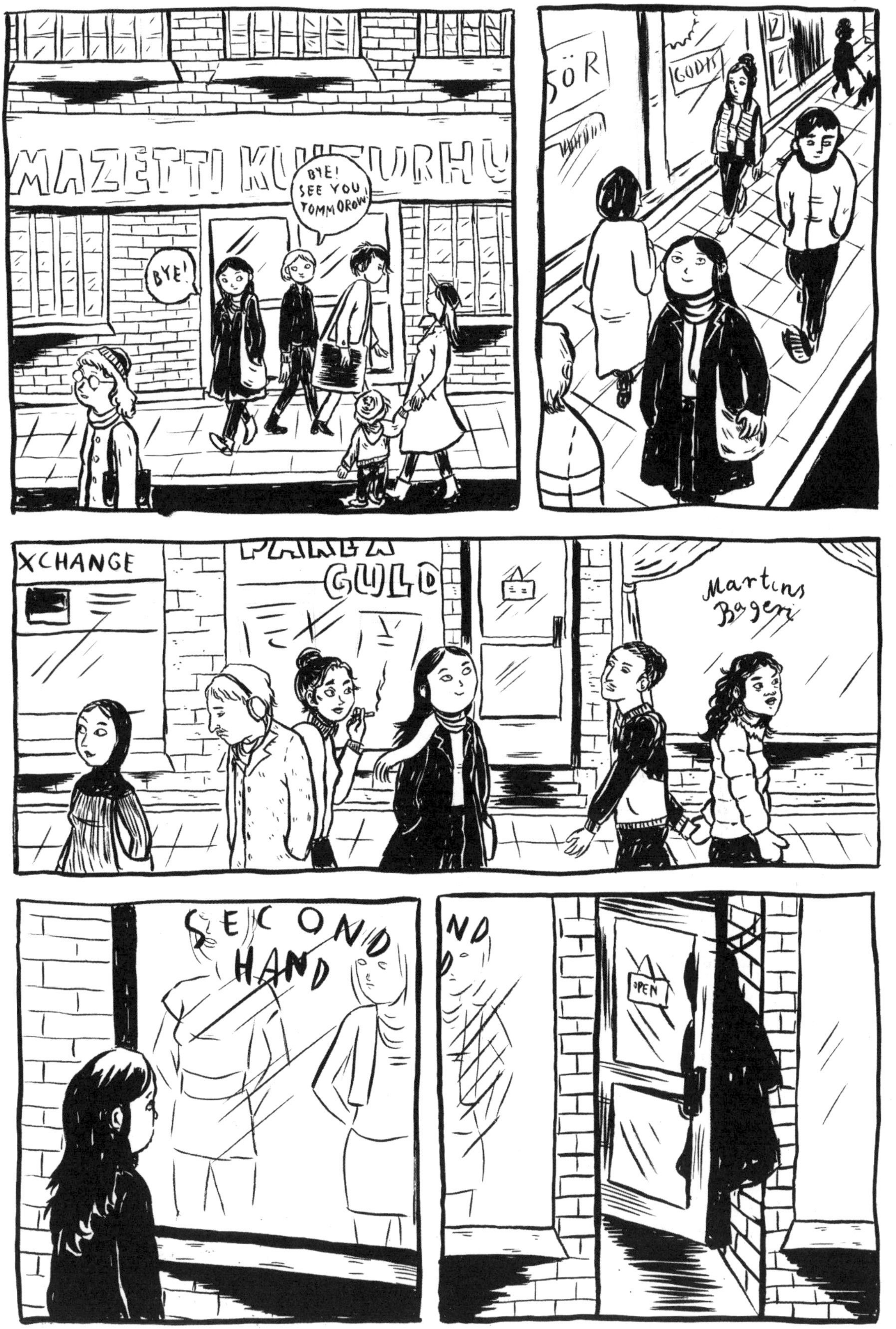
MAZETTI KULTURHU
BYE! SEE YOU TOMMOROW!
BYE!
SÖR
GODIS
XCHANGE
GULD
Martins Bageri
SECOND HAND
ND
OPEN

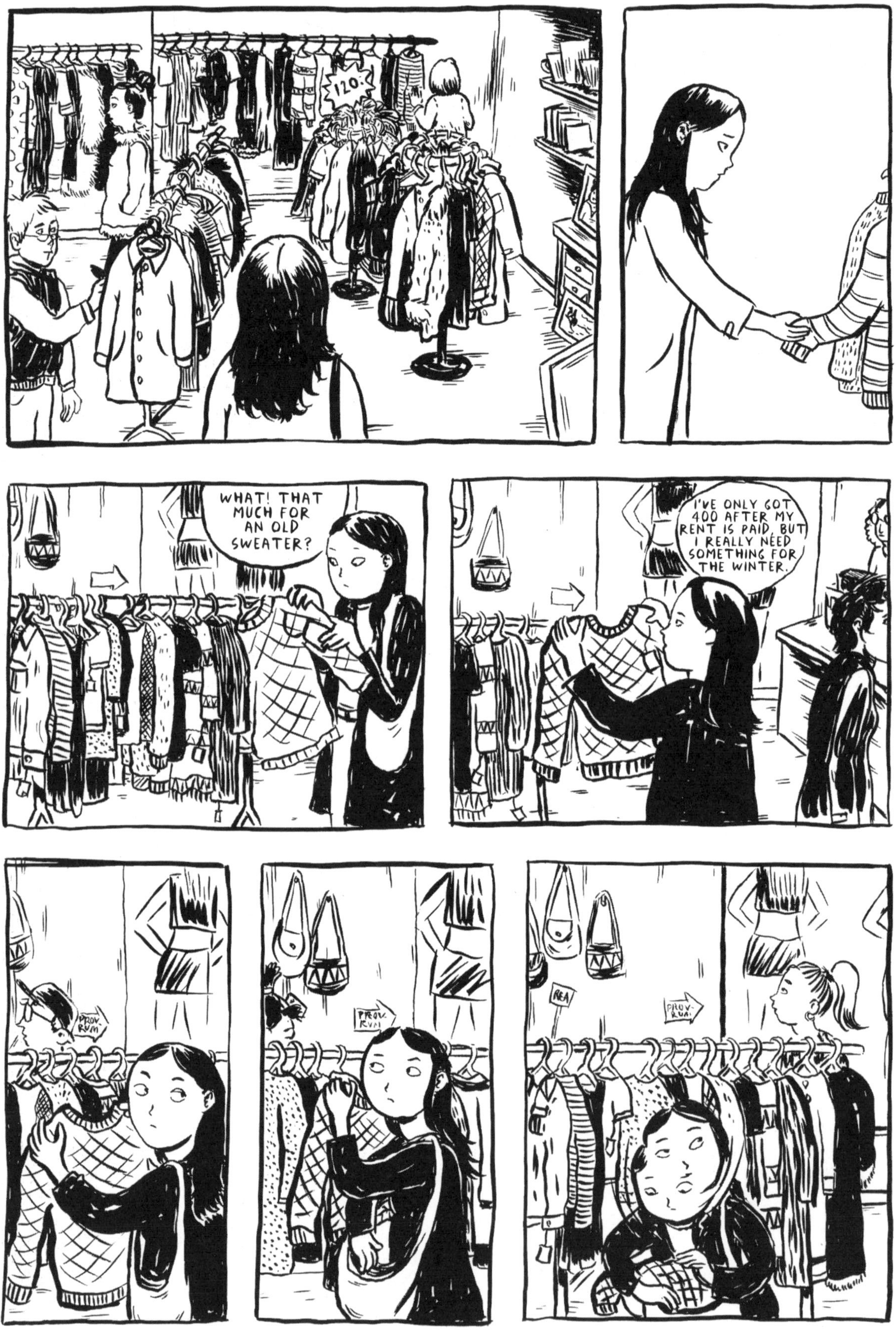
120:
WHAT! THAT MUCH FOR AN OLD SWEATER?
I'VE ONLY GOT 400 AFTER MY RENT IS PAID, BUT I REALLY NEED SOMETHING FOR THE WINTER.
PROV-RUM
REA

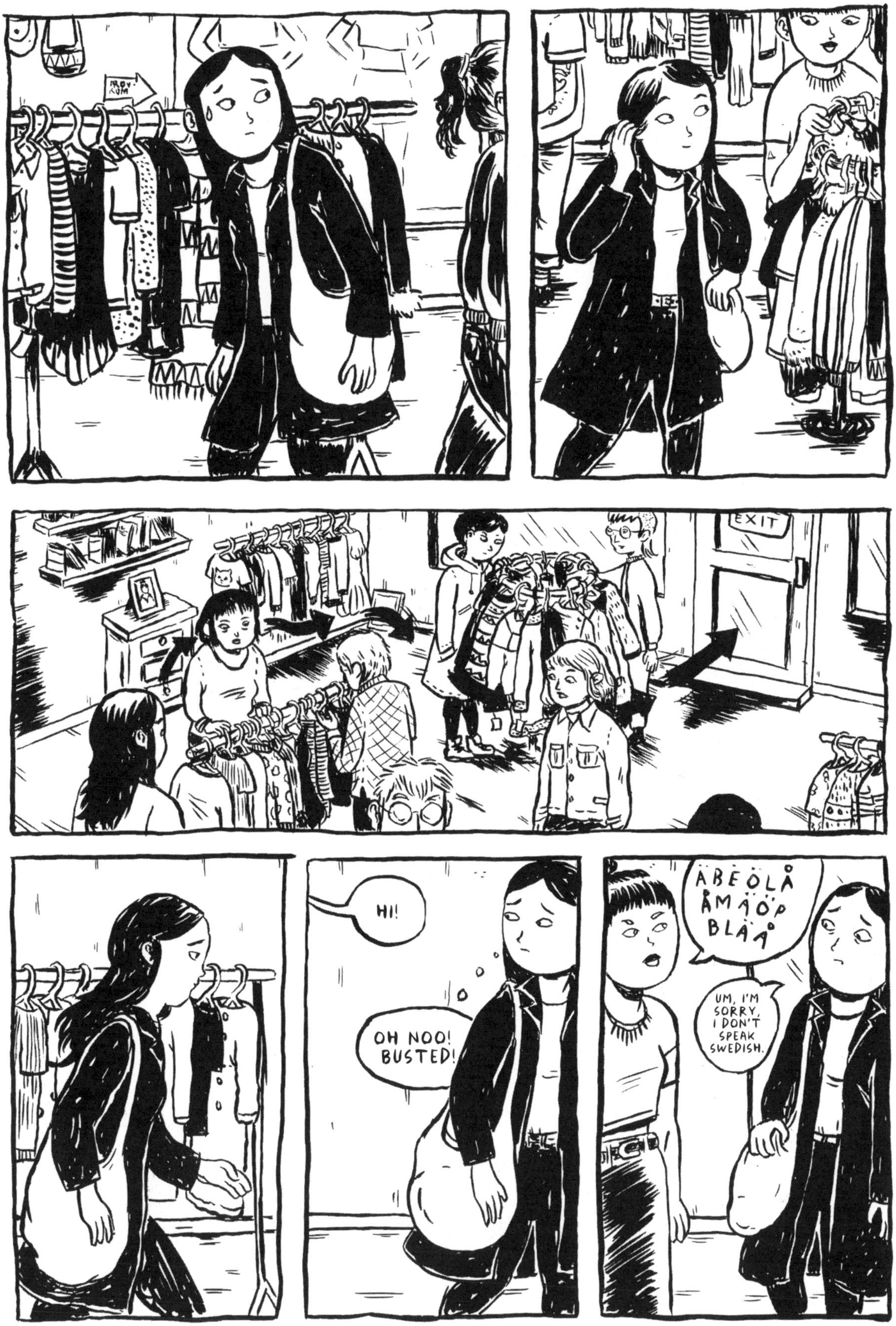
EXIT
HI!
OH NOO! BUSTED!
ÄBËÖLÅ ÅMÄÖP BLÄÅ
UM, I'M SORRY, I DON'T SPEAK SWEDISH.

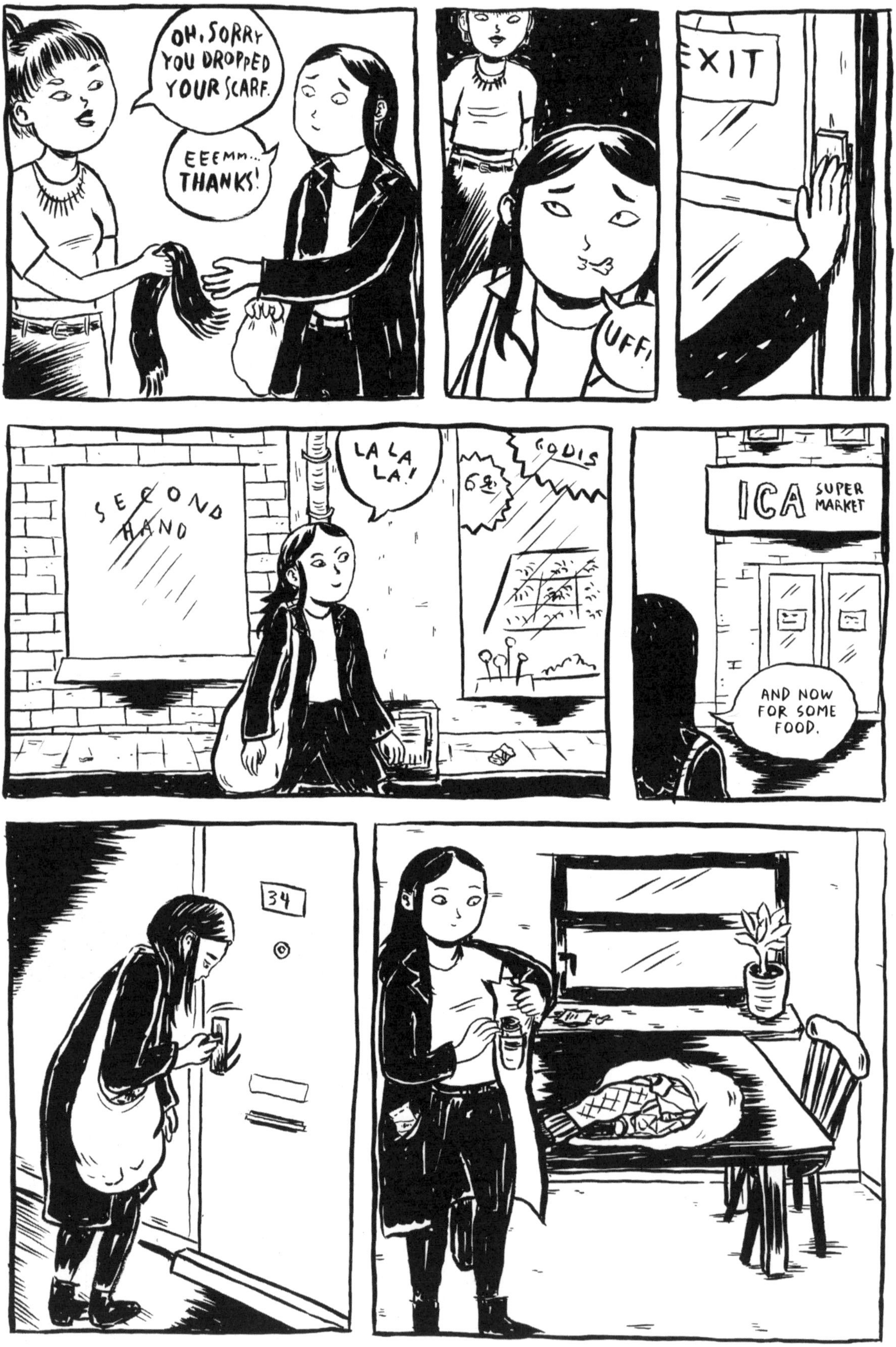
OH, SORRY YOU DROPPED YOUR SCARF.
EEEMM... THANKS!
UFF!
EXIT
SECOND HAND
LA LA LA!
GODIS
ICA SUPER MARKET
AND NOW FOR SOME FOOD.
34

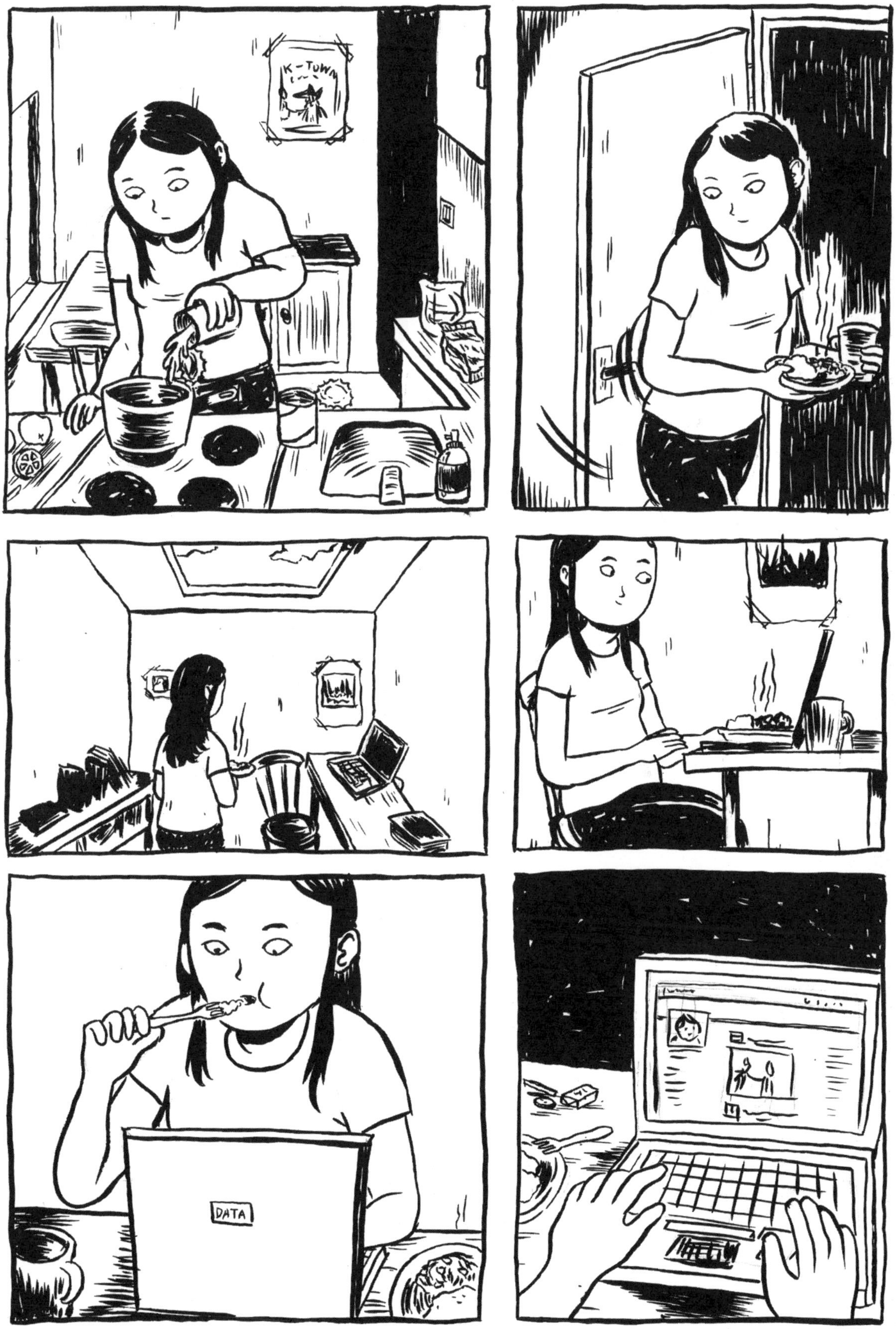
K-TOWN
DATA

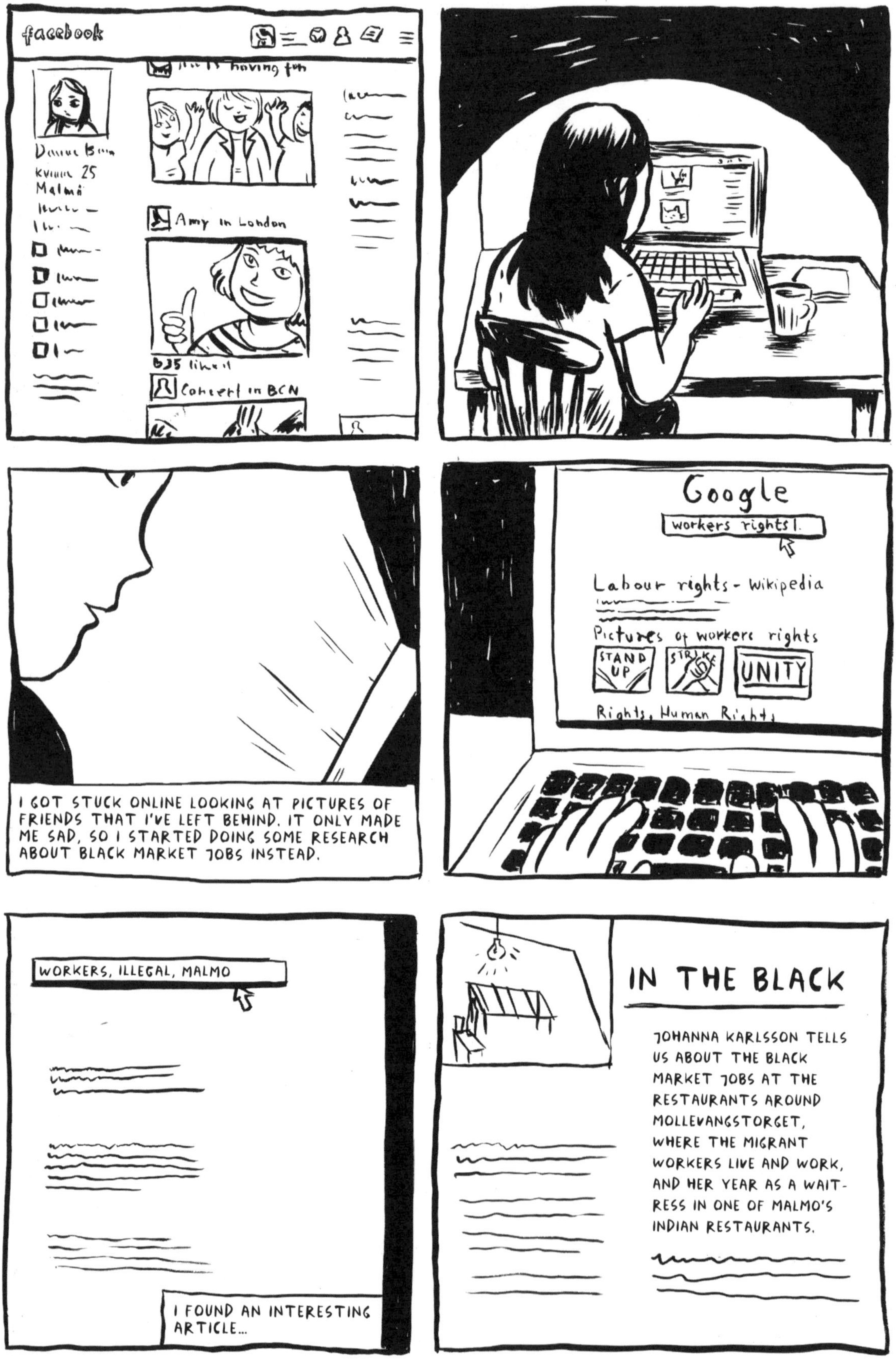
facebook
Amy in London
Concert in BCN
I GOT STUCK ONLINE LOOKING AT PICTURES OF FRIENDS THAT I'VE LEFT BEHIND. IT ONLY MADE ME SAD, SO I STARTED DOING SOME RESEARCH ABOUT BLACK MARKET JOBS INSTEAD.
Google
workers rights
Labour rights - Wikipedia
Pictures of workers rights
STAND UP
STRIKE
UNITY
WORKERS, ILLEGAL, MALMO
I FOUND AN INTERESTING ARTICLE...
IN THE BLACK
JOHANNA KARLSSON TELLS US ABOUT THE BLACK MARKET JOBS AT THE RESTAURANTS AROUND MOLLEVANGSTORGET, WHERE THE MIGRANT WORKERS LIVE AND WORK, AND HER YEAR AS A WAIT-RESS IN ONE OF MALMO'S INDIAN RESTAURANTS.

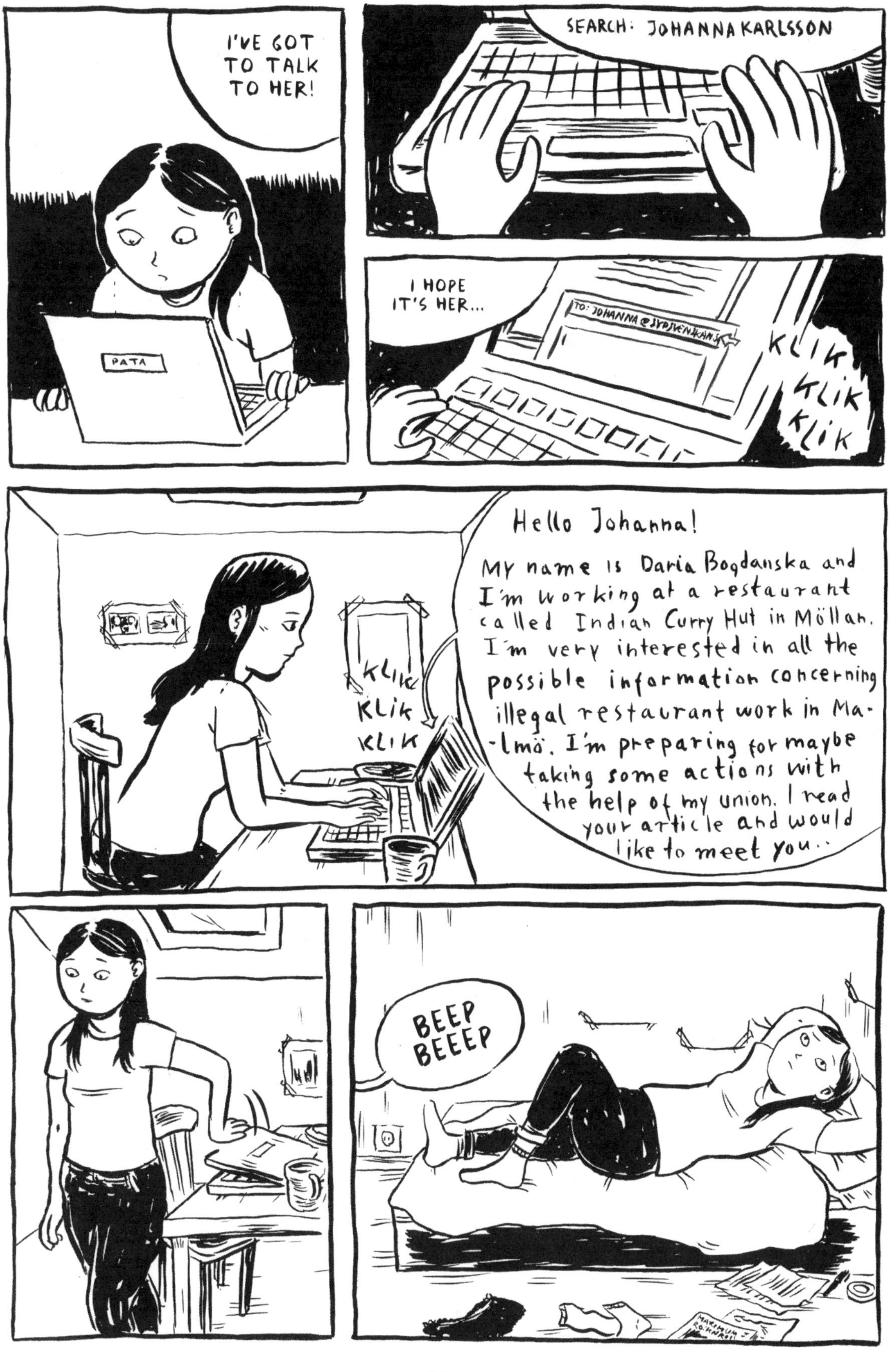

I'VE GOT TO TALK TO HER!
PATA
SEARCH: JOHANNA KARLSSON
I HOPE IT'S HER...
TO: JOHANNA@SYDSVENSKANS
KLIK KLIK KLIK
Hello Johanna!
My name is Daria Bogdanska and I'm working at a restaurant called Indian Curry Hut in Möllan. I'm very interested in all the possible information concerning illegal restaurant work in Ma-lmö. I'm preparing for maybe taking some actions with the help of my union. I read your article and would like to meet you..
KLIK KLIK KLIK
BEEP BEEEP

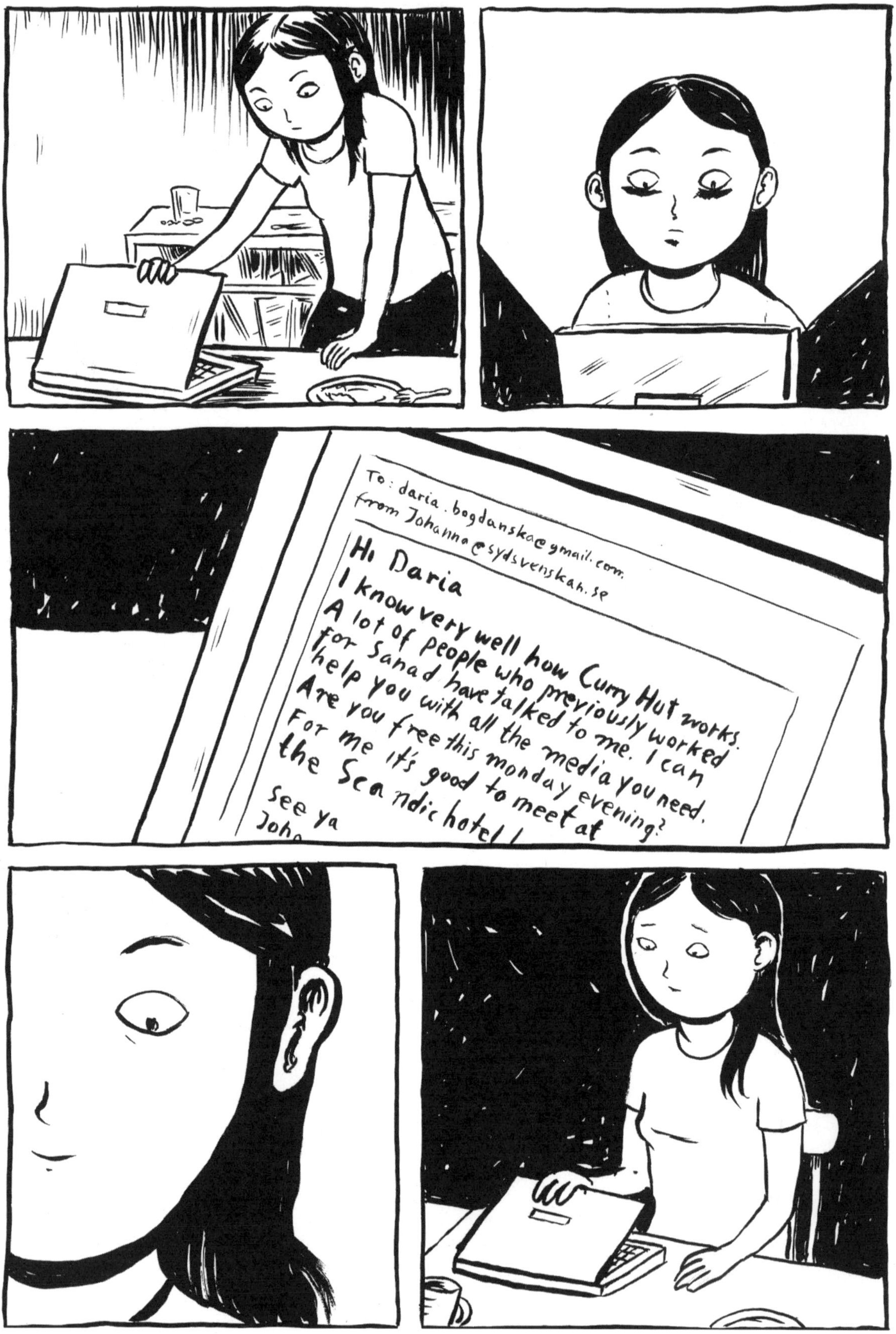
To: daria.bogdanska@gmail.com
from Johanna@sydsvenskan.se
Hi Daria
I know very well how Curry Hut works.
A lot of people who previously worked
for Sanad have talked to me. I can
help you with all the media you need.
Are you free this monday evening?
For me it's good to meet at
the Scandic hotel!
See ya

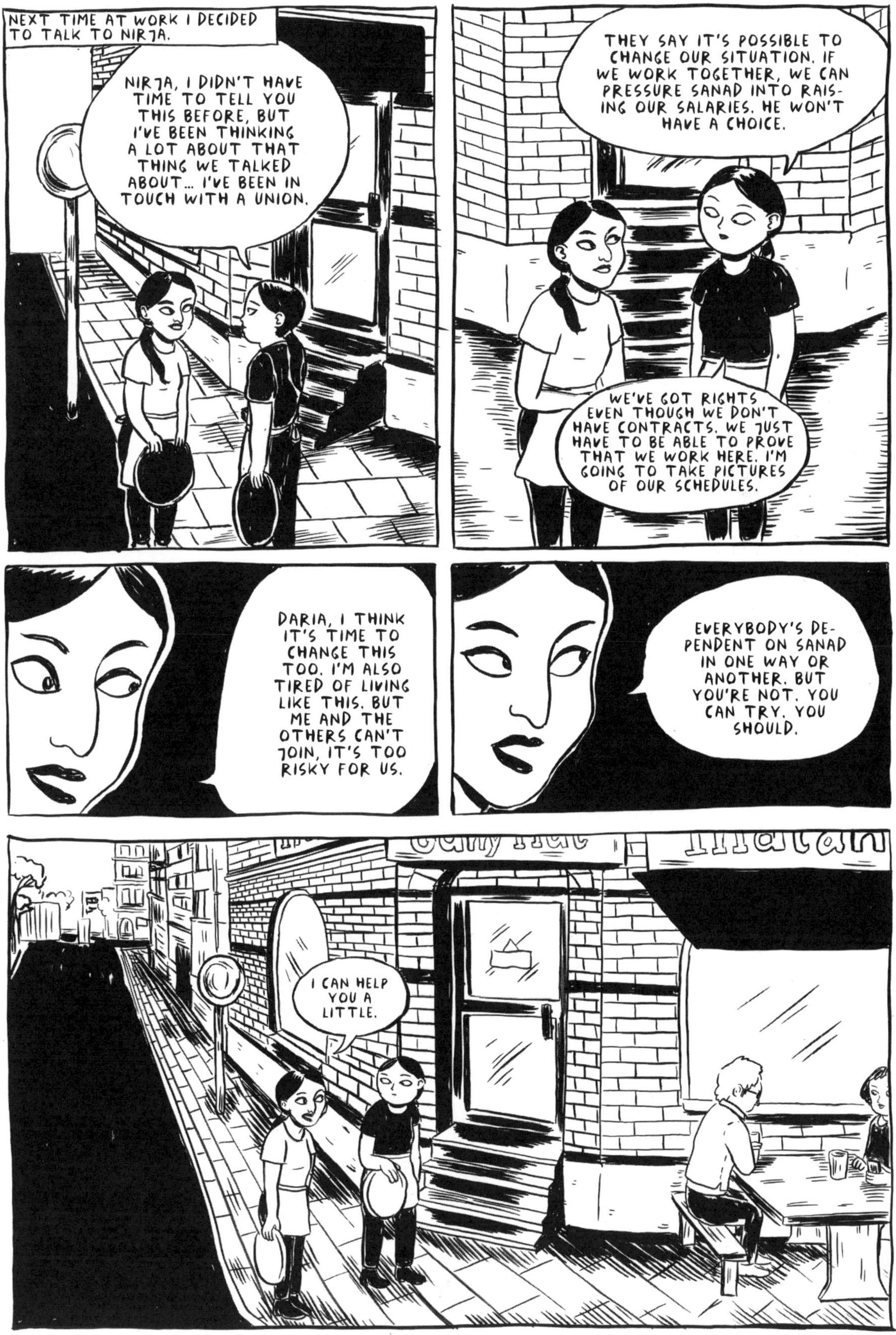
NEXT TIME AT WORK I DECIDED TO TALK TO NIRJA.
NIRJA, I DIDN'T HAVE TIME TO TELL YOU THIS BEFORE, BUT I'VE BEEN THINKING A LOT ABOUT THAT THING WE TALKED ABOUT... I'VE BEEN IN TOUCH WITH A UNION.
THEY SAY IT'S POSSIBLE TO CHANGE OUR SITUATION. IF WE WORK TOGETHER, WE CAN PRESSURE SANAD INTO RAISING OUR SALARIES. HE WON'T HAVE A CHOICE.
WE'VE GOT RIGHTS EVEN THOUGH WE DON'T HAVE CONTRACTS. WE JUST HAVE TO BE ABLE TO PROVE THAT WE WORK HERE. I'M GOING TO TAKE PICTURES OF OUR SCHEDULES.
DARIA, I THINK IT'S TIME TO CHANGE THIS TOO. I'M ALSO TIRED OF LIVING LIKE THIS. BUT ME AND THE OTHERS CAN'T JOIN, IT'S TOO RISKY FOR US.
EVERYBODY'S DEPENDENT ON SANAD IN ONE WAY OR ANOTHER. BUT YOU'RE NOT. YOU CAN TRY. YOU SHOULD.
I CAN HELP YOU A LITTLE.

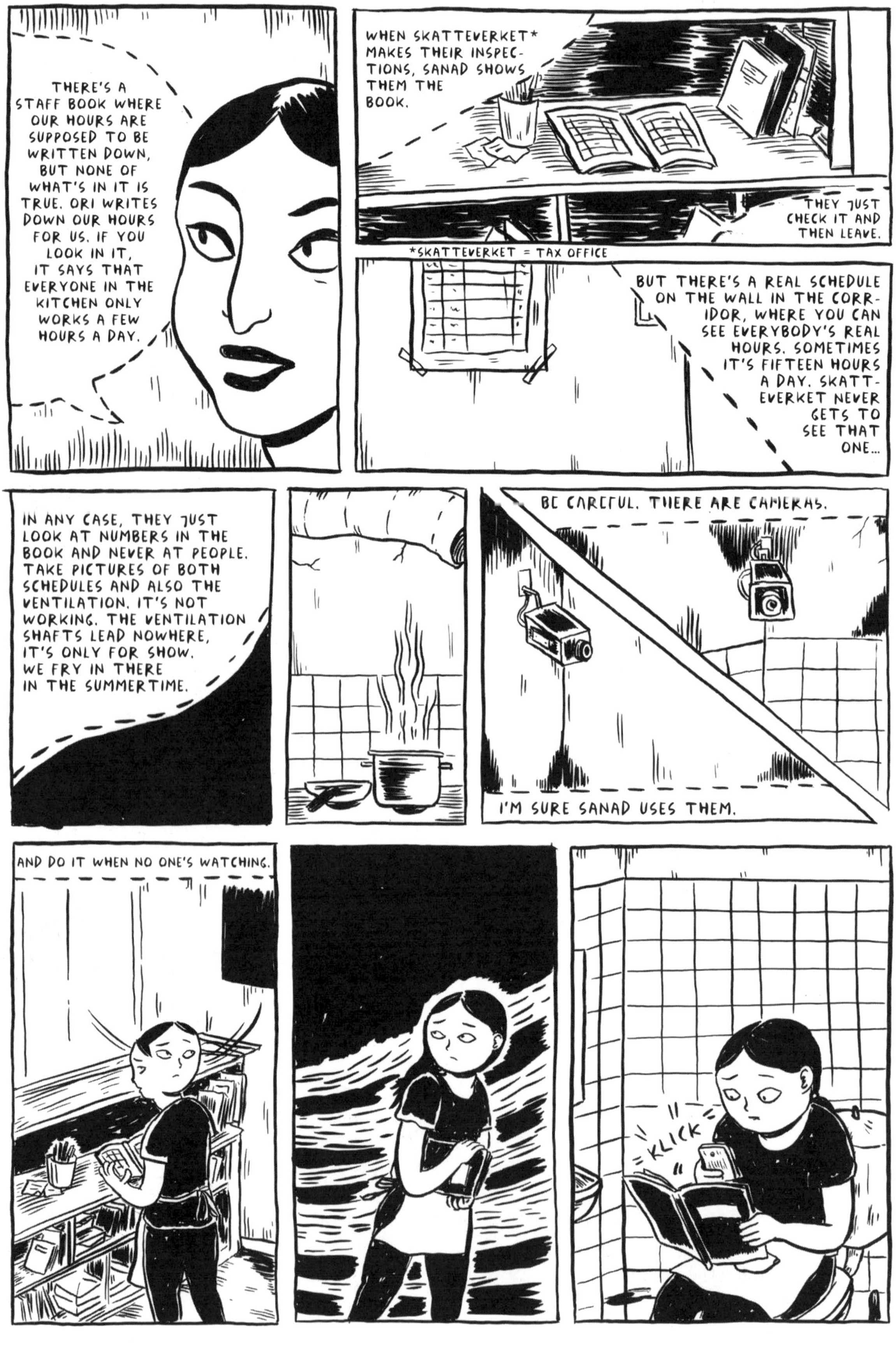
THERE'S A STAFF BOOK WHERE OUR HOURS ARE SUPPOSED TO BE WRITTEN DOWN, BUT NONE OF WHAT'S IN IT IS TRUE. ORI WRITES DOWN OUR HOURS FOR US. IF YOU LOOK IN IT, IT SAYS THAT EVERYONE IN THE KITCHEN ONLY WORKS A FEW HOURS A DAY.
WHEN SKATTEVERKET* MAKES THEIR INSPECTIONS, SANAD SHOWS THEM THE BOOK.
THEY JUST CHECK IT AND THEN LEAVE.
*SKATTEVERKET = TAX OFFICE
BUT THERE'S A REAL SCHEDULE ON THE WALL IN THE CORRIDOR, WHERE YOU CAN SEE EVERYBODY'S REAL HOURS. SOMETIMES IT'S FIFTEEN HOURS A DAY. SKATTEVERKET NEVER GETS TO SEE THAT ONE...
IN ANY CASE, THEY JUST LOOK AT NUMBERS IN THE BOOK AND NEVER AT PEOPLE. TAKE PICTURES OF BOTH SCHEDULES AND ALSO THE VENTILATION. IT'S NOT WORKING. THE VENTILATION SHAFTS LEAD NOWHERE, IT'S ONLY FOR SHOW. WE FRY IN THERE IN THE SUMMERTIME.
BE CAREFUL. THERE ARE CAMERAS.
I'M SURE SANAD USES THEM.
AND DO IT WHEN NO ONE'S WATCHING.
KLICK

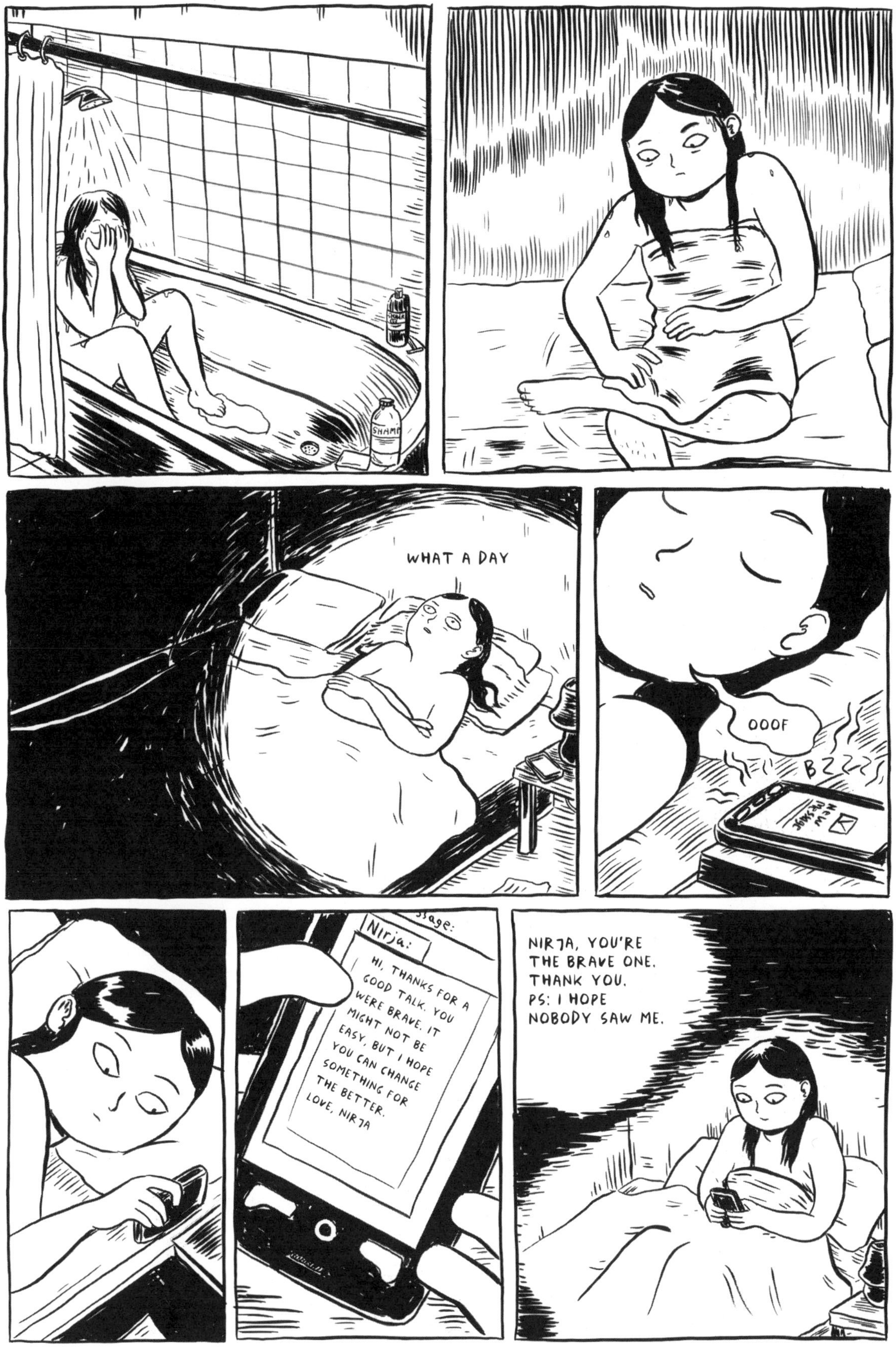
WHAT A DAY
OOOF
BZZZZ
NEW MESSAGE
Nirja:
HI, THANKS FOR A GOOD TALK. YOU WERE BRAVE. IT MIGHT NOT BE EASY, BUT I HOPE YOU CAN CHANGE SOMETHING FOR THE BETTER.
LOVE, NIRJA
NIRJA, YOU'RE THE BRAVE ONE. THANK YOU.
PS: I HOPE NOBODY SAW ME.

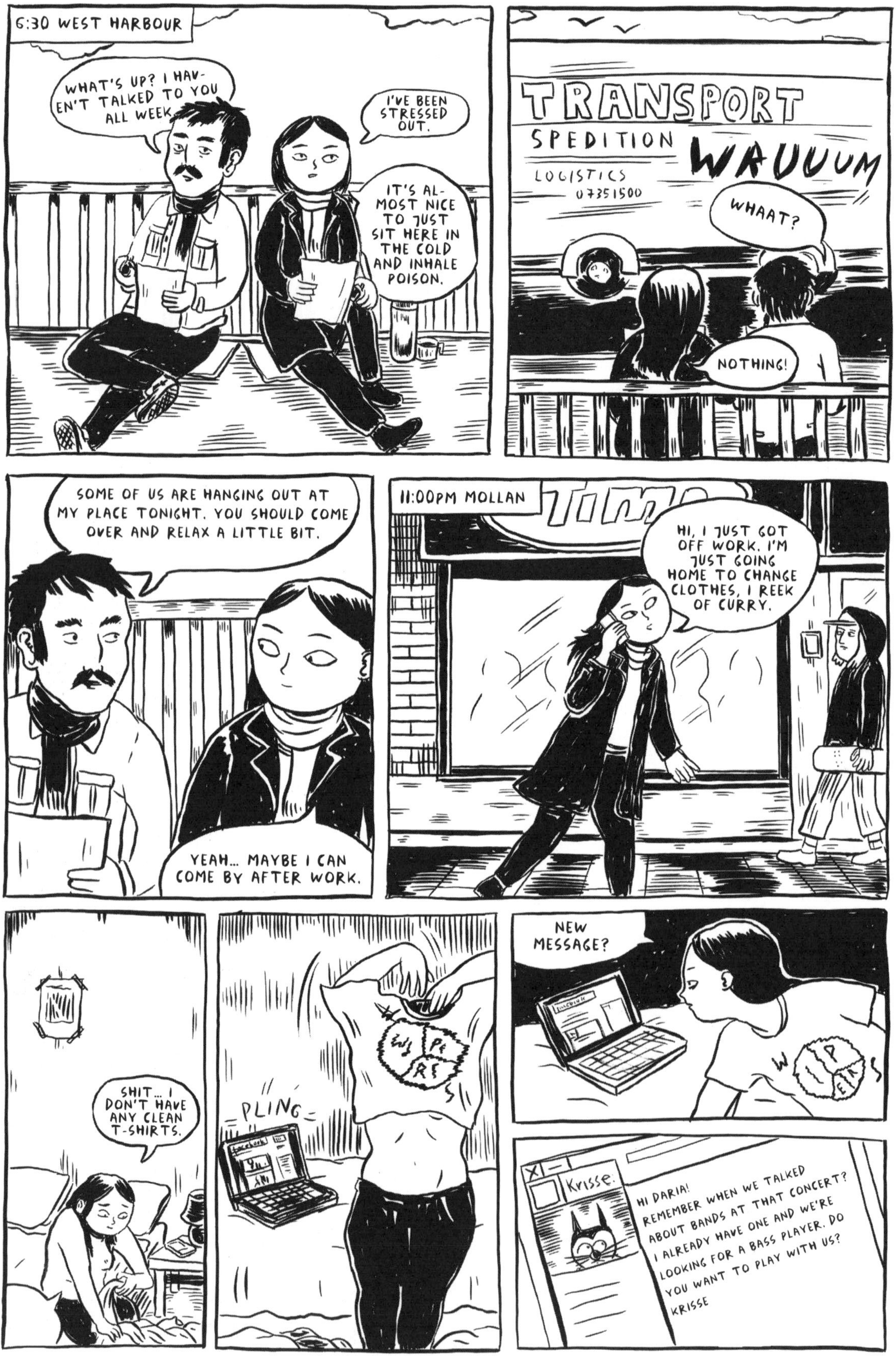
6:30 WEST HARBOUR
WHAT'S UP? I HAVEN'T TALKED TO YOU ALL WEEK.
I'VE BEEN STRESSED OUT.
IT'S ALMOST NICE TO JUST SIT HERE IN THE COLD AND INHALE POISON.
TRANSPORT
SPEDITION
LOGISTICS
07351500
WAUUUM
WHAAT?
NOTHING!
SOME OF US ARE HANGING OUT AT MY PLACE TONIGHT. YOU SHOULD COME OVER AND RELAX A LITTLE BIT.
YEAH... MAYBE I CAN COME BY AFTER WORK.
11:00PM MOLLAN
HI, I JUST GOT OFF WORK. I'M JUST GOING HOME TO CHANGE CLOTHES, I REEK OF CURRY.
SHIT... I DON'T HAVE ANY CLEAN T-SHIRTS.
PLING
NEW MESSAGE?
Krisse.
HI DARIA!
REMEMBER WHEN WE TALKED ABOUT BANDS AT THAT CONCERT? I ALREADY HAVE ONE AND WE'RE LOOKING FOR A BASS PLAYER. DO YOU WANT TO PLAY WITH US?
KRISSE

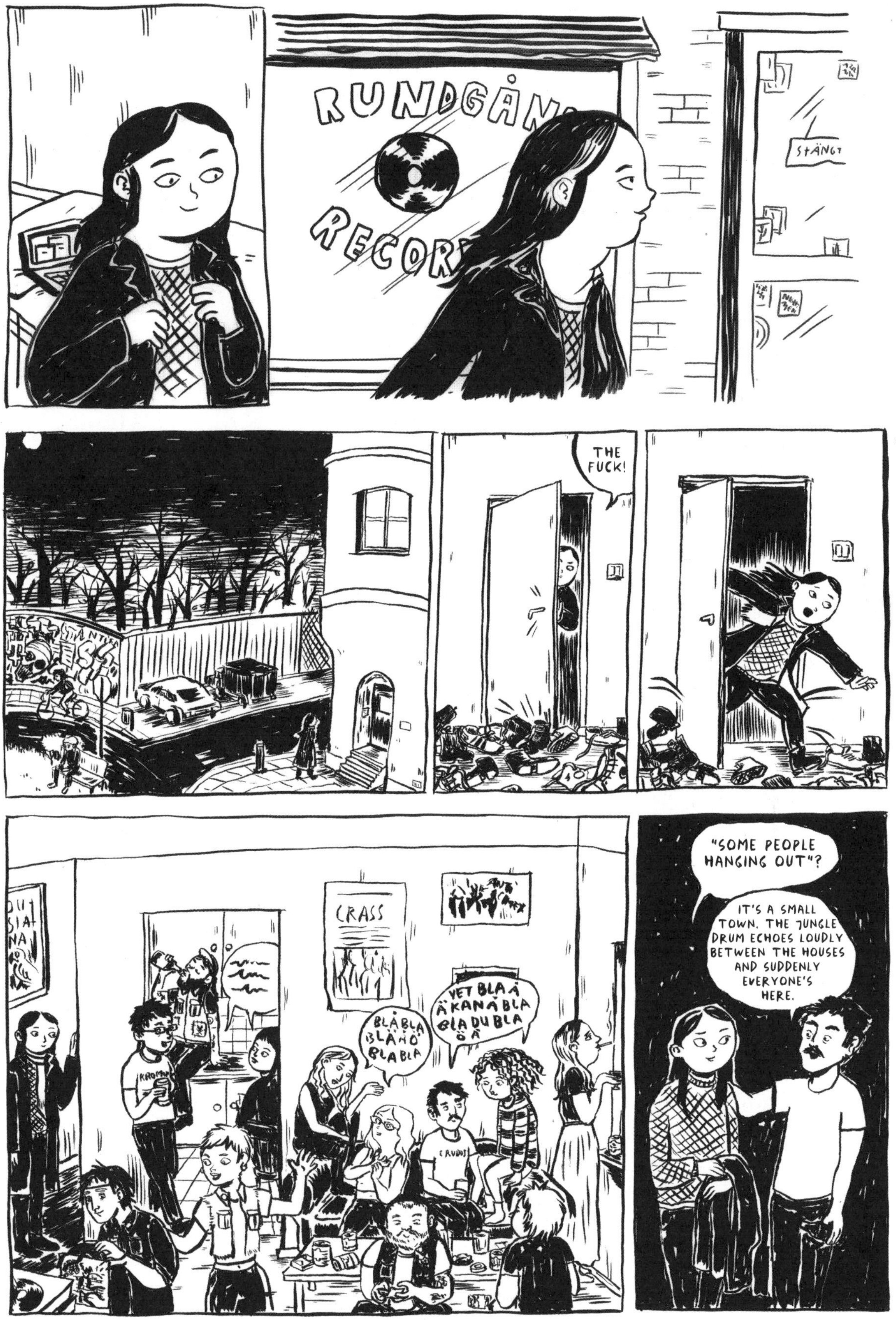
STÄNGT
THE FUCK!
CRASS
BLÅBLA BLÅHÖ BLABLA
VET BLA Ä ÄKANÄBLA BLADUBLA ÖÄ
"SOME PEOPLE HANGING OUT"?
IT'S A SMALL TOWN. THE JUNGLE DRUM ECHOES LOUDLY BETWEEN THE HOUSES AND SUDDENLY EVERYONE'S HERE.

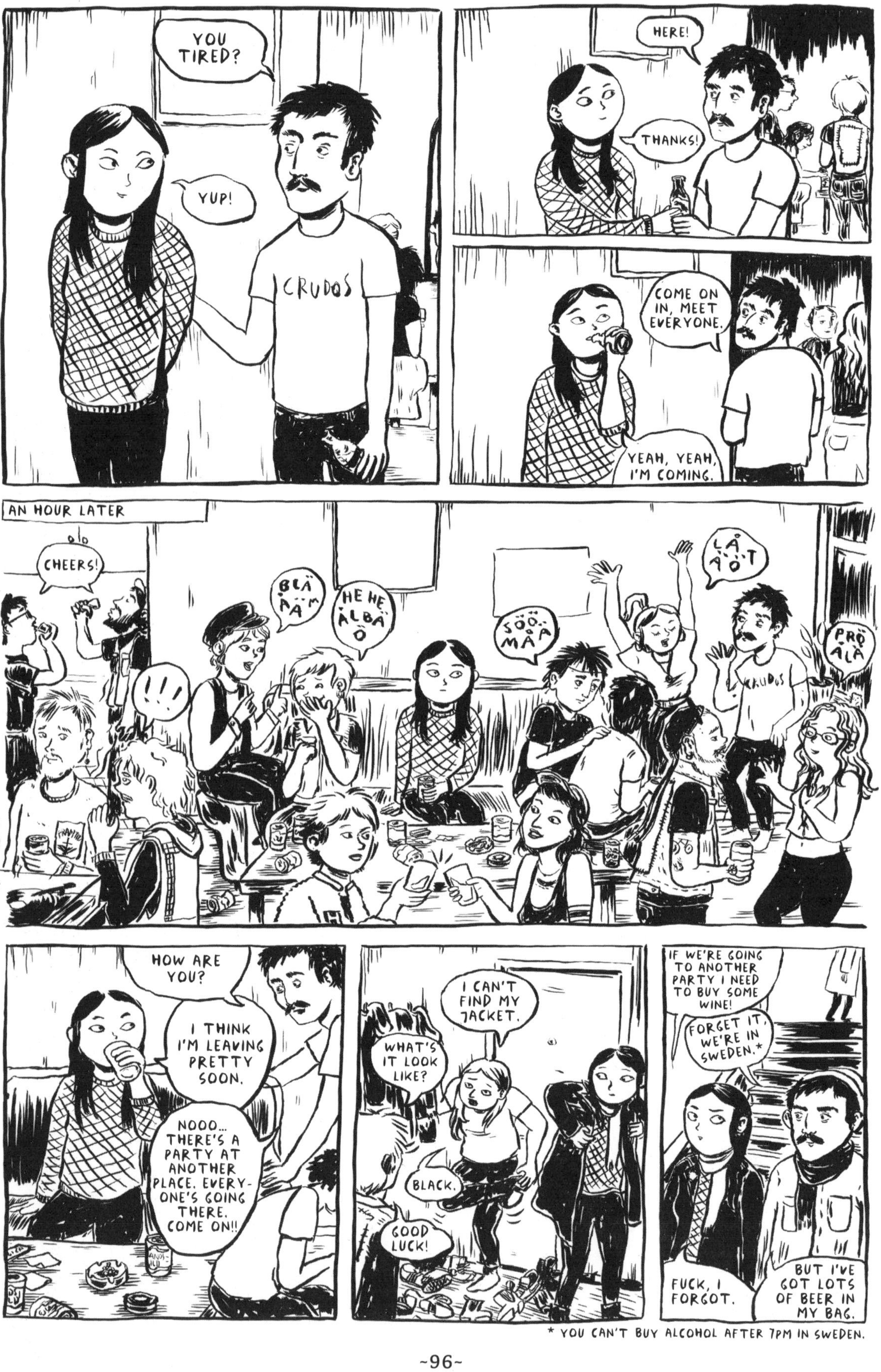

YOU TIRED?
YUP!
CRUDOS
HERE!
THANKS!
COME ON IN, MEET EVERYONE.
YEAH, YEAH, I'M COMING.
AN HOUR LATER
CHEERS!
BLÄ PÅ M
HE HE ÄLBÄ Ö
!!!
SÖÖ MÅ A
LÅ T ÅÖ
PRÖ ÅLÄ
CRUDOS
HOW ARE YOU?
I THINK I'M LEAVING PRETTY SOON.
NOOO... THERE'S A PARTY AT ANOTHER PLACE. EVERY-ONE'S GOING THERE. COME ON!!
I CAN'T FIND MY JACKET.
WHAT'S IT LOOK LIKE?
BLACK.
GOOD LUCK!
IF WE'RE GOING TO ANOTHER PARTY I NEED TO BUY SOME WINE!
FORGET IT, WE'RE IN SWEDEN.*
FUCK, I FORGOT.
BUT I'VE GOT LOTS OF BEER IN MY BAG.

* YOU CAN'T BUY ALCOHOL AFTER 7PM IN SWEDEN.

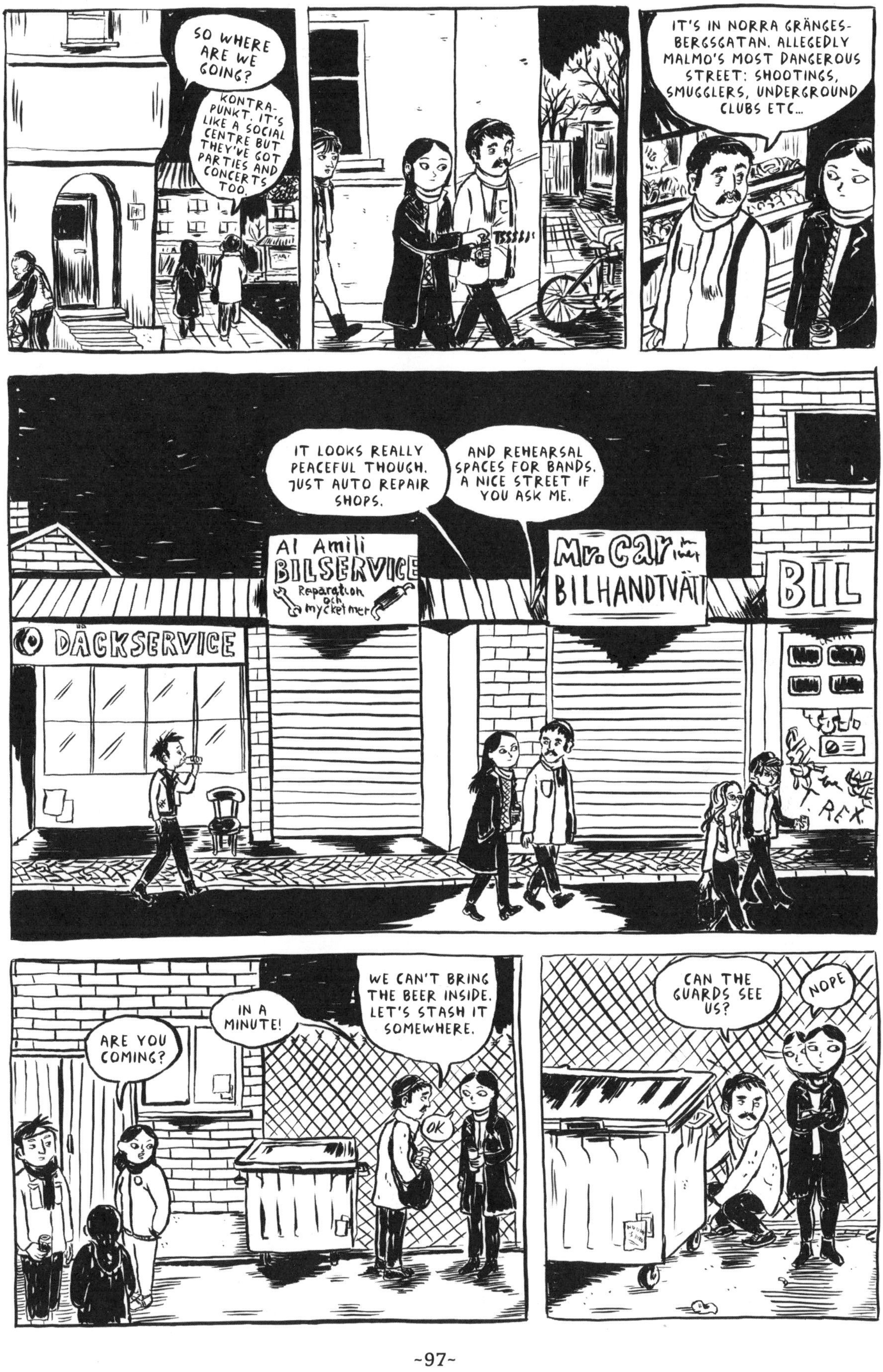
SO WHERE ARE WE GOING?
KONTRA-PUNKT. IT'S LIKE A SOCIAL CENTRE BUT THEY'VE GOT PARTIES AND CONCERTS TOO.
TSSSS!!
IT'S IN NORRA GRÄNGES-BERGSGATAN. ALLEGEDLY MALMO'S MOST DANGEROUS STREET: SHOOTINGS, SMUGGLERS, UNDERGROUND CLUBS ETC...
IT LOOKS REALLY PEACEFUL THOUGH. JUST AUTO REPAIR SHOPS.
AND REHEARSAL SPACES FOR BANDS. A NICE STREET IF YOU ASK ME.
Al Amili
BILSERVICE
Reparation och mycket mer
Mr. Car
BILHANDTVÄTT
BIL
DÄCKSERVICE
REX
ARE YOU COMING?
IN A MINUTE!
WE CAN'T BRING THE BEER INSIDE. LET'S STASH IT SOMEWHERE.
OK
CAN THE GUARDS SEE US?
NOPE

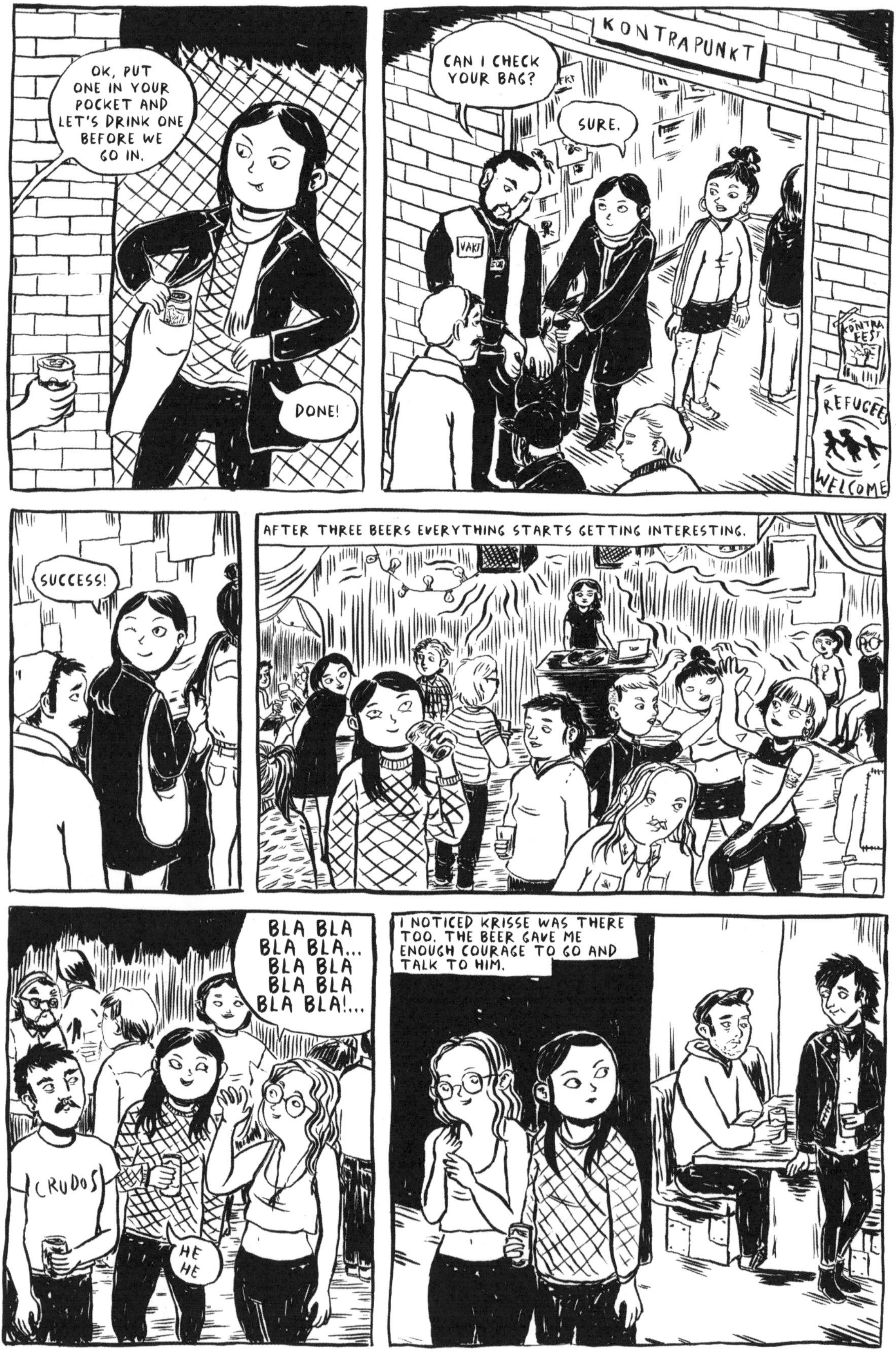
OK, PUT ONE IN YOUR POCKET AND LET'S DRINK ONE BEFORE WE GO IN.
DONE!
KONTRAPUNKT
CAN I CHECK YOUR BAG?
SURE.
VAKT
KONTRA FEST
REFUGEES WELCOME
SUCCESS!
AFTER THREE BEERS EVERYTHING STARTS GETTING INTERESTING.
BLA BLA BLA BLA... BLA BLA BLA BLA BLA BLA!...
CRUDOS
HE HE
I NOTICED KRISSE WAS THERE TOO. THE BEER GAVE ME ENOUGH COURAGE TO GO AND TALK TO HIM.

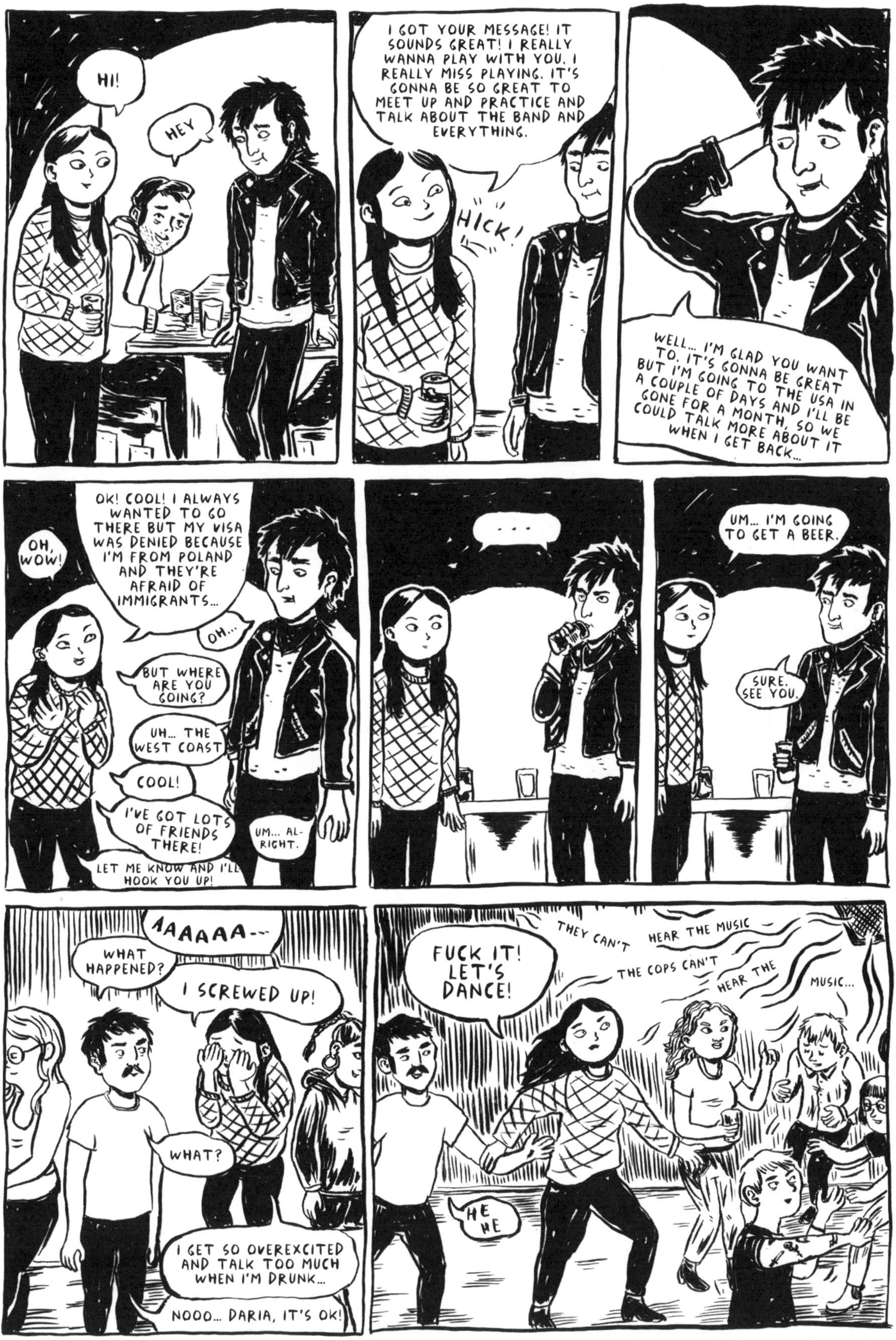
HI!
HEY
I GOT YOUR MESSAGE! IT SOUNDS GREAT! I REALLY WANNA PLAY WITH YOU. I REALLY MISS PLAYING. IT'S GONNA BE SO GREAT TO MEET UP AND PRACTICE AND TALK ABOUT THE BAND AND EVERYTHING.
HICK!
WELL... I'M GLAD YOU WANT TO. IT'S GONNA BE GREAT BUT I'M GOING TO THE USA IN A COUPLE OF DAYS AND I'LL BE GONE FOR A MONTH, SO WE COULD TALK MORE ABOUT IT WHEN I GET BACK...
OH, WOW!
OK! COOL! I ALWAYS WANTED TO GO THERE BUT MY VISA WAS DENIED BECAUSE I'M FROM POLAND AND THEY'RE AFRAID OF IMMIGRANTS...
OH...
BUT WHERE ARE YOU GOING?
UH... THE WEST COAST
COOL!
I'VE GOT LOTS OF FRIENDS THERE!
LET ME KNOW AND I'LL HOOK YOU UP!
UM... AL-RIGHT.
. . .
UM... I'M GOING TO GET A BEER.
SURE. SEE YOU.
AAAAAA---
WHAT HAPPENED?
I SCREWED UP!
WHAT?
I GET SO OVEREXCITED AND TALK TOO MUCH WHEN I'M DRUNK...
NOOO... DARIA, IT'S OK!
FUCK IT! LET'S DANCE!
THEY CAN'T HEAR THE MUSIC
THE COPS CAN'T HEAR THE MUSIC...
HE HE

SONG: "MASSHYSTERI DE KAN INTE HÖRA MUSIKEN"

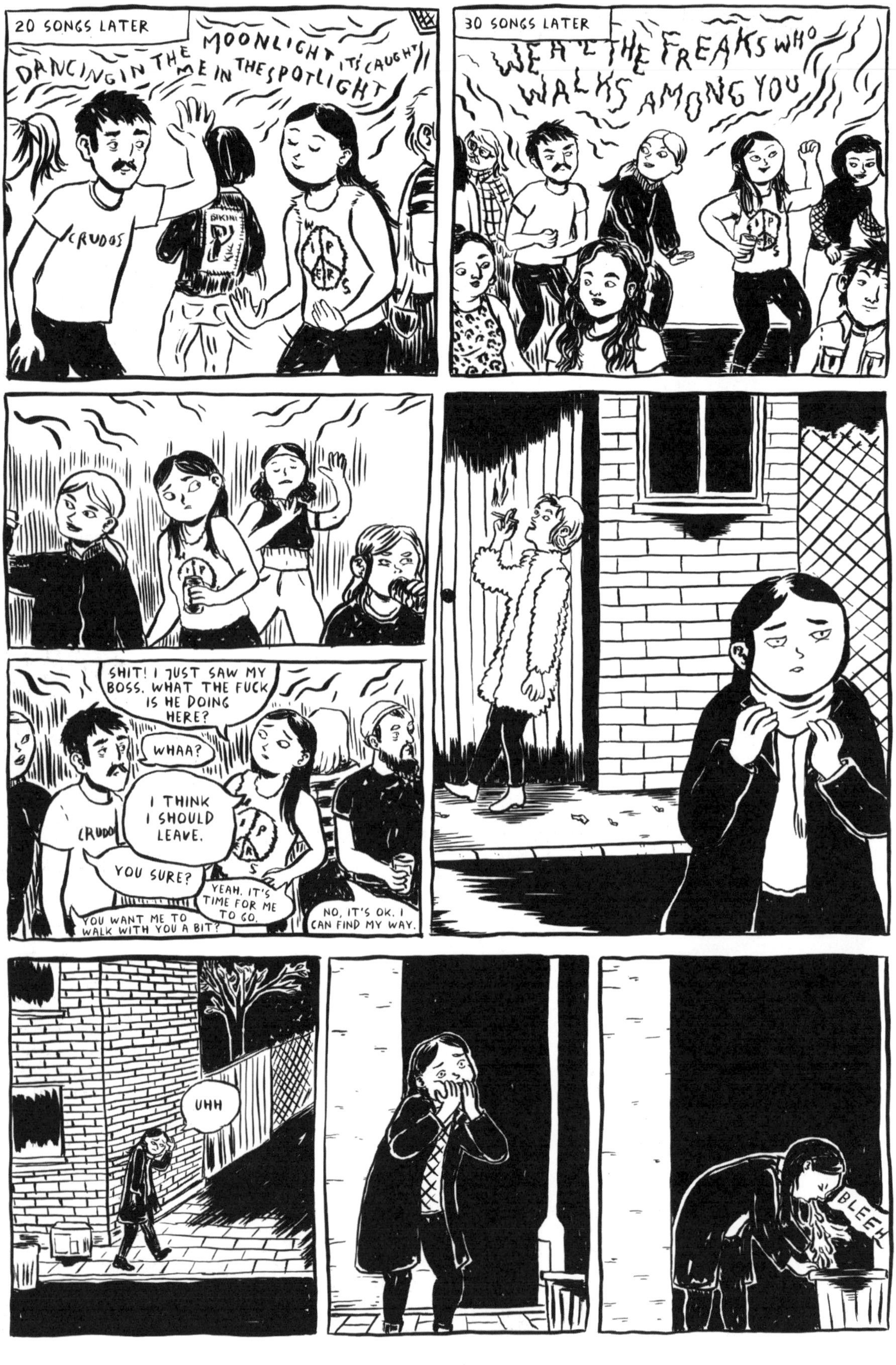
20 SONGS LATER
DANCING IN THE MOONLIGHT IT'S CAUGHT ME IN THE SPOTLIGHT
CRUDOS
BIKINI
30 SONGS LATER
WE'RE THE FREAKS WHO WALKS AMONG YOU
SHIT! I JUST SAW MY BOSS. WHAT THE FUCK IS HE DOING HERE?
WHAA?
I THINK I SHOULD LEAVE.
YOU SURE?
YEAH. IT'S TIME FOR ME TO GO.
YOU WANT ME TO WALK WITH YOU A BIT?
NO, IT'S OK. I CAN FIND MY WAY.
UHH
BLEEH

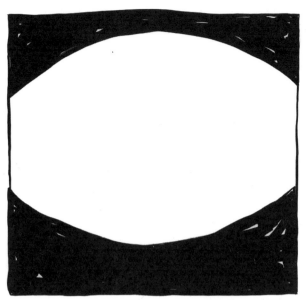

OOO... MY HEAD...

UUUG...

WHAT TIME IS IT?

OH, FUCK!

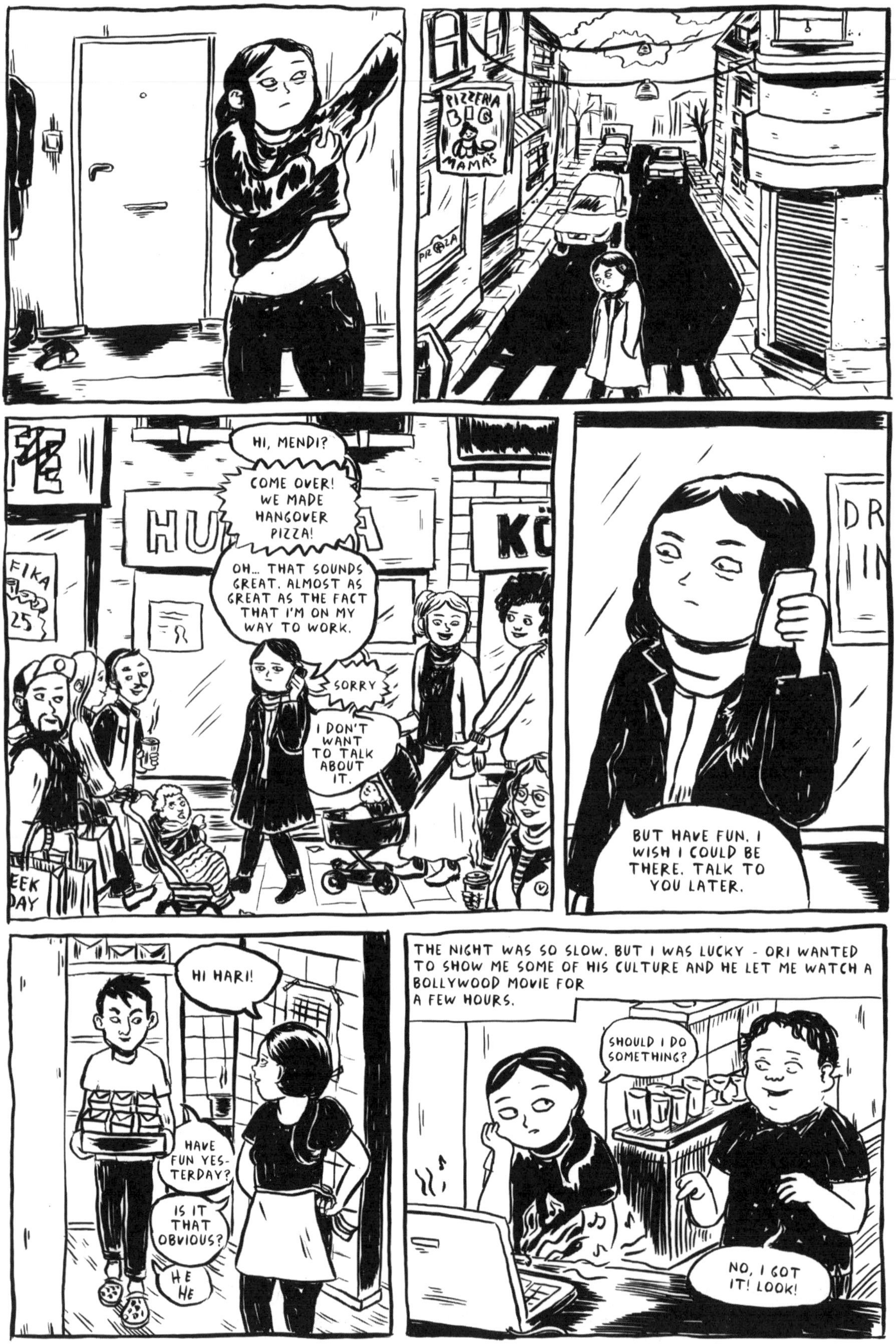
PIZZERIA BIG MAMA'S
PIZZA
HI, MENDI?
COME OVER! WE MADE HANGOVER PIZZA!
OH... THAT SOUNDS GREAT. ALMOST AS GREAT AS THE FACT THAT I'M ON MY WAY TO WORK.
SORRY
I DON'T WANT TO TALK ABOUT IT.
FIKA 25
HU
KÖ
EEK DAY
DR IN
BUT HAVE FUN. I WISH I COULD BE THERE. TALK TO YOU LATER.
HI HARI!
HAVE FUN YESTERDAY?
IS IT THAT OBVIOUS?
HE HE
THE NIGHT WAS SO SLOW. BUT I WAS LUCKY - ORI WANTED TO SHOW ME SOME OF HIS CULTURE AND HE LET ME WATCH A BOLLYWOOD MOVIE FOR A FEW HOURS.
SHOULD I DO SOMETHING?
NO, I GOT IT! LOOK!

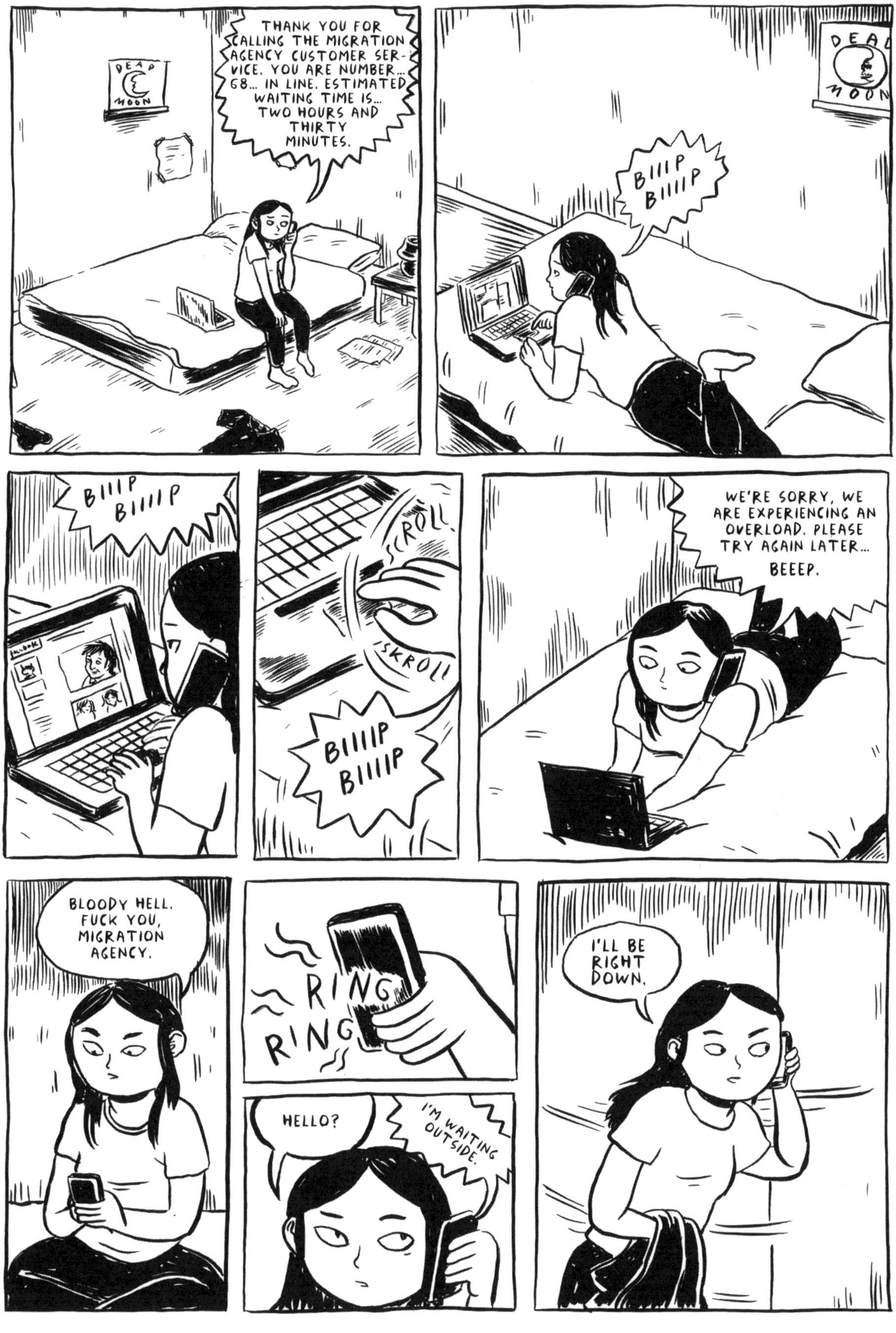
THANK YOU FOR CALLING THE MIGRATION AGENCY CUSTOMER SERVICE. YOU ARE NUMBER... 68... IN LINE. ESTIMATED WAITING TIME IS... TWO HOURS AND THIRTY MINUTES.
DEAD MOON
BIIIP BIIIIP
DEAD MOON
BIIIP BIIIIP
SCROLL
SKROLL
BIIIIP BIIIIP
WE'RE SORRY, WE ARE EXPERIENCING AN OVERLOAD. PLEASE TRY AGAIN LATER...
BEEEP.
BLOODY HELL. FUCK YOU, MIGRATION AGENCY.
RING
RING
HELLO?
I'M WAITING OUTSIDE.
I'LL BE RIGHT DOWN.

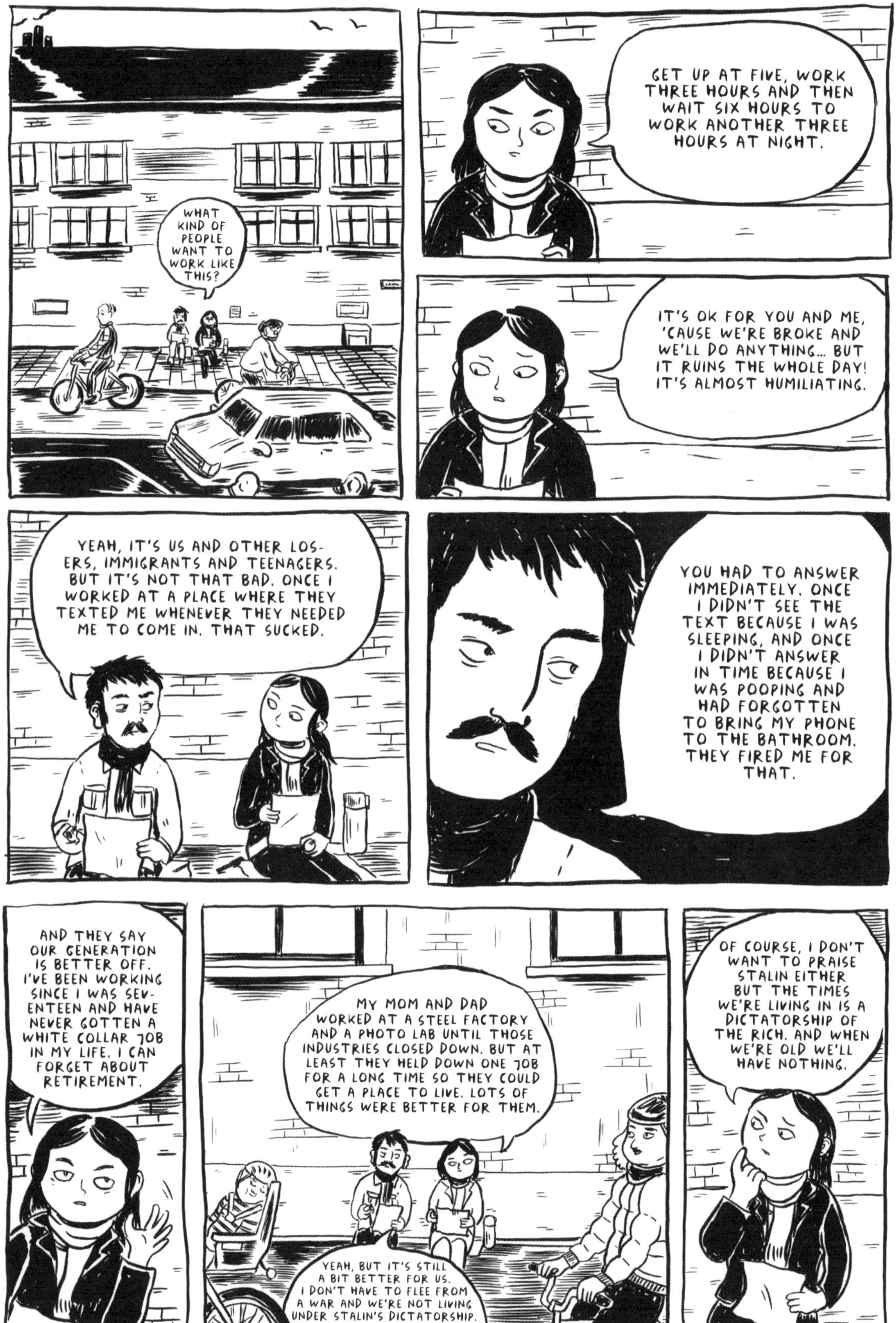
WHAT KIND OF PEOPLE WANT TO WORK LIKE THIS?
GET UP AT FIVE, WORK THREE HOURS AND THEN WAIT SIX HOURS TO WORK ANOTHER THREE HOURS AT NIGHT.
IT'S OK FOR YOU AND ME, 'CAUSE WE'RE BROKE AND WE'LL DO ANYTHING... BUT IT RUINS THE WHOLE DAY! IT'S ALMOST HUMILIATING.
YEAH, IT'S US AND OTHER LOS-ERS, IMMIGRANTS AND TEENAGERS. BUT IT'S NOT THAT BAD. ONCE I WORKED AT A PLACE WHERE THEY TEXTED ME WHENEVER THEY NEEDED ME TO COME IN. THAT SUCKED.
YOU HAD TO ANSWER IMMEDIATELY. ONCE I DIDN'T SEE THE TEXT BECAUSE I WAS SLEEPING, AND ONCE I DIDN'T ANSWER IN TIME BECAUSE I WAS POOPING AND HAD FORGOTTEN TO BRING MY PHONE TO THE BATHROOM. THEY FIRED ME FOR THAT.
AND THEY SAY OUR GENERATION IS BETTER OFF. I'VE BEEN WORKING SINCE I WAS SEV-ENTEEN AND HAVE NEVER GOTTEN A WHITE COLLAR JOB IN MY LIFE. I CAN FORGET ABOUT RETIREMENT.
MY MOM AND DAD WORKED AT A STEEL FACTORY AND A PHOTO LAB UNTIL THOSE INDUSTRIES CLOSED DOWN. BUT AT LEAST THEY HELD DOWN ONE JOB FOR A LONG TIME SO THEY COULD GET A PLACE TO LIVE. LOTS OF THINGS WERE BETTER FOR THEM.
YEAH, BUT IT'S STILL A BIT BETTER FOR US. I DON'T HAVE TO FLEE FROM A WAR AND WE'RE NOT LIVING UNDER STALIN'S DICTATORSHIP.
OF COURSE, I DON'T WANT TO PRAISE STALIN EITHER BUT THE TIMES WE'RE LIVING IN IS A DICTATORSHIP OF THE RICH. AND WHEN WE'RE OLD WE'LL HAVE NOTHING.

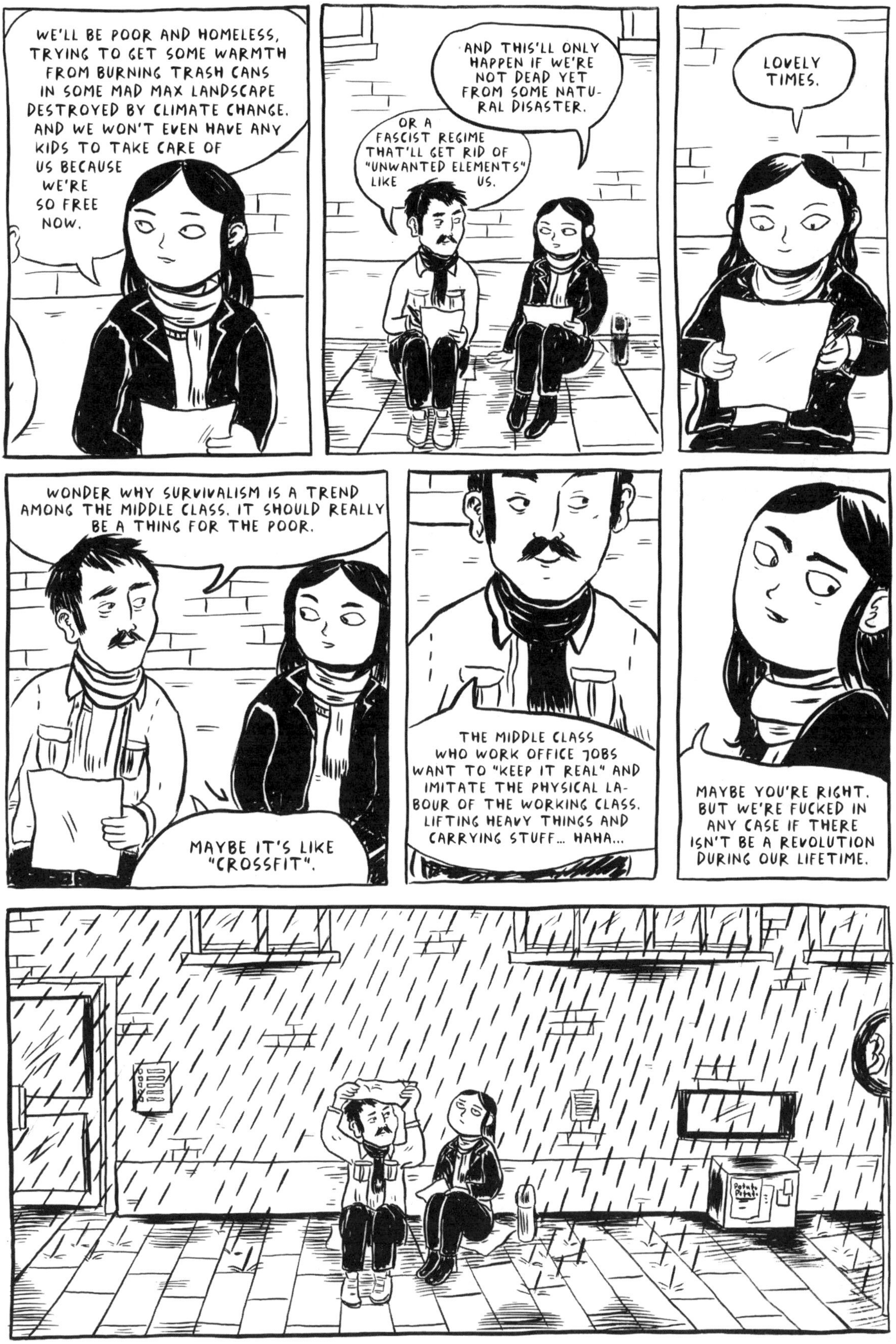
WE'LL BE POOR AND HOMELESS, TRYING TO GET SOME WARMTH FROM BURNING TRASH CANS IN SOME MAD MAX LANDSCAPE DESTROYED BY CLIMATE CHANGE. AND WE WON'T EVEN HAVE ANY KIDS TO TAKE CARE OF US BECAUSE WE'RE SO FREE NOW.
AND THIS'LL ONLY HAPPEN IF WE'RE NOT DEAD YET FROM SOME NATURAL DISASTER.
OR A FASCIST REGIME THAT'LL GET RID OF "UNWANTED ELEMENTS" LIKE US.
LOVELY TIMES.
WONDER WHY SURVIVALISM IS A TREND AMONG THE MIDDLE CLASS. IT SHOULD REALLY BE A THING FOR THE POOR.
MAYBE IT'S LIKE "CROSSFIT".
THE MIDDLE CLASS WHO WORK OFFICE JOBS WANT TO "KEEP IT REAL" AND IMITATE THE PHYSICAL LABOUR OF THE WORKING CLASS. LIFTING HEAVY THINGS AND CARRYING STUFF... HAHA...
MAYBE YOU'RE RIGHT. BUT WE'RE FUCKED IN ANY CASE IF THERE ISN'T BE A REVOLUTION DURING OUR LIFETIME.

A FEW DAYS LATER I GOT A TEXT FROM NIRJA.

Nirja:

DARIA, I'M SORRY I HAVEN'T BEEN IN TOUCH, I HAD TO BORROW MONEY AND TAKE TIME OFF TO HANDLE SCHOOL. I DON'T KNOW WHEN I'LL BE BACK. DON'T TELL ANYONE YOU DON'T TRUST ABOUT WHAT WE TALKED ABOUT. SANAD MUSTN'T KNOW.
LOVE, N

I KNEW THAT IF I WANTED TO PROCEED, I HAD TO FIND SOMEONE WHO COULD JOIN ME. I TRIED TO CONVINCE IDA, THE SWEDISH WAITRESS.

THANKS FOR COMING.

I TOLD HER EVERYTHING NIRJA HAD TOLD ME AND THAT I NEEDED HER HELP.

OH, THAT'S TERRIBLE! I DIDN'T KNOW.

I THINK IF THE TWO OF US DID SOMETHING, WE COULD HELP THE OTHERS.

OH, ABSOLUTELY, OF COURSE I'LL HELP, IT'S A GOOD IDEA!

YOU CAN START BY JOINING THE UNION, AND THEN WE CAN TALK ABOUT HOW TO MOVE FORWARD.

SURE, I'LL DO THAT.

BUT LATER, WHEN I TRIED CALLING HER SHE DIDN'T PICK UP.

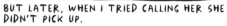

Calling Ida

BIIIP BIIIP

BIIP BIIP BIIP BIIP

BIIP BIIP BIIP BIIP

I HAVEN'T SEEN HER AT CURRY HUT AGAIN, BUT ONE DAY I SAW HER BEHIND THE BAR AT HANG BAR.

Häng Bar

ONE DOWN...

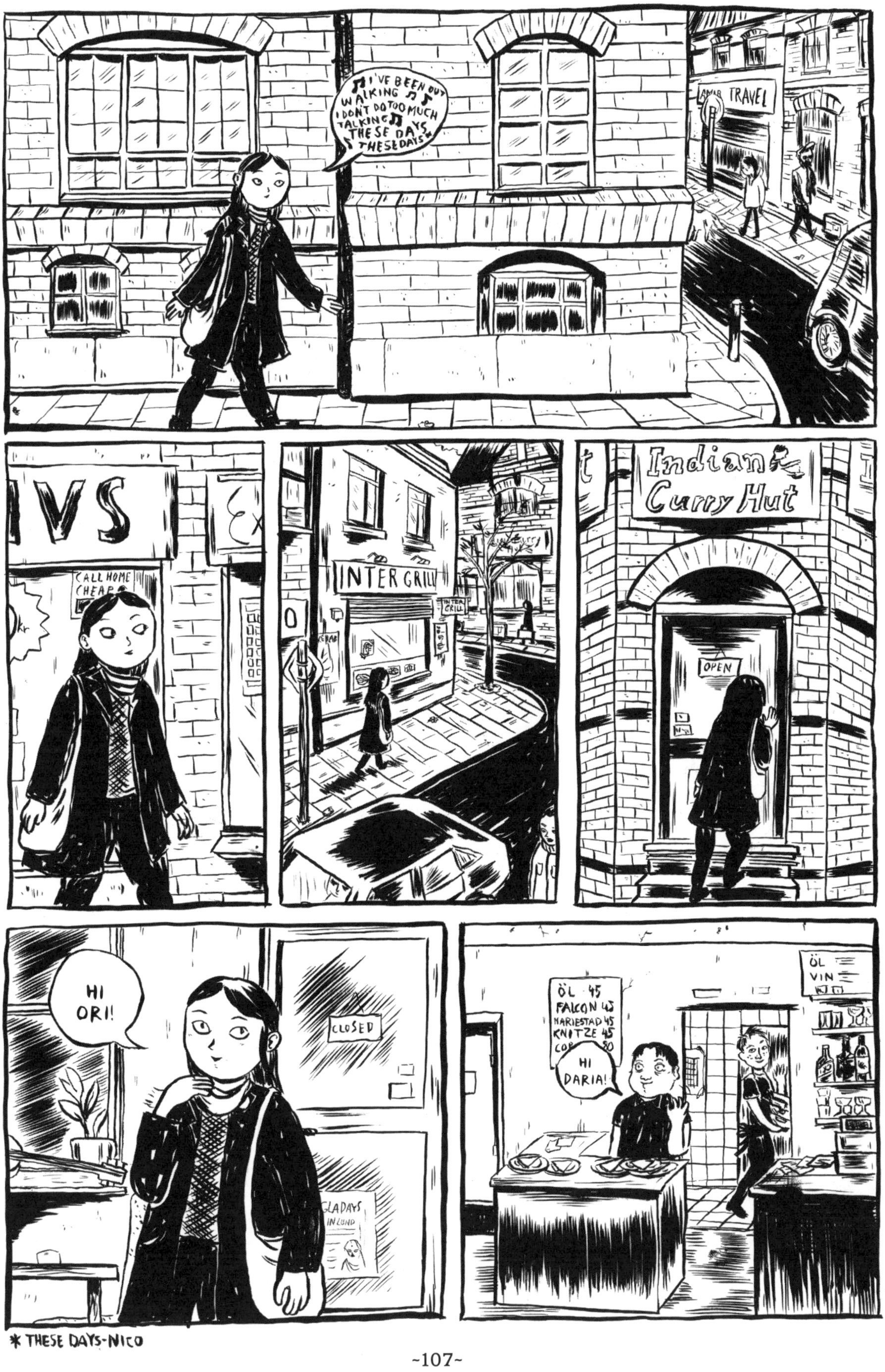

I'VE BEEN OUT WALKING I DON'T DO TOO MUCH TALKING THESE DAYS THESE DAYS*
TRAVEL
CALL HOME CHEAP
INTER GRILL
Indian Curry Hut
OPEN
HI ORI!
CLOSED
HI DARIA!
ÖL VIN
ÖL 45
FALCON 45

* THESE DAYS-NICO

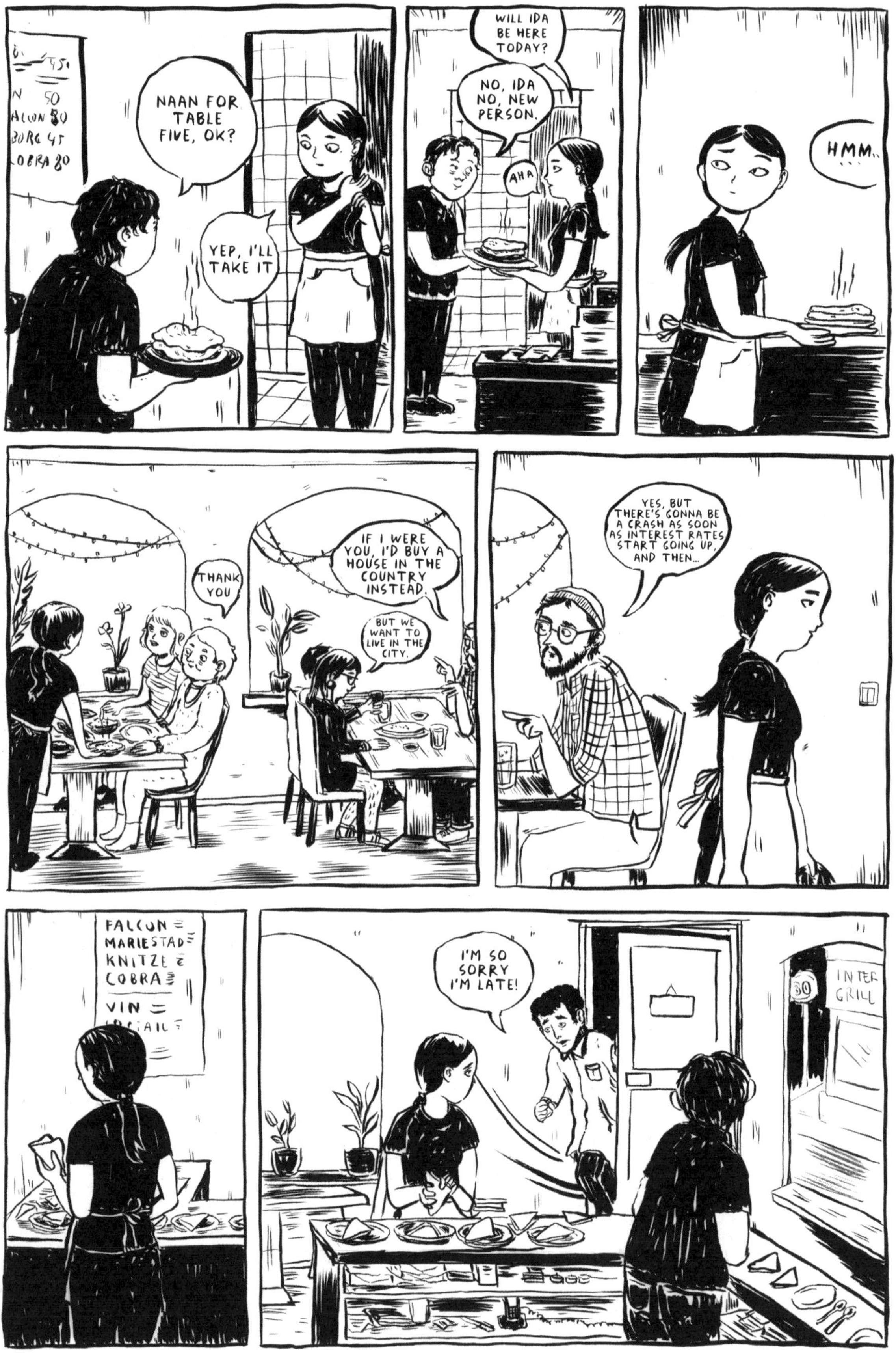
NAAN FOR TABLE FIVE, OK?
YEP, I'LL TAKE IT
WILL IDA BE HERE TODAY?
NO, IDA NO, NEW PERSON.
AHA
HMM..
THANK YOU
IF I WERE YOU, I'D BUY A HOUSE IN THE COUNTRY INSTEAD.
BUT WE WANT TO LIVE IN THE CITY.
YES, BUT THERE'S GONNA BE A CRASH AS SOON AS INTEREST RATES START GOING UP, AND THEN...
FALCON
MARIESTAD
KNITZE
COBRA
VIN
I'M SO SORRY I'M LATE!
30
INTER GRILL

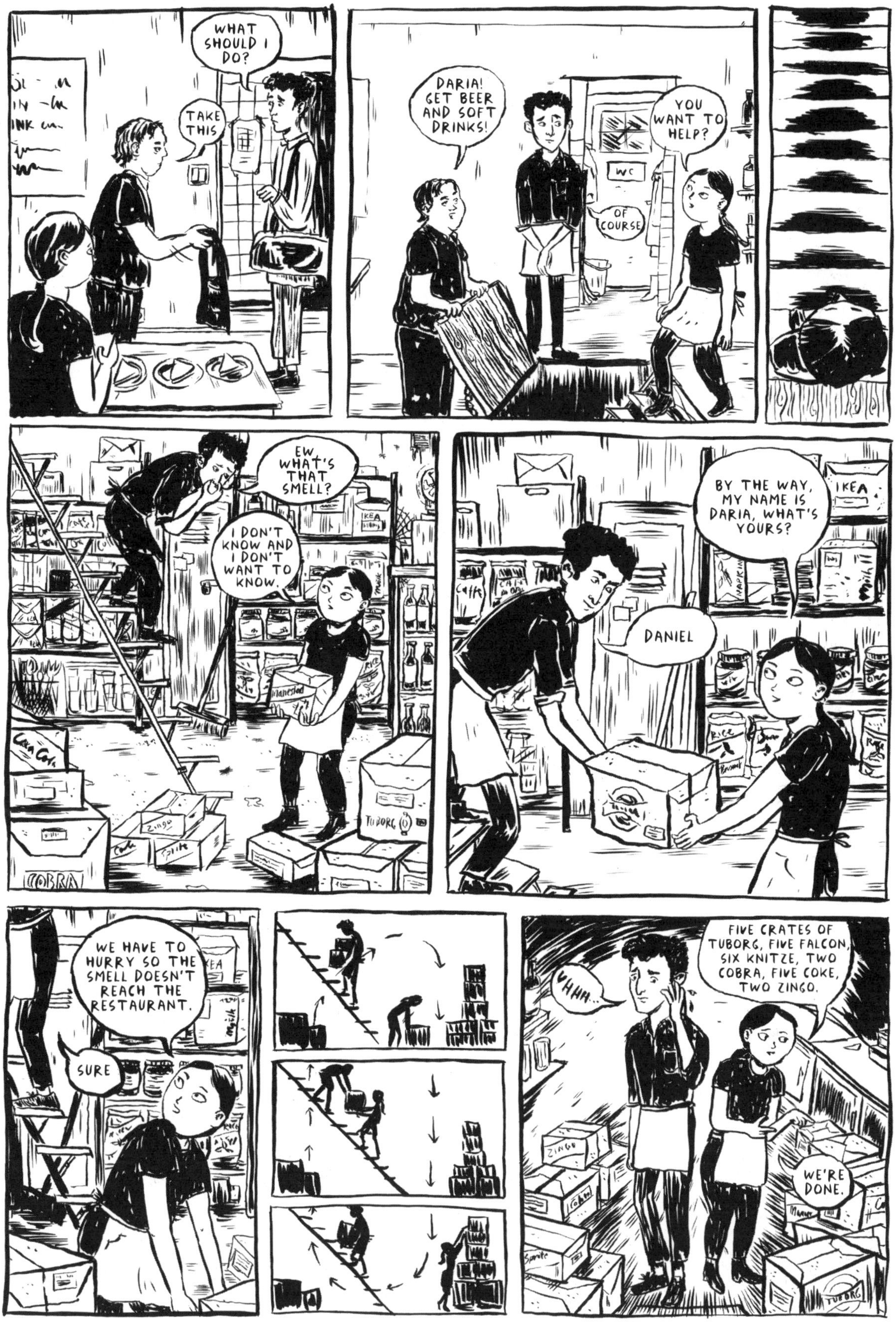
WHAT SHOULD I DO?
TAKE THIS
DARIA! GET BEER AND SOFT DRINKS!
YOU WANT TO HELP?
OF COURSE
EW WHAT'S THAT SMELL?
I DON'T KNOW AND I DON'T WANT TO KNOW.
BY THE WAY, MY NAME IS DARIA, WHAT'S YOURS?
DANIEL
WE HAVE TO HURRY SO THE SMELL DOESN'T REACH THE RESTAURANT.
SURE
FIVE CRATES OF TUBORG, FIVE FALCON, SIX KNITZE, TWO COBRA, FIVE COKE, TWO ZINGO.
UHHH...
WE'RE DONE.

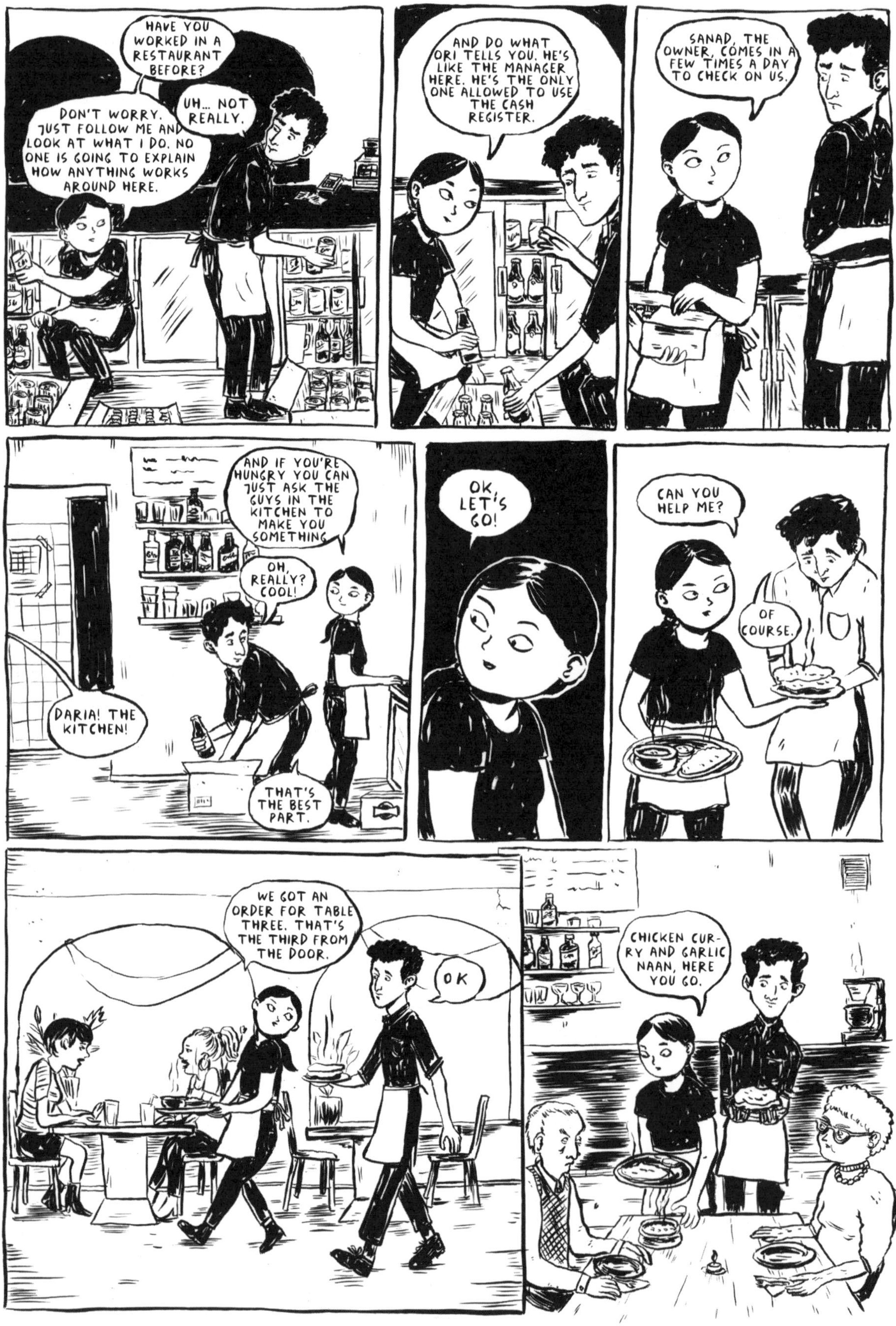
HAVE YOU WORKED IN A RESTAURANT BEFORE?
UH... NOT REALLY.
DON'T WORRY. JUST FOLLOW ME AND LOOK AT WHAT I DO. NO ONE IS GOING TO EXPLAIN HOW ANYTHING WORKS AROUND HERE.
AND DO WHAT ORI TELLS YOU. HE'S LIKE THE MANAGER HERE. HE'S THE ONLY ONE ALLOWED TO USE THE CASH REGISTER.
SANAD, THE OWNER, COMES IN A FEW TIMES A DAY TO CHECK ON US.
AND IF YOU'RE HUNGRY YOU CAN JUST ASK THE GUYS IN THE KITCHEN TO MAKE YOU SOMETHING
OH, REALLY? COOL!
DARIA! THE KITCHEN!
THAT'S THE BEST PART.
OK, LET'S GO!
CAN YOU HELP ME?
OF COURSE.
WE GOT AN ORDER FOR TABLE THREE. THAT'S THE THIRD FROM THE DOOR.
OK
CHICKEN CURRY AND GARLIC NAAN, HERE YOU GO.

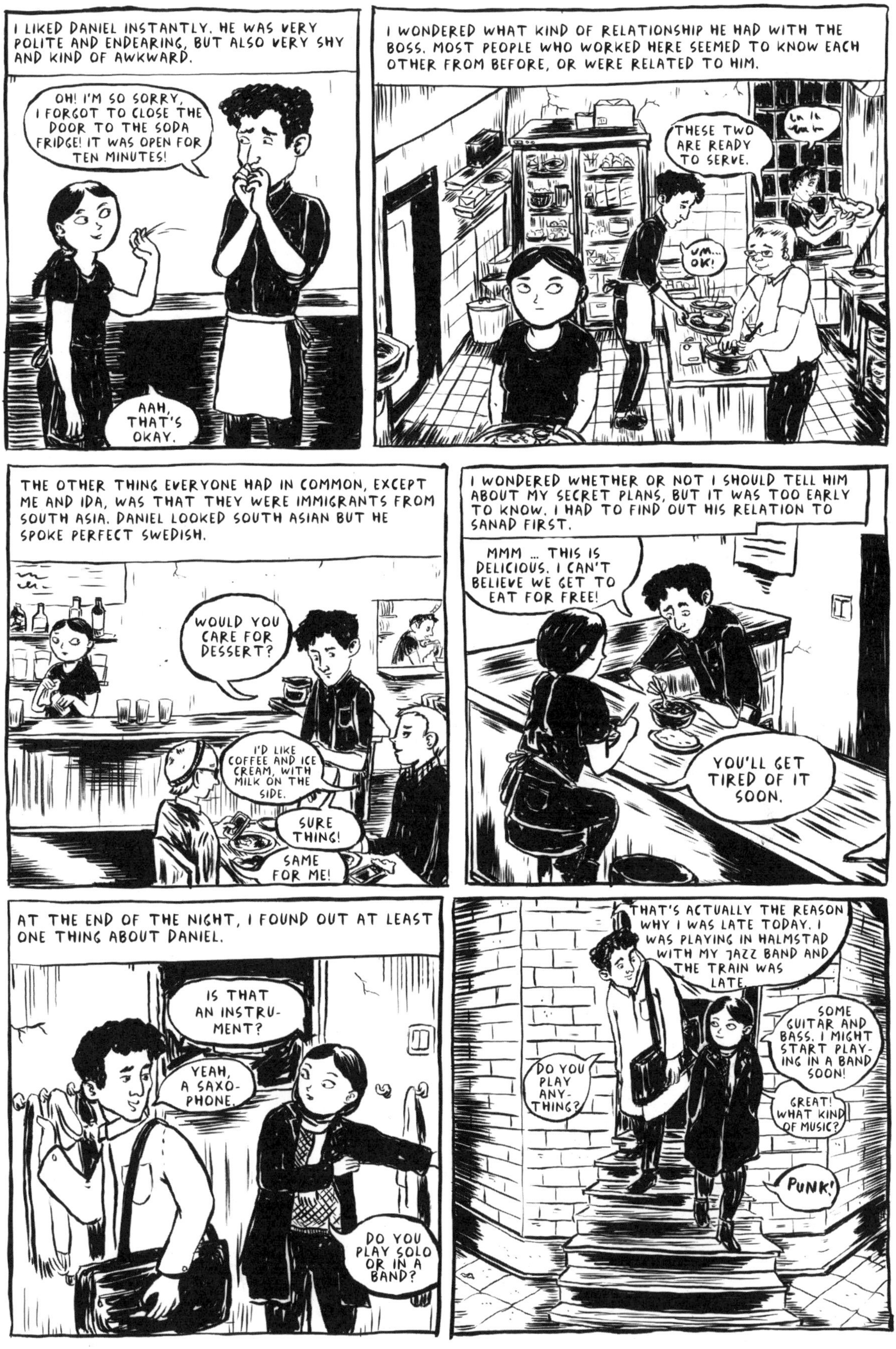

I LIKED DANIEL INSTANTLY. HE WAS VERY POLITE AND ENDEARING, BUT ALSO VERY SHY AND KIND OF AWKWARD.
OH! I'M SO SORRY, I FORGOT TO CLOSE THE DOOR TO THE SODA FRIDGE! IT WAS OPEN FOR TEN MINUTES!
AAH, THAT'S OKAY.
I WONDERED WHAT KIND OF RELATIONSHIP HE HAD WITH THE BOSS. MOST PEOPLE WHO WORKED HERE SEEMED TO KNOW EACH OTHER FROM BEFORE, OR WERE RELATED TO HIM.
THESE TWO ARE READY TO SERVE.
UM... OK!
THE OTHER THING EVERYONE HAD IN COMMON, EXCEPT ME AND IDA, WAS THAT THEY WERE IMMIGRANTS FROM SOUTH ASIA. DANIEL LOOKED SOUTH ASIAN BUT HE SPOKE PERFECT SWEDISH.
WOULD YOU CARE FOR DESSERT?
I'D LIKE COFFEE AND ICE CREAM, WITH MILK ON THE SIDE.
SURE THING!
SAME FOR ME!
I WONDERED WHETHER OR NOT I SHOULD TELL HIM ABOUT MY SECRET PLANS, BUT IT WAS TOO EARLY TO KNOW. I HAD TO FIND OUT HIS RELATION TO SANAD FIRST.
MMM ... THIS IS DELICIOUS. I CAN'T BELIEVE WE GET TO EAT FOR FREE!
YOU'LL GET TIRED OF IT SOON.
AT THE END OF THE NIGHT, I FOUND OUT AT LEAST ONE THING ABOUT DANIEL.
IS THAT AN INSTRU-MENT?
YEAH, A SAXO-PHONE.
DO YOU PLAY SOLO OR IN A BAND?
THAT'S ACTUALLY THE REASON WHY I WAS LATE TODAY. I WAS PLAYING IN HALMSTAD WITH MY JAZZ BAND AND THE TRAIN WAS LATE.
DO YOU PLAY ANY-THING?
SOME GUITAR AND BASS. I MIGHT START PLAY-ING IN A BAND SOON!
GREAT! WHAT KIND OF MUSIC?
PUNK!

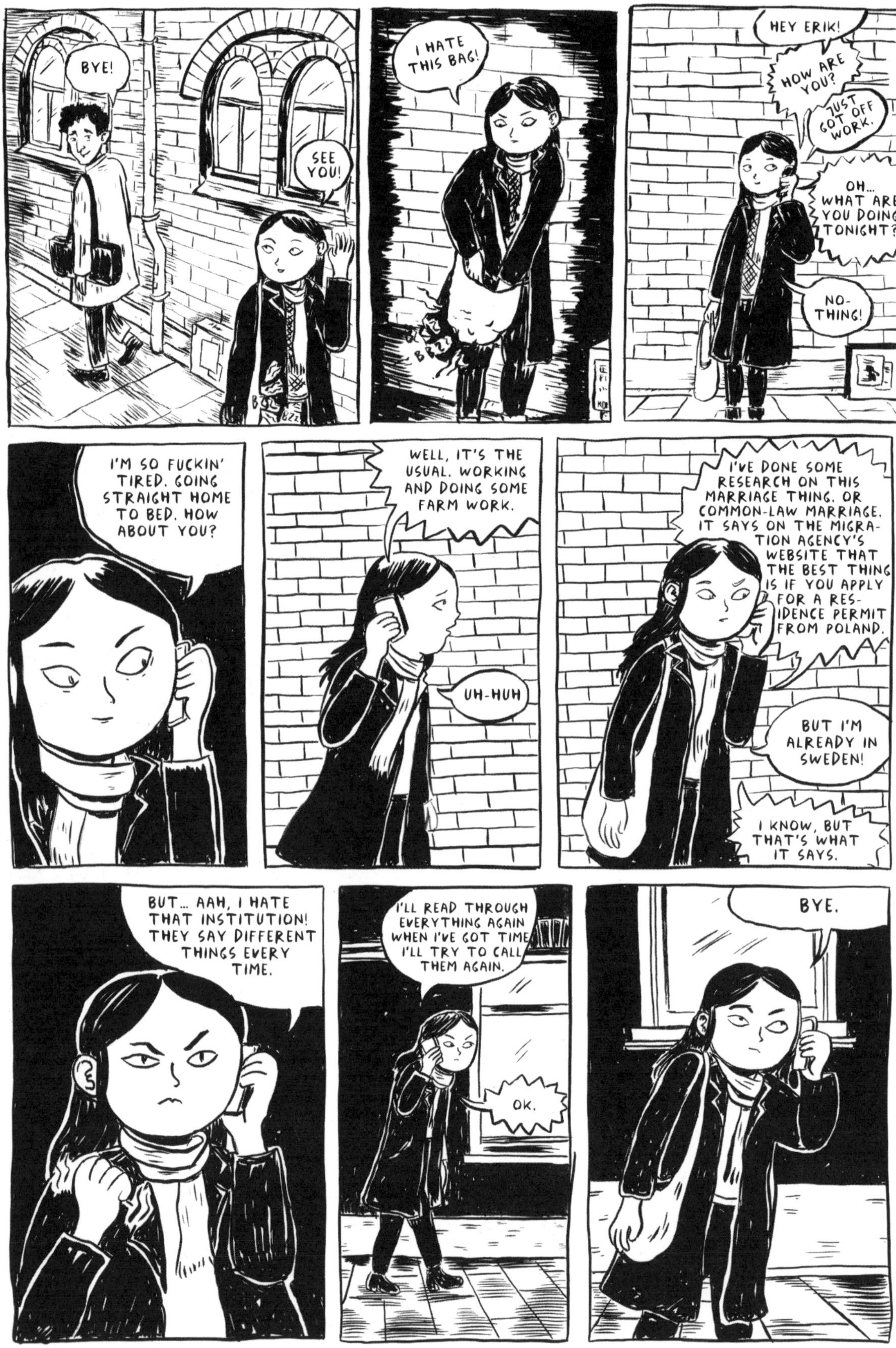
BYE!
SEE YOU!
I HATE THIS BAG!
HEY ERIK!
HOW ARE YOU?
JUST GOT OFF WORK.
OH... WHAT ARE YOU DOING TONIGHT?
NO-THING!
I'M SO FUCKIN' TIRED. GOING STRAIGHT HOME TO BED. HOW ABOUT YOU?
WELL, IT'S THE USUAL. WORKING AND DOING SOME FARM WORK.
UH-HUH
I'VE DONE SOME RESEARCH ON THIS MARRIAGE THING. OR COMMON-LAW MARRIAGE. IT SAYS ON THE MIGRATION AGENCY'S WEBSITE THAT THE BEST THING IS IF YOU APPLY FOR A RESIDENCE PERMIT FROM POLAND.
BUT I'M ALREADY IN SWEDEN!
I KNOW, BUT THAT'S WHAT IT SAYS.
BUT... AAH, I HATE THAT INSTITUTION! THEY SAY DIFFERENT THINGS EVERY TIME.
I'LL READ THROUGH EVERYTHING AGAIN WHEN I'VE GOT TIME. I'LL TRY TO CALL THEM AGAIN.
OK.
BYE.

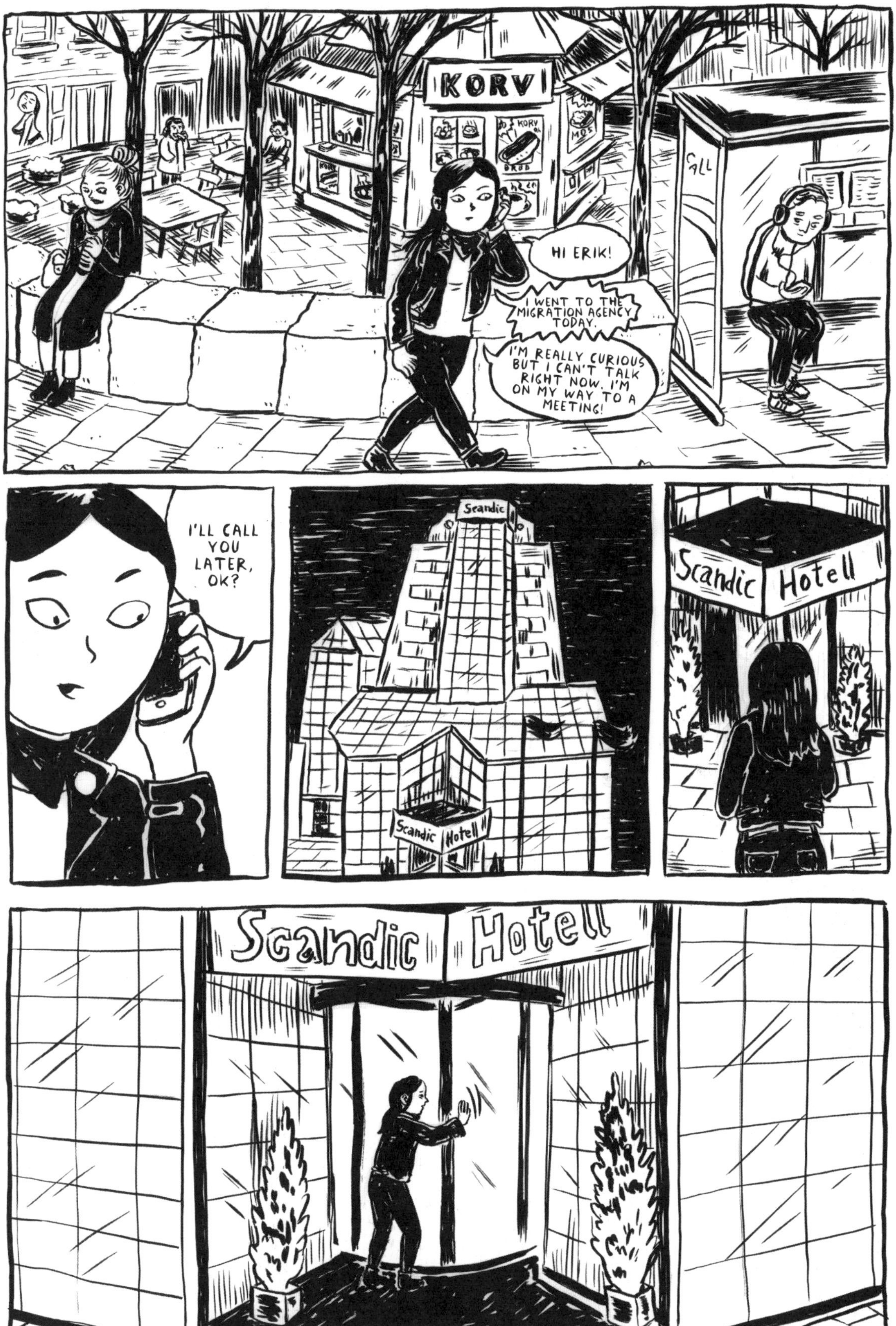
KORV
KORV
BRÖD
MOS
CALL
HI ERIK!
I WENT TO THE MIGRATION AGENCY TODAY.
I'M REALLY CURIOUS BUT I CAN'T TALK RIGHT NOW. I'M ON MY WAY TO A MEETING!
I'LL CALL YOU LATER, OK?
Scandic
Scandic Hotell
Scandic Hotell
Scandic Hotell

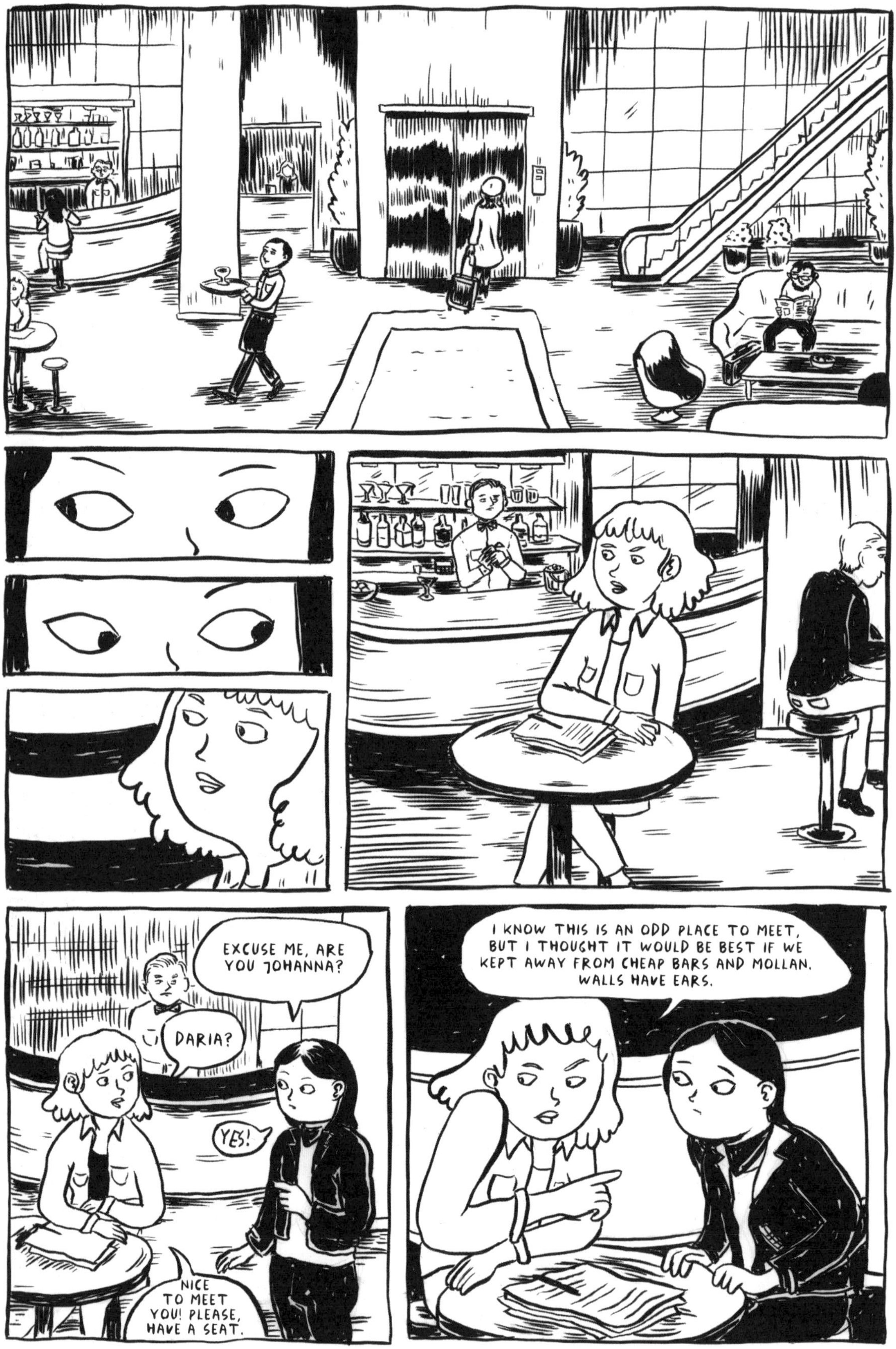
EXCUSE ME, ARE YOU JOHANNA?
DARIA?
YES!
NICE TO MEET YOU! PLEASE, HAVE A SEAT.
I KNOW THIS IS AN ODD PLACE TO MEET, BUT I THOUGHT IT WOULD BE BEST IF WE KEPT AWAY FROM CHEAP BARS AND MOLLAN. WALLS HAVE EARS.

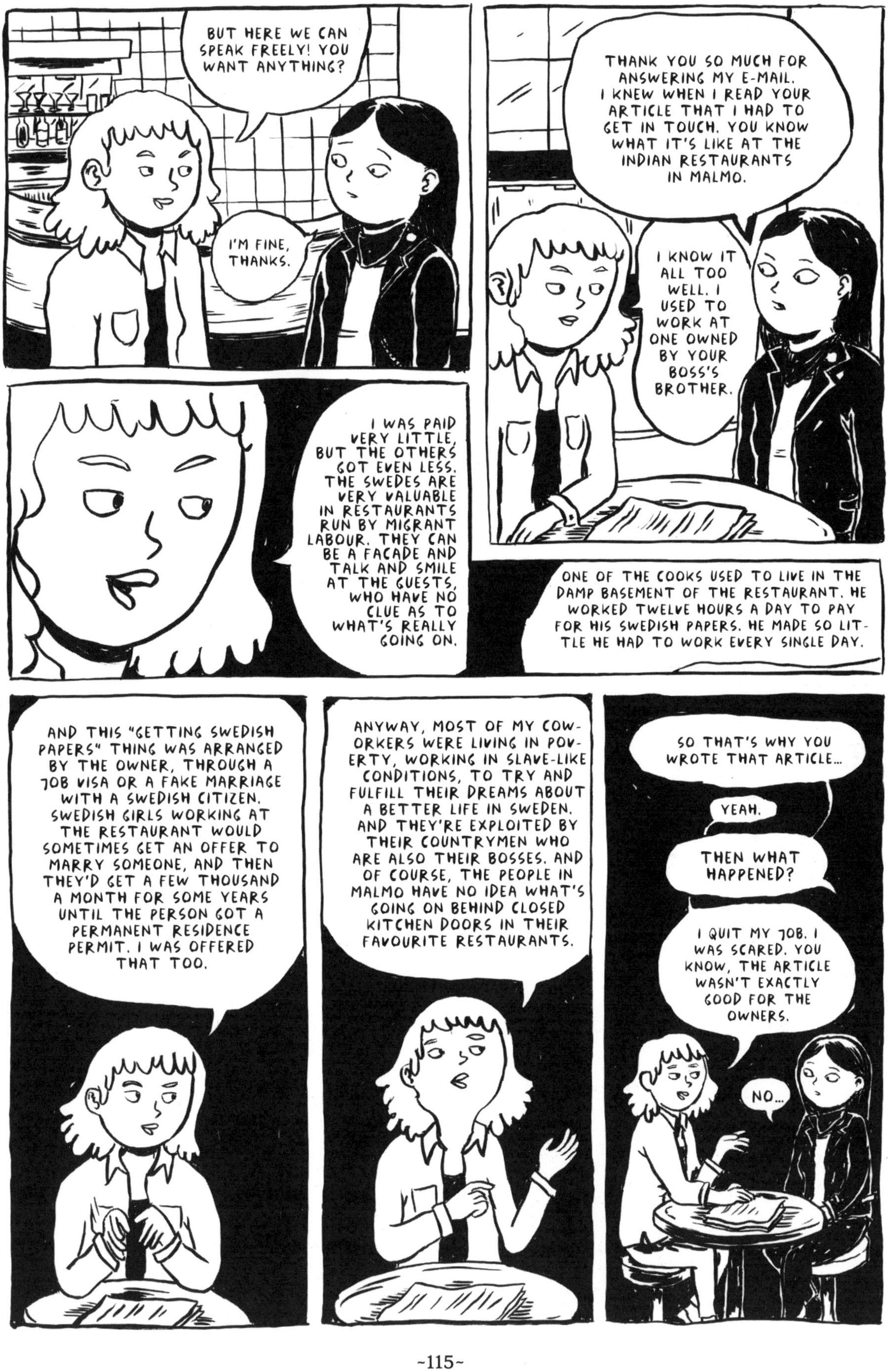
BUT HERE WE CAN SPEAK FREELY! YOU WANT ANYTHING?
I'M FINE, THANKS.
THANK YOU SO MUCH FOR ANSWERING MY E-MAIL. I KNEW WHEN I READ YOUR ARTICLE THAT I HAD TO GET IN TOUCH. YOU KNOW WHAT IT'S LIKE AT THE INDIAN RESTAURANTS IN MALMO.
I KNOW IT ALL TOO WELL. I USED TO WORK AT ONE OWNED BY YOUR BOSS'S BROTHER.
I WAS PAID VERY LITTLE, BUT THE OTHERS GOT EVEN LESS. THE SWEDES ARE VERY VALUABLE IN RESTAURANTS RUN BY MIGRANT LABOUR. THEY CAN BE A FACADE AND TALK AND SMILE AT THE GUESTS, WHO HAVE NO CLUE AS TO WHAT'S REALLY GOING ON.
ONE OF THE COOKS USED TO LIVE IN THE DAMP BASEMENT OF THE RESTAURANT. HE WORKED TWELVE HOURS A DAY TO PAY FOR HIS SWEDISH PAPERS. HE MADE SO LITTLE HE HAD TO WORK EVERY SINGLE DAY.
AND THIS "GETTING SWEDISH PAPERS" THING WAS ARRANGED BY THE OWNER, THROUGH A JOB VISA OR A FAKE MARRIAGE WITH A SWEDISH CITIZEN. SWEDISH GIRLS WORKING AT THE RESTAURANT WOULD SOMETIMES GET AN OFFER TO MARRY SOMEONE, AND THEN THEY'D GET A FEW THOUSAND A MONTH FOR SOME YEARS UNTIL THE PERSON GOT A PERMANENT RESIDENCE PERMIT. I WAS OFFERED THAT TOO.
ANYWAY, MOST OF MY COWORKERS WERE LIVING IN POVERTY, WORKING IN SLAVE-LIKE CONDITIONS, TO TRY AND FULFILL THEIR DREAMS ABOUT A BETTER LIFE IN SWEDEN. AND THEY'RE EXPLOITED BY THEIR COUNTRYMEN WHO ARE ALSO THEIR BOSSES. AND OF COURSE, THE PEOPLE IN MALMO HAVE NO IDEA WHAT'S GOING ON BEHIND CLOSED KITCHEN DOORS IN THEIR FAVOURITE RESTAURANTS.
SO THAT'S WHY YOU WROTE THAT ARTICLE...
YEAH.
THEN WHAT HAPPENED?
I QUIT MY JOB. I WAS SCARED. YOU KNOW, THE ARTICLE WASN'T EXACTLY GOOD FOR THE OWNERS.
NO...

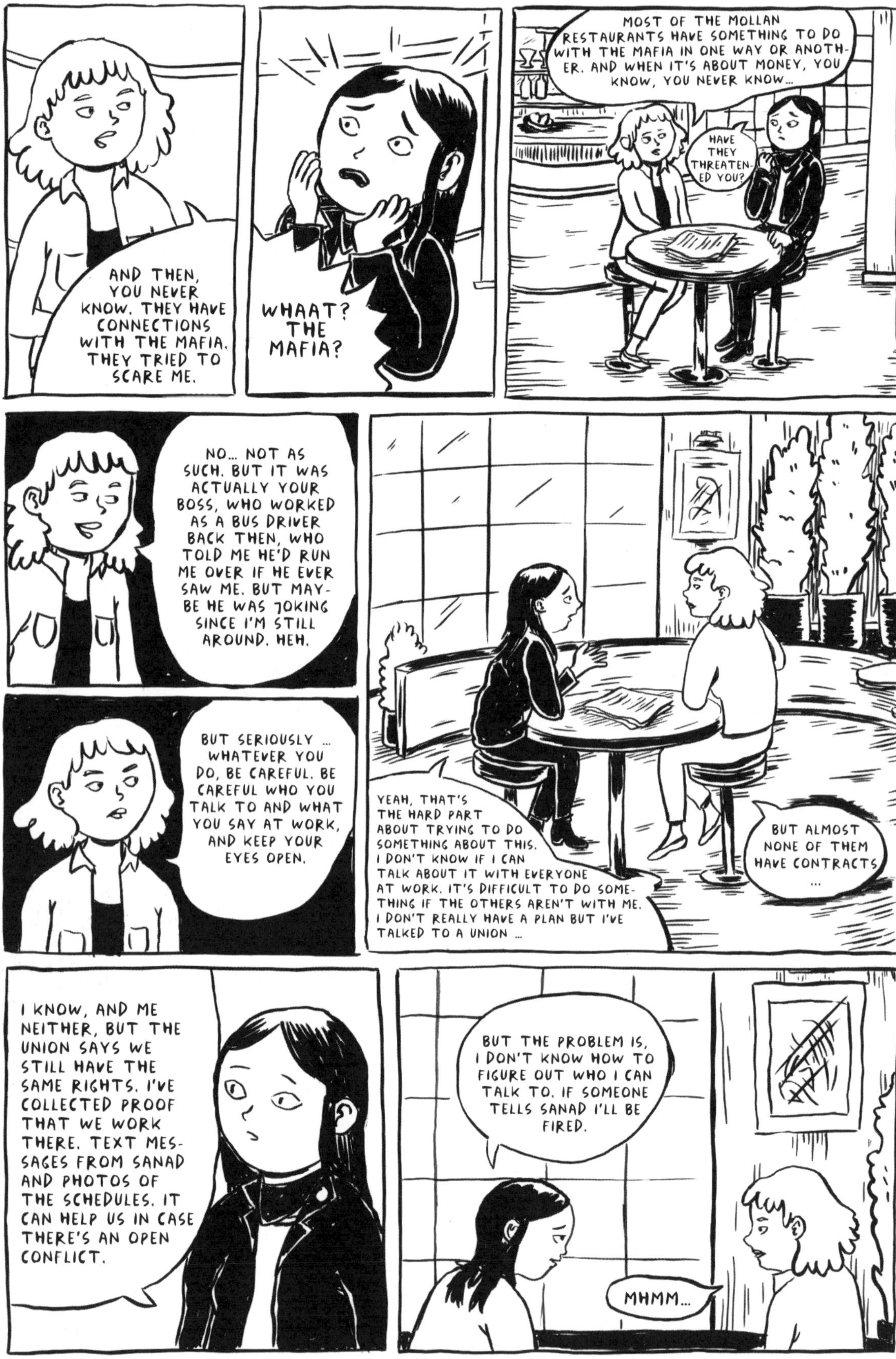
AND THEN, YOU NEVER KNOW. THEY HAVE CONNECTIONS WITH THE MAFIA. THEY TRIED TO SCARE ME.
WHAAT? THE MAFIA?
MOST OF THE MOLLAN RESTAURANTS HAVE SOMETHING TO DO WITH THE MAFIA IN ONE WAY OR ANOTHER. AND WHEN IT'S ABOUT MONEY, YOU KNOW, YOU NEVER KNOW...
HAVE THEY THREATENED YOU?
NO... NOT AS SUCH. BUT IT WAS ACTUALLY YOUR BOSS, WHO WORKED AS A BUS DRIVER BACK THEN, WHO TOLD ME HE'D RUN ME OVER IF HE EVER SAW ME. BUT MAYBE HE WAS JOKING SINCE I'M STILL AROUND. HEH.
BUT SERIOUSLY ... WHATEVER YOU DO, BE CAREFUL. BE CAREFUL WHO YOU TALK TO AND WHAT YOU SAY AT WORK, AND KEEP YOUR EYES OPEN.
YEAH, THAT'S THE HARD PART ABOUT TRYING TO DO SOMETHING ABOUT THIS. I DON'T KNOW IF I CAN TALK ABOUT IT WITH EVERYONE AT WORK. IT'S DIFFICULT TO DO SOMETHING IF THE OTHERS AREN'T WITH ME. I DON'T REALLY HAVE A PLAN BUT I'VE TALKED TO A UNION ...
BUT ALMOST NONE OF THEM HAVE CONTRACTS ...
I KNOW, AND ME NEITHER, BUT THE UNION SAYS WE STILL HAVE THE SAME RIGHTS. I'VE COLLECTED PROOF THAT WE WORK THERE. TEXT MESSAGES FROM SANAD AND PHOTOS OF THE SCHEDULES. IT CAN HELP US IN CASE THERE'S AN OPEN CONFLICT.
BUT THE PROBLEM IS, I DON'T KNOW HOW TO FIGURE OUT WHO I CAN TALK TO. IF SOMEONE TELLS SANAD I'LL BE FIRED.
MHMM...

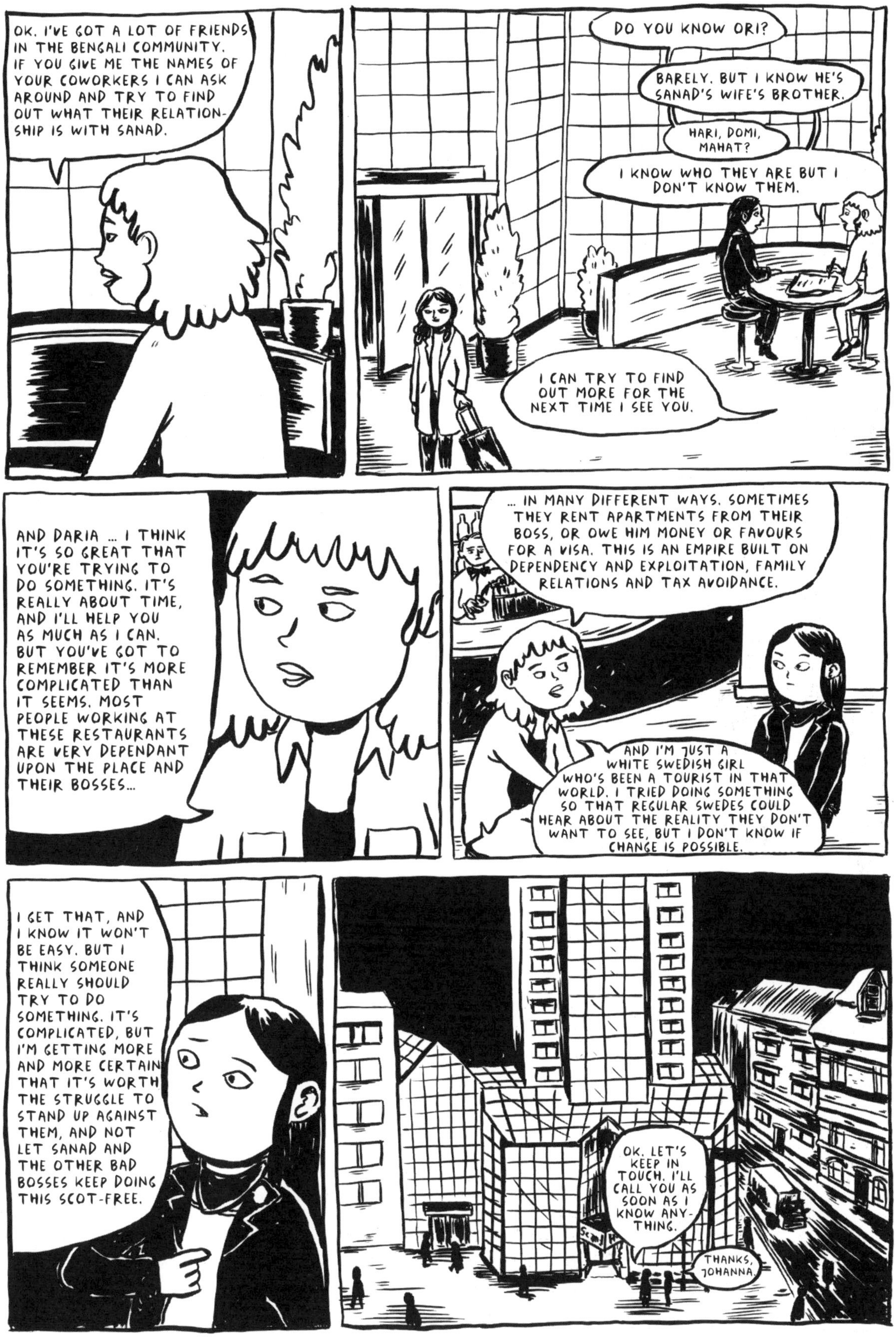
OK. I'VE GOT A LOT OF FRIENDS IN THE BENGALI COMMUNITY. IF YOU GIVE ME THE NAMES OF YOUR COWORKERS I CAN ASK AROUND AND TRY TO FIND OUT WHAT THEIR RELATIONSHIP IS WITH SANAD.
DO YOU KNOW ORI?
BARELY. BUT I KNOW HE'S SANAD'S WIFE'S BROTHER.
HARI, DOMI, MAHAT?
I KNOW WHO THEY ARE BUT I DON'T KNOW THEM.
I CAN TRY TO FIND OUT MORE FOR THE NEXT TIME I SEE YOU.
AND DARIA ... I THINK IT'S SO GREAT THAT YOU'RE TRYING TO DO SOMETHING. IT'S REALLY ABOUT TIME, AND I'LL HELP YOU AS MUCH AS I CAN. BUT YOU'VE GOT TO REMEMBER IT'S MORE COMPLICATED THAN IT SEEMS. MOST PEOPLE WORKING AT THESE RESTAURANTS ARE VERY DEPENDANT UPON THE PLACE AND THEIR BOSSES...
... IN MANY DIFFERENT WAYS. SOMETIMES THEY RENT APARTMENTS FROM THEIR BOSS, OR OWE HIM MONEY OR FAVOURS FOR A VISA. THIS IS AN EMPIRE BUILT ON DEPENDENCY AND EXPLOITATION, FAMILY RELATIONS AND TAX AVOIDANCE.
AND I'M JUST A WHITE SWEDISH GIRL WHO'S BEEN A TOURIST IN THAT WORLD. I TRIED DOING SOMETHING SO THAT REGULAR SWEDES COULD HEAR ABOUT THE REALITY THEY DON'T WANT TO SEE, BUT I DON'T KNOW IF CHANGE IS POSSIBLE.
I GET THAT, AND I KNOW IT WON'T BE EASY. BUT I THINK SOMEONE REALLY SHOULD TRY TO DO SOMETHING. IT'S COMPLICATED, BUT I'M GETTING MORE AND MORE CERTAIN THAT IT'S WORTH THE STRUGGLE TO STAND UP AGAINST THEM, AND NOT LET SANAD AND THE OTHER BAD BOSSES KEEP DOING THIS SCOT-FREE.
OK. LET'S KEEP IN TOUCH. I'LL CALL YOU AS SOON AS I KNOW ANYTHING.
THANKS, JOHANNA.

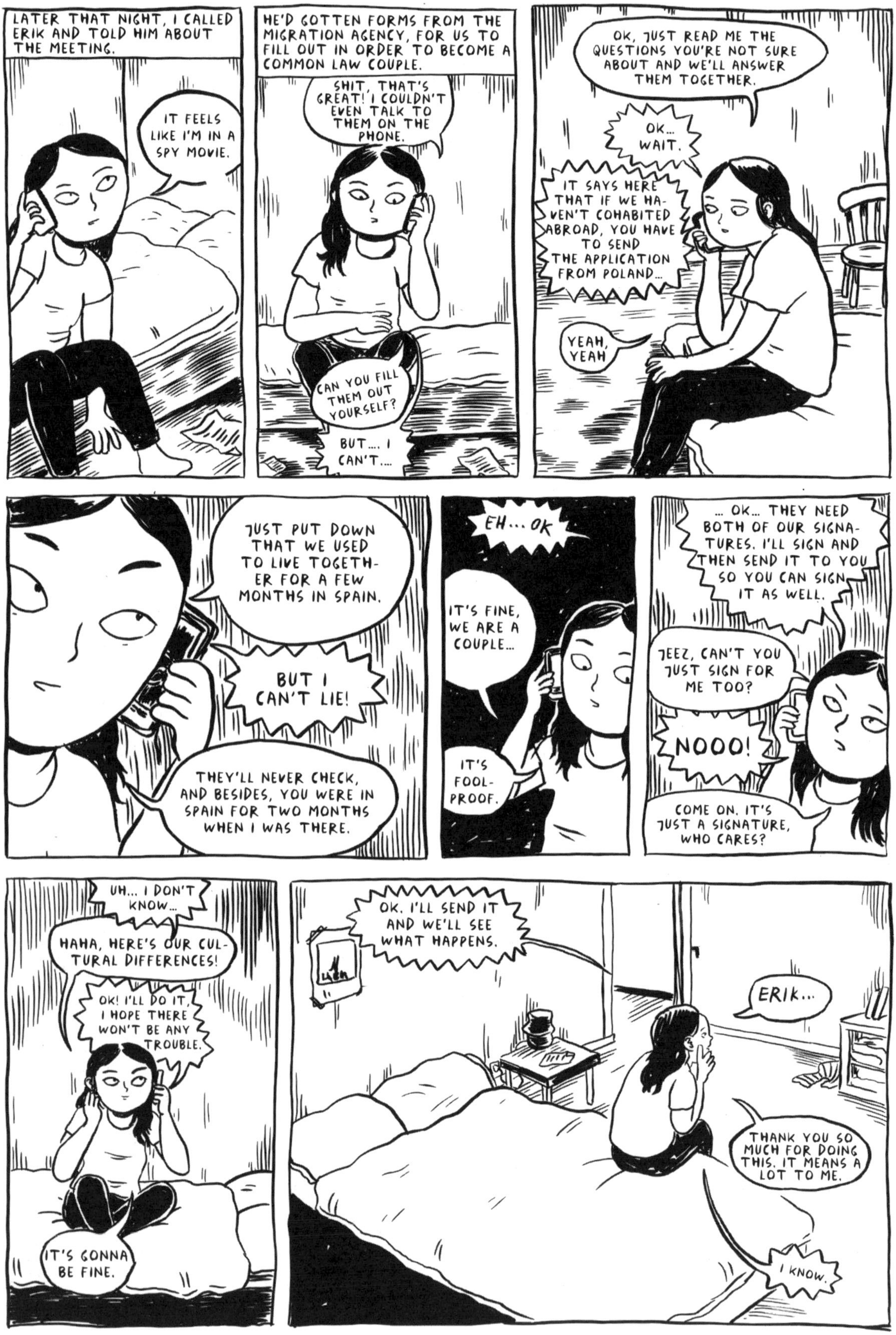

LATER THAT NIGHT, I CALLED ERIK AND TOLD HIM ABOUT THE MEETING.
IT FEELS LIKE I'M IN A SPY MOVIE.
HE'D GOTTEN FORMS FROM THE MIGRATION AGENCY, FOR US TO FILL OUT IN ORDER TO BECOME A COMMON LAW COUPLE.
SHIT, THAT'S GREAT! I COULDN'T EVEN TALK TO THEM ON THE PHONE.
CAN YOU FILL THEM OUT YOURSELF?
BUT.... I CAN'T....
OK, JUST READ ME THE QUESTIONS YOU'RE NOT SURE ABOUT AND WE'LL ANSWER THEM TOGETHER.
OK... WAIT.
IT SAYS HERE THAT IF WE HAVEN'T COHABITED ABROAD, YOU HAVE TO SEND THE APPLICATION FROM POLAND...
YEAH, YEAH
JUST PUT DOWN THAT WE USED TO LIVE TOGETHER FOR A FEW MONTHS IN SPAIN.
BUT I CAN'T LIE!
THEY'LL NEVER CHECK, AND BESIDES, YOU WERE IN SPAIN FOR TWO MONTHS WHEN I WAS THERE.
EH... OK
IT'S FINE, WE ARE A COUPLE...
IT'S FOOLPROOF.
... OK... THEY NEED BOTH OF OUR SIGNATURES. I'LL SIGN AND THEN SEND IT TO YOU SO YOU CAN SIGN IT AS WELL.
JEEZ, CAN'T YOU JUST SIGN FOR ME TOO?
NOOO!
COME ON. IT'S JUST A SIGNATURE, WHO CARES?
UH... I DON'T KNOW...
HAHA, HERE'S OUR CULTURAL DIFFERENCES!
OK! I'LL DO IT, I HOPE THERE WON'T BE ANY TROUBLE.
IT'S GONNA BE FINE.
OK. I'LL SEND IT AND WE'LL SEE WHAT HAPPENS.
ERIK...
THANK YOU SO MUCH FOR DOING THIS. IT MEANS A LOT TO ME.
I KNOW.

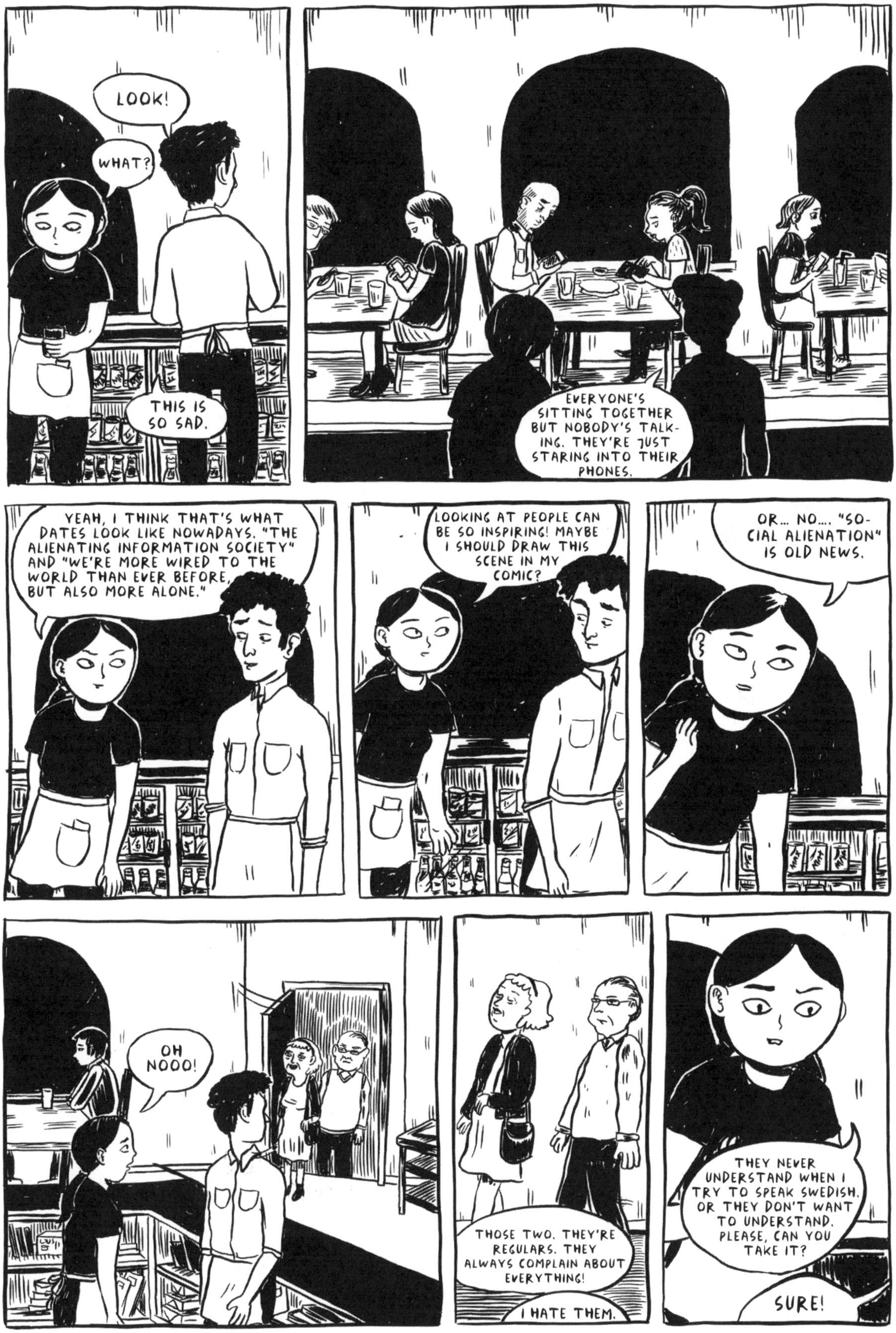
LOOK!
WHAT?
THIS IS SO SAD.
EVERYONE'S SITTING TOGETHER BUT NOBODY'S TALK-ING. THEY'RE JUST STARING INTO THEIR PHONES.
YEAH, I THINK THAT'S WHAT DATES LOOK LIKE NOWADAYS. "THE ALIENATING INFORMATION SOCIETY" AND "WE'RE MORE WIRED TO THE WORLD THAN EVER BEFORE, BUT ALSO MORE ALONE."
LOOKING AT PEOPLE CAN BE SO INSPIRING! MAYBE I SHOULD DRAW THIS SCENE IN MY COMIC?
OR... NO.... "SO-CIAL ALIENATION" IS OLD NEWS.
OH NOOO!
THOSE TWO. THEY'RE REGULARS. THEY ALWAYS COMPLAIN ABOUT EVERYTHING!
I HATE THEM.
THEY NEVER UNDERSTAND WHEN I TRY TO SPEAK SWEDISH. OR THEY DON'T WANT TO UNDERSTAND. PLEASE, CAN YOU TAKE IT?
SURE!

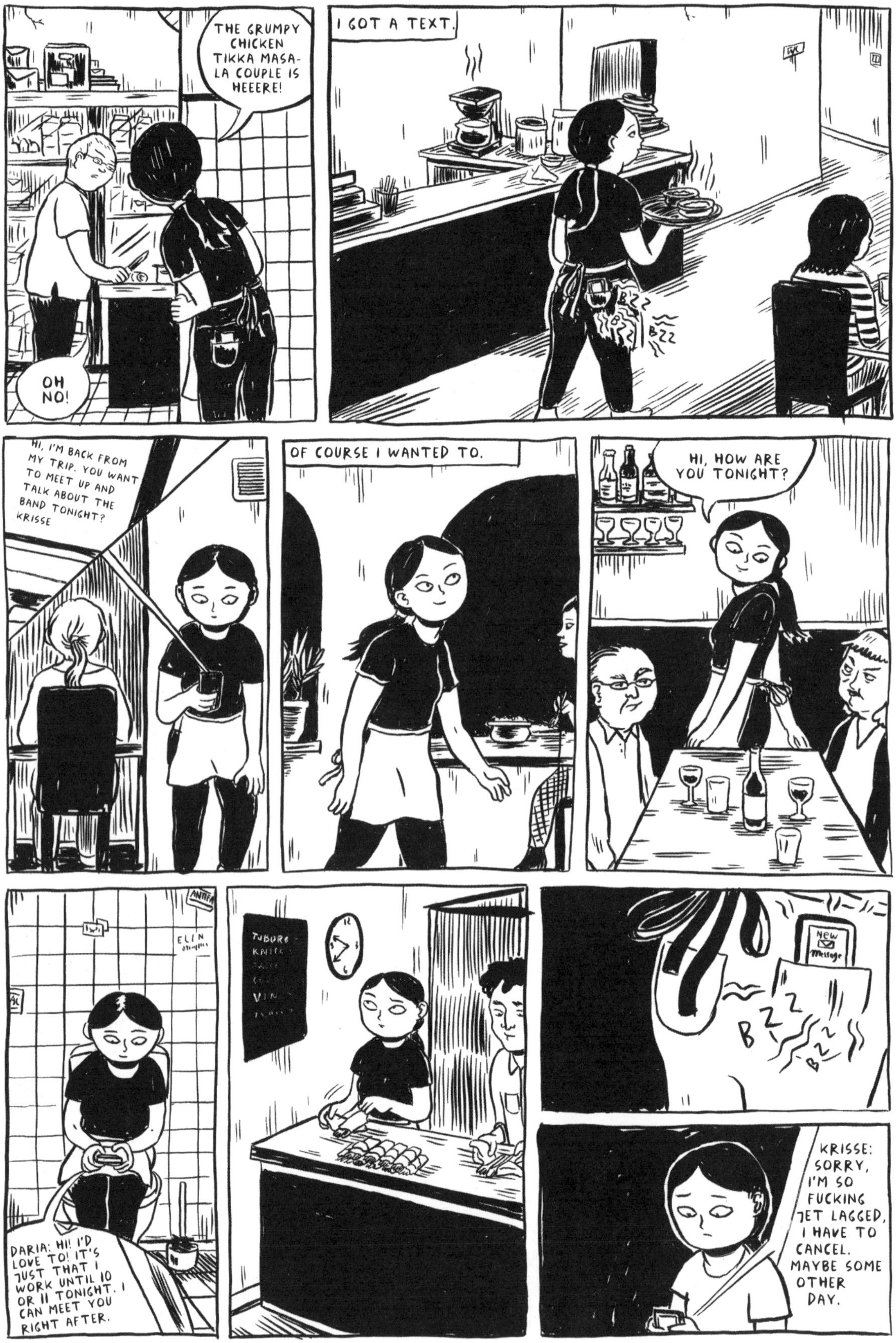
THE GRUMPY CHICKEN TIKKA MASA-LA COUPLE IS HEEERE!
OH NO!
I GOT A TEXT.
BZZ BZZ BZZ
HI, I'M BACK FROM MY TRIP. YOU WANT TO MEET UP AND TALK ABOUT THE BAND TONIGHT? KRISSE
OF COURSE I WANTED TO.
HI, HOW ARE YOU TONIGHT?
DARIA: HI! I'D LOVE TO! IT'S JUST THAT I WORK UNTIL 10 OR 11 TONIGHT. I CAN MEET YOU RIGHT AFTER.
NEW MESSAGE
BZZ BZZ
KRISSE: SORRY, I'M SO FUCKING JET LAGGED, I HAVE TO CANCEL. MAYBE SOME OTHER DAY.

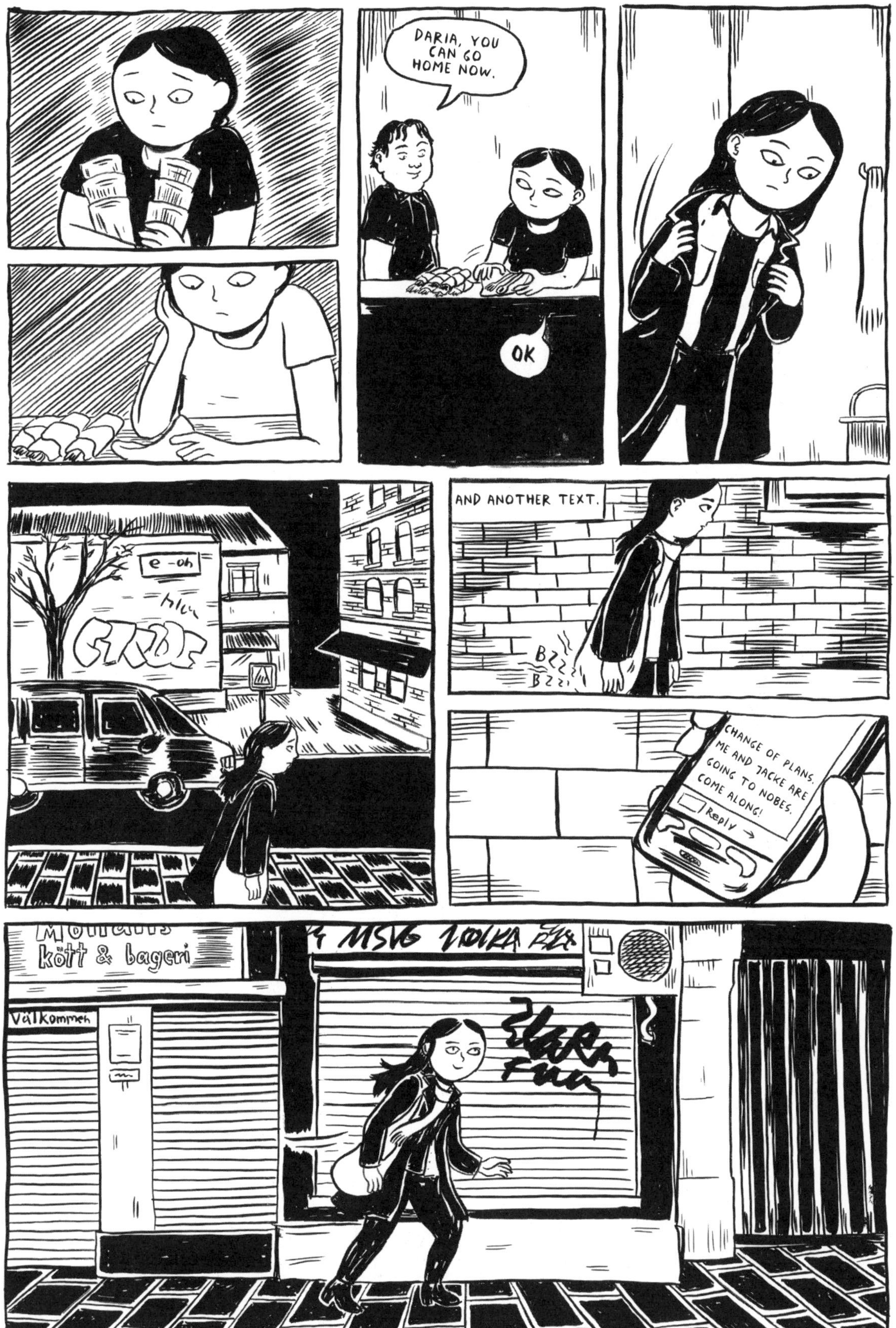
DARIA, YOU CAN GO HOME NOW.
OK
AND ANOTHER TEXT.
BZZZ
BZZZ
CHANGE OF PLANS. ME AND JACKE ARE GOING TO NOBES. COME ALONG!
Reply →
kött & bageri
Välkommen

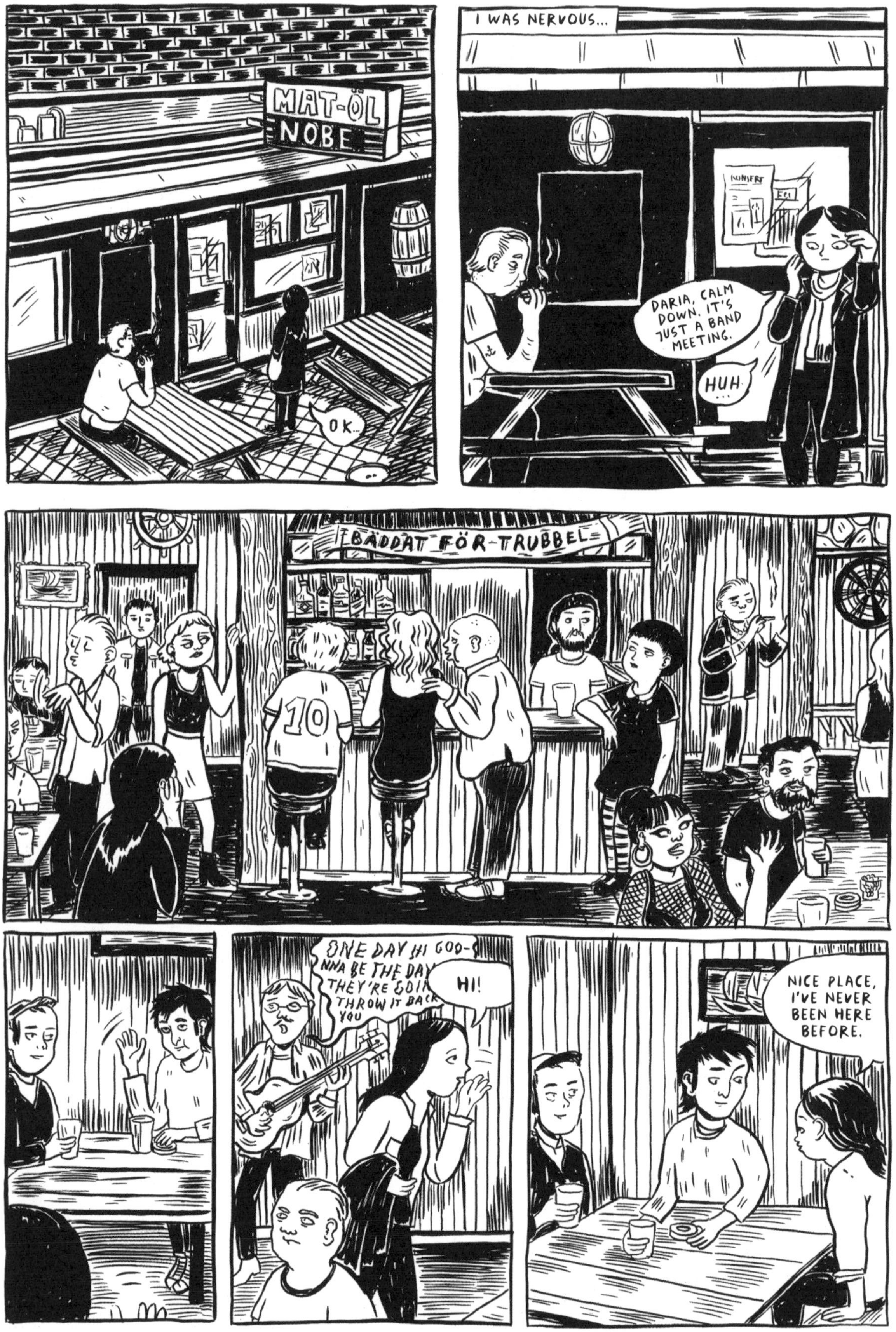
MAT-ÖL
NOBE
OK...
I WAS NERVOUS...
DARIA, CALM DOWN. IT'S JUST A BAND MEETING.
HUH...
BÄDDAT FÖR TRUBBEL
ONE DAY GOO-NNA BE THE DAY THEY'RE GOI THROW IT BACK YOU
HI!
NICE PLACE, I'VE NEVER BEEN HERE BEFORE.

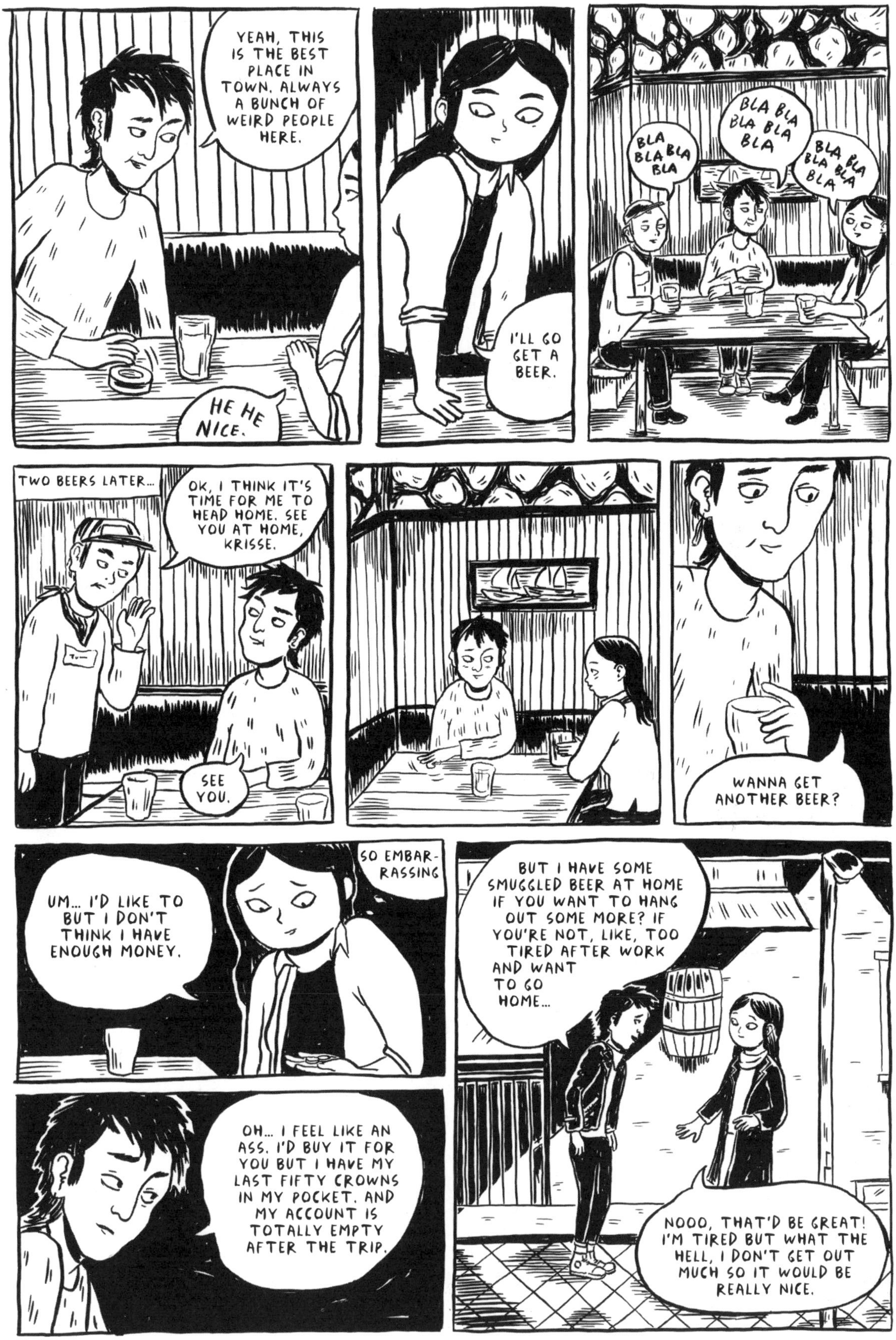
YEAH, THIS IS THE BEST PLACE IN TOWN. ALWAYS A BUNCH OF WEIRD PEOPLE HERE.
HE HE NICE.
I'LL GO GET A BEER.
BLA BLA BLA BLA
BLA BLA BLA BLA BLA
BLA BLA BLA BLA BLA
TWO BEERS LATER...
OK, I THINK IT'S TIME FOR ME TO HEAD HOME. SEE YOU AT HOME, KRISSE.
SEE YOU.
WANNA GET ANOTHER BEER?
UM... I'D LIKE TO BUT I DON'T THINK I HAVE ENOUGH MONEY.
SO EMBARRASSING
OH... I FEEL LIKE AN ASS. I'D BUY IT FOR YOU BUT I HAVE MY LAST FIFTY CROWNS IN MY POCKET. AND MY ACCOUNT IS TOTALLY EMPTY AFTER THE TRIP.
BUT I HAVE SOME SMUGGLED BEER AT HOME IF YOU WANT TO HANG OUT SOME MORE? IF YOU'RE NOT, LIKE, TOO TIRED AFTER WORK AND WANT TO GO HOME...
NOOO, THAT'D BE GREAT! I'M TIRED BUT WHAT THE HELL, I DON'T GET OUT MUCH SO IT WOULD BE REALLY NICE.

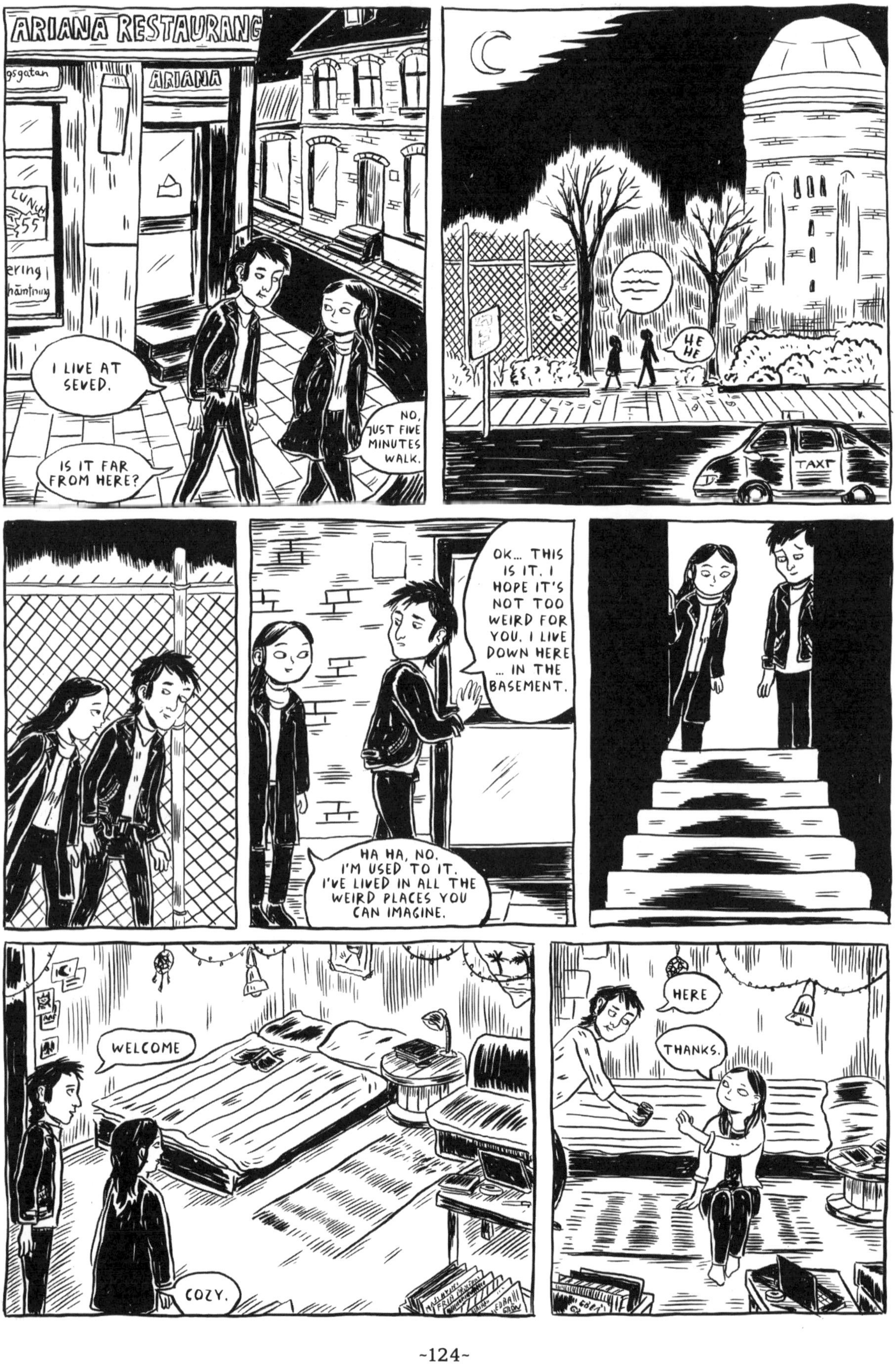
ARIANA RESTAURANG
gsgatan
ARIANA
I LIVE AT SEVED.
IS IT FAR FROM HERE?
NO, JUST FIVE MINUTES WALK.
HE HE
TAXI
OK... THIS IS IT. I HOPE IT'S NOT TOO WEIRD FOR YOU. I LIVE DOWN HERE ... IN THE BASEMENT.
HA HA, NO. I'M USED TO IT. I'VE LIVED IN ALL THE WEIRD PLACES YOU CAN IMAGINE.
WELCOME
COZY.
HERE
THANKS.

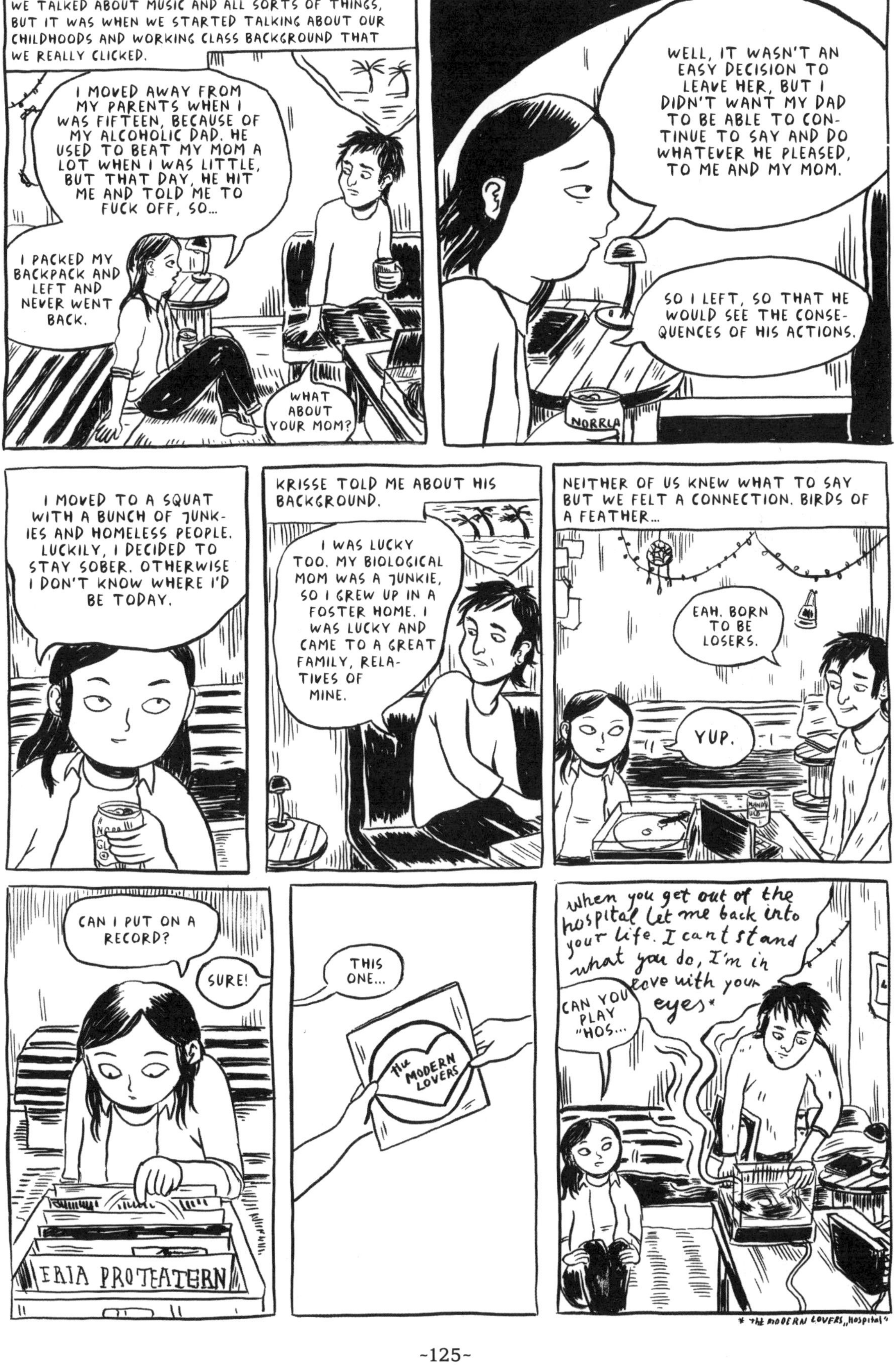
WE TALKED ABOUT MUSIC AND ALL SORTS OF THINGS, BUT IT WAS WHEN WE STARTED TALKING ABOUT OUR CHILDHOODS AND WORKING CLASS BACKGROUND THAT WE REALLY CLICKED.
I MOVED AWAY FROM MY PARENTS WHEN I WAS FIFTEEN, BECAUSE OF MY ALCOHOLIC DAD. HE USED TO BEAT MY MOM A LOT WHEN I WAS LITTLE, BUT THAT DAY, HE HIT ME AND TOLD ME TO FUCK OFF, SO...
I PACKED MY BACKPACK AND LEFT AND NEVER WENT BACK.
WHAT ABOUT YOUR MOM?
WELL, IT WASN'T AN EASY DECISION TO LEAVE HER, BUT I DIDN'T WANT MY DAD TO BE ABLE TO CONTINUE TO SAY AND DO WHATEVER HE PLEASED, TO ME AND MY MOM.
SO I LEFT, SO THAT HE WOULD SEE THE CONSEQUENCES OF HIS ACTIONS.
NORRLA
I MOVED TO A SQUAT WITH A BUNCH OF JUNKIES AND HOMELESS PEOPLE. LUCKILY, I DECIDED TO STAY SOBER. OTHERWISE I DON'T KNOW WHERE I'D BE TODAY.
KRISSE TOLD ME ABOUT HIS BACKGROUND.
I WAS LUCKY TOO. MY BIOLOGICAL MOM WAS A JUNKIE, SO I GREW UP IN A FOSTER HOME. I WAS LUCKY AND CAME TO A GREAT FAMILY, RELATIVES OF MINE.
NEITHER OF US KNEW WHAT TO SAY BUT WE FELT A CONNECTION. BIRDS OF A FEATHER...
EAH. BORN TO BE LOSERS.
YUP.
CAN I PUT ON A RECORD?
SURE!
ERIA PROTEATERN
THIS ONE...
the MODERN LOVERS
when you get out of the hospital let me back into your life. I cant stand what you do, I'm in love with your eyes*
CAN YOU PLAY "HOS...
* THE MODERN LOVERS „Hospital"

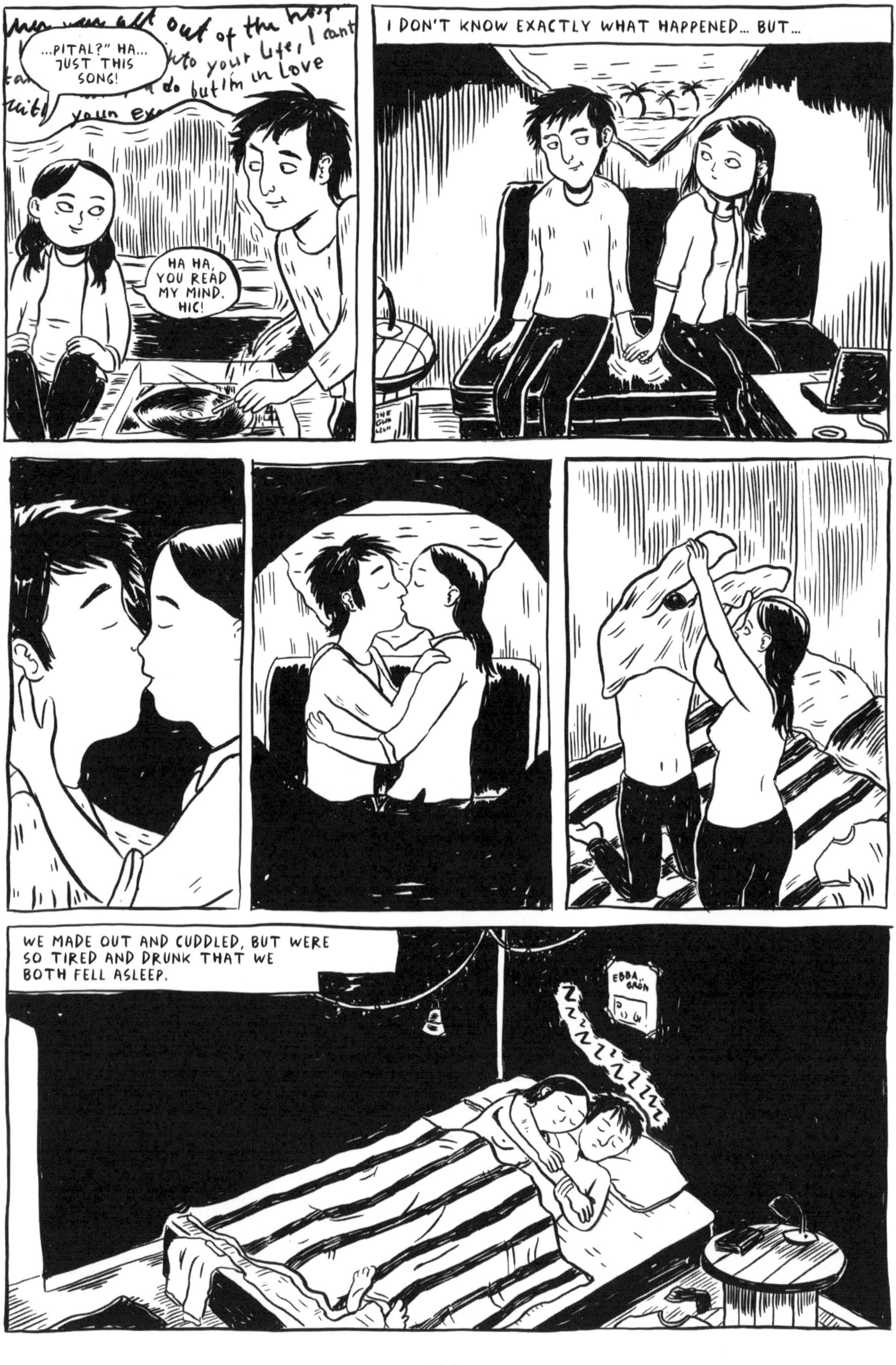
...PITAL?" HA... JUST THIS SONG!
HA HA, YOU READ MY MIND. HIC!
I DON'T KNOW EXACTLY WHAT HAPPENED... BUT...
WE MADE OUT AND CUDDLED, BUT WERE SO TIRED AND DRUNK THAT WE BOTH FELL ASLEEP.
EBBA.. GRÖN
ZZZZZZZZZZ

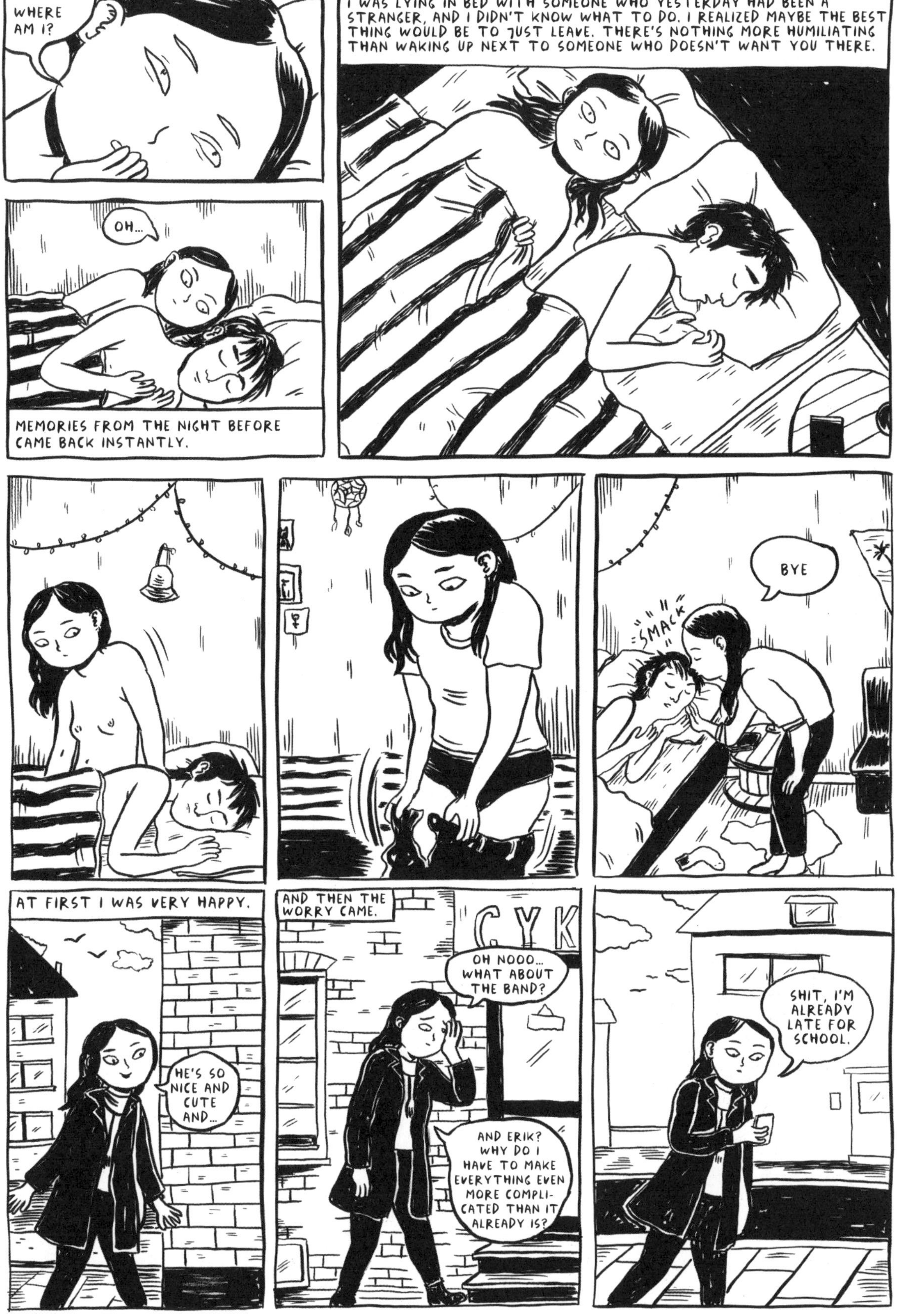
WHERE AM I?
I WAS LYING IN BED WITH SOMEONE WHO YESTERDAY HAD BEEN A STRANGER, AND I DIDN'T KNOW WHAT TO DO. I REALIZED MAYBE THE BEST THING WOULD BE TO JUST LEAVE. THERE'S NOTHING MORE HUMILIATING THAN WAKING UP NEXT TO SOMEONE WHO DOESN'T WANT YOU THERE.
OH...
MEMORIES FROM THE NIGHT BEFORE CAME BACK INSTANTLY.
SMACK
BYE
AT FIRST I WAS VERY HAPPY.
HE'S SO NICE AND CUTE AND...
AND THEN THE WORRY CAME.
CYK
OH NOOO... WHAT ABOUT THE BAND?
AND ERIK? WHY DO I HAVE TO MAKE EVERYTHING EVEN MORE COMPLICATED THAN IT ALREADY IS?
SHIT, I'M ALREADY LATE FOR SCHOOL.

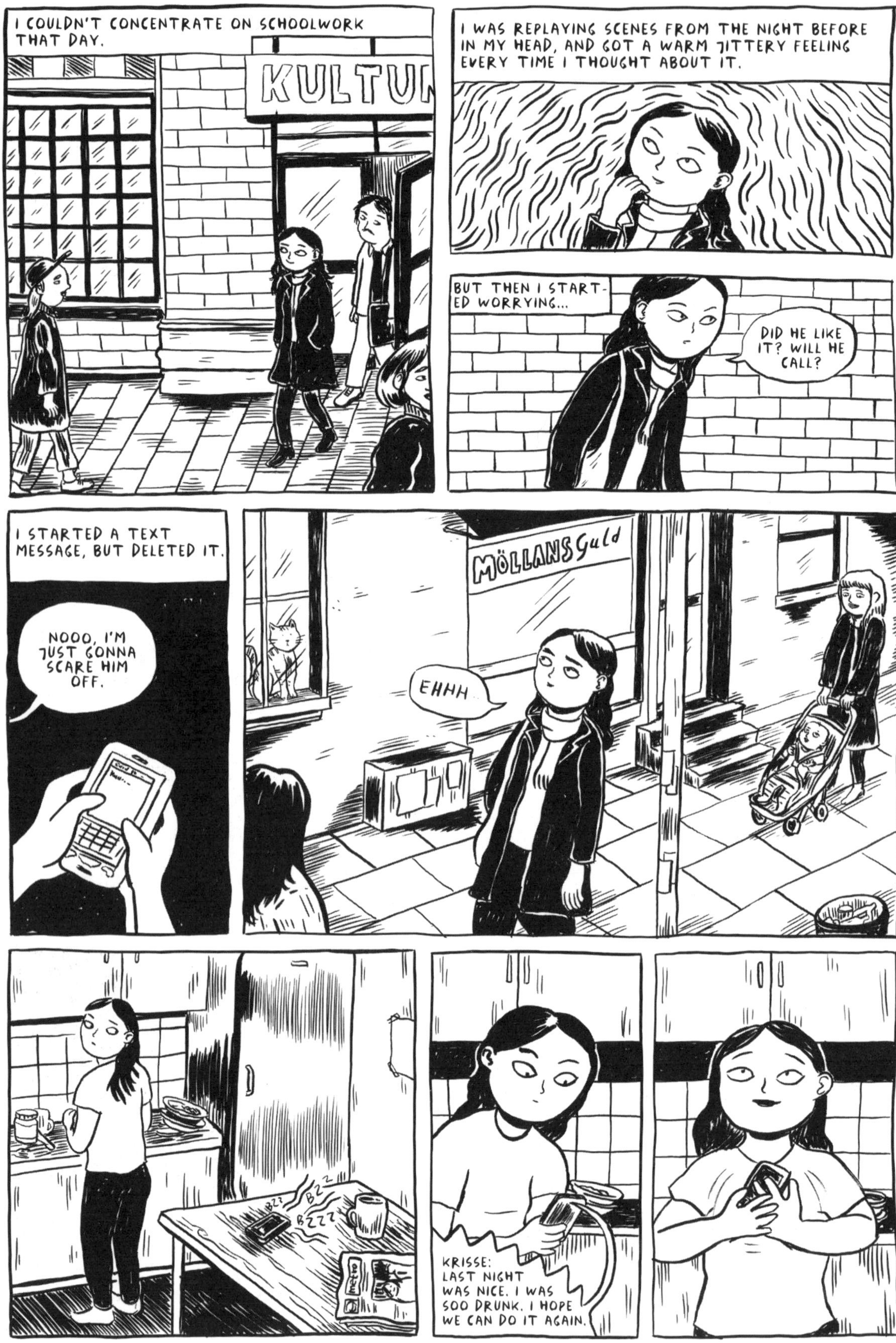
I COULDN'T CONCENTRATE ON SCHOOLWORK THAT DAY.
KULTU
I WAS REPLAYING SCENES FROM THE NIGHT BEFORE IN MY HEAD, AND GOT A WARM JITTERY FEELING EVERY TIME I THOUGHT ABOUT IT.
BUT THEN I STARTED WORRYING...
DID HE LIKE IT? WILL HE CALL?
I STARTED A TEXT MESSAGE, BUT DELETED IT.
NOOO, I'M JUST GONNA SCARE HIM OFF.
MÖLLANS Guld
EHHH
BZZ
BZZ
BZZZ
KRISSE: LAST NIGHT WAS NICE. I WAS SOO DRUNK. I HOPE WE CAN DO IT AGAIN.

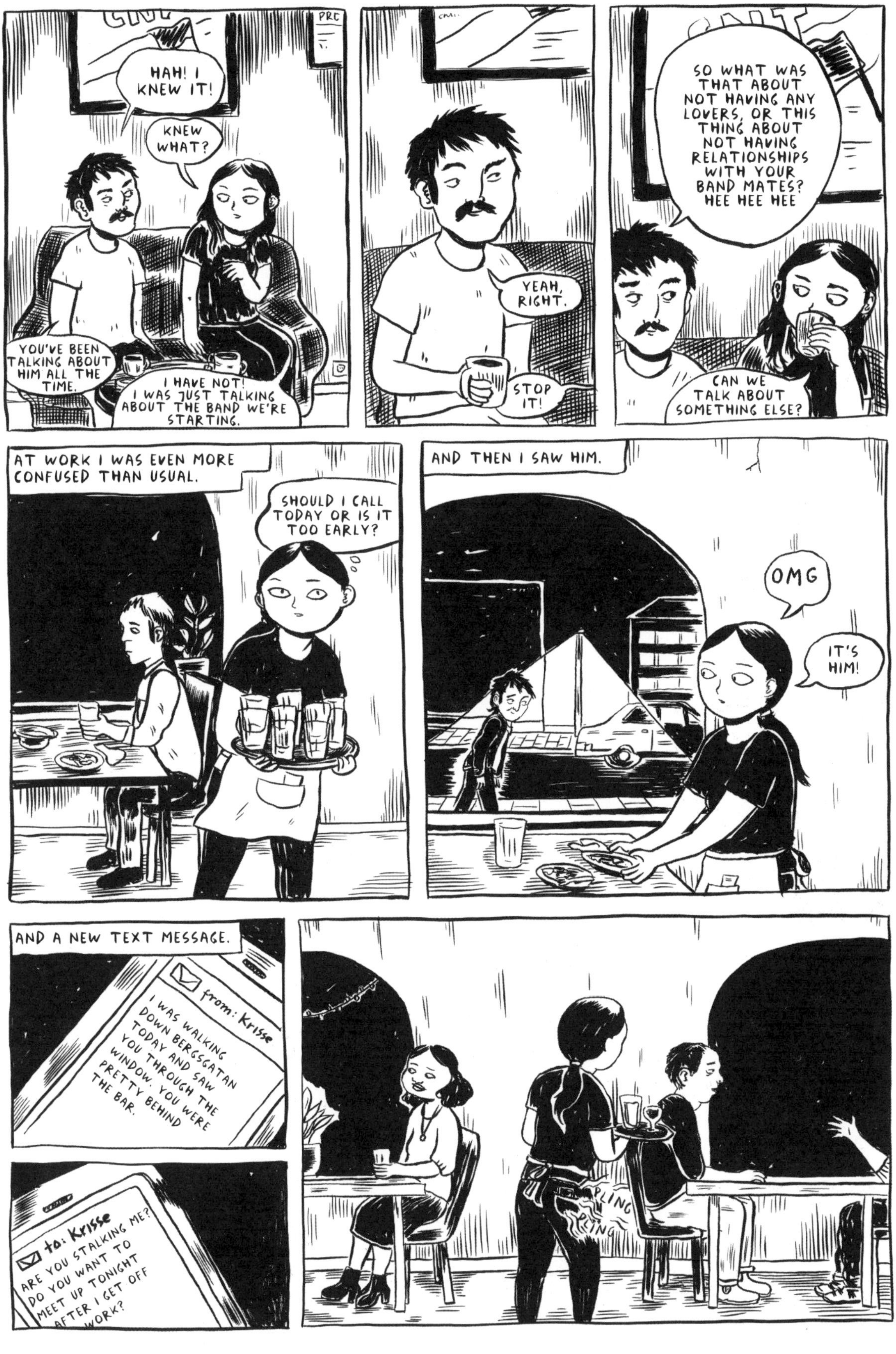
HAH! I KNEW IT!
KNEW WHAT?
YOU'VE BEEN TALKING ABOUT HIM ALL THE TIME.
I HAVE NOT! I WAS JUST TALKING ABOUT THE BAND WE'RE STARTING.
YEAH, RIGHT.
STOP IT!
SO WHAT WAS THAT ABOUT NOT HAVING ANY LOVERS, OR THIS THING ABOUT NOT HAVING RELATIONSHIPS WITH YOUR BAND MATES? HEE HEE HEE
CAN WE TALK ABOUT SOMETHING ELSE?
AT WORK I WAS EVEN MORE CONFUSED THAN USUAL.
SHOULD I CALL TODAY OR IS IT TOO EARLY?
AND THEN I SAW HIM.
OMG
IT'S HIM!
AND A NEW TEXT MESSAGE.
from: Krisse
I WAS WALKING DOWN BERGSGATAN TODAY AND SAW YOU THROUGH THE WINDOW. YOU WERE PRETTY BEHIND THE BAR.
to: Krisse
ARE YOU STALKING ME? DO YOU WANT TO MEET UP TONIGHT AFTER I GET OFF WORK?
PLING PLING

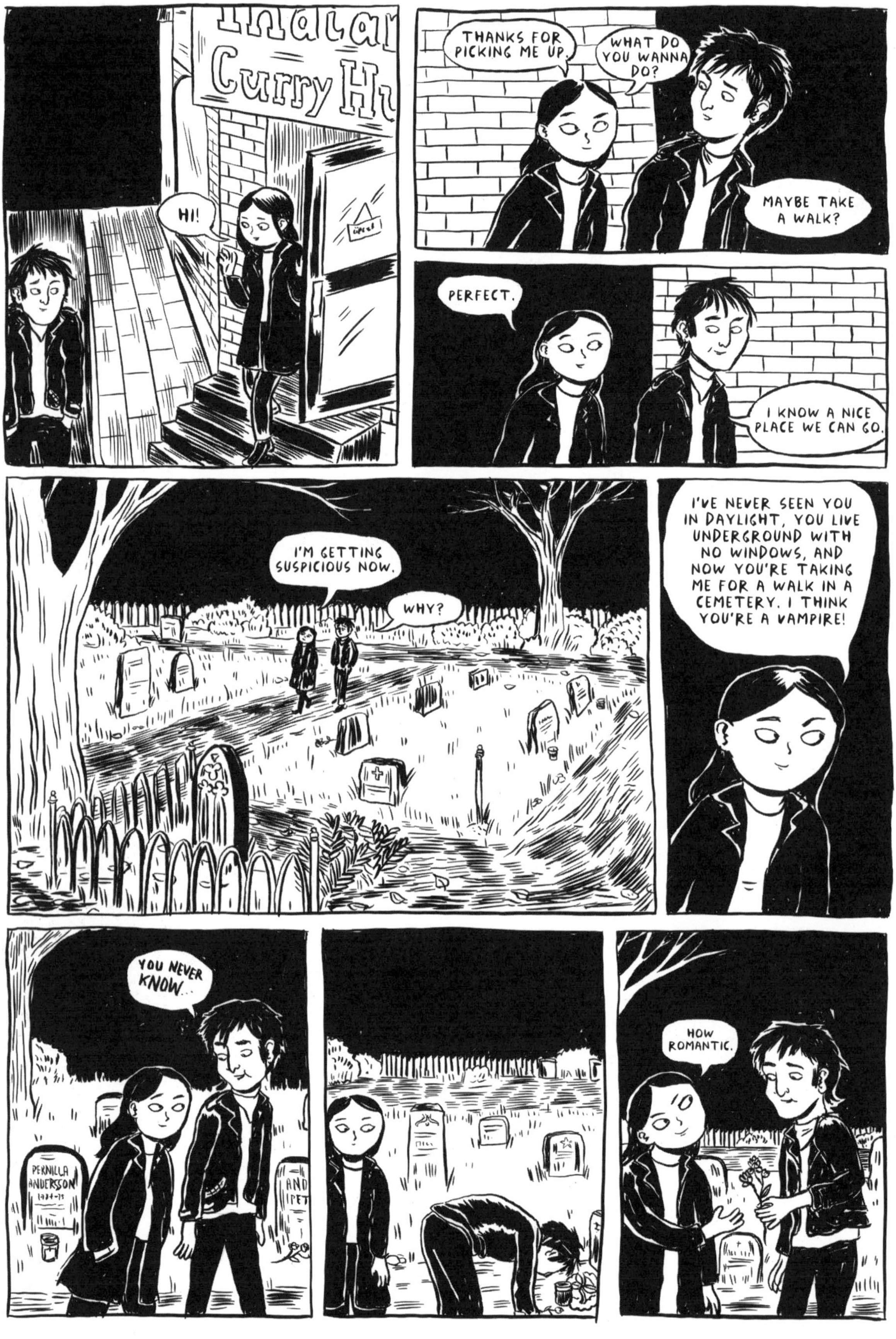
Indian
Curry Hu
HI!
THANKS FOR PICKING ME UP.
WHAT DO YOU WANNA DO?
MAYBE TAKE A WALK?
PERFECT.
I KNOW A NICE PLACE WE CAN GO.
I'M GETTING SUSPICIOUS NOW.
WHY?
I'VE NEVER SEEN YOU IN DAYLIGHT, YOU LIVE UNDERGROUND WITH NO WINDOWS, AND NOW YOU'RE TAKING ME FOR A WALK IN A CEMETERY. I THINK YOU'RE A VAMPIRE!
YOU NEVER KNOW...
PERNILLA ANDERSSON
HOW ROMANTIC.

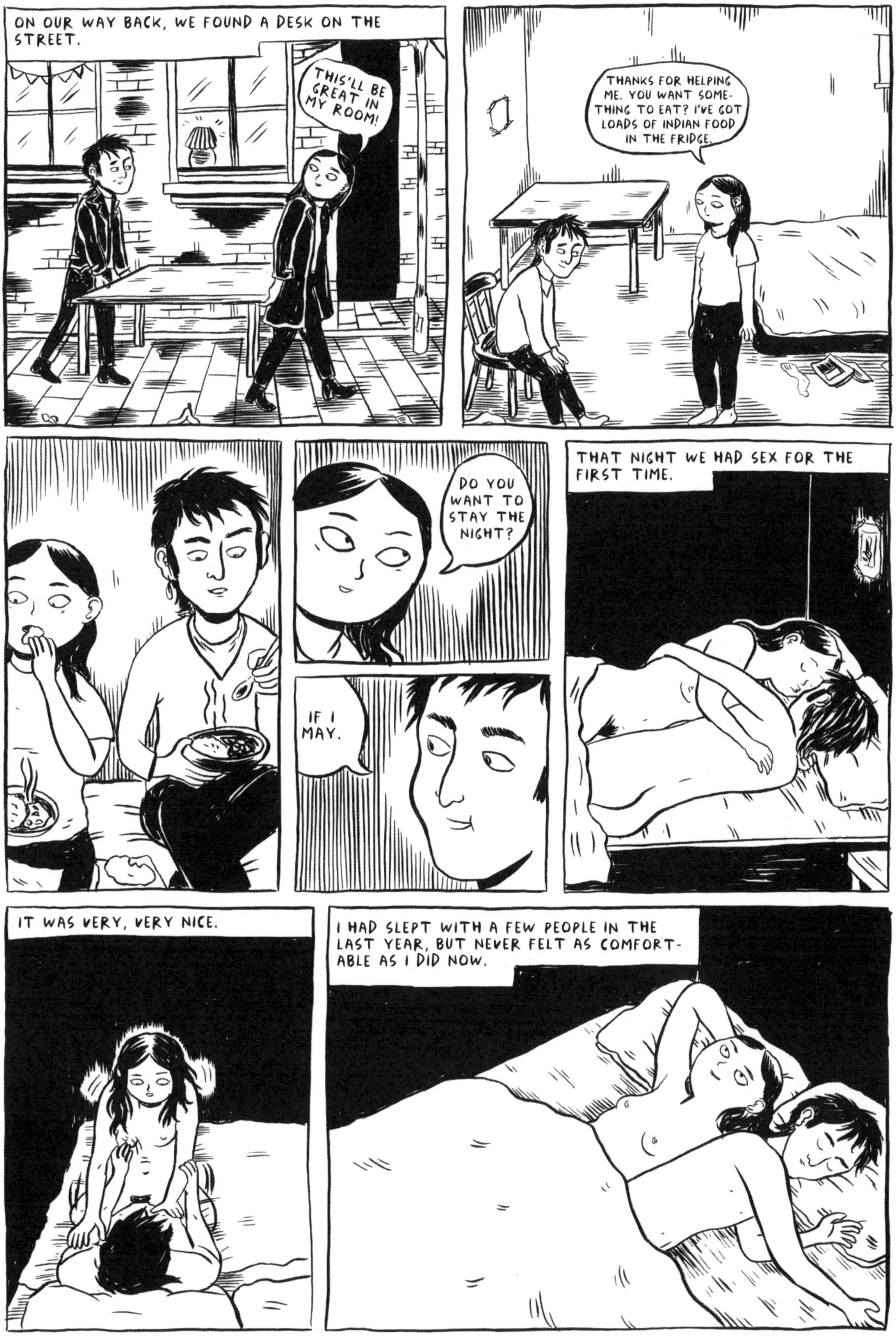
ON OUR WAY BACK, WE FOUND A DESK ON THE STREET.
THIS'LL BE GREAT IN MY ROOM!
THANKS FOR HELPING ME. YOU WANT SOMETHING TO EAT? I'VE GOT LOADS OF INDIAN FOOD IN THE FRIDGE.
DO YOU WANT TO STAY THE NIGHT?
IF I MAY.
THAT NIGHT WE HAD SEX FOR THE FIRST TIME.
IT WAS VERY, VERY NICE.
I HAD SLEPT WITH A FEW PEOPLE IN THE LAST YEAR, BUT NEVER FELT AS COMFORTABLE AS I DID NOW.

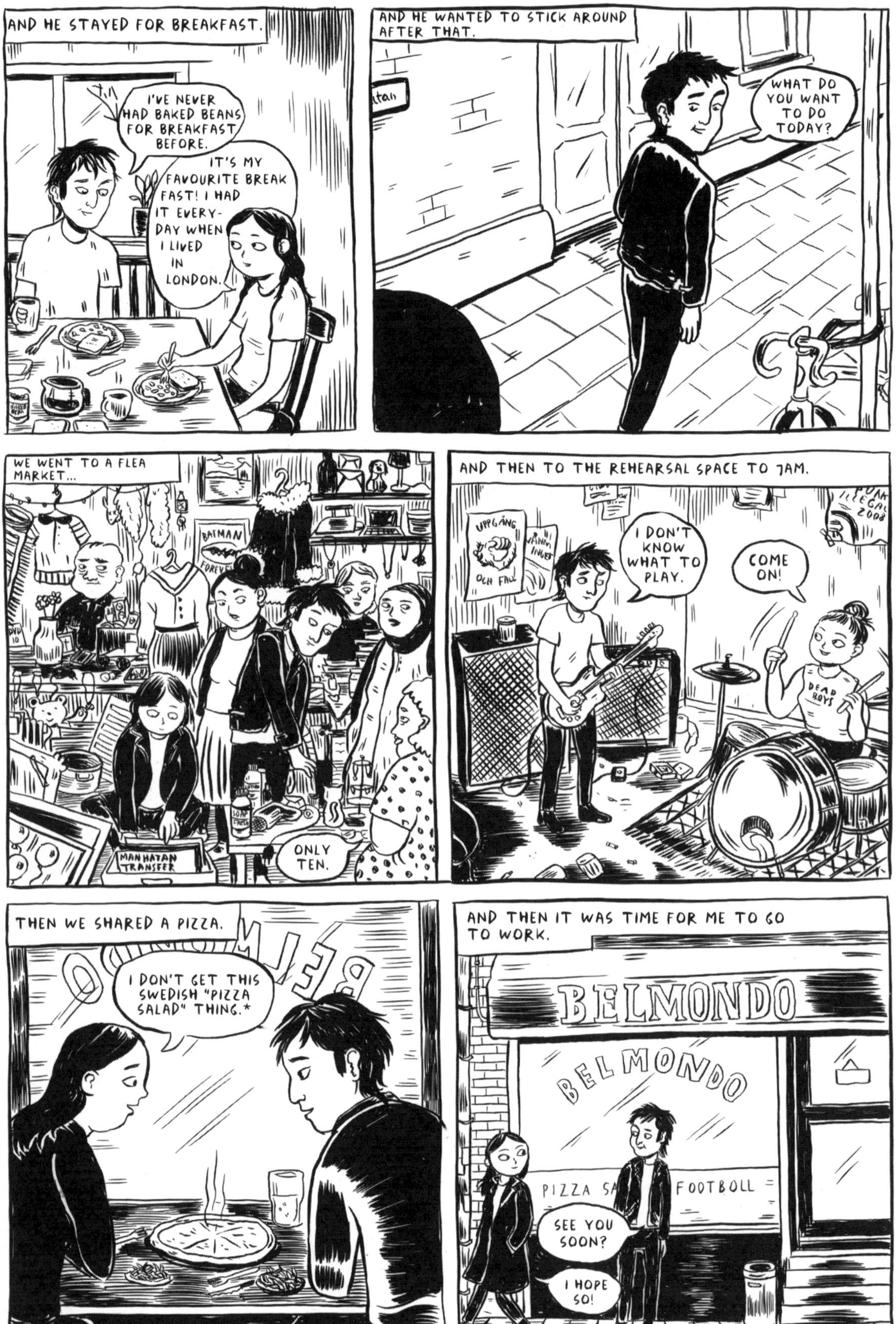
AND HE STAYED FOR BREAKFAST.
I'VE NEVER HAD BAKED BEANS FOR BREAKFAST BEFORE.
IT'S MY FAVOURITE BREAK FAST! I HAD IT EVERY-DAY WHEN I LIVED IN LONDON.
AND HE WANTED TO STICK AROUND AFTER THAT.
WHAT DO YOU WANT TO DO TODAY?
WE WENT TO A FLEA MARKET...
BATMAN
MANHATAN TRANSFER
ONLY TEN.
AND THEN TO THE REHEARSAL SPACE TO JAM.
I DON'T KNOW WHAT TO PLAY.
COME ON!
DEAD BOYS
THEN WE SHARED A PIZZA.
I DON'T GET THIS SWEDISH "PIZZA SALAD" THING.*
AND THEN IT WAS TIME FOR ME TO GO TO WORK.
BELMONDO
BELMONDO
PIZZA SA FOOTBOLL
SEE YOU SOON?
I HOPE SO!

*IN SWEDEN IF YOU ORDER A PIZZA CABBAGE SALAD ALWAYS COMES ON THE SIDE.

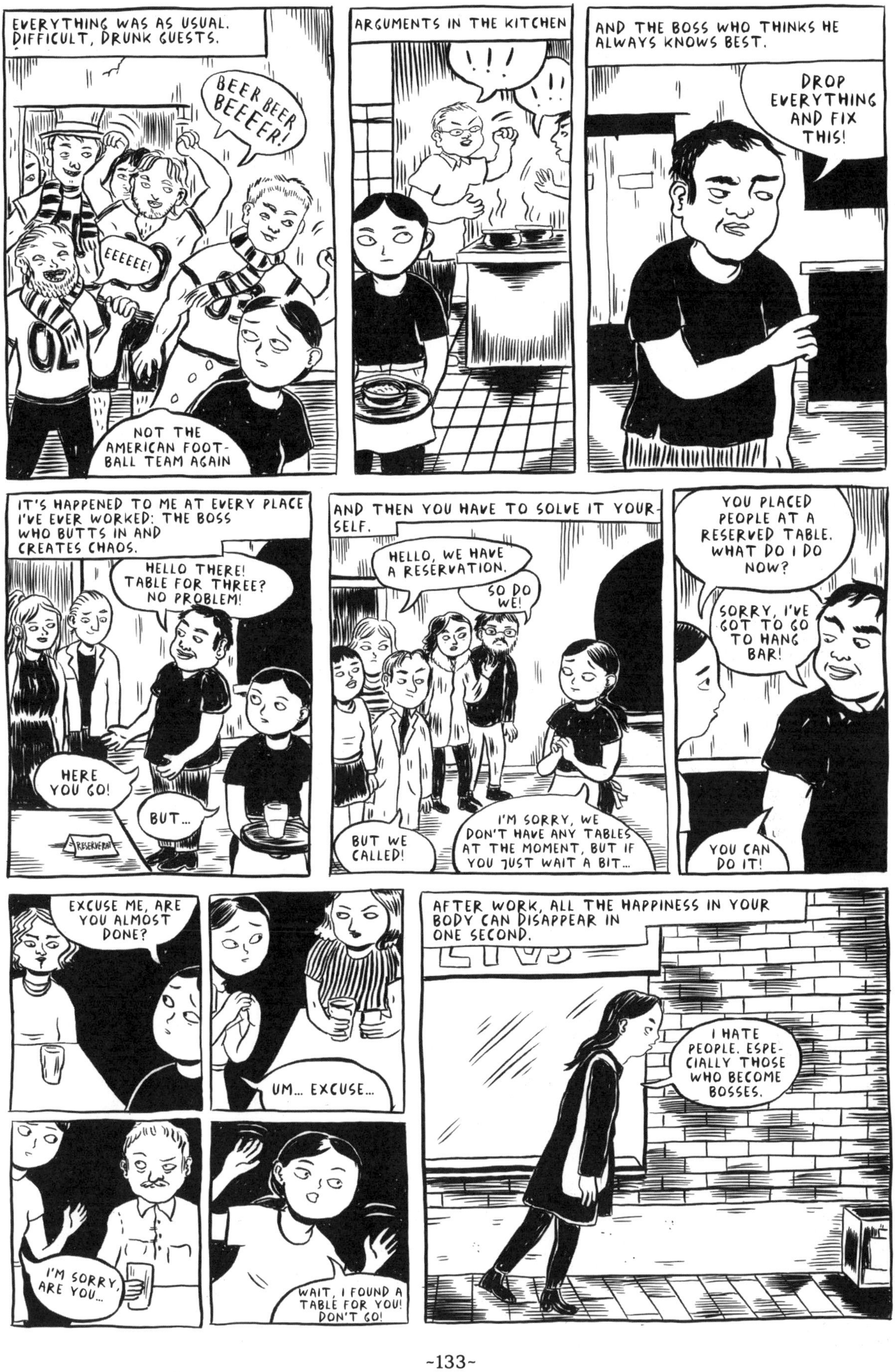
EVERYTHING WAS AS USUAL. DIFFICULT, DRUNK GUESTS.
BEER BEER BEEEER!
EEEEEE!
NOT THE AMERICAN FOOT-BALL TEAM AGAIN
ARGUMENTS IN THE KITCHEN
!!!
!!
AND THE BOSS WHO THINKS HE ALWAYS KNOWS BEST.
DROP EVERYTHING AND FIX THIS!
IT'S HAPPENED TO ME AT EVERY PLACE I'VE EVER WORKED: THE BOSS WHO BUTTS IN AND CREATES CHAOS.
HELLO THERE! TABLE FOR THREE? NO PROBLEM!
HERE YOU GO!
BUT...
RESERVERAT
AND THEN YOU HAVE TO SOLVE IT YOUR-SELF.
HELLO, WE HAVE A RESERVATION.
SO DO WE!
BUT WE CALLED!
I'M SORRY, WE DON'T HAVE ANY TABLES AT THE MOMENT, BUT IF YOU JUST WAIT A BIT...
YOU PLACED PEOPLE AT A RESERVED TABLE. WHAT DO I DO NOW?
SORRY, I'VE GOT TO GO TO HANG BAR!
YOU CAN DO IT!
EXCUSE ME, ARE YOU ALMOST DONE?
UM... EXCUSE...
I'M SORRY, ARE YOU...
WAIT, I FOUND A TABLE FOR YOU! DON'T GO!
AFTER WORK, ALL THE HAPPINESS IN YOUR BODY CAN DISAPPEAR IN ONE SECOND.
I HATE PEOPLE. ESPE-CIALLY THOSE WHO BECOME BOSSES.

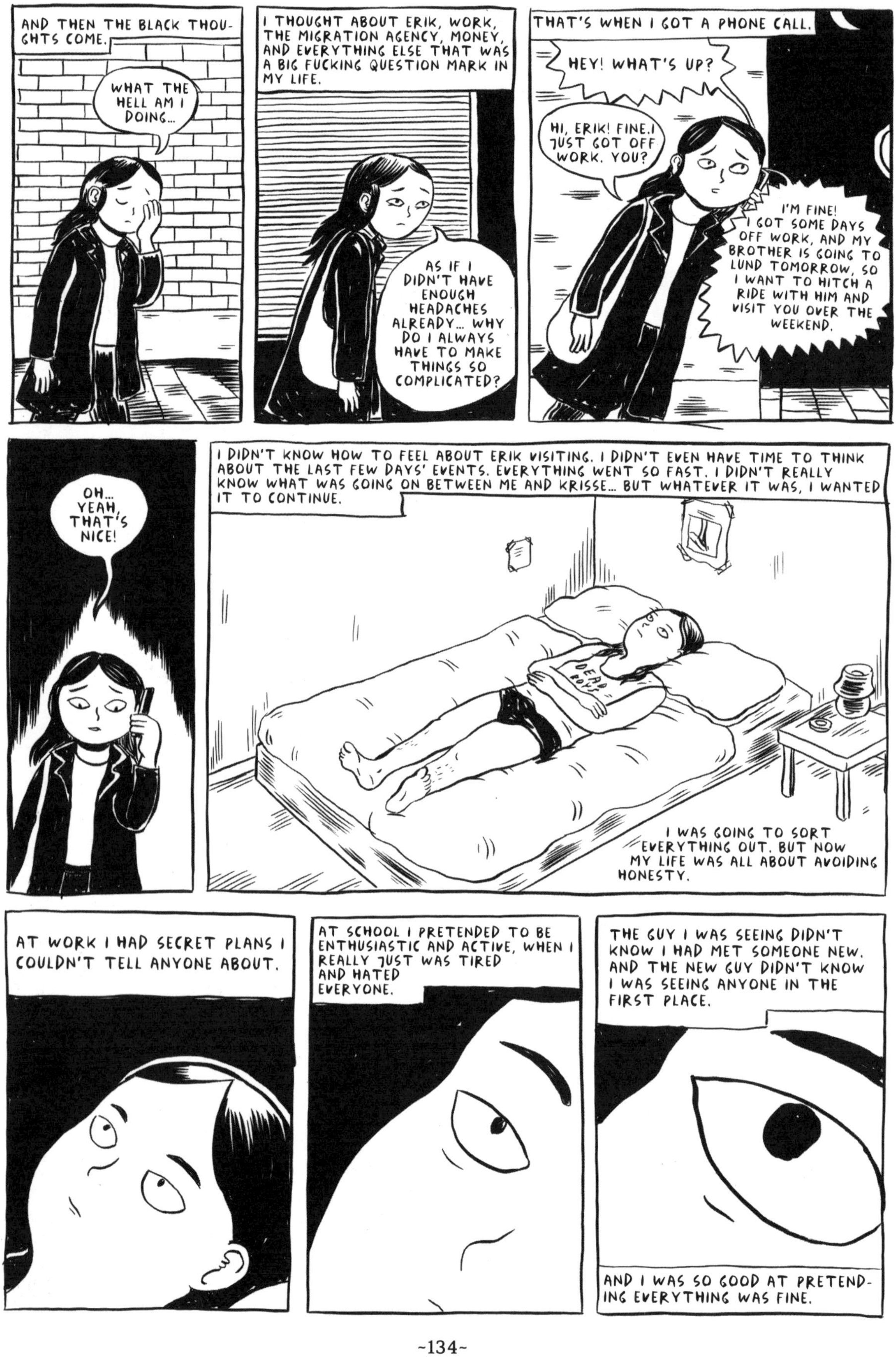
AND THEN THE BLACK THOUGHTS COME.
WHAT THE HELL AM I DOING...
I THOUGHT ABOUT ERIK, WORK, THE MIGRATION AGENCY, MONEY, AND EVERYTHING ELSE THAT WAS A BIG FUCKING QUESTION MARK IN MY LIFE.
AS IF I DIDN'T HAVE ENOUGH HEADACHES ALREADY... WHY DO I ALWAYS HAVE TO MAKE THINGS SO COMPLICATED?
THAT'S WHEN I GOT A PHONE CALL.
HEY! WHAT'S UP?
HI, ERIK! FINE. I JUST GOT OFF WORK. YOU?
I'M FINE! I GOT SOME DAYS OFF WORK, AND MY BROTHER IS GOING TO LUND TOMORROW, SO I WANT TO HITCH A RIDE WITH HIM AND VISIT YOU OVER THE WEEKEND.
OH... YEAH, THAT'S NICE!
I DIDN'T KNOW HOW TO FEEL ABOUT ERIK VISITING. I DIDN'T EVEN HAVE TIME TO THINK ABOUT THE LAST FEW DAYS' EVENTS. EVERYTHING WENT SO FAST. I DIDN'T REALLY KNOW WHAT WAS GOING ON BETWEEN ME AND KRISSE... BUT WHATEVER IT WAS, I WANTED IT TO CONTINUE.
DEAD BOYS
I WAS GOING TO SORT EVERYTHING OUT. BUT NOW MY LIFE WAS ALL ABOUT AVOIDING HONESTY.
AT WORK I HAD SECRET PLANS I COULDN'T TELL ANYONE ABOUT.
AT SCHOOL I PRETENDED TO BE ENTHUSIASTIC AND ACTIVE, WHEN I REALLY JUST WAS TIRED AND HATED EVERYONE.
THE GUY I WAS SEEING DIDN'T KNOW I HAD MET SOMEONE NEW. AND THE NEW GUY DIDN'T KNOW I WAS SEEING ANYONE IN THE FIRST PLACE.
AND I WAS SO GOOD AT PRETENDING EVERYTHING WAS FINE.

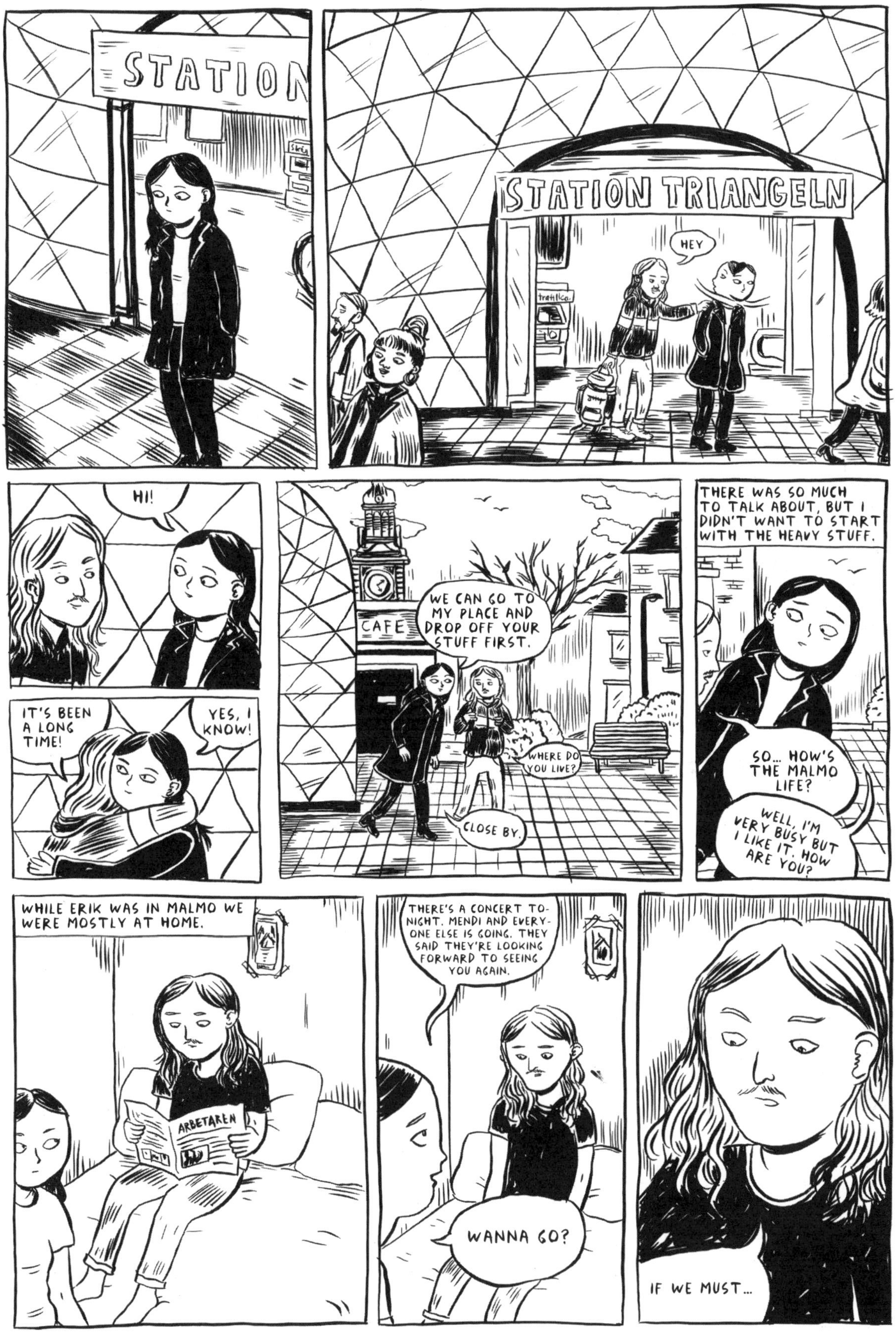
STATION
STATION TRIANGELN
HEY
HI!
IT'S BEEN A LONG TIME!
YES, I KNOW!
WE CAN GO TO MY PLACE AND DROP OFF YOUR STUFF FIRST.
CAFE
WHERE DO YOU LIVE?
CLOSE BY.
THERE WAS SO MUCH TO TALK ABOUT, BUT I DIDN'T WANT TO START WITH THE HEAVY STUFF.
SO... HOW'S THE MALMO LIFE?
WELL, I'M VERY BUSY BUT I LIKE IT. HOW ARE YOU?
WHILE ERIK WAS IN MALMO WE WERE MOSTLY AT HOME.
ARBETAREN
THERE'S A CONCERT TO-NIGHT. MENDI AND EVERY-ONE ELSE IS GOING. THEY SAID THEY'RE LOOKING FORWARD TO SEEING YOU AGAIN.
WANNA GO?
IF WE MUST...

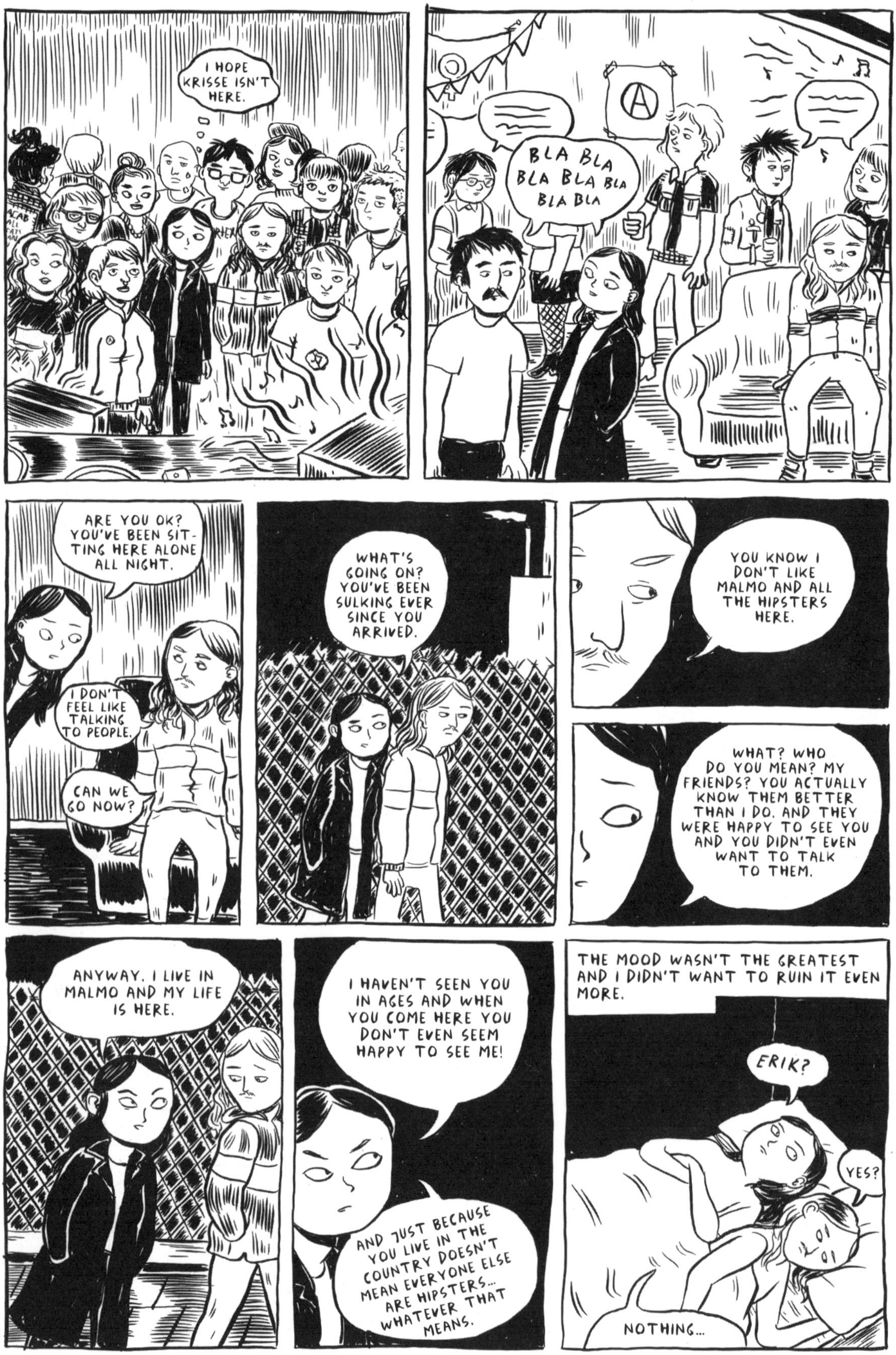
I HOPE KRISSE ISN'T HERE.
BLA BLA BLA BLA BLA BLA BLA
ARE YOU OK? YOU'VE BEEN SITTING HERE ALONE ALL NIGHT.
I DON'T FEEL LIKE TALKING TO PEOPLE.
CAN WE GO NOW?
WHAT'S GOING ON? YOU'VE BEEN SULKING EVER SINCE YOU ARRIVED.
YOU KNOW I DON'T LIKE MALMO AND ALL THE HIPSTERS HERE.
WHAT? WHO DO YOU MEAN? MY FRIENDS? YOU ACTUALLY KNOW THEM BETTER THAN I DO. AND THEY WERE HAPPY TO SEE YOU AND YOU DIDN'T EVEN WANT TO TALK TO THEM.
ANYWAY, I LIVE IN MALMO AND MY LIFE IS HERE.
I HAVEN'T SEEN YOU IN AGES AND WHEN YOU COME HERE YOU DON'T EVEN SEEM HAPPY TO SEE ME!
AND JUST BECAUSE YOU LIVE IN THE COUNTRY DOESN'T MEAN EVERYONE ELSE ARE HIPSTERS... WHATEVER THAT MEANS.
THE MOOD WASN'T THE GREATEST AND I DIDN'T WANT TO RUIN IT EVEN MORE.
ERIK?
YES?
NOTHING...

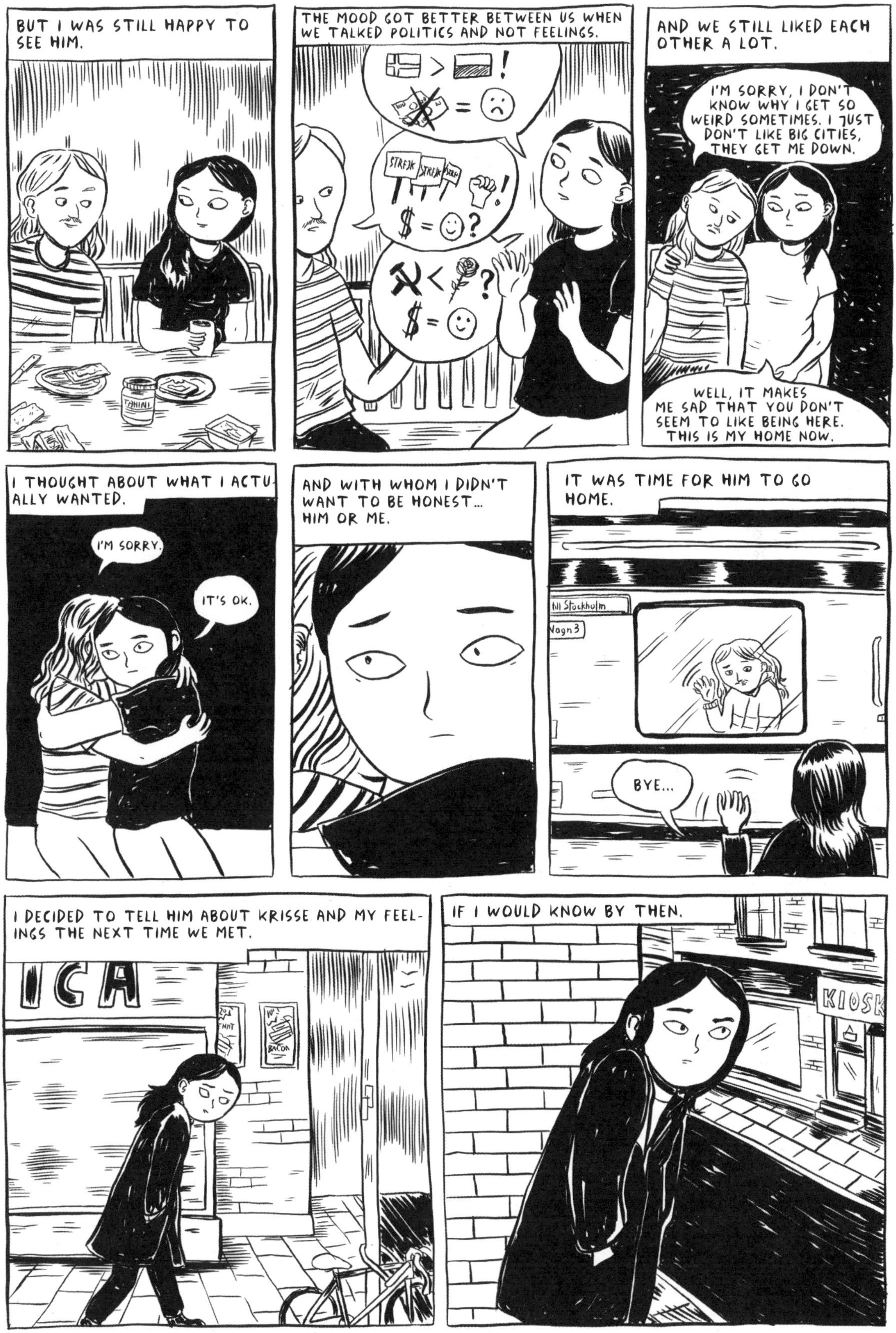
BUT I WAS STILL HAPPY TO SEE HIM.
TAHINI
THE MOOD GOT BETTER BETWEEN US WHEN WE TALKED POLITICS AND NOT FEELINGS.
STREJK STREJK STREJK
AND WE STILL LIKED EACH OTHER A LOT.
I'M SORRY, I DON'T KNOW WHY I GET SO WEIRD SOMETIMES. I JUST DON'T LIKE BIG CITIES, THEY GET ME DOWN.
WELL, IT MAKES ME SAD THAT YOU DON'T SEEM TO LIKE BEING HERE. THIS IS MY HOME NOW.
I THOUGHT ABOUT WHAT I ACTUALLY WANTED.
I'M SORRY.
IT'S OK.
AND WITH WHOM I DIDN'T WANT TO BE HONEST... HIM OR ME.
IT WAS TIME FOR HIM TO GO HOME.
till Stockholm
Vagn 3
BYE...
I DECIDED TO TELL HIM ABOUT KRISSE AND MY FEELINGS THE NEXT TIME WE MET.
ICA
BACON
IF I WOULD KNOW BY THEN.
KIOSK

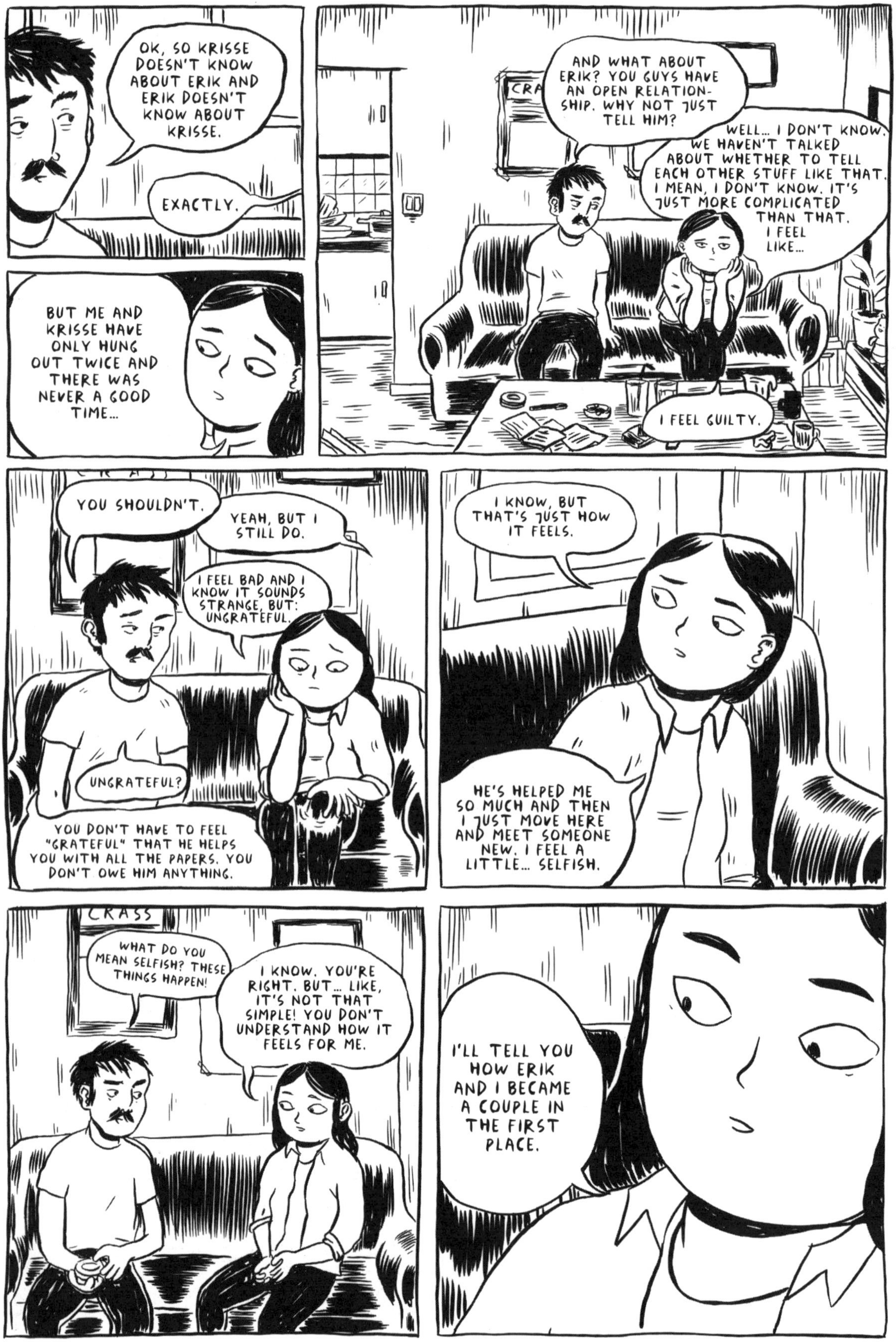
OK, SO KRISSE DOESN'T KNOW ABOUT ERIK AND ERIK DOESN'T KNOW ABOUT KRISSE.
EXACTLY.
BUT ME AND KRISSE HAVE ONLY HUNG OUT TWICE AND THERE WAS NEVER A GOOD TIME...
CRA
AND WHAT ABOUT ERIK? YOU GUYS HAVE AN OPEN RELATIONSHIP. WHY NOT JUST TELL HIM?
WELL... I DON'T KNOW. WE HAVEN'T TALKED ABOUT WHETHER TO TELL EACH OTHER STUFF LIKE THAT. I MEAN, I DON'T KNOW. IT'S JUST MORE COMPLICATED THAN THAT. I FEEL LIKE...
I FEEL GUILTY.
YOU SHOULDN'T.
YEAH, BUT I STILL DO.
I FEEL BAD AND I KNOW IT SOUNDS STRANGE, BUT: UNGRATEFUL.
UNGRATEFUL?
YOU DON'T HAVE TO FEEL "GRATEFUL" THAT HE HELPS YOU WITH ALL THE PAPERS. YOU DON'T OWE HIM ANYTHING.
I KNOW, BUT THAT'S JUST HOW IT FEELS.
HE'S HELPED ME SO MUCH AND THEN I JUST MOVE HERE AND MEET SOMEONE NEW. I FEEL A LITTLE... SELFISH.
CRASS
WHAT DO YOU MEAN SELFISH? THESE THINGS HAPPEN!
I KNOW. YOU'RE RIGHT. BUT... LIKE, IT'S NOT THAT SIMPLE! YOU DON'T UNDERSTAND HOW IT FEELS FOR ME.
I'LL TELL YOU HOW ERIK AND I BECAME A COUPLE IN THE FIRST PLACE.

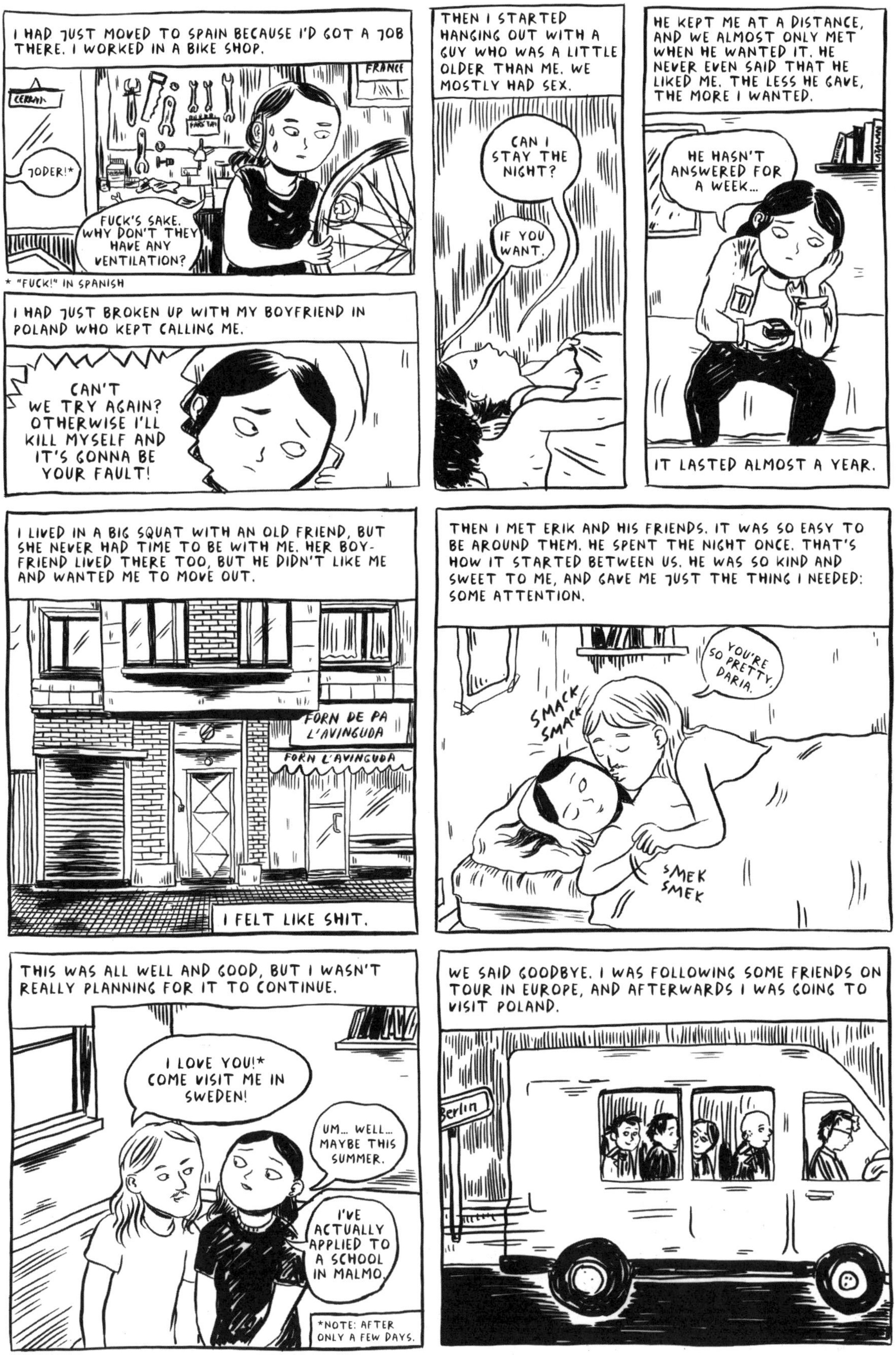
I HAD JUST MOVED TO SPAIN BECAUSE I'D GOT A JOB THERE. I WORKED IN A BIKE SHOP.
JODER!*
FUCK'S SAKE. WHY DON'T THEY HAVE ANY VENTILATION?
* "FUCK!" IN SPANISH
I HAD JUST BROKEN UP WITH MY BOYFRIEND IN POLAND WHO KEPT CALLING ME.
CAN'T WE TRY AGAIN? OTHERWISE I'LL KILL MYSELF AND IT'S GONNA BE YOUR FAULT!
THEN I STARTED HANGING OUT WITH A GUY WHO WAS A LITTLE OLDER THAN ME. WE MOSTLY HAD SEX.
CAN I STAY THE NIGHT?
IF YOU WANT.
HE KEPT ME AT A DISTANCE, AND WE ALMOST ONLY MET WHEN HE WANTED IT. HE NEVER EVEN SAID THAT HE LIKED ME. THE LESS HE GAVE, THE MORE I WANTED.
HE HASN'T ANSWERED FOR A WEEK...
IT LASTED ALMOST A YEAR.
I LIVED IN A BIG SQUAT WITH AN OLD FRIEND, BUT SHE NEVER HAD TIME TO BE WITH ME. HER BOY-FRIEND LIVED THERE TOO, BUT HE DIDN'T LIKE ME AND WANTED ME TO MOVE OUT.
FORN DE PA L'AVINGUDA
FORN L'AVINGUDA
I FELT LIKE SHIT.
THEN I MET ERIK AND HIS FRIENDS. IT WAS SO EASY TO BE AROUND THEM. HE SPENT THE NIGHT ONCE. THAT'S HOW IT STARTED BETWEEN US. HE WAS SO KIND AND SWEET TO ME, AND GAVE ME JUST THE THING I NEEDED: SOME ATTENTION.
YOU'RE SO PRETTY, DARIA.
SMACK SMACK
SMEK SMEK
THIS WAS ALL WELL AND GOOD, BUT I WASN'T REALLY PLANNING FOR IT TO CONTINUE.
I LOVE YOU!* COME VISIT ME IN SWEDEN!
UM... WELL... MAYBE THIS SUMMER.
I'VE ACTUALLY APPLIED TO A SCHOOL IN MALMO.
*NOTE: AFTER ONLY A FEW DAYS.
WE SAID GOODBYE. I WAS FOLLOWING SOME FRIENDS ON TOUR IN EUROPE, AND AFTERWARDS I WAS GOING TO VISIT POLAND.
Berlin

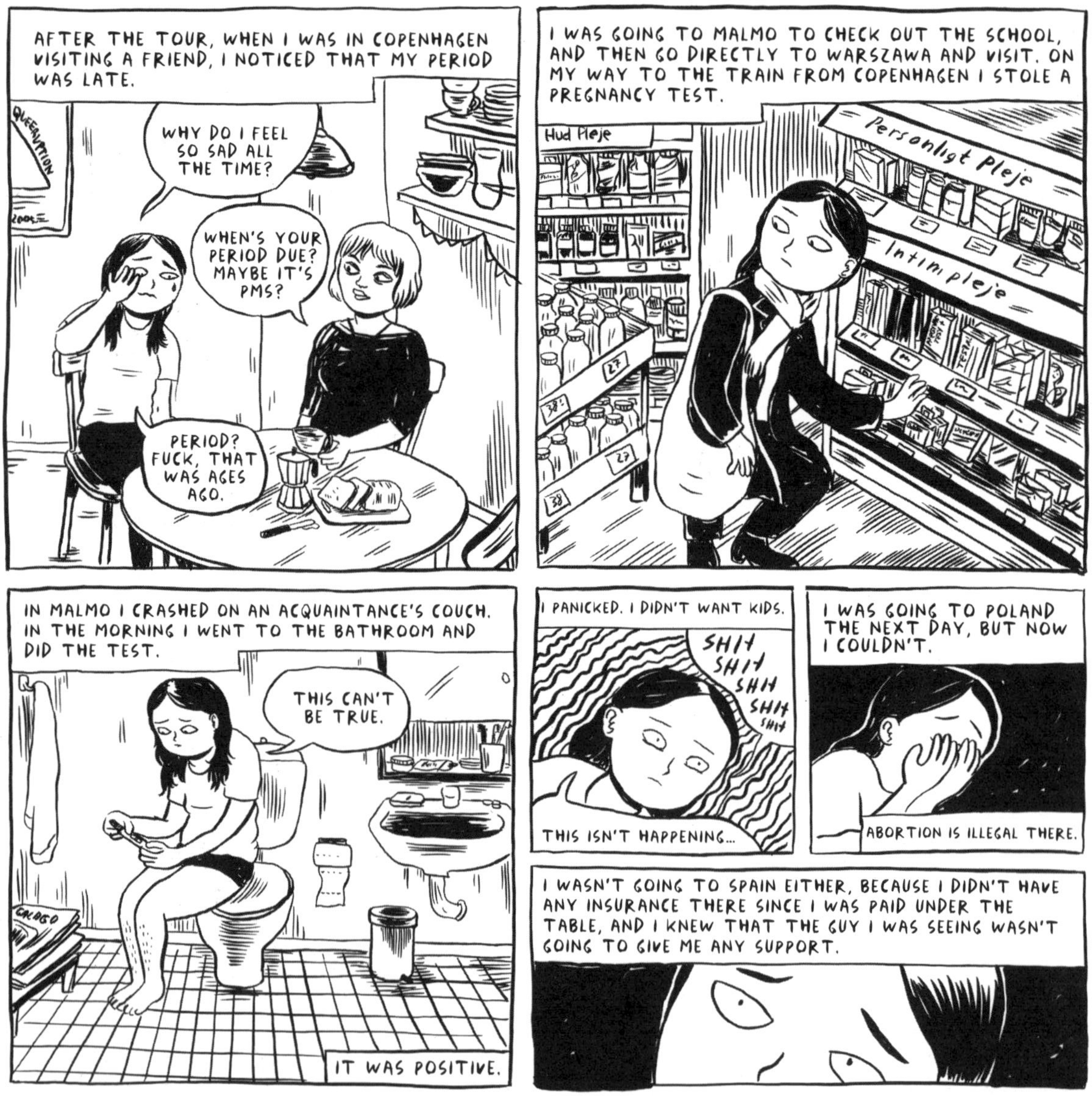
AFTER THE TOUR, WHEN I WAS IN COPENHAGEN VISITING A FRIEND, I NOTICED THAT MY PERIOD WAS LATE.
QUEERUPTION
WHY DO I FEEL SO SAD ALL THE TIME?
WHEN'S YOUR PERIOD DUE? MAYBE IT'S PMS?
PERIOD? FUCK, THAT WAS AGES AGO.
I WAS GOING TO MALMO TO CHECK OUT THE SCHOOL, AND THEN GO DIRECTLY TO WARSZAWA AND VISIT. ON MY WAY TO THE TRAIN FROM COPENHAGEN I STOLE A PREGNANCY TEST.
Hud Pleje
Personligt Pleje
Intimpleje
IN MALMO I CRASHED ON AN ACQUAINTANCE'S COUCH. IN THE MORNING I WENT TO THE BATHROOM AND DID THE TEST.
THIS CAN'T BE TRUE.
IT WAS POSITIVE.
I PANICKED. I DIDN'T WANT KIDS.
SHIT SHIT SHIT SHIT SHIT
THIS ISN'T HAPPENING...
I WAS GOING TO POLAND THE NEXT DAY, BUT NOW I COULDN'T.
ABORTION IS ILLEGAL THERE.
I WASN'T GOING TO SPAIN EITHER, BECAUSE I DIDN'T HAVE ANY INSURANCE THERE SINCE I WAS PAID UNDER THE TABLE, AND I KNEW THAT THE GUY I WAS SEEING WASN'T GOING TO GIVE ME ANY SUPPORT.
IT WAS WINTER. VERY COLD AND GREY AND I WAS IN MALMO FOR THE FIRST TIME. I FELT ALONE AND DIDN'T KNOW WHAT TO DO.
JULA
TELEFON
SKOR
SO I CALLED ERIK.
HE WAS STILL ON VACATION IN SPAIN AND A LITTLE DRUNK WHEN I CALLED.
CAN I, LIKE, CALL YOU LATER?
NOT REALLY. I'M IN SWEDEN AND CALLING FROM A PAY PHONE.
I'M PREGNANT AND I NEED HELP.
HE SAID HE'D GET ON THE FIRST FLIGHT BACK TO SWEDEN.
THANK YOU ERIK.

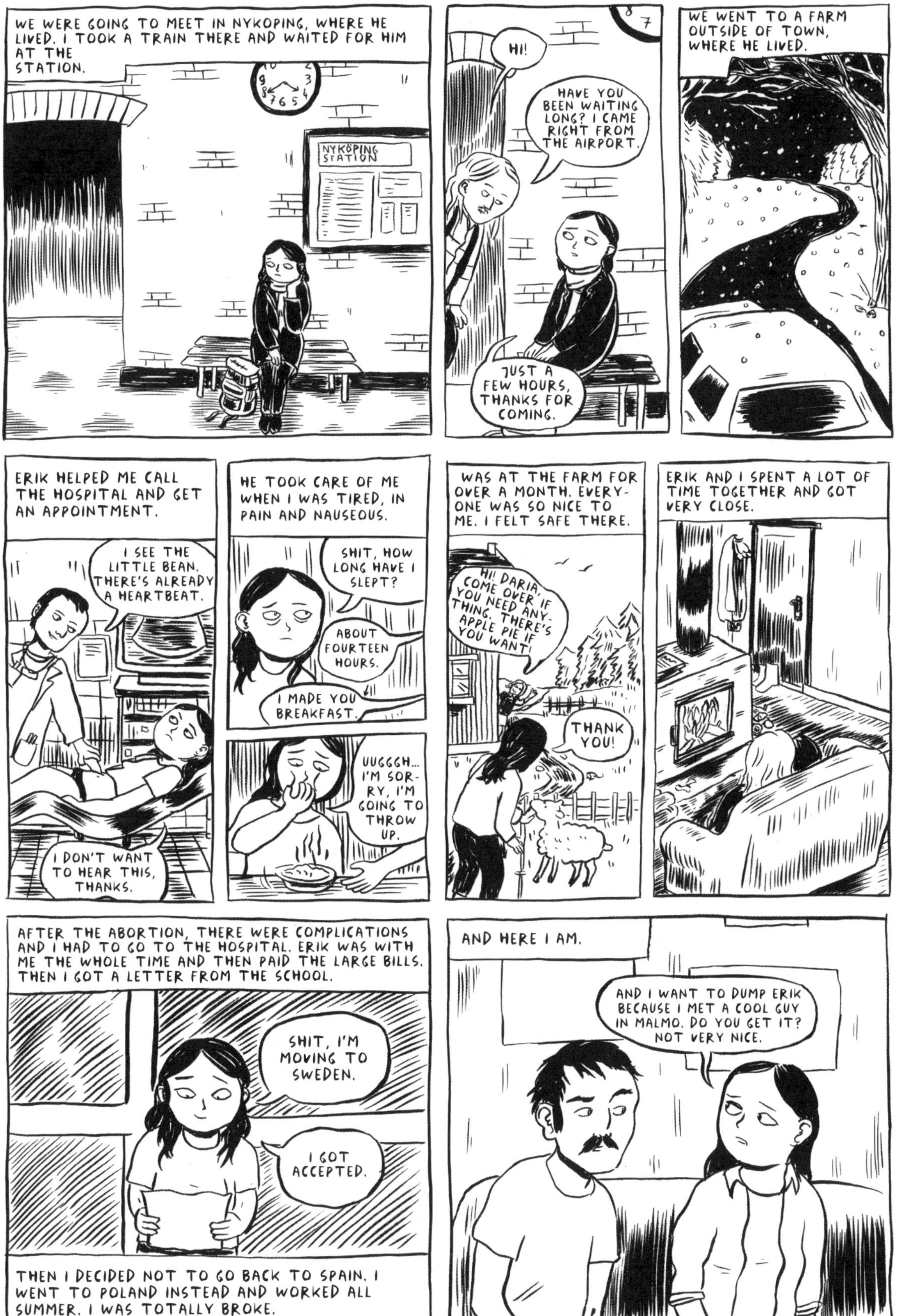
WE WERE GOING TO MEET IN NYKOPING, WHERE HE LIVED. I TOOK A TRAIN THERE AND WAITED FOR HIM AT THE STATION.
NYKÖPING STATION
HI!
HAVE YOU BEEN WAITING LONG? I CAME RIGHT FROM THE AIRPORT.
JUST A FEW HOURS, THANKS FOR COMING.
WE WENT TO A FARM OUTSIDE OF TOWN, WHERE HE LIVED.
ERIK HELPED ME CALL THE HOSPITAL AND GET AN APPOINTMENT.
I SEE THE LITTLE BEAN. THERE'S ALREADY A HEARTBEAT.
I DON'T WANT TO HEAR THIS, THANKS.
HE TOOK CARE OF ME WHEN I WAS TIRED, IN PAIN AND NAUSEOUS.
SHIT, HOW LONG HAVE I SLEPT?
ABOUT FOURTEEN HOURS.
I MADE YOU BREAKFAST.
UUGGGH... I'M SORRY, I'M GOING TO THROW UP.
WAS AT THE FARM FOR OVER A MONTH. EVERYONE WAS SO NICE TO ME. I FELT SAFE THERE.
HI! DARIA, COME OVER IF YOU NEED ANYTHING. THERE'S APPLE PIE IF YOU WANT!
THANK YOU!
ERIK AND I SPENT A LOT OF TIME TOGETHER AND GOT VERY CLOSE.
AFTER THE ABORTION, THERE WERE COMPLICATIONS AND I HAD TO GO TO THE HOSPITAL. ERIK WAS WITH ME THE WHOLE TIME AND THEN PAID THE LARGE BILLS. THEN I GOT A LETTER FROM THE SCHOOL.
SHIT, I'M MOVING TO SWEDEN.
I GOT ACCEPTED.
THEN I DECIDED NOT TO GO BACK TO SPAIN. I WENT TO POLAND INSTEAD AND WORKED ALL SUMMER. I WAS TOTALLY BROKE.
AND HERE I AM.
AND I WANT TO DUMP ERIK BECAUSE I MET A COOL GUY IN MALMO. DO YOU GET IT? NOT VERY NICE.

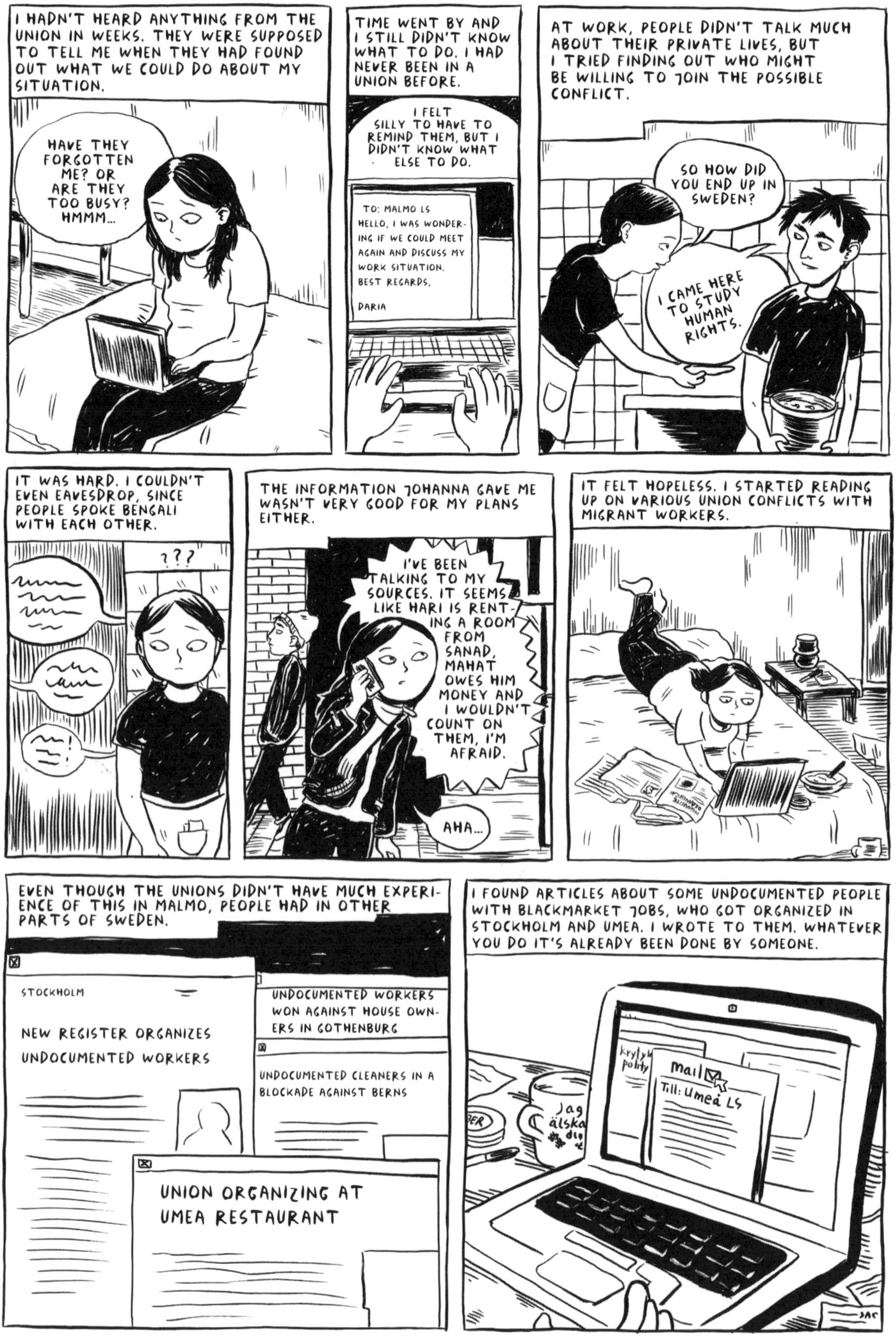
I HADN'T HEARD ANYTHING FROM THE UNION IN WEEKS. THEY WERE SUPPOSED TO TELL ME WHEN THEY HAD FOUND OUT WHAT WE COULD DO ABOUT MY SITUATION.
HAVE THEY FORGOTTEN ME? OR ARE THEY TOO BUSY? HMMM...
TIME WENT BY AND I STILL DIDN'T KNOW WHAT TO DO. I HAD NEVER BEEN IN A UNION BEFORE.
I FELT SILLY TO HAVE TO REMIND THEM, BUT I DIDN'T KNOW WHAT ELSE TO DO.
TO: MALMO LS
HELLO, I WAS WONDERING IF WE COULD MEET AGAIN AND DISCUSS MY WORK SITUATION.
BEST REGARDS,
DARIA
AT WORK, PEOPLE DIDN'T TALK MUCH ABOUT THEIR PRIVATE LIVES, BUT I TRIED FINDING OUT WHO MIGHT BE WILLING TO JOIN THE POSSIBLE CONFLICT.
SO HOW DID YOU END UP IN SWEDEN?
I CAME HERE TO STUDY HUMAN RIGHTS.
IT WAS HARD. I COULDN'T EVEN EAVESDROP, SINCE PEOPLE SPOKE BENGALI WITH EACH OTHER.
???
THE INFORMATION JOHANNA GAVE ME WASN'T VERY GOOD FOR MY PLANS EITHER.
I'VE BEEN TALKING TO MY SOURCES. IT SEEMS LIKE HARI IS RENTING A ROOM FROM SANAD, MAHAT OWES HIM MONEY AND I WOULDN'T COUNT ON THEM, I'M AFRAID.
AHA...
IT FELT HOPELESS. I STARTED READING UP ON VARIOUS UNION CONFLICTS WITH MIGRANT WORKERS.
EVEN THOUGH THE UNIONS DIDN'T HAVE MUCH EXPERIENCE OF THIS IN MALMO, PEOPLE HAD IN OTHER PARTS OF SWEDEN.
STOCKHOLM
NEW REGISTER ORGANIZES UNDOCUMENTED WORKERS
UNDOCUMENTED WORKERS WON AGAINST HOUSE OWNERS IN GOTHENBURG
UNDOCUMENTED CLEANERS IN A BLOCKADE AGAINST BERNS
UNION ORGANIZING AT UMEA RESTAURANT
I FOUND ARTICLES ABOUT SOME UNDOCUMENTED PEOPLE WITH BLACKMARKET JOBS, WHO GOT ORGANIZED IN STOCKHOLM AND UMEA. I WROTE TO THEM. WHATEVER YOU DO IT'S ALREADY BEEN DONE BY SOMEONE.
Mail
Till: Umeå LS
Jag älska dig

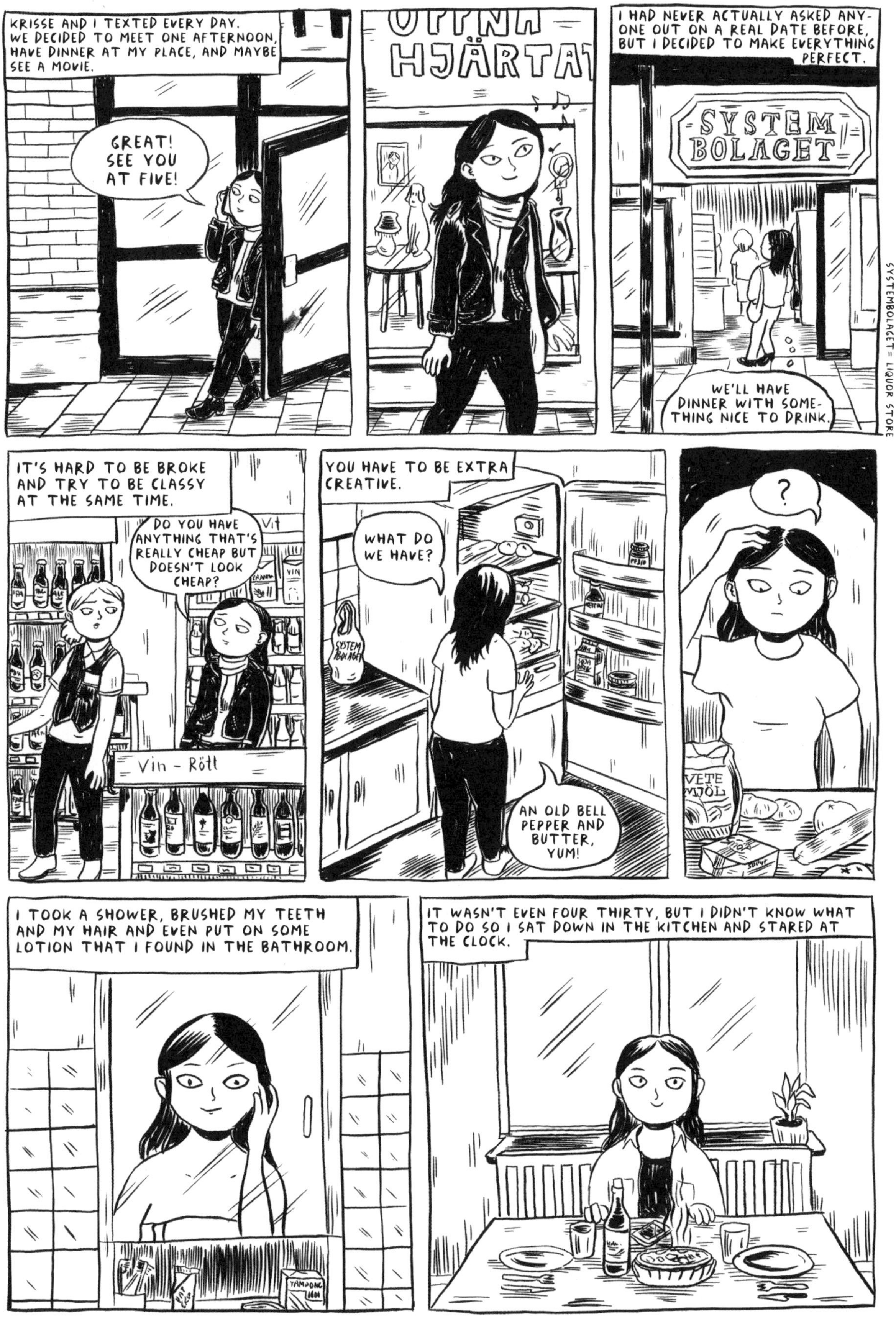
KRISSE AND I TEXTED EVERY DAY. WE DECIDED TO MEET ONE AFTERNOON, HAVE DINNER AT MY PLACE, AND MAYBE SEE A MOVIE.
GREAT! SEE YOU AT FIVE!
HJÄRTA
I HAD NEVER ACTUALLY ASKED ANYONE OUT ON A REAL DATE BEFORE, BUT I DECIDED TO MAKE EVERYTHING PERFECT.
SYSTEM BOLAGET
WE'LL HAVE DINNER WITH SOMETHING NICE TO DRINK.
SYSTEMBOLAGET = LIQUOR STORE
IT'S HARD TO BE BROKE AND TRY TO BE CLASSY AT THE SAME TIME.
DO YOU HAVE ANYTHING THAT'S REALLY CHEAP BUT DOESN'T LOOK CHEAP?
Vin - Rött
YOU HAVE TO BE EXTRA CREATIVE.
WHAT DO WE HAVE?
AN OLD BELL PEPPER AND BUTTER, YUM!
?
VETE MJÖL
I TOOK A SHOWER, BRUSHED MY TEETH AND MY HAIR AND EVEN PUT ON SOME LOTION THAT I FOUND IN THE BATHROOM.
IT WASN'T EVEN FOUR THIRTY, BUT I DIDN'T KNOW WHAT TO DO SO I SAT DOWN IN THE KITCHEN AND STARED AT THE CLOCK.

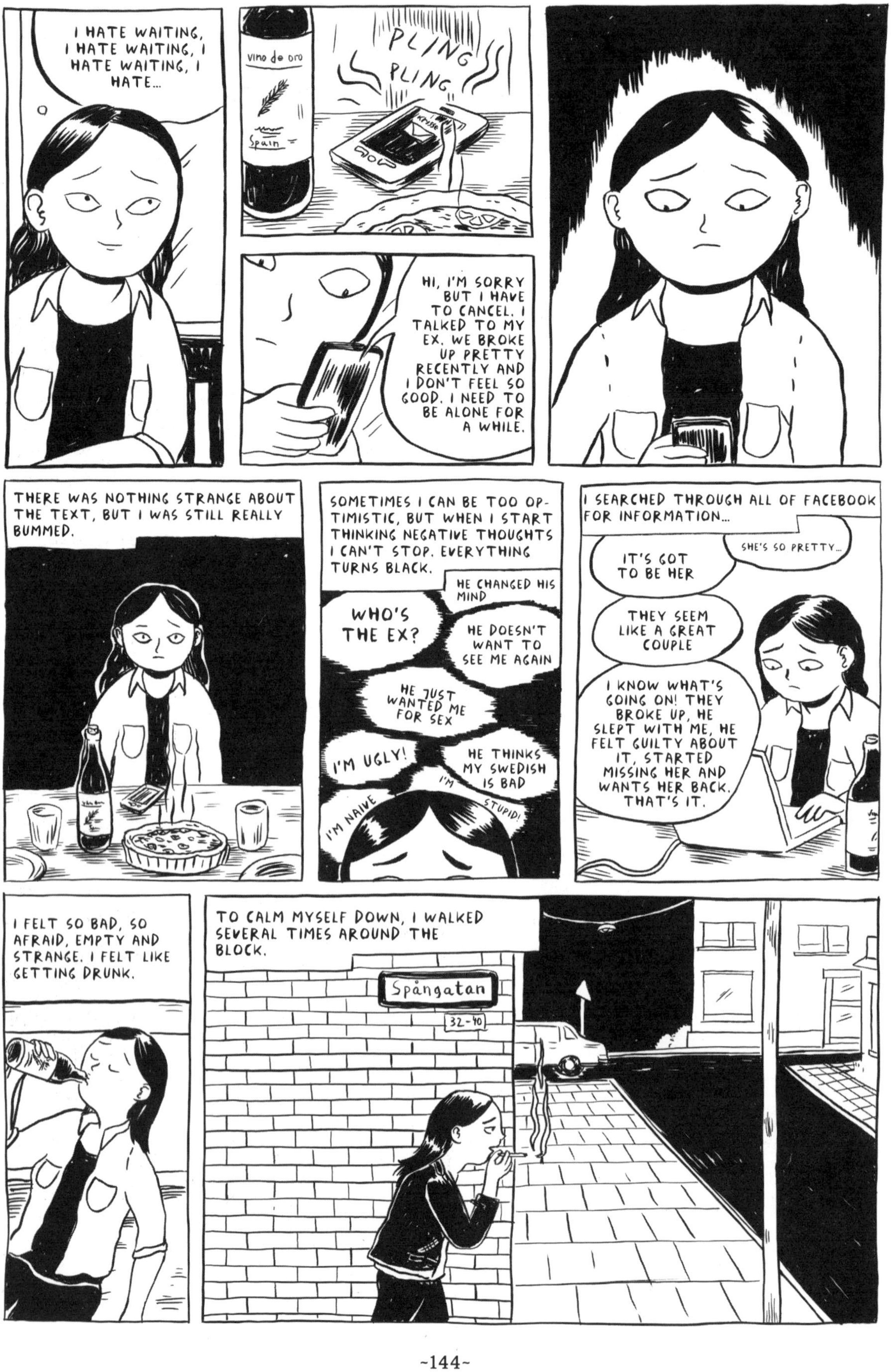
I HATE WAITING, I HATE WAITING, I HATE WAITING, I HATE...
vino de oro
Spain
PLING
PLING
HI, I'M SORRY BUT I HAVE TO CANCEL. I TALKED TO MY EX. WE BROKE UP PRETTY RECENTLY AND I DON'T FEEL SO GOOD. I NEED TO BE ALONE FOR A WHILE.
THERE WAS NOTHING STRANGE ABOUT THE TEXT, BUT I WAS STILL REALLY BUMMED.
SOMETIMES I CAN BE TOO OPTIMISTIC, BUT WHEN I START THINKING NEGATIVE THOUGHTS I CAN'T STOP. EVERYTHING TURNS BLACK.
HE CHANGED HIS MIND
WHO'S THE EX?
HE DOESN'T WANT TO SEE ME AGAIN
HE JUST WANTED ME FOR SEX
I'M UGLY!
HE THINKS MY SWEDISH IS BAD
I'M STUPID!
I'M NAIVE
I SEARCHED THROUGH ALL OF FACEBOOK FOR INFORMATION...
SHE'S SO PRETTY...
IT'S GOT TO BE HER
THEY SEEM LIKE A GREAT COUPLE
I KNOW WHAT'S GOING ON! THEY BROKE UP, HE SLEPT WITH ME, HE FELT GUILTY ABOUT IT, STARTED MISSING HER AND WANTS HER BACK. THAT'S IT.
I FELT SO BAD, SO AFRAID, EMPTY AND STRANGE. I FELT LIKE GETTING DRUNK.
TO CALM MYSELF DOWN, I WALKED SEVERAL TIMES AROUND THE BLOCK.
Spångatan
32-40

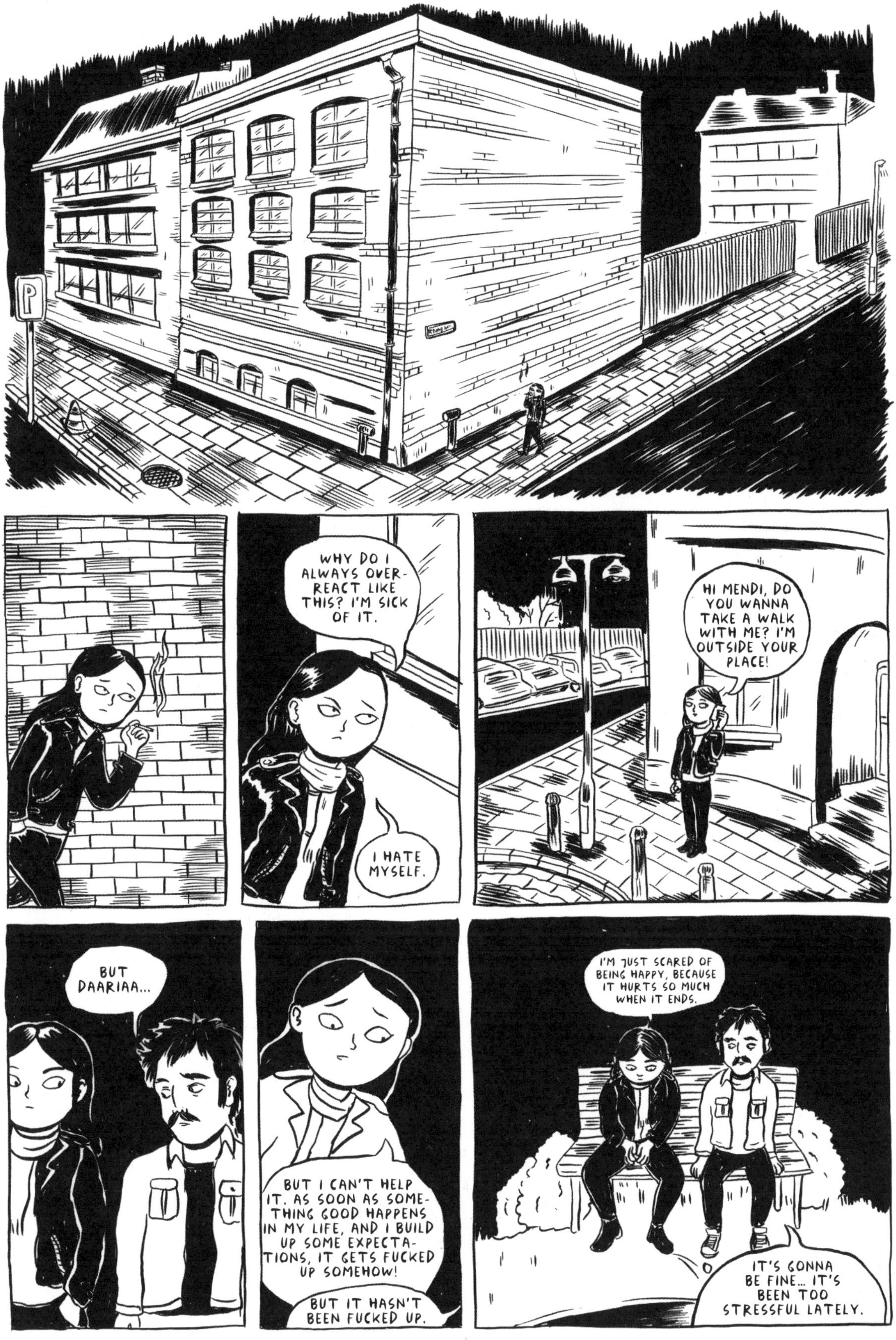
WHY DO I ALWAYS OVER-REACT LIKE THIS? I'M SICK OF IT.
I HATE MYSELF.
HI MENDI, DO YOU WANNA TAKE A WALK WITH ME? I'M OUTSIDE YOUR PLACE!
BUT DAARIAA...
BUT I CAN'T HELP IT. AS SOON AS SOME-THING GOOD HAPPENS IN MY LIFE, AND I BUILD UP SOME EXPECTA-TIONS, IT GETS FUCKED UP SOMEHOW!
BUT IT HASN'T BEEN FUCKED UP.
I'M JUST SCARED OF BEING HAPPY, BECAUSE IT HURTS SO MUCH WHEN IT ENDS.
IT'S GONNA BE FINE... IT'S BEEN TOO STRESSFUL LATELY.

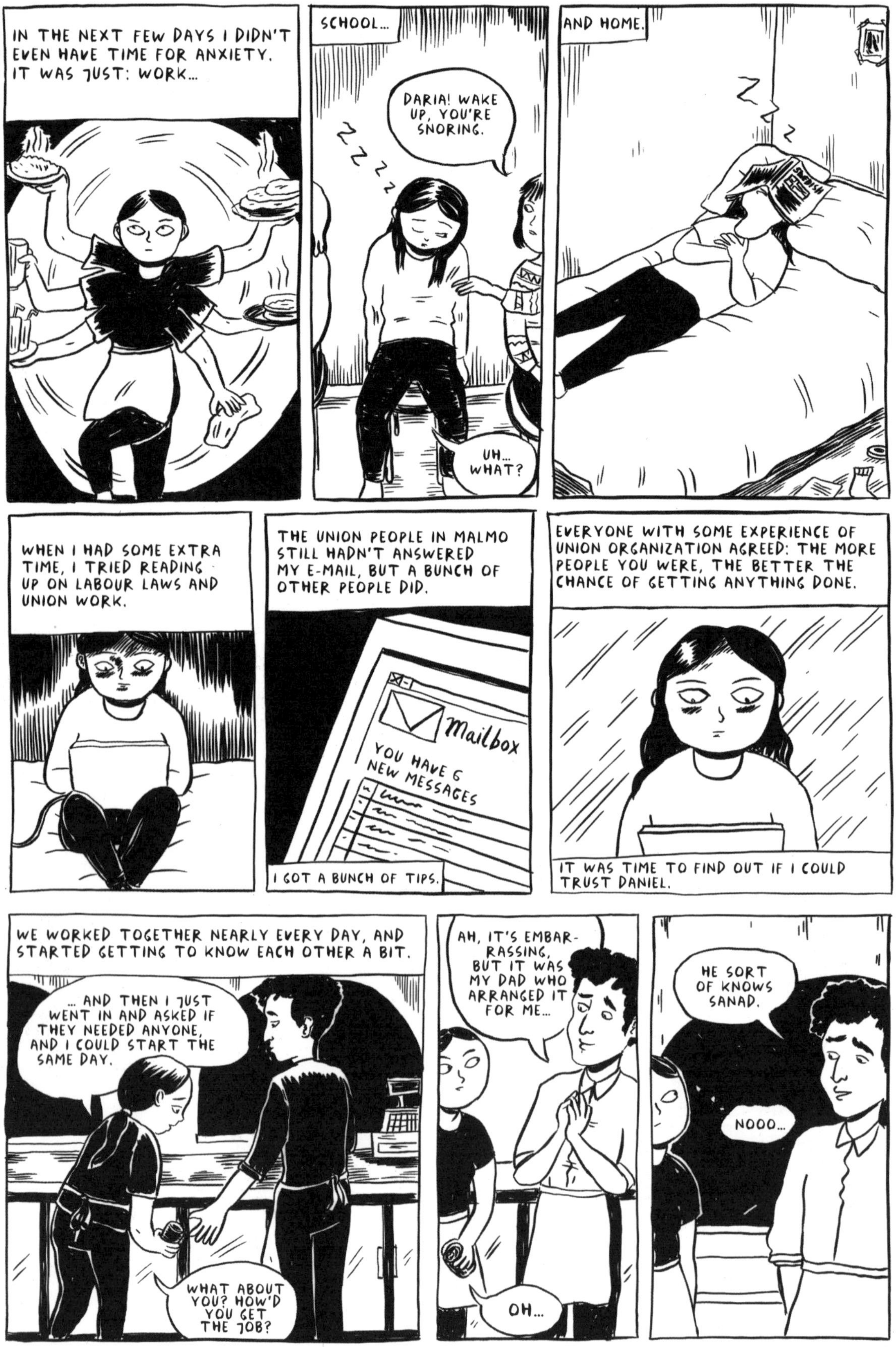
IN THE NEXT FEW DAYS I DIDN'T EVEN HAVE TIME FOR ANXIETY. IT WAS JUST: WORK...
SCHOOL...
DARIA! WAKE UP, YOU'RE SNORING.
UH... WHAT?
AND HOME.
WHEN I HAD SOME EXTRA TIME, I TRIED READING UP ON LABOUR LAWS AND UNION WORK.
THE UNION PEOPLE IN MALMO STILL HADN'T ANSWERED MY E-MAIL, BUT A BUNCH OF OTHER PEOPLE DID.
Mailbox
YOU HAVE 6 NEW MESSAGES
I GOT A BUNCH OF TIPS.
EVERYONE WITH SOME EXPERIENCE OF UNION ORGANIZATION AGREED: THE MORE PEOPLE YOU WERE, THE BETTER THE CHANCE OF GETTING ANYTHING DONE.
IT WAS TIME TO FIND OUT IF I COULD TRUST DANIEL.
WE WORKED TOGETHER NEARLY EVERY DAY, AND STARTED GETTING TO KNOW EACH OTHER A BIT.
... AND THEN I JUST WENT IN AND ASKED IF THEY NEEDED ANYONE, AND I COULD START THE SAME DAY.
WHAT ABOUT YOU? HOW'D YOU GET THE JOB?
AH, IT'S EMBARRASSING, BUT IT WAS MY DAD WHO ARRANGED IT FOR ME...
OH...
HE SORT OF KNOWS SANAD.
NOOO...

LIKE... NOT REALLY, BUT MY DAD ALWAYS COMES HERE AND THEY ALWAYS TALK.

!!!

DAD THOUGHT IT WAS TIME FOR ME TO GET A JOB AND MOVE OUT, SO HE ASKED IF THEY NEEDED ANYONE HERE.

SO IT WAS LIKE I HAD HOPED! DANIEL DIDN'T HAVE A REAL CONNECTION WITH SANAD. IT WAS NOW OR NEVER.

BYE EVERY-ONE!

Curry Hut   Curry Hut

HEY, DANIEL! WAIT!

WHERE ARE YOU HEADED?

NOBELVAGEN, YOU?

ME TOO. I'LL WALK WITH YOU.

I WANT TO TALK TO YOU ABOUT SOME-THING.

OH, OK.

Häng Bar

WAIT, I DON'T WANT TO PASS BY HANG BAR, CAN WE TAKE THE NEXT STREET?

...THERE'S THIS THING I'VE BEEN WANTING TO TALK TO YOU ABOUT. MAY I BE DIRECT AND ASK YOU SOMETHING?

I HOPE HE DOESN'T THINK I'M COMING ON TO HIM

UM... OKAY...

HOW MUCH DO YOU MAKE?

UM... WHY? I ACTUALLY DON'T KNOW EXACTLY. I HAVEN'T BEEN ABLE TO TALK TO SANAD ABOUT IT.

OK, LISTEN, YOU DON'T HAVE A CONTRACT EITHER RIGHT?

NO, WE HAVEN'T REALLY TALKED ABOUT THAT EITHER.

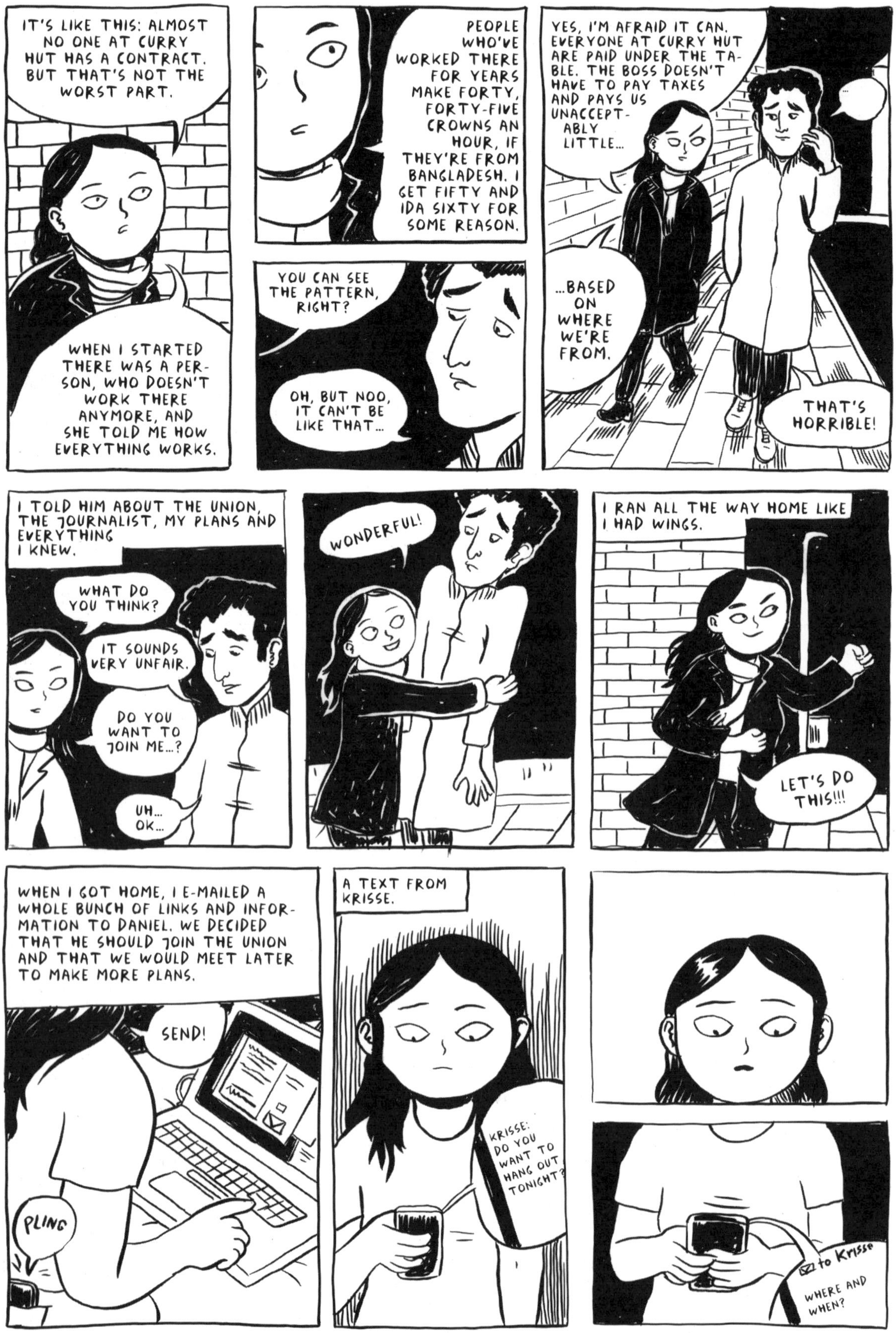
IT'S LIKE THIS: ALMOST NO ONE AT CURRY HUT HAS A CONTRACT. BUT THAT'S NOT THE WORST PART.
WHEN I STARTED THERE WAS A PERSON, WHO DOESN'T WORK THERE ANYMORE, AND SHE TOLD ME HOW EVERYTHING WORKS.
PEOPLE WHO'VE WORKED THERE FOR YEARS MAKE FORTY, FORTY-FIVE CROWNS AN HOUR, IF THEY'RE FROM BANGLADESH. I GET FIFTY AND IDA SIXTY FOR SOME REASON.
YOU CAN SEE THE PATTERN, RIGHT?
OH, BUT NOO, IT CAN'T BE LIKE THAT...
YES, I'M AFRAID IT CAN. EVERYONE AT CURRY HUT ARE PAID UNDER THE TABLE. THE BOSS DOESN'T HAVE TO PAY TAXES AND PAYS US UNACCEPTABLY LITTLE...
...
...BASED ON WHERE WE'RE FROM.
THAT'S HORRIBLE!
I TOLD HIM ABOUT THE UNION, THE JOURNALIST, MY PLANS AND EVERYTHING I KNEW.
WHAT DO YOU THINK?
IT SOUNDS VERY UNFAIR.
DO YOU WANT TO JOIN ME...?
UH... OK...
WONDERFUL!
I RAN ALL THE WAY HOME LIKE I HAD WINGS.
LET'S DO THIS!!!
WHEN I GOT HOME, I E-MAILED A WHOLE BUNCH OF LINKS AND INFORMATION TO DANIEL. WE DECIDED THAT HE SHOULD JOIN THE UNION AND THAT WE WOULD MEET LATER TO MAKE MORE PLANS.
SEND!
PLING
A TEXT FROM KRISSE.
KRISSE: DO YOU WANT TO HANG OUT TONIGHT?
to Krisse
WHERE AND WHEN?

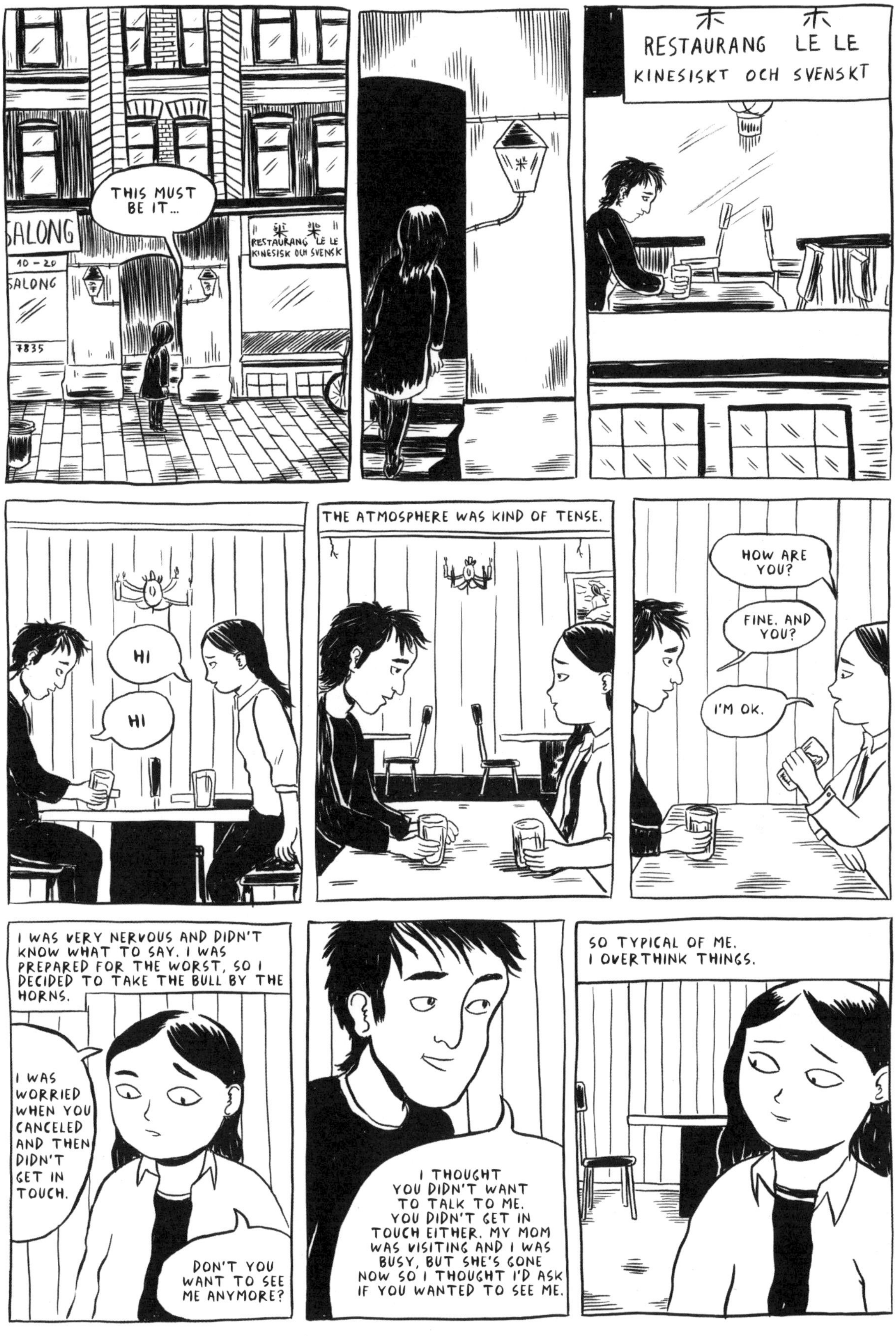
THIS MUST BE IT...
SALONG
10 – 20
SALONG
7835
RESTAURANG LE LE KINESISK OCH SVENSK
RESTAURANG LE LE
KINESISKT OCH SVENSKT
HI
HI
THE ATMOSPHERE WAS KIND OF TENSE.
HOW ARE YOU?
FINE. AND YOU?
I'M OK.
I WAS VERY NERVOUS AND DIDN'T KNOW WHAT TO SAY. I WAS PREPARED FOR THE WORST, SO I DECIDED TO TAKE THE BULL BY THE HORNS.
I WAS WORRIED WHEN YOU CANCELED AND THEN DIDN'T GET IN TOUCH.
DON'T YOU WANT TO SEE ME ANYMORE?
I THOUGHT YOU DIDN'T WANT TO TALK TO ME. YOU DIDN'T GET IN TOUCH EITHER. MY MOM WAS VISITING AND I WAS BUSY, BUT SHE'S GONE NOW SO I THOUGHT I'D ASK IF YOU WANTED TO SEE ME.
SO TYPICAL OF ME. I OVERTHINK THINGS.

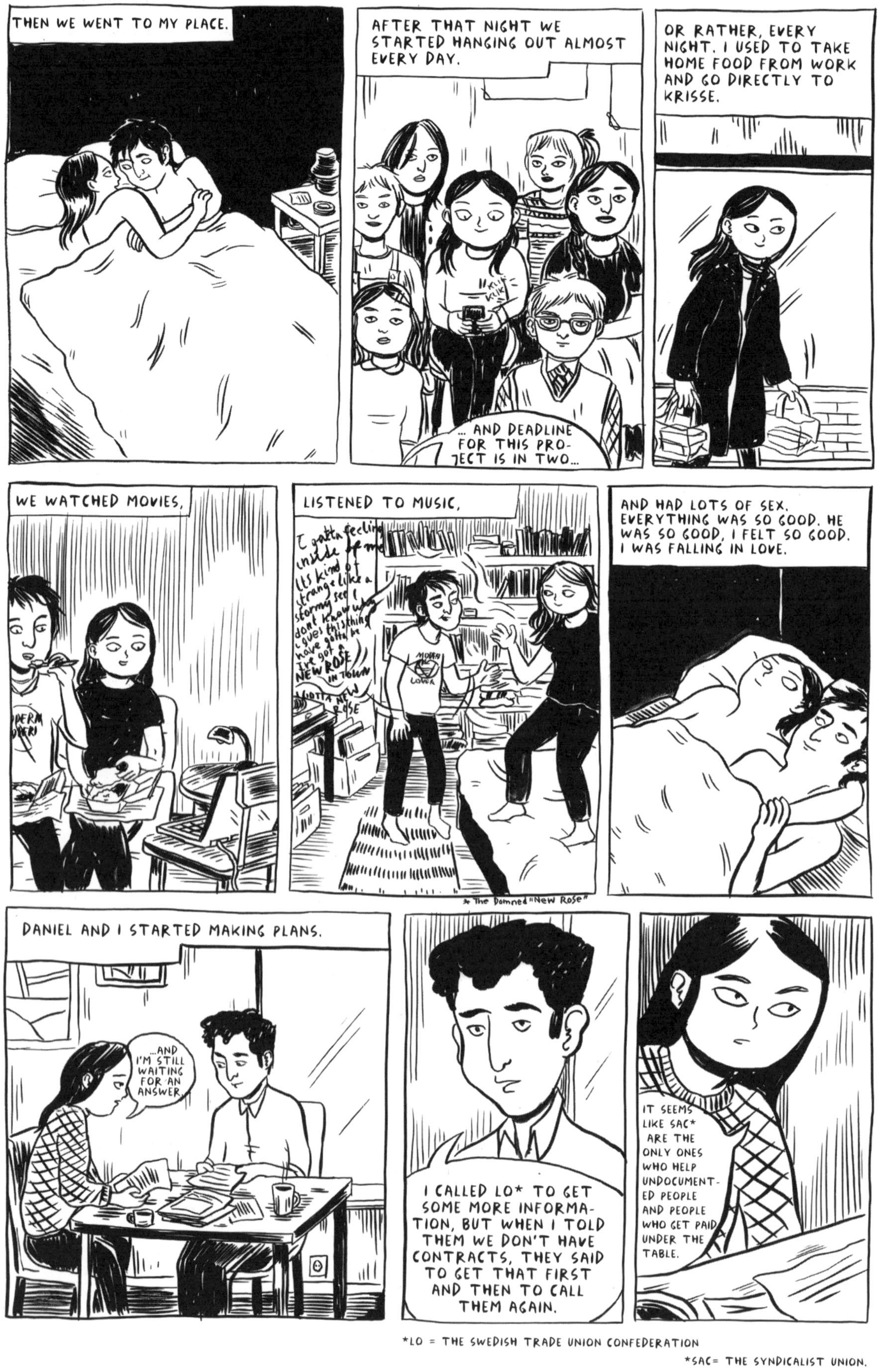
THEN WE WENT TO MY PLACE.
AFTER THAT NIGHT WE STARTED HANGING OUT ALMOST EVERY DAY.
...AND DEADLINE FOR THIS PROJECT IS IN TWO...
OR RATHER, EVERY NIGHT. I USED TO TAKE HOME FOOD FROM WORK AND GO DIRECTLY TO KRISSE.
WE WATCHED MOVIES,
LISTENED TO MUSIC,
NEW ROSE IN TOWN
* The Damned "New Rose"
AND HAD LOTS OF SEX. EVERYTHING WAS SO GOOD. HE WAS SO GOOD, I FELT SO GOOD. I WAS FALLING IN LOVE.
DANIEL AND I STARTED MAKING PLANS.
...AND I'M STILL WAITING FOR AN ANSWER.
I CALLED LO* TO GET SOME MORE INFORMATION, BUT WHEN I TOLD THEM WE DON'T HAVE CONTRACTS, THEY SAID TO GET THAT FIRST AND THEN TO CALL THEM AGAIN.
IT SEEMS LIKE SAC* ARE THE ONLY ONES WHO HELP UNDOCUMENTED PEOPLE AND PEOPLE WHO GET PAID UNDER THE TABLE.

*LO = THE SWEDISH TRADE UNION CONFEDERATION

*SAC= THE SYNDICALIST UNION.

YOU HAVE RIGHTS

YOUR WORKING CONDITIONS ARE NOT SOMETHING VAGUE OR UNCERTAIN. THOSE WHO WANT AND DARE TO CHANGE THINGS CAN DO IT. WE CAN ALL MAKE A DIFFERENCE.

UNION

NO ONE GETS IT BETTER UNLESS EVERYONE DOES.

THE EMPLOYEES ARE ALWAYS OPPOSED TO THE MANAGEMENT. MANAGEMENT WANTS EMPLOYEES TO WORK MORE AND TAKE ON MORE TASKS, BUT INCUR AS FEW COSTS AS POSSIBLE. WE WANT TO CREATE UNITY AMONG EMPLOYEES AND TOGETHER FIGHT THE MANAGEMENT.

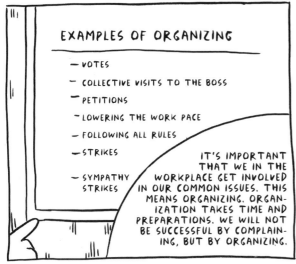

EXAMPLES OF ORGANIZING

- VOTES
- COLLECTIVE VISITS TO THE BOSS
- PETITIONS
- LOWERING THE WORK PACE
- FOLLOWING ALL RULES
- STRIKES
- SYMPATHY STRIKES

IT'S IMPORTANT THAT WE IN THE WORKPLACE GET INVOLVED IN OUR COMMON ISSUES. THIS MEANS ORGANIZING. ORGANIZATION TAKES TIME AND PREPARATIONS. WE WILL NOT BE SUCCESSFUL BY COMPLAINING, BUT BY ORGANIZING.

BOSSES

- MANAGEMENT
- CLOSE LEADERSHIP
- LOYALTY

MANAGEMENT MEANS THE BOSSES' STRATEGIES TO DISRUPT OUR AWARENESS, UNITY AND SOLIDARITY. THE PURPOSE OF MANAGEMENT IS TO MAKE US FEEL EMOTIONAL LOYALTY TO THE BOSS AND THE COMPANY, INSTEAD OF TO OUR COWORKERS.

SOLIDARITY IN THE WORKPLACE

- HAVE YOUR COWORKERS BACKS
- SOLVE INTERNAL CONFLICTS WITHOUT INVOLVING MANAGEMENT
- DIVIDE YOUR WORKLOAD EQUALLY
- DON'T BE FRIENDS WITH THE BOSS OR TALK DEROGATORILY ABOUT YOUR COWORKERS.

YOU CAN STRENGTHEN THE GROUP'S SOLIDARITY BY TALKING ABOUT WHAT BEHAVIOURS ARE GOOD FOR THE GROUP. YOU CAN ALSO ACT WITH SOLIDARITY AND ENCOURAGE OTHERS TO DO THE SAME.

I SAT THERE LISTENING AND THOUGHT IT ALL SOUNDED SO SERIOUS. LIKE THE WORD "ORGANIZING". IN FACT, IT WAS SOMETHING I'D BEEN DOING IN ALL THE PLACES I'D WORKED.

BUT IT ALWAYS ENDED THE SAME WAY.

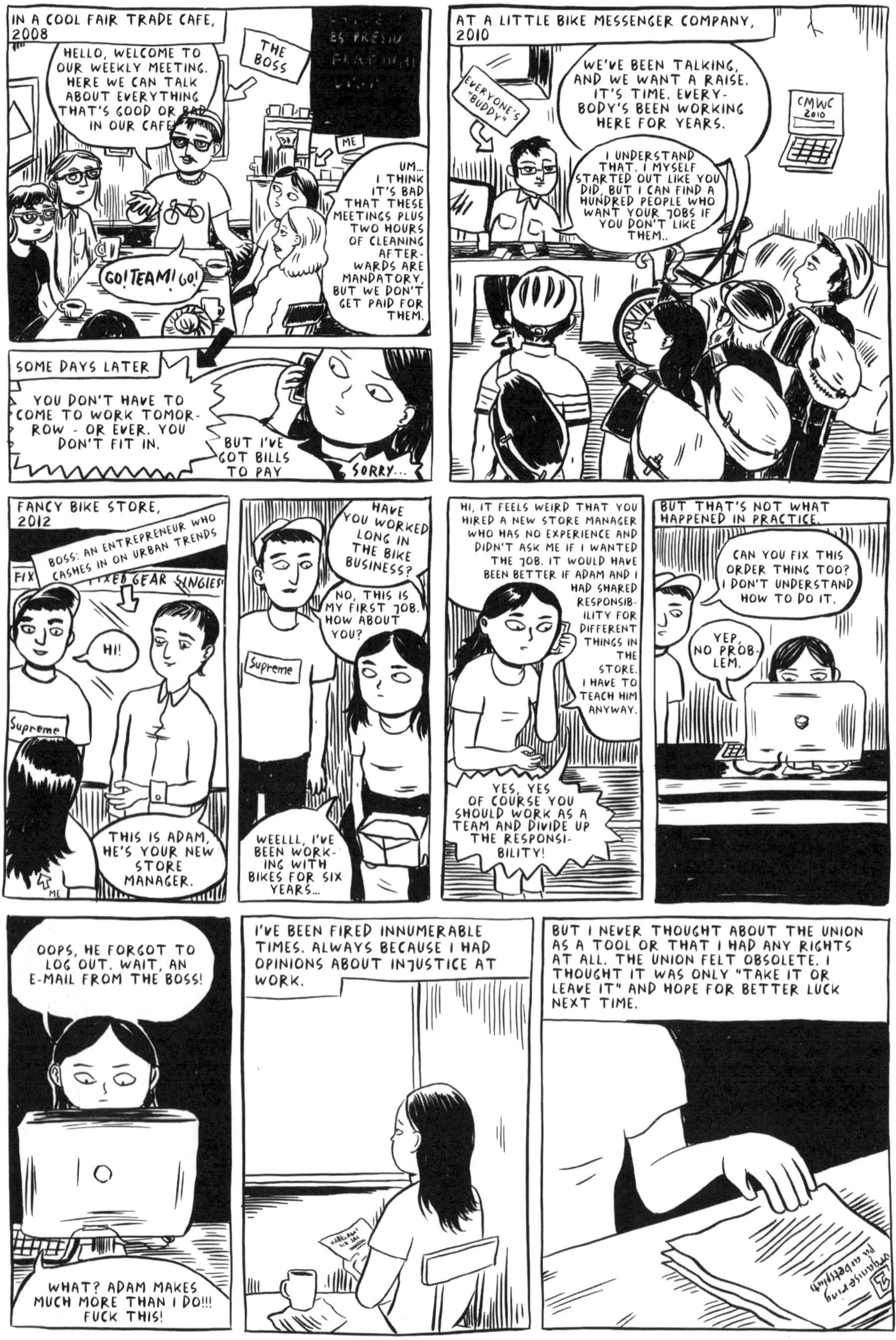

IN A COOL FAIR TRADE CAFE, 2008
HELLO, WELCOME TO OUR WEEKLY MEETING. HERE WE CAN TALK ABOUT EVERYTHING THAT'S GOOD OR BAD IN OUR CAFE.
THE BOSS
ME
UM... I THINK IT'S BAD THAT THESE MEETINGS PLUS TWO HOURS OF CLEANING AFTER-WARDS ARE MANDATORY, BUT WE DON'T GET PAID FOR THEM.
GO! TEAM! GO!
SOME DAYS LATER
YOU DON'T HAVE TO COME TO WORK TOMOR-ROW - OR EVER. YOU DON'T FIT IN.
BUT I'VE GOT BILLS TO PAY
SORRY...
AT A LITTLE BIKE MESSENGER COMPANY, 2010
EVERYONE'S "BUDDY"
WE'VE BEEN TALKING, AND WE WANT A RAISE. IT'S TIME. EVERY-BODY'S BEEN WORKING HERE FOR YEARS.
CMWC 2010
I UNDERSTAND THAT. I MYSELF STARTED OUT LIKE YOU DID, BUT I CAN FIND A HUNDRED PEOPLE WHO WANT YOUR JOBS IF YOU DON'T LIKE THEM..
FANCY BIKE STORE, 2012
BOSS: AN ENTREPRENEUR WHO CASHES IN ON URBAN TRENDS
FIX
FIXED GEAR SINGLES!
HI!
Supreme
THIS IS ADAM, HE'S YOUR NEW STORE MANAGER.
ME
HAVE YOU WORKED LONG IN THE BIKE BUSINESS?
NO, THIS IS MY FIRST JOB. HOW ABOUT YOU?
Supreme
WEELLL, I'VE BEEN WORK-ING WITH BIKES FOR SIX YEARS...
HI, IT FEELS WEIRD THAT YOU HIRED A NEW STORE MANAGER WHO HAS NO EXPERIENCE AND DIDN'T ASK ME IF I WANTED THE JOB. IT WOULD HAVE BEEN BETTER IF ADAM AND I HAD SHARED RESPONSIB-ILITY FOR DIFFERENT THINGS IN THE STORE. I HAVE TO TEACH HIM ANYWAY.
YES, YES OF COURSE YOU SHOULD WORK AS A TEAM AND DIVIDE UP THE RESPONSI-BILITY!
BUT THAT'S NOT WHAT HAPPENED IN PRACTICE.
CAN YOU FIX THIS ORDER THING TOO? I DON'T UNDERSTAND HOW TO DO IT.
YEP, NO PROB-LEM.
OOPS, HE FORGOT TO LOG OUT. WAIT, AN E-MAIL FROM THE BOSS!
WHAT? ADAM MAKES MUCH MORE THAN I DO!!! FUCK THIS!
I'VE BEEN FIRED INNUMERABLE TIMES. ALWAYS BECAUSE I HAD OPINIONS ABOUT INJUSTICE AT WORK.
BUT I NEVER THOUGHT ABOUT THE UNION AS A TOOL OR THAT I HAD ANY RIGHTS AT ALL. THE UNION FELT OBSOLETE. I THOUGHT IT WAS ONLY "TAKE IT OR LEAVE IT" AND HOPE FOR BETTER LUCK NEXT TIME.

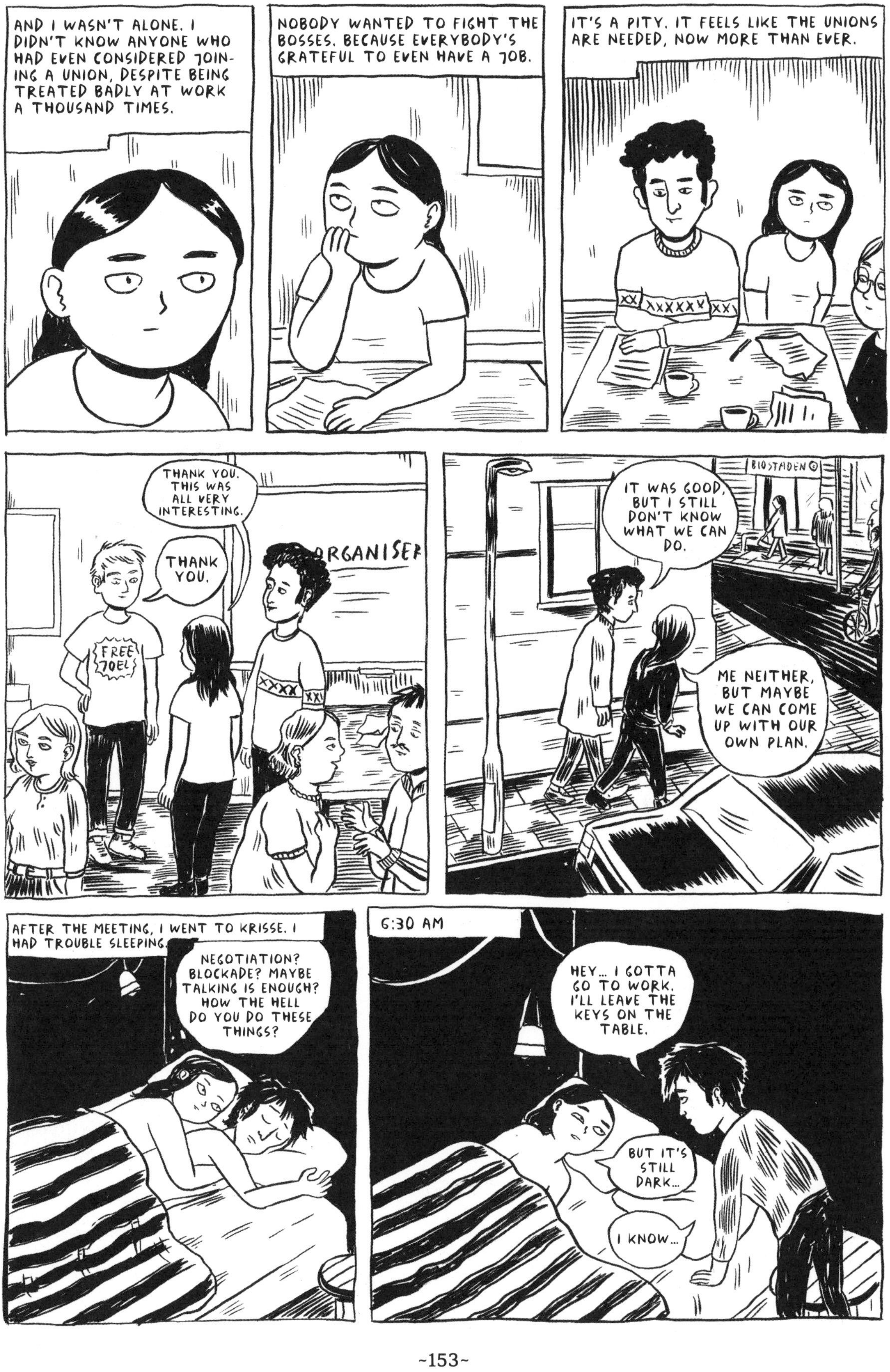
AND I WASN'T ALONE. I DIDN'T KNOW ANYONE WHO HAD EVEN CONSIDERED JOINING A UNION, DESPITE BEING TREATED BADLY AT WORK A THOUSAND TIMES.
NOBODY WANTED TO FIGHT THE BOSSES. BECAUSE EVERYBODY'S GRATEFUL TO EVEN HAVE A JOB.
IT'S A PITY. IT FEELS LIKE THE UNIONS ARE NEEDED, NOW MORE THAN EVER.
THANK YOU. THIS WAS ALL VERY INTERESTING.
THANK YOU.
FREE JOEL
ORGANISER
BIOSTADEN
IT WAS GOOD, BUT I STILL DON'T KNOW WHAT WE CAN DO.
ME NEITHER, BUT MAYBE WE CAN COME UP WITH OUR OWN PLAN.
AFTER THE MEETING, I WENT TO KRISSE. I HAD TROUBLE SLEEPING.
NEGOTIATION? BLOCKADE? MAYBE TALKING IS ENOUGH? HOW THE HELL DO YOU DO THESE THINGS?
6:30 AM
HEY... I GOTTA GO TO WORK. I'LL LEAVE THE KEYS ON THE TABLE.
BUT IT'S STILL DARK...
I KNOW...

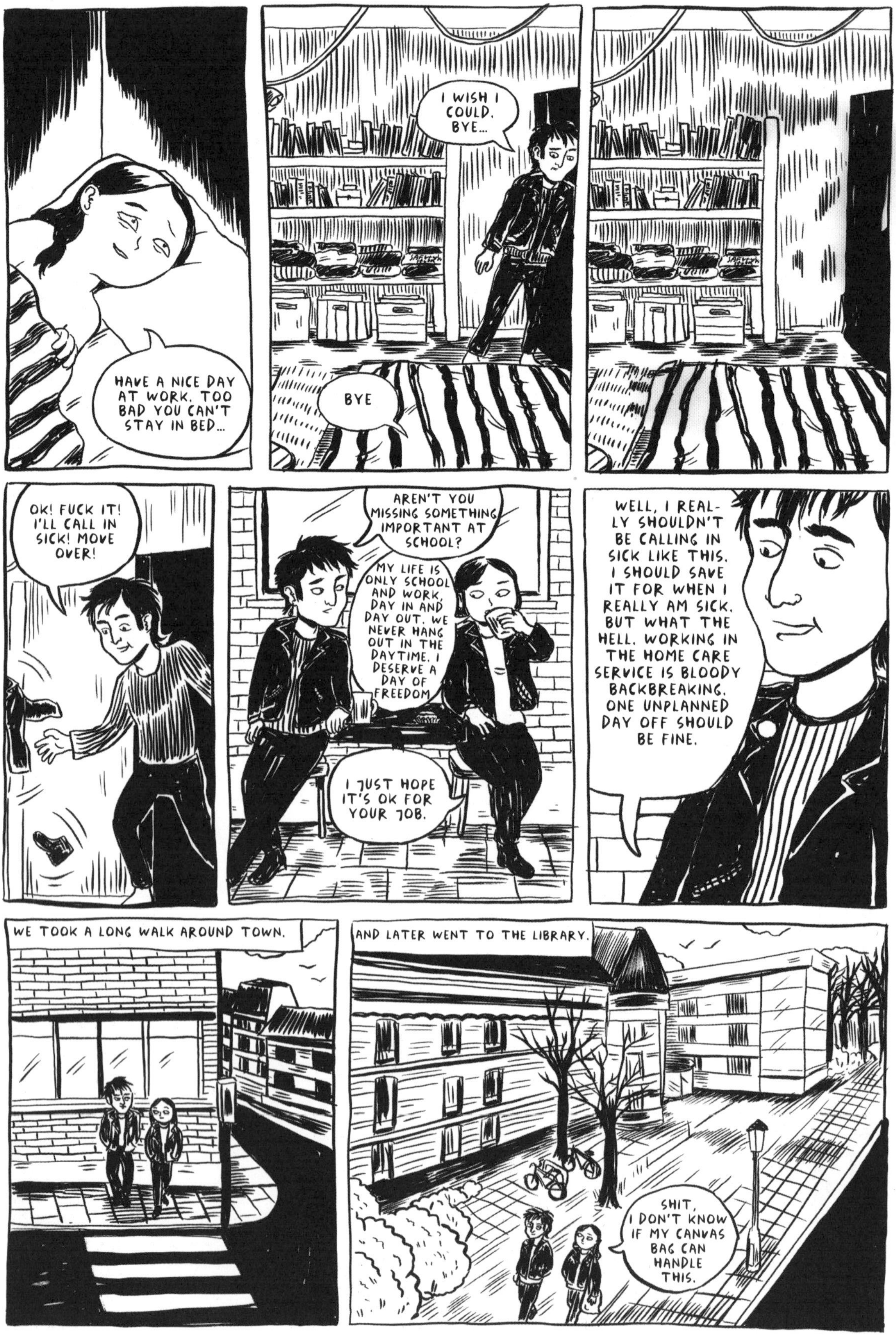
HAVE A NICE DAY AT WORK. TOO BAD YOU CAN'T STAY IN BED...
I WISH I COULD. BYE...
BYE
OK! FUCK IT! I'LL CALL IN SICK! MOVE OVER!
AREN'T YOU MISSING SOMETHING IMPORTANT AT SCHOOL?
MY LIFE IS ONLY SCHOOL AND WORK, DAY IN AND DAY OUT. WE NEVER HANG OUT IN THE DAYTIME. I DESERVE A DAY OF FREEDOM
I JUST HOPE IT'S OK FOR YOUR JOB.
WELL, I REALLY SHOULDN'T BE CALLING IN SICK LIKE THIS. I SHOULD SAVE IT FOR WHEN I REALLY AM SICK. BUT WHAT THE HELL. WORKING IN THE HOME CARE SERVICE IS BLOODY BACKBREAKING. ONE UNPLANNED DAY OFF SHOULD BE FINE.
WE TOOK A LONG WALK AROUND TOWN.
AND LATER WENT TO THE LIBRARY.
SHIT, I DON'T KNOW IF MY CANVAS BAG CAN HANDLE THIS.

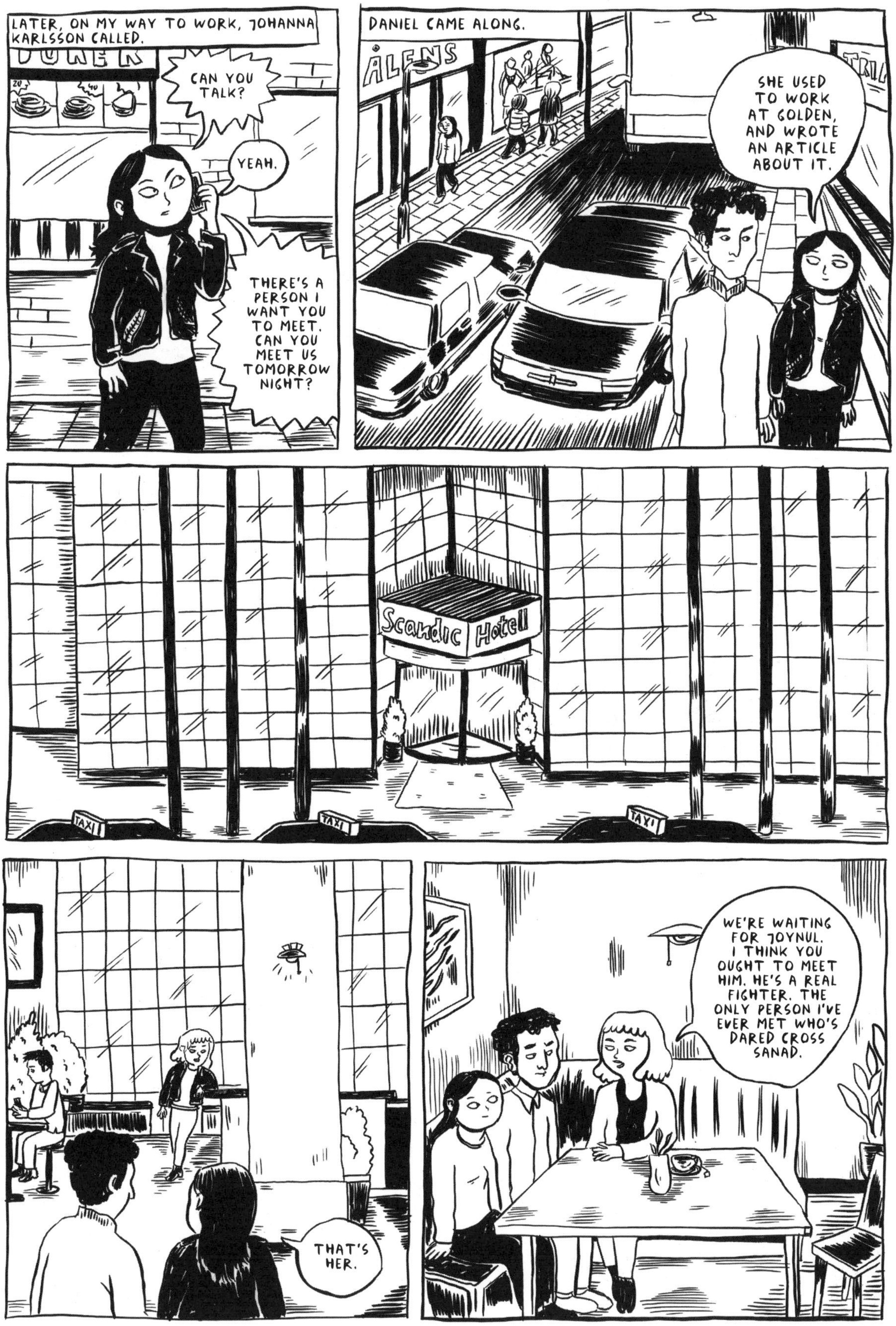
LATER, ON MY WAY TO WORK, JOHANNA KARLSSON CALLED.
DÖNER
CAN YOU TALK?
YEAH.
THERE'S A PERSON I WANT YOU TO MEET. CAN YOU MEET US TOMORROW NIGHT?
DANIEL CAME ALONG.
ÅLENS
SHE USED TO WORK AT GOLDEN, AND WROTE AN ARTICLE ABOUT IT.
Scandic Hotell
TAXI
TAXI
TAXI
THAT'S HER.
WE'RE WAITING FOR JOYNUL. I THINK YOU OUGHT TO MEET HIM. HE'S A REAL FIGHTER. THE ONLY PERSON I'VE EVER MET WHO'S DARED CROSS SANAD.

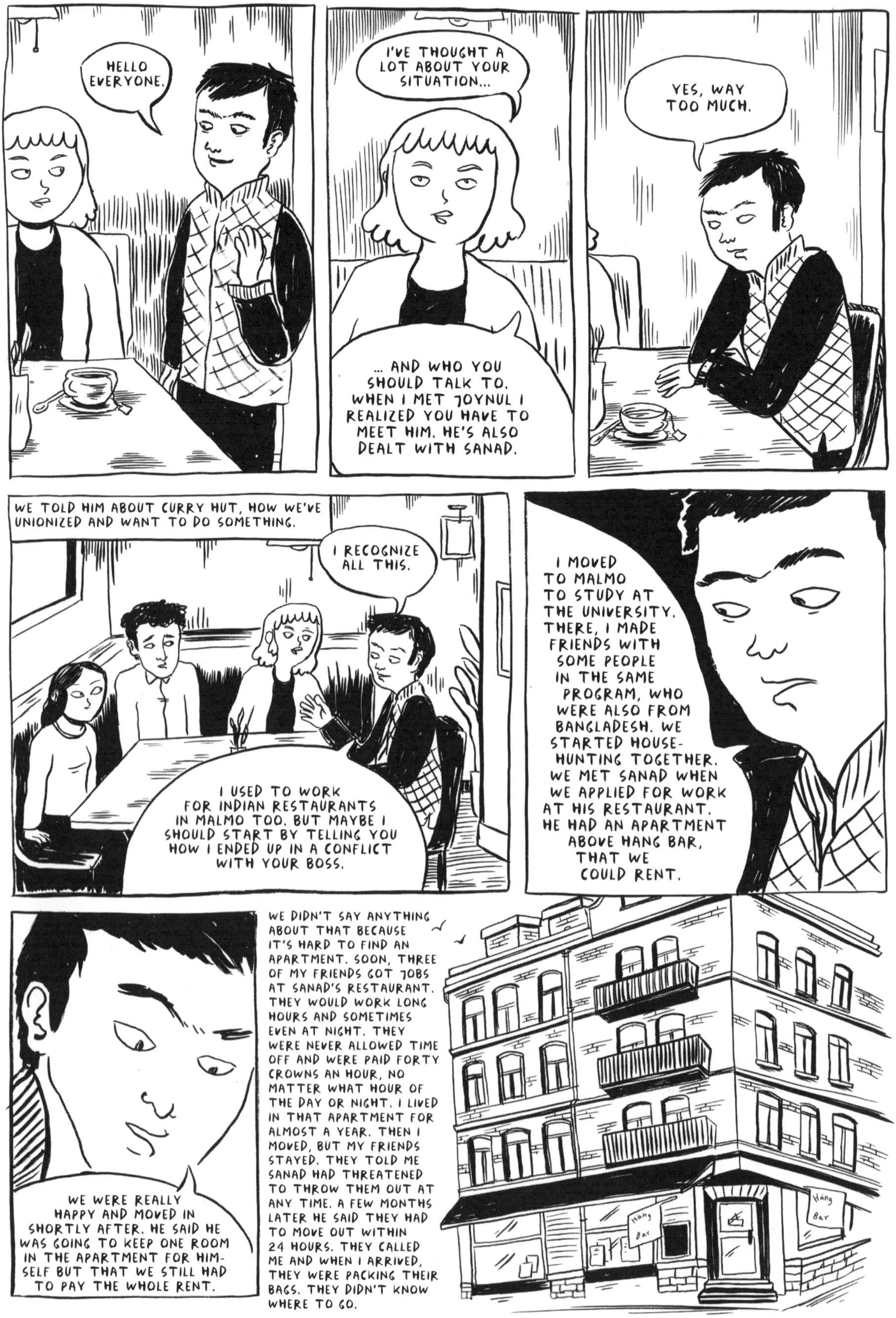
HELLO EVERYONE.
I'VE THOUGHT A LOT ABOUT YOUR SITUATION...
... AND WHO YOU SHOULD TALK TO. WHEN I MET JOYNUL I REALIZED YOU HAVE TO MEET HIM. HE'S ALSO DEALT WITH SANAD.
YES, WAY TOO MUCH.
WE TOLD HIM ABOUT CURRY HUT, HOW WE'VE UNIONIZED AND WANT TO DO SOMETHING.
I RECOGNIZE ALL THIS.
I USED TO WORK FOR INDIAN RESTAURANTS IN MALMO TOO. BUT MAYBE I SHOULD START BY TELLING YOU HOW I ENDED UP IN A CONFLICT WITH YOUR BOSS.
I MOVED TO MALMO TO STUDY AT THE UNIVERSITY. THERE, I MADE FRIENDS WITH SOME PEOPLE IN THE SAME PROGRAM, WHO WERE ALSO FROM BANGLADESH. WE STARTED HOUSE-HUNTING TOGETHER. WE MET SANAD WHEN WE APPLIED FOR WORK AT HIS RESTAURANT. HE HAD AN APARTMENT ABOVE HANG BAR, THAT WE COULD RENT.
WE WERE REALLY HAPPY AND MOVED IN SHORTLY AFTER. HE SAID HE WAS GOING TO KEEP ONE ROOM IN THE APARTMENT FOR HIM-SELF BUT THAT WE STILL HAD TO PAY THE WHOLE RENT.
WE DIDN'T SAY ANYTHING ABOUT THAT BECAUSE IT'S HARD TO FIND AN APARTMENT. SOON, THREE OF MY FRIENDS GOT JOBS AT SANAD'S RESTAURANT. THEY WOULD WORK LONG HOURS AND SOMETIMES EVEN AT NIGHT. THEY WERE NEVER ALLOWED TIME OFF AND WERE PAID FORTY CROWNS AN HOUR, NO MATTER WHAT HOUR OF THE DAY OR NIGHT. I LIVED IN THAT APARTMENT FOR ALMOST A YEAR. THEN I MOVED, BUT MY FRIENDS STAYED. THEY TOLD ME SANAD HAD THREATENED TO THROW THEM OUT AT ANY TIME. A FEW MONTHS LATER HE SAID THEY HAD TO MOVE OUT WITHIN 24 HOURS. THEY CALLED ME AND WHEN I ARRIVED, THEY WERE PACKING THEIR BAGS. THEY DIDN'T KNOW WHERE TO GO.
Hang Bar
Hang Bar

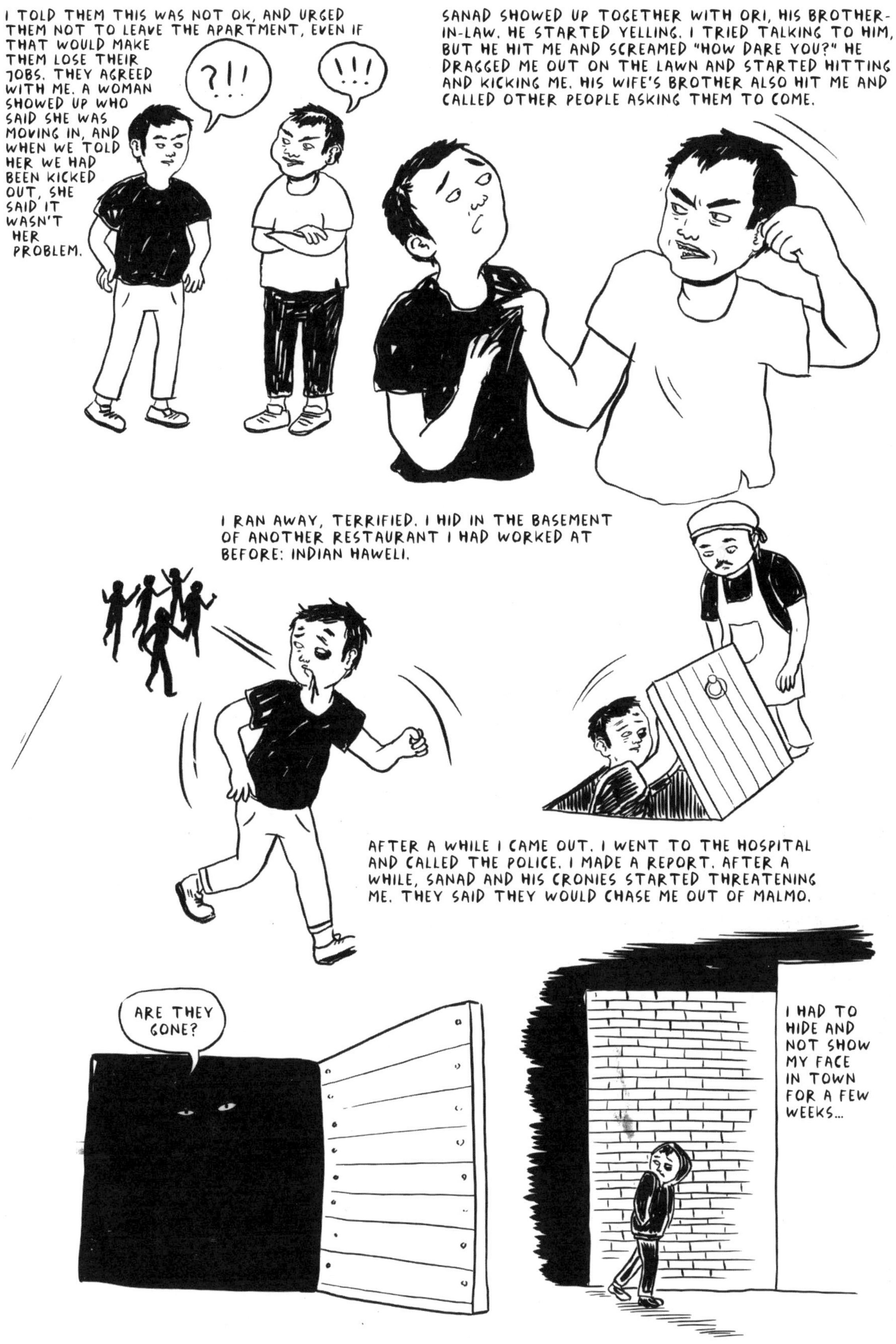
I TOLD THEM THIS WAS NOT OK, AND URGED THEM NOT TO LEAVE THE APARTMENT, EVEN IF THAT WOULD MAKE THEM LOSE THEIR JOBS. THEY AGREED WITH ME. A WOMAN SHOWED UP WHO SAID SHE WAS MOVING IN, AND WHEN WE TOLD HER WE HAD BEEN KICKED OUT, SHE SAID IT WASN'T HER PROBLEM.
?!!
!!!
SANAD SHOWED UP TOGETHER WITH ORI, HIS BROTHER-IN-LAW. HE STARTED YELLING. I TRIED TALKING TO HIM, BUT HE HIT ME AND SCREAMED "HOW DARE YOU?" HE DRAGGED ME OUT ON THE LAWN AND STARTED HITTING AND KICKING ME. HIS WIFE'S BROTHER ALSO HIT ME AND CALLED OTHER PEOPLE ASKING THEM TO COME.
I RAN AWAY, TERRIFIED. I HID IN THE BASEMENT OF ANOTHER RESTAURANT I HAD WORKED AT BEFORE: INDIAN HAWELI.
AFTER A WHILE I CAME OUT. I WENT TO THE HOSPITAL AND CALLED THE POLICE. I MADE A REPORT. AFTER A WHILE, SANAD AND HIS CRONIES STARTED THREATENING ME. THEY SAID THEY WOULD CHASE ME OUT OF MALMO.
ARE THEY GONE?
I HAD TO HIDE AND NOT SHOW MY FACE IN TOWN FOR A FEW WEEKS...

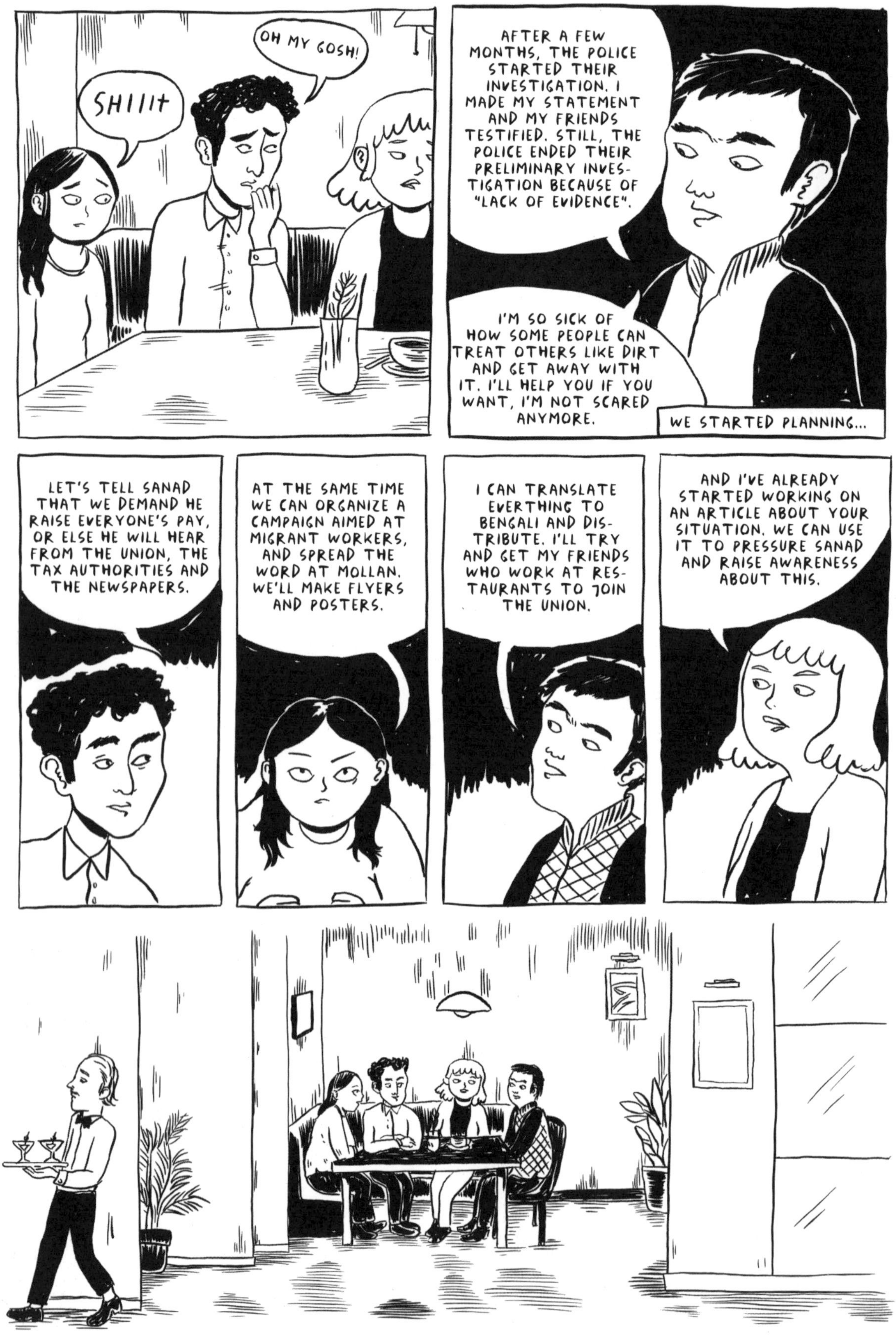
SHIIIt
OH MY GOSH!
AFTER A FEW MONTHS, THE POLICE STARTED THEIR INVESTIGATION. I MADE MY STATEMENT AND MY FRIENDS TESTIFIED. STILL, THE POLICE ENDED THEIR PRELIMINARY INVESTIGATION BECAUSE OF "LACK OF EVIDENCE".
I'M SO SICK OF HOW SOME PEOPLE CAN TREAT OTHERS LIKE DIRT AND GET AWAY WITH IT. I'LL HELP YOU IF YOU WANT, I'M NOT SCARED ANYMORE.
WE STARTED PLANNING...
LET'S TELL SANAD THAT WE DEMAND HE RAISE EVERYONE'S PAY, OR ELSE HE WILL HEAR FROM THE UNION, THE TAX AUTHORITIES AND THE NEWSPAPERS.
AT THE SAME TIME WE CAN ORGANIZE A CAMPAIGN AIMED AT MIGRANT WORKERS, AND SPREAD THE WORD AT MOLLAN. WE'LL MAKE FLYERS AND POSTERS.
I CAN TRANSLATE EVERTHING TO BENGALI AND DISTRIBUTE. I'LL TRY AND GET MY FRIENDS WHO WORK AT RESTAURANTS TO JOIN THE UNION.
AND I'VE ALREADY STARTED WORKING ON AN ARTICLE ABOUT YOUR SITUATION. WE CAN USE IT TO PRESSURE SANAD AND RAISE AWARENESS ABOUT THIS.

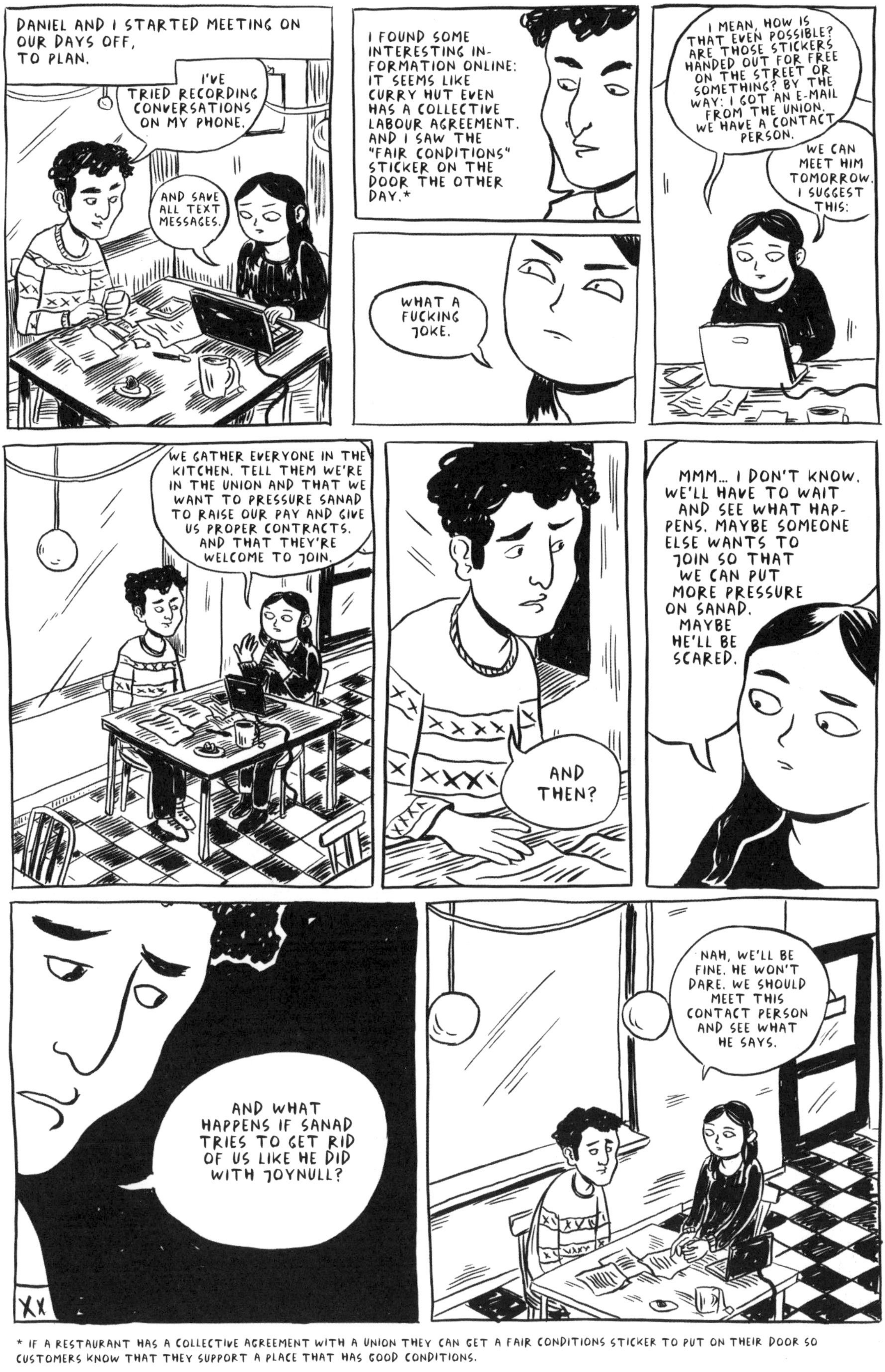
DANIEL AND I STARTED MEETING ON OUR DAYS OFF, TO PLAN.
I'VE TRIED RECORDING CONVERSATIONS ON MY PHONE.
AND SAVE ALL TEXT MESSAGES.
I FOUND SOME INTERESTING INFORMATION ONLINE: IT SEEMS LIKE CURRY HUT EVEN HAS A COLLECTIVE LABOUR AGREEMENT. AND I SAW THE "FAIR CONDITIONS" STICKER ON THE DOOR THE OTHER DAY.*
WHAT A FUCKING JOKE.
I MEAN, HOW IS THAT EVEN POSSIBLE? ARE THOSE STICKERS HANDED OUT FOR FREE ON THE STREET OR SOMETHING? BY THE WAY: I GOT AN E-MAIL FROM THE UNION. WE HAVE A CONTACT PERSON.
WE CAN MEET HIM TOMORROW. I SUGGEST THIS:
WE GATHER EVERYONE IN THE KITCHEN. TELL THEM WE'RE IN THE UNION AND THAT WE WANT TO PRESSURE SANAD TO RAISE OUR PAY AND GIVE US PROPER CONTRACTS. AND THAT THEY'RE WELCOME TO JOIN.
AND THEN?
MMM... I DON'T KNOW. WE'LL HAVE TO WAIT AND SEE WHAT HAPPENS. MAYBE SOMEONE ELSE WANTS TO JOIN SO THAT WE CAN PUT MORE PRESSURE ON SANAD. MAYBE HE'LL BE SCARED.
AND WHAT HAPPENS IF SANAD TRIES TO GET RID OF US LIKE HE DID WITH JOYNULL?
NAH, WE'LL BE FINE. HE WON'T DARE. WE SHOULD MEET THIS CONTACT PERSON AND SEE WHAT HE SAYS.

* IF A RESTAURANT HAS A COLLECTIVE AGREEMENT WITH A UNION THEY CAN GET A FAIR CONDITIONS STICKER TO PUT ON THEIR DOOR SO CUSTOMERS KNOW THAT THEY SUPPORT A PLACE THAT HAS GOOD CONDITIONS.

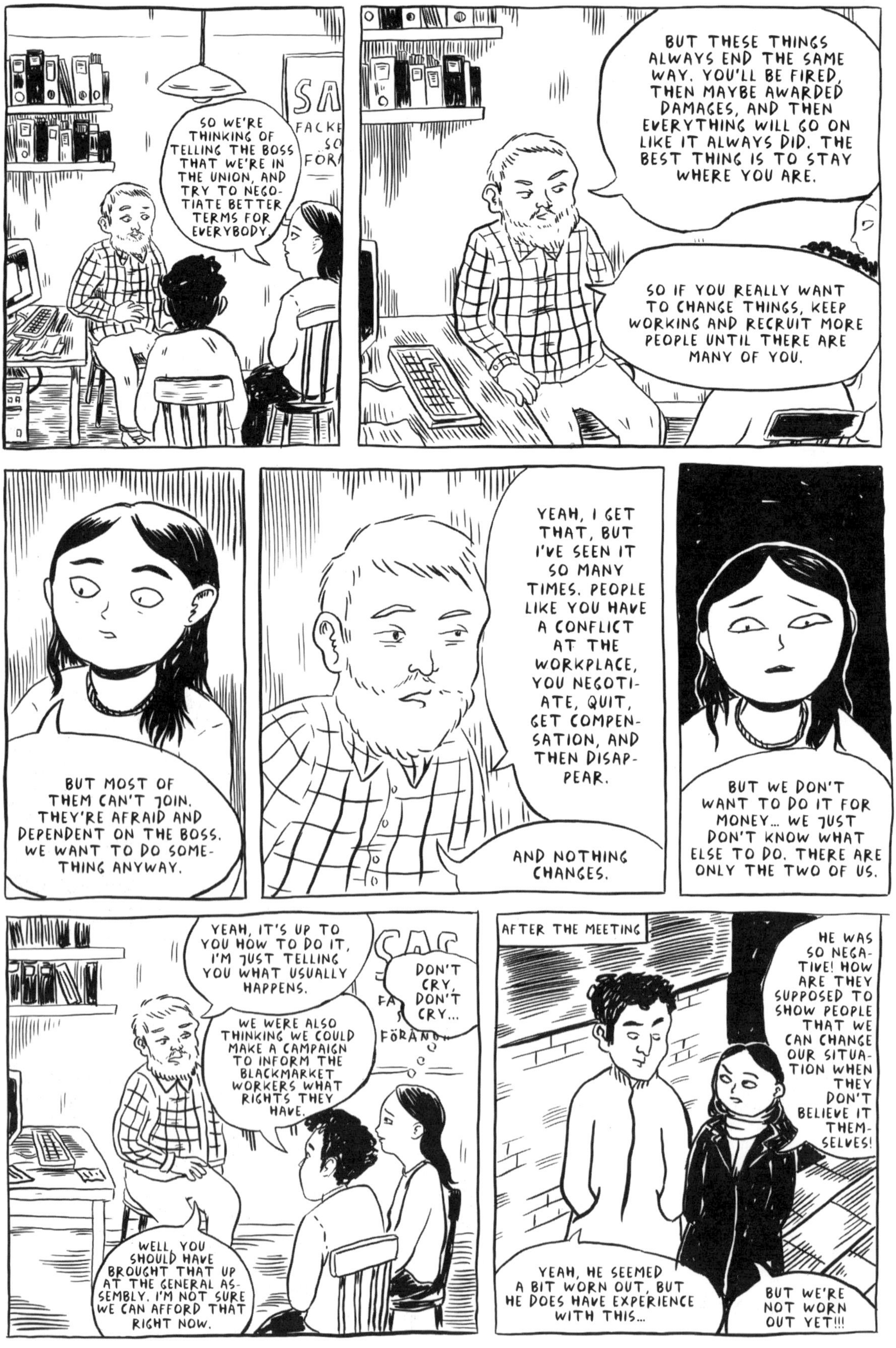

SO WE'RE THINKING OF TELLING THE BOSS THAT WE'RE IN THE UNION, AND TRY TO NEGOTIATE BETTER TERMS FOR EVERYBODY.
BUT THESE THINGS ALWAYS END THE SAME WAY. YOU'LL BE FIRED, THEN MAYBE AWARDED DAMAGES, AND THEN EVERYTHING WILL GO ON LIKE IT ALWAYS DID. THE BEST THING IS TO STAY WHERE YOU ARE.
SO IF YOU REALLY WANT TO CHANGE THINGS, KEEP WORKING AND RECRUIT MORE PEOPLE UNTIL THERE ARE MANY OF YOU.
BUT MOST OF THEM CAN'T JOIN. THEY'RE AFRAID AND DEPENDENT ON THE BOSS. WE WANT TO DO SOMETHING ANYWAY.
YEAH, I GET THAT, BUT I'VE SEEN IT SO MANY TIMES. PEOPLE LIKE YOU HAVE A CONFLICT AT THE WORKPLACE, YOU NEGOTIATE, QUIT, GET COMPENSATION, AND THEN DISAPPEAR.
AND NOTHING CHANGES.
BUT WE DON'T WANT TO DO IT FOR MONEY... WE JUST DON'T KNOW WHAT ELSE TO DO. THERE ARE ONLY THE TWO OF US.
YEAH, IT'S UP TO YOU HOW TO DO IT, I'M JUST TELLING YOU WHAT USUALLY HAPPENS.
DON'T CRY, DON'T CRY...
WE WERE ALSO THINKING WE COULD MAKE A CAMPAIGN TO INFORM THE BLACKMARKET WORKERS WHAT RIGHTS THEY HAVE.
WELL, YOU SHOULD HAVE BROUGHT THAT UP AT THE GENERAL ASSEMBLY. I'M NOT SURE WE CAN AFFORD THAT RIGHT NOW.
AFTER THE MEETING
HE WAS SO NEGATIVE! HOW ARE THEY SUPPOSED TO SHOW PEOPLE THAT WE CAN CHANGE OUR SITUATION WHEN THEY DON'T BELIEVE IT THEMSELVES!
YEAH, HE SEEMED A BIT WORN OUT, BUT HE DOES HAVE EXPERIENCE WITH THIS...
BUT WE'RE NOT WORN OUT YET!!!

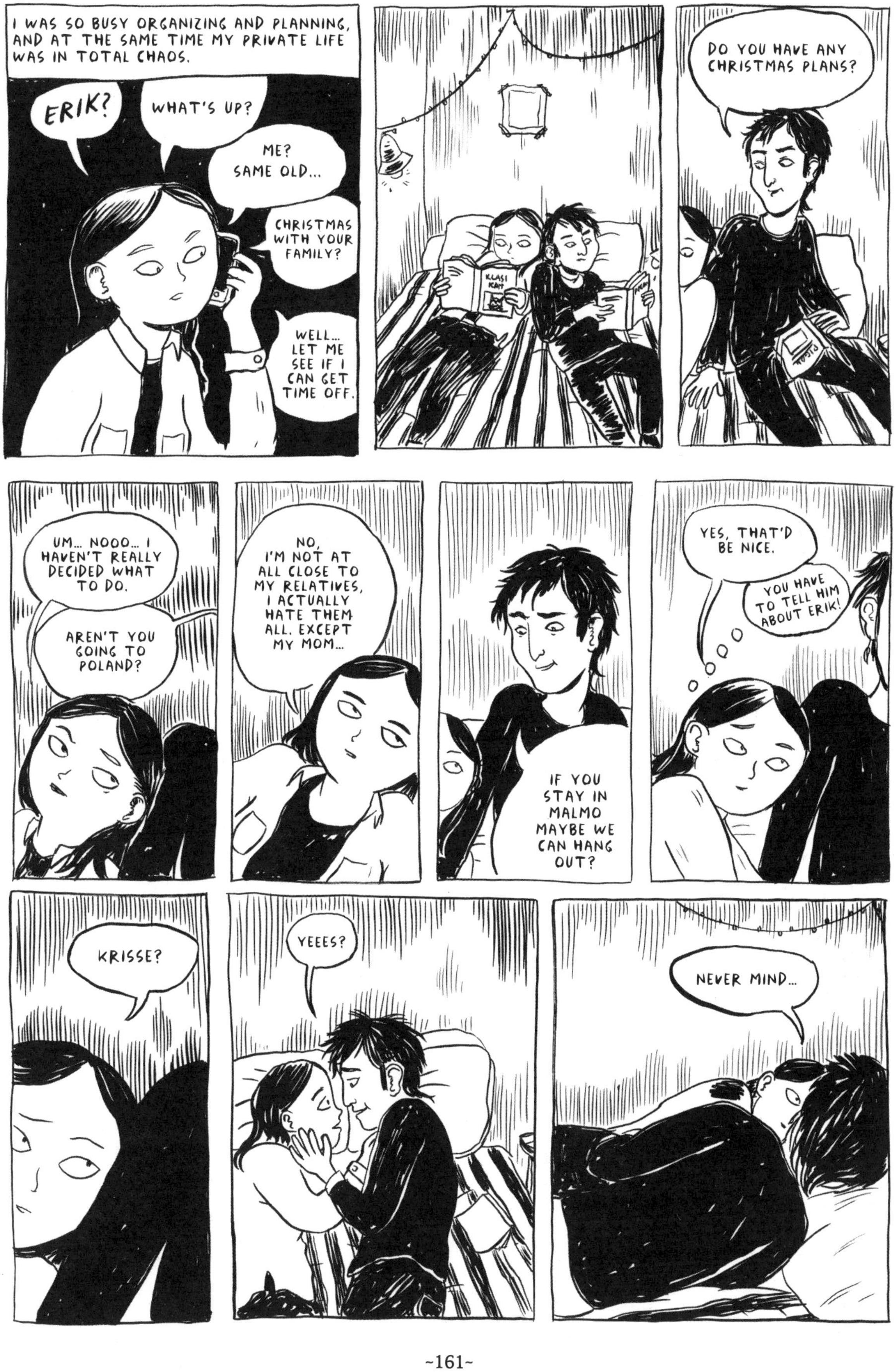
I WAS SO BUSY ORGANIZING AND PLANNING, AND AT THE SAME TIME MY PRIVATE LIFE WAS IN TOTAL CHAOS.
ERIK?
WHAT'S UP?
ME? SAME OLD...
CHRISTMAS WITH YOUR FAMILY?
WELL... LET ME SEE IF I CAN GET TIME OFF.
DO YOU HAVE ANY CHRISTMAS PLANS?
UM... NOOO... I HAVEN'T REALLY DECIDED WHAT TO DO.
AREN'T YOU GOING TO POLAND?
NO, I'M NOT AT ALL CLOSE TO MY RELATIVES, I ACTUALLY HATE THEM ALL. EXCEPT MY MOM...
IF YOU STAY IN MALMO MAYBE WE CAN HANG OUT?
YES, THAT'D BE NICE.
YOU HAVE TO TELL HIM ABOUT ERIK!
KRISSE?
YEEES?
NEVER MIND...

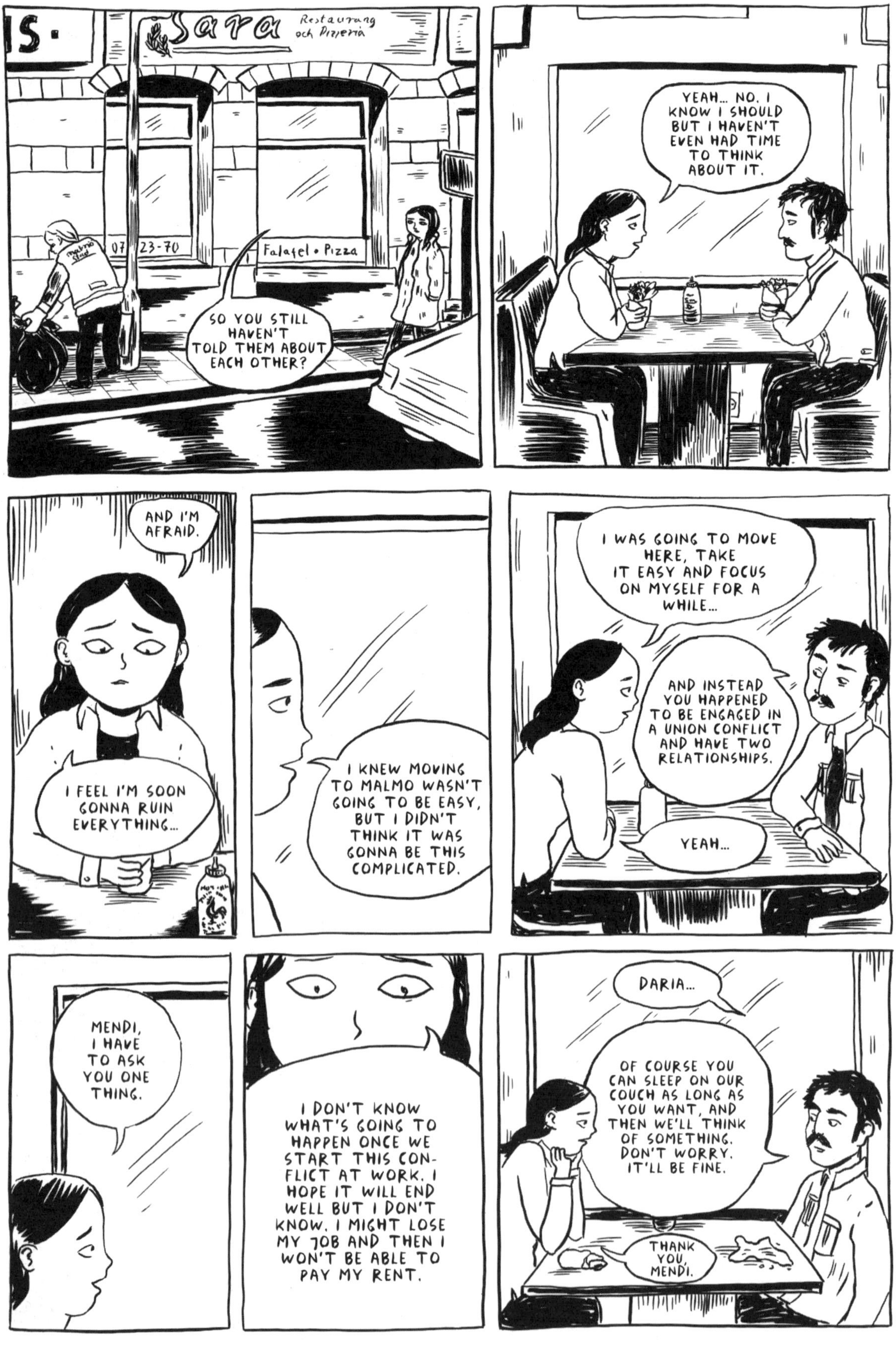
Sara Restaurang och Pizzeria
07 23-70
Falafel • Pizza
SO YOU STILL HAVEN'T TOLD THEM ABOUT EACH OTHER?
YEAH... NO. I KNOW I SHOULD BUT I HAVEN'T EVEN HAD TIME TO THINK ABOUT IT.
AND I'M AFRAID.
I FEEL I'M SOON GONNA RUIN EVERYTHING...
I KNEW MOVING TO MALMO WASN'T GOING TO BE EASY, BUT I DIDN'T THINK IT WAS GONNA BE THIS COMPLICATED.
I WAS GOING TO MOVE HERE, TAKE IT EASY AND FOCUS ON MYSELF FOR A WHILE...
AND INSTEAD YOU HAPPENED TO BE ENGAGED IN A UNION CONFLICT AND HAVE TWO RELATIONSHIPS.
YEAH...
MENDI, I HAVE TO ASK YOU ONE THING.
I DON'T KNOW WHAT'S GOING TO HAPPEN ONCE WE START THIS CONFLICT AT WORK. I HOPE IT WILL END WELL BUT I DON'T KNOW. I MIGHT LOSE MY JOB AND THEN I WON'T BE ABLE TO PAY MY RENT.
DARIA...
OF COURSE YOU CAN SLEEP ON OUR COUCH AS LONG AS YOU WANT, AND THEN WE'LL THINK OF SOMETHING. DON'T WORRY. IT'LL BE FINE.
THANK YOU, MENDI.

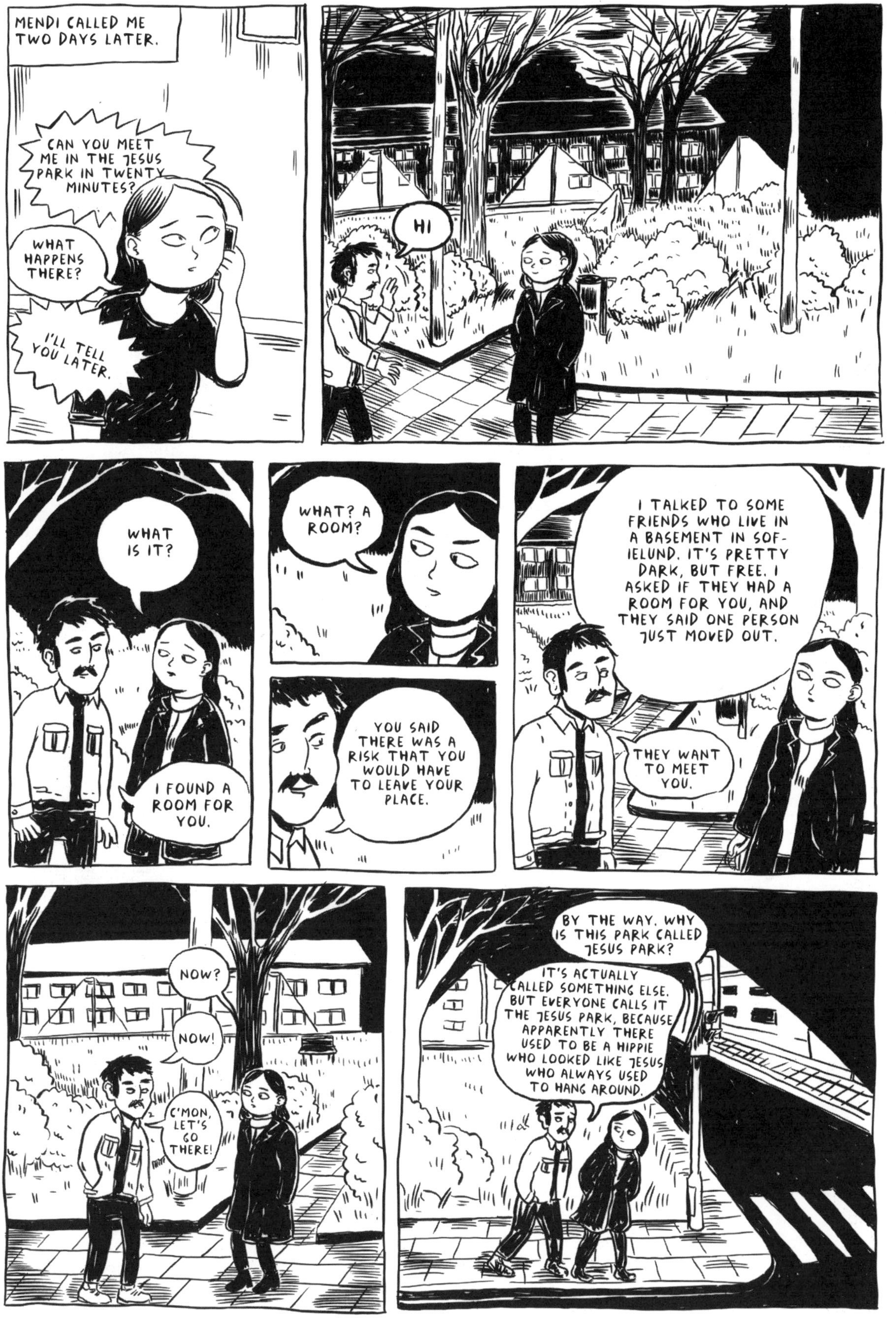
MENDI CALLED ME TWO DAYS LATER.
CAN YOU MEET ME IN THE JESUS PARK IN TWENTY MINUTES?
WHAT HAPPENS THERE?
I'LL TELL YOU LATER.
HI
WHAT IS IT?
I FOUND A ROOM FOR YOU.
WHAT? A ROOM?
YOU SAID THERE WAS A RISK THAT YOU WOULD HAVE TO LEAVE YOUR PLACE.
I TALKED TO SOME FRIENDS WHO LIVE IN A BASEMENT IN SOF-IELUND. IT'S PRETTY DARK, BUT FREE. I ASKED IF THEY HAD A ROOM FOR YOU, AND THEY SAID ONE PERSON JUST MOVED OUT.
THEY WANT TO MEET YOU.
NOW?
NOW!
C'MON, LET'S GO THERE!
BY THE WAY, WHY IS THIS PARK CALLED JESUS PARK?
IT'S ACTUALLY CALLED SOMETHING ELSE. BUT EVERYONE CALLS IT THE JESUS PARK, BECAUSE APPARENTLY THERE USED TO BE A HIPPIE WHO LOOKED LIKE JESUS WHO ALWAYS USED TO HANG AROUND.

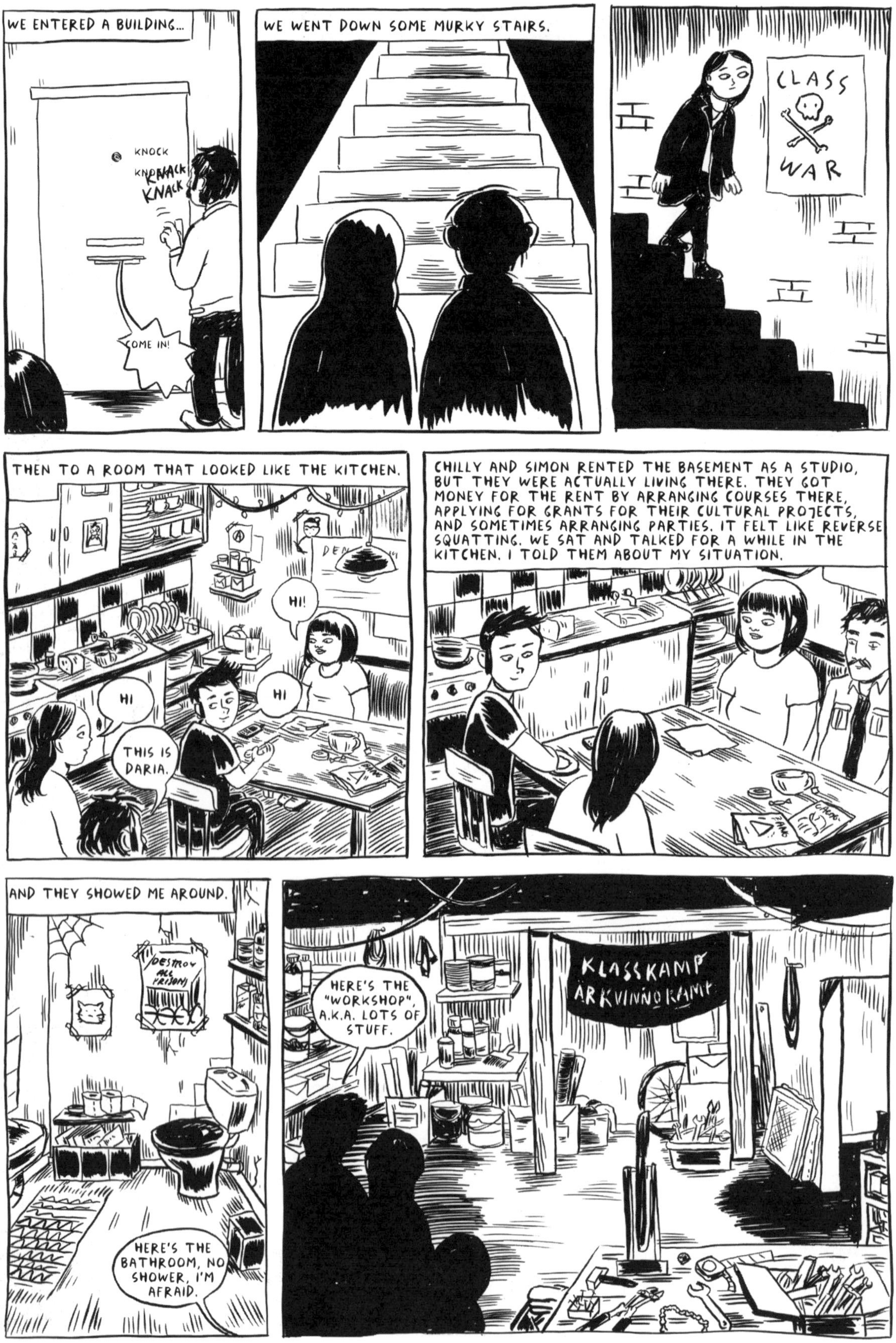
WE ENTERED A BUILDING...
KNOCK
KNOCK
KNACK
KNACK
COME IN!
WE WENT DOWN SOME MURKY STAIRS.
CLASS WAR
THEN TO A ROOM THAT LOOKED LIKE THE KITCHEN.
HI!
HI
HI
THIS IS DARIA.
CHILLY AND SIMON RENTED THE BASEMENT AS A STUDIO, BUT THEY WERE ACTUALLY LIVING THERE. THEY GOT MONEY FOR THE RENT BY ARRANGING COURSES THERE, APPLYING FOR GRANTS FOR THEIR CULTURAL PROJECTS, AND SOMETIMES ARRANGING PARTIES. IT FELT LIKE REVERSE SQUATTING. WE SAT AND TALKED FOR A WHILE IN THE KITCHEN. I TOLD THEM ABOUT MY SITUATION.
AND THEY SHOWED ME AROUND.
DESTROY ALL PRISONS
HERE'S THE BATHROOM, NO SHOWER, I'M AFRAID.
KLASSKAMP ÄR KVINNOKAMP
HERE'S THE "WORKSHOP", A.K.A. LOTS OF STUFF.

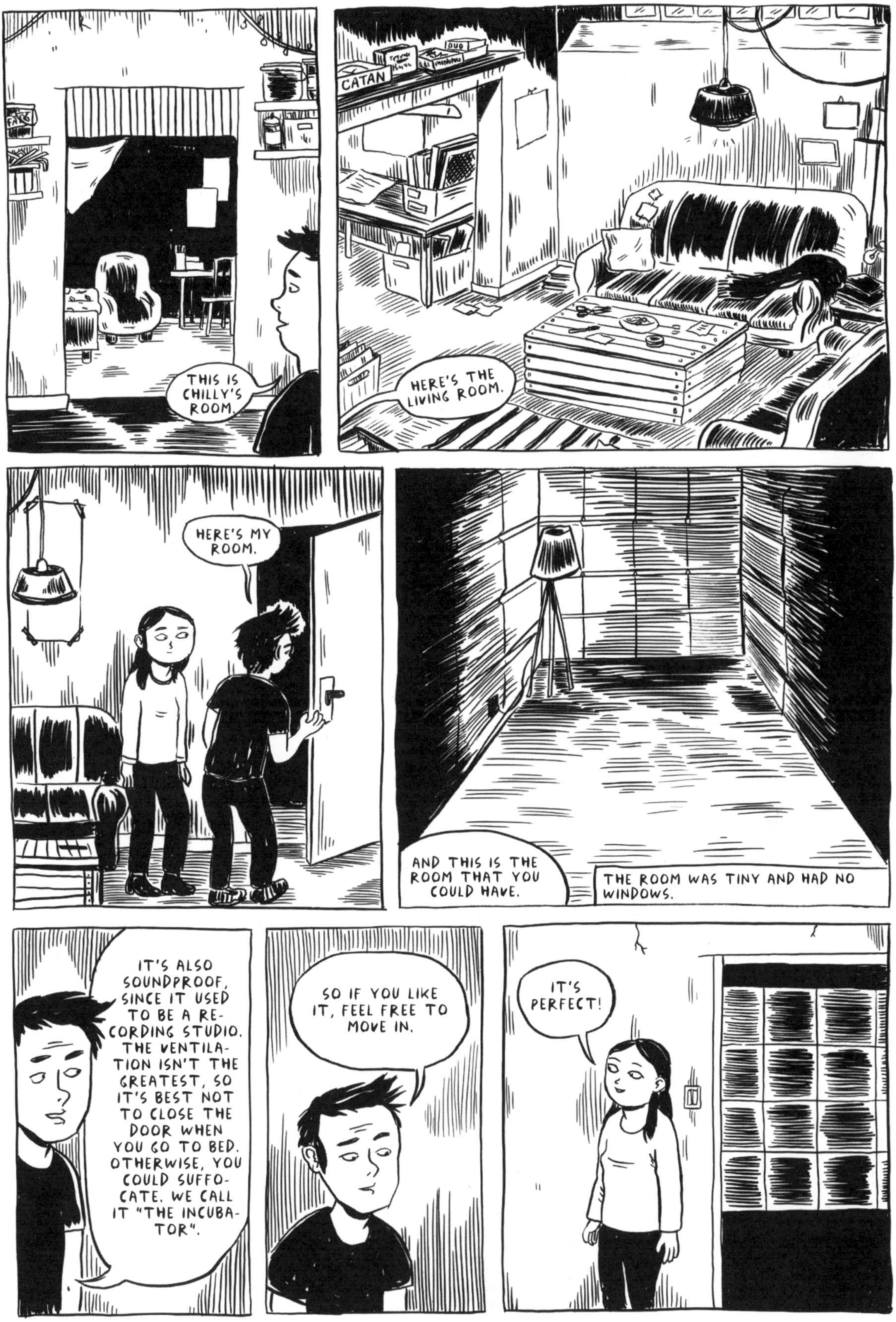
CATAN
DUO
THIS IS CHILLY'S ROOM.
HERE'S THE LIVING ROOM.
HERE'S MY ROOM.
AND THIS IS THE ROOM THAT YOU COULD HAVE.
THE ROOM WAS TINY AND HAD NO WINDOWS.
IT'S ALSO SOUNDPROOF, SINCE IT USED TO BE A RECORDING STUDIO. THE VENTILATION ISN'T THE GREATEST, SO IT'S BEST NOT TO CLOSE THE DOOR WHEN YOU GO TO BED. OTHERWISE, YOU COULD SUFFOCATE. WE CALL IT "THE INCUBATOR".
SO IF YOU LIKE IT, FEEL FREE TO MOVE IN.
IT'S PERFECT!

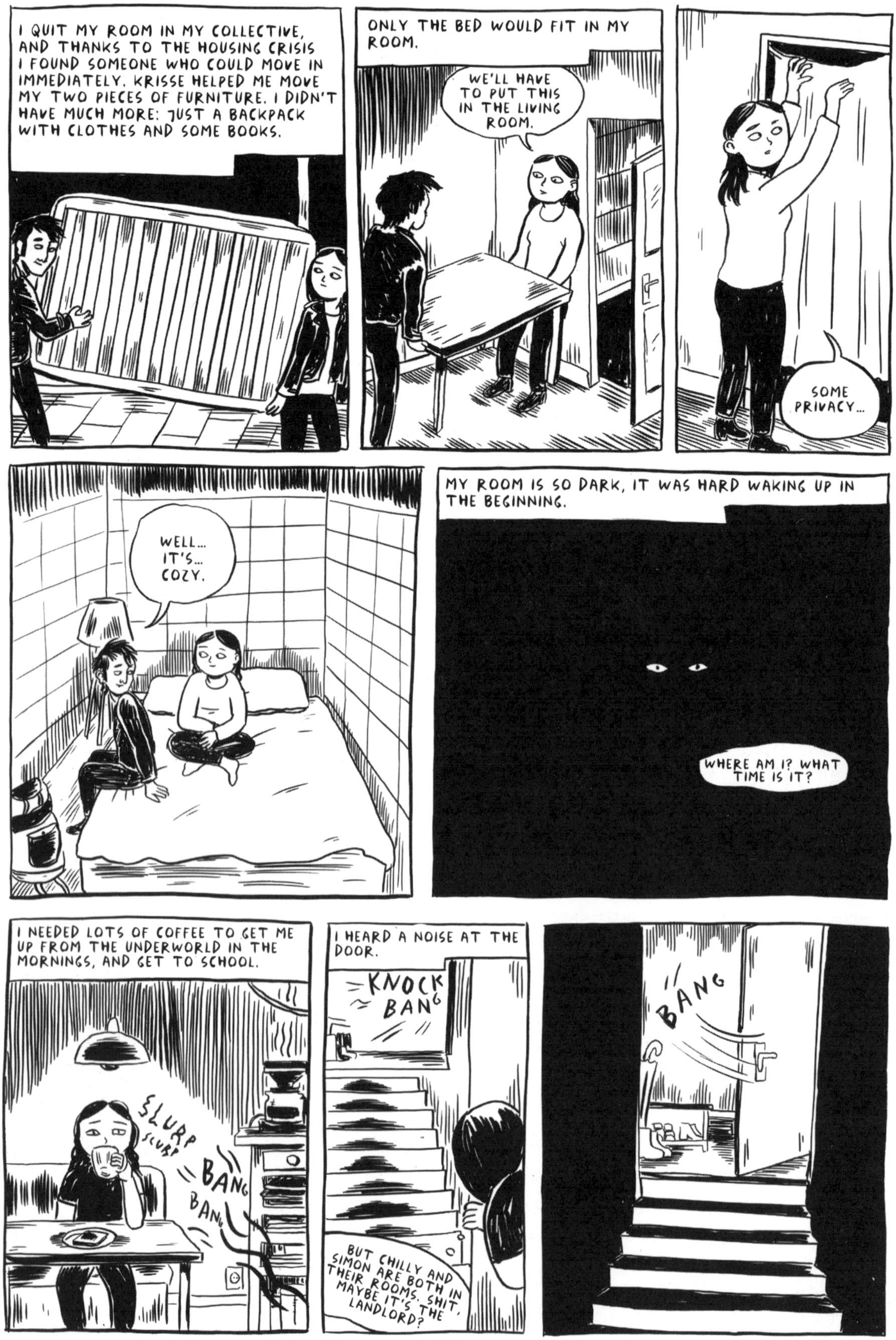

I QUIT MY ROOM IN MY COLLECTIVE, AND THANKS TO THE HOUSING CRISIS I FOUND SOMEONE WHO COULD MOVE IN IMMEDIATELY. KRISSE HELPED ME MOVE MY TWO PIECES OF FURNITURE. I DIDN'T HAVE MUCH MORE: JUST A BACKPACK WITH CLOTHES AND SOME BOOKS.
ONLY THE BED WOULD FIT IN MY ROOM.
WE'LL HAVE TO PUT THIS IN THE LIVING ROOM.
SOME PRIVACY...
WELL... IT'S... COZY.
MY ROOM IS SO DARK, IT WAS HARD WAKING UP IN THE BEGINNING.
WHERE AM I? WHAT TIME IS IT?
I NEEDED LOTS OF COFFEE TO GET ME UP FROM THE UNDERWORLD IN THE MORNINGS, AND GET TO SCHOOL.
SLURP
SLURP
BANG
BANG
I HEARD A NOISE AT THE DOOR.
KNOCK
BANG
BUT CHILLY AND SIMON ARE BOTH IN THEIR ROOMS. SHIT, MAYBE IT'S THE LANDLORD?
BANG

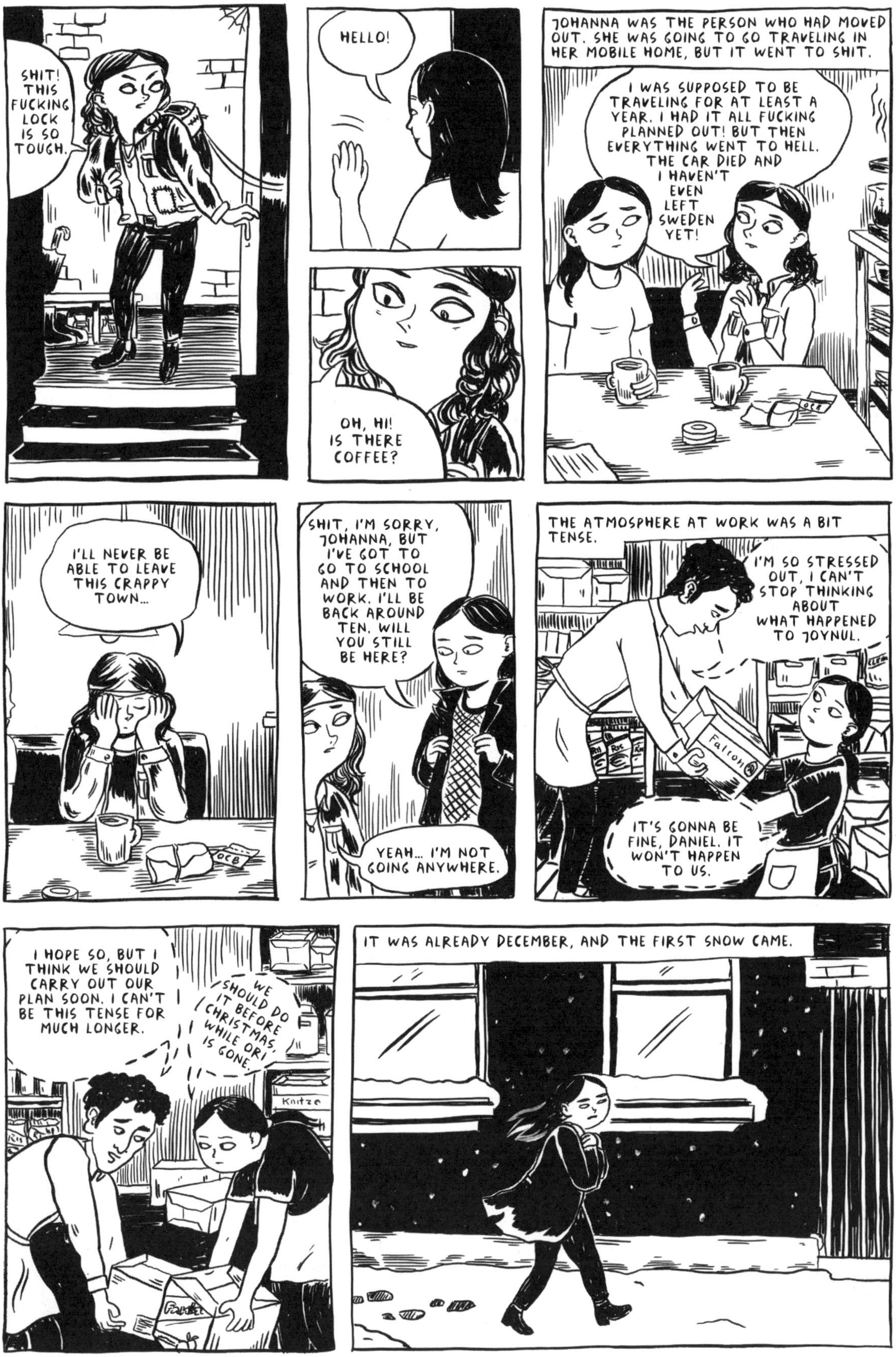
SHIT! THIS FUCKING LOCK IS SO TOUGH.
HELLO!
OH, HI! IS THERE COFFEE?
JOHANNA WAS THE PERSON WHO HAD MOVED OUT. SHE WAS GOING TO GO TRAVELING IN HER MOBILE HOME, BUT IT WENT TO SHIT.
I WAS SUPPOSED TO BE TRAVELING FOR AT LEAST A YEAR. I HAD IT ALL FUCKING PLANNED OUT! BUT THEN EVERYTHING WENT TO HELL. THE CAR DIED AND I HAVEN'T EVEN LEFT SWEDEN YET!
OCB
I'LL NEVER BE ABLE TO LEAVE THIS CRAPPY TOWN...
OCB
SHIT, I'M SORRY, JOHANNA, BUT I'VE GOT TO GO TO SCHOOL AND THEN TO WORK. I'LL BE BACK AROUND TEN. WILL YOU STILL BE HERE?
YEAH... I'M NOT GOING ANYWHERE.
THE ATMOSPHERE AT WORK WAS A BIT TENSE.
I'M SO STRESSED OUT, I CAN'T STOP THINKING ABOUT WHAT HAPPENED TO JOYNUL.
Falcon
IT'S GONNA BE FINE, DANIEL. IT WON'T HAPPEN TO US.
I HOPE SO, BUT I THINK WE SHOULD CARRY OUT OUR PLAN SOON. I CAN'T BE THIS TENSE FOR MUCH LONGER.
WE SHOULD DO IT BEFORE CHRISTMAS, WHILE ORI IS GONE.
Knitze
IT WAS ALREADY DECEMBER, AND THE FIRST SNOW CAME.

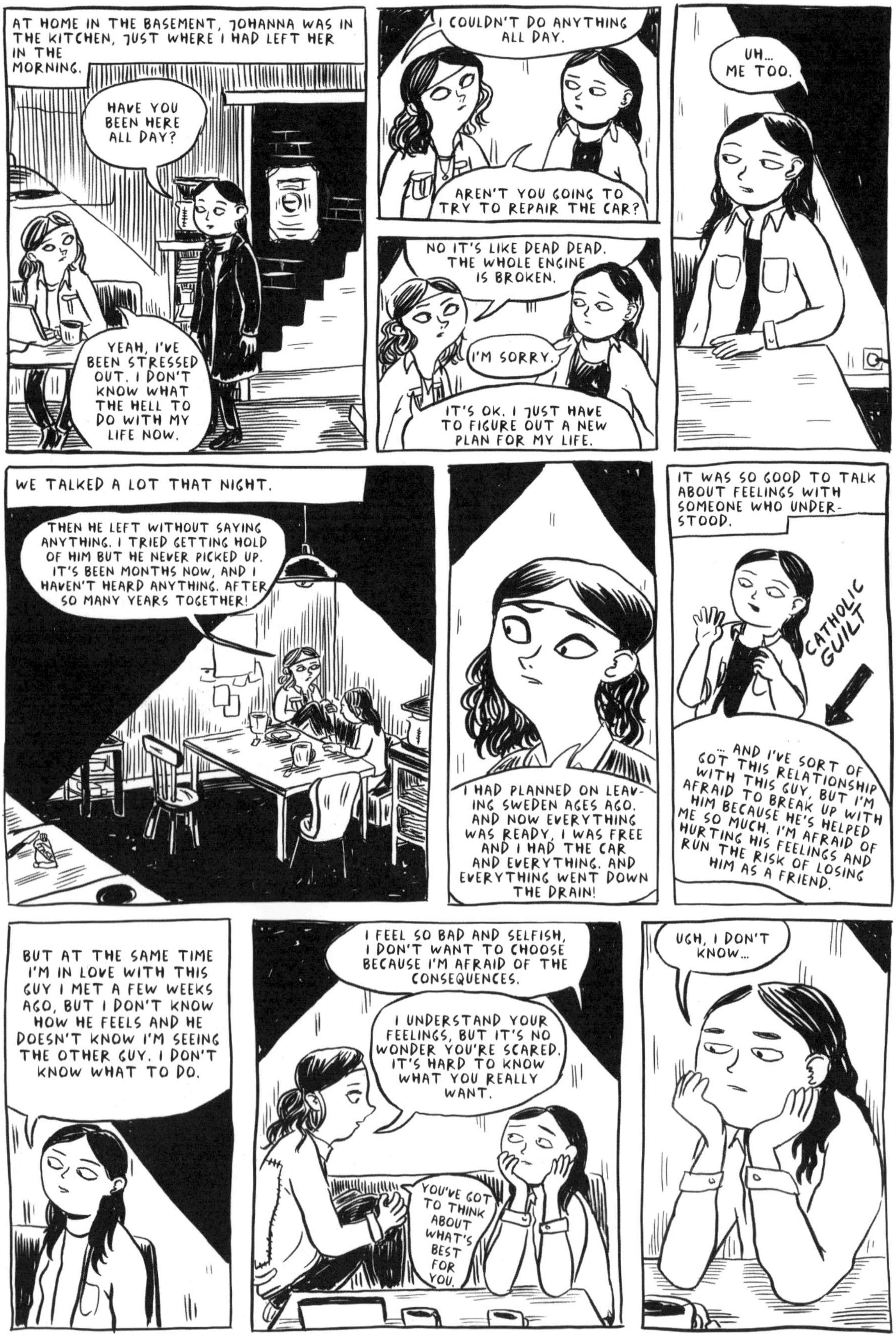

AT HOME IN THE BASEMENT, JOHANNA WAS IN THE KITCHEN, JUST WHERE I HAD LEFT HER IN THE MORNING.
HAVE YOU BEEN HERE ALL DAY?
YEAH, I'VE BEEN STRESSED OUT. I DON'T KNOW WHAT THE HELL TO DO WITH MY LIFE NOW.
I COULDN'T DO ANYTHING ALL DAY.
AREN'T YOU GOING TO TRY TO REPAIR THE CAR?
NO IT'S LIKE DEAD DEAD. THE WHOLE ENGINE IS BROKEN.
I'M SORRY.
IT'S OK. I JUST HAVE TO FIGURE OUT A NEW PLAN FOR MY LIFE.
UH... ME TOO.
WE TALKED A LOT THAT NIGHT.
THEN HE LEFT WITHOUT SAYING ANYTHING. I TRIED GETTING HOLD OF HIM BUT HE NEVER PICKED UP. IT'S BEEN MONTHS NOW, AND I HAVEN'T HEARD ANYTHING. AFTER SO MANY YEARS TOGETHER!
I HAD PLANNED ON LEAVING SWEDEN AGES AGO. AND NOW EVERYTHING WAS READY, I WAS FREE AND I HAD THE CAR AND EVERYTHING. AND EVERYTHING WENT DOWN THE DRAIN!
IT WAS SO GOOD TO TALK ABOUT FEELINGS WITH SOMEONE WHO UNDERSTOOD.
CATHOLIC GUILT
... AND I'VE SORT OF GOT THIS RELATIONSHIP WITH THIS GUY, BUT I'M AFRAID TO BREAK UP WITH HIM BECAUSE HE'S HELPED ME SO MUCH. I'M AFRAID OF HURTING HIS FEELINGS AND RUN THE RISK OF LOSING HIM AS A FRIEND.
BUT AT THE SAME TIME I'M IN LOVE WITH THIS GUY I MET A FEW WEEKS AGO, BUT I DON'T KNOW HOW HE FEELS AND HE DOESN'T KNOW I'M SEEING THE OTHER GUY. I DON'T KNOW WHAT TO DO.
I FEEL SO BAD AND SELFISH, I DON'T WANT TO CHOOSE BECAUSE I'M AFRAID OF THE CONSEQUENCES.
I UNDERSTAND YOUR FEELINGS, BUT IT'S NO WONDER YOU'RE SCARED. IT'S HARD TO KNOW WHAT YOU REALLY WANT.
YOU'VE GOT TO THINK ABOUT WHAT'S BEST FOR YOU.
UGH, I DON'T KNOW...

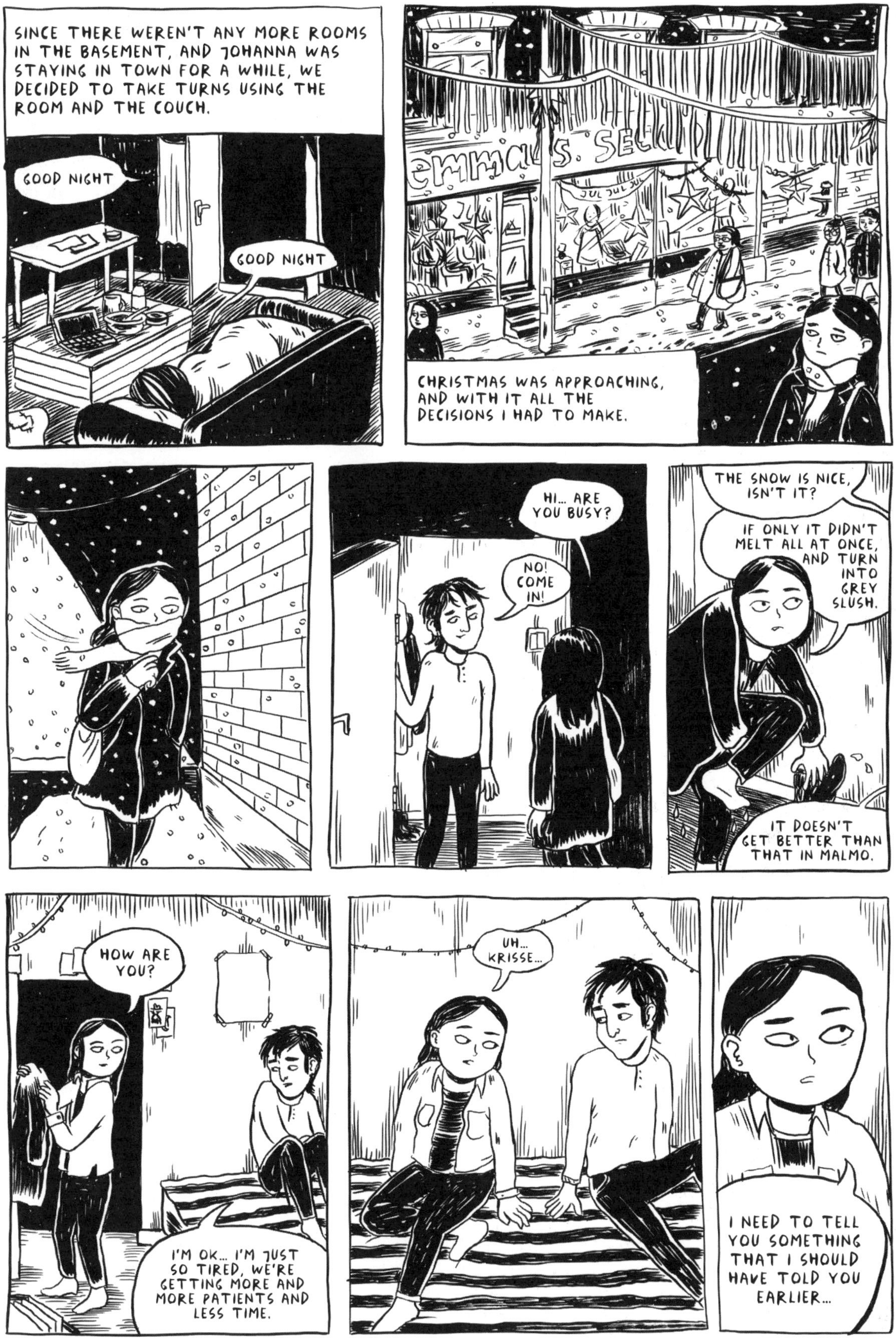
SINCE THERE WEREN'T ANY MORE ROOMS IN THE BASEMENT, AND JOHANNA WAS STAYING IN TOWN FOR A WHILE, WE DECIDED TO TAKE TURNS USING THE ROOM AND THE COUCH.
GOOD NIGHT
GOOD NIGHT
CHRISTMAS WAS APPROACHING, AND WITH IT ALL THE DECISIONS I HAD TO MAKE.
HI... ARE YOU BUSY?
NO! COME IN!
THE SNOW IS NICE, ISN'T IT?
IF ONLY IT DIDN'T MELT ALL AT ONCE, AND TURN INTO GREY SLUSH.
IT DOESN'T GET BETTER THAN THAT IN MALMO.
HOW ARE YOU?
I'M OK... I'M JUST SO TIRED, WE'RE GETTING MORE AND MORE PATIENTS AND LESS TIME.
UH... KRISSE...
I NEED TO TELL YOU SOMETHING THAT I SHOULD HAVE TOLD YOU EARLIER...

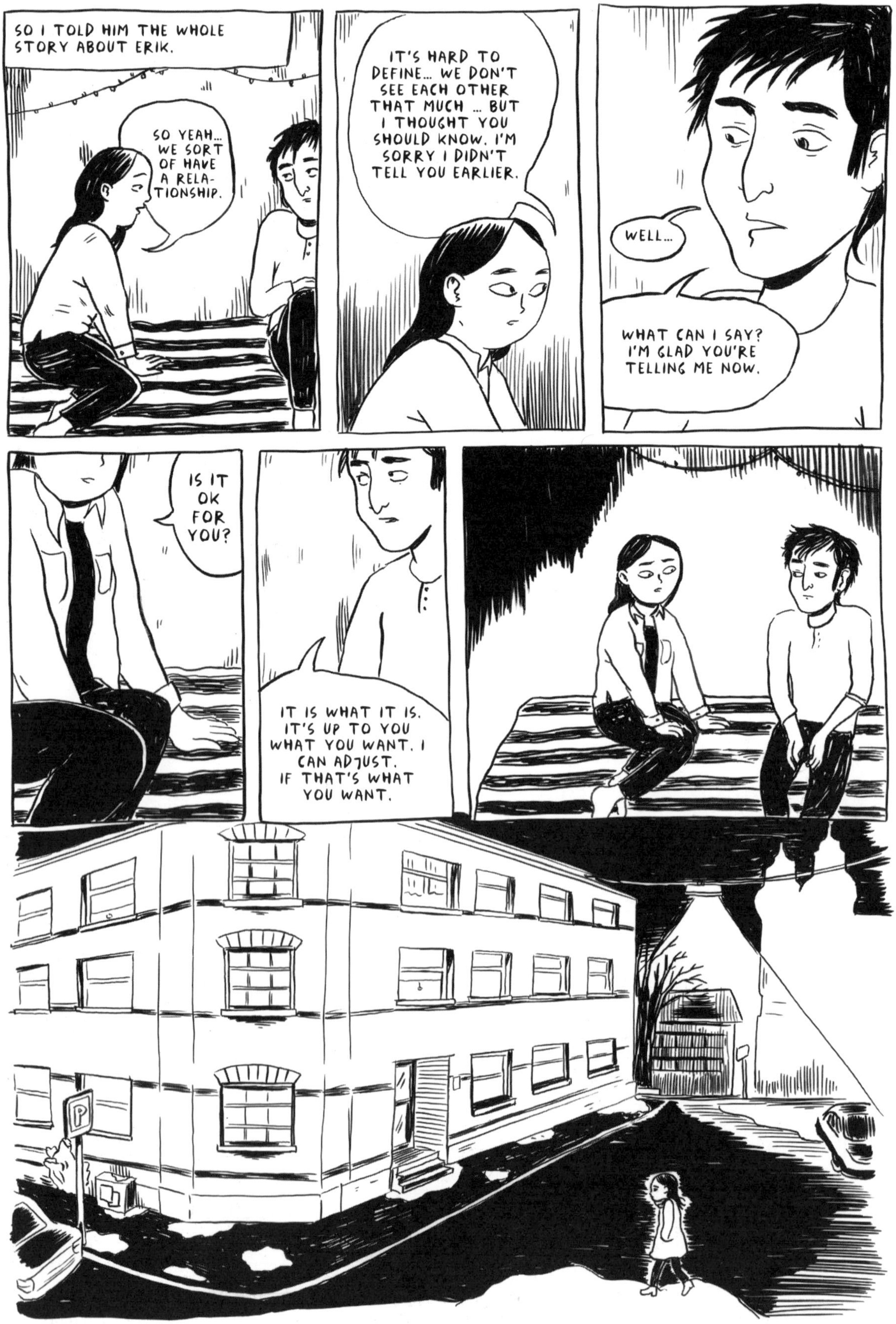
SO I TOLD HIM THE WHOLE STORY ABOUT ERIK.
SO YEAH... WE SORT OF HAVE A RELA-TIONSHIP.
IT'S HARD TO DEFINE... WE DON'T SEE EACH OTHER THAT MUCH ... BUT I THOUGHT YOU SHOULD KNOW. I'M SORRY I DIDN'T TELL YOU EARLIER.
WELL...
WHAT CAN I SAY? I'M GLAD YOU'RE TELLING ME NOW.
IS IT OK FOR YOU?
IT IS WHAT IT IS. IT'S UP TO YOU WHAT YOU WANT. I CAN ADJUST. IF THAT'S WHAT YOU WANT.
P

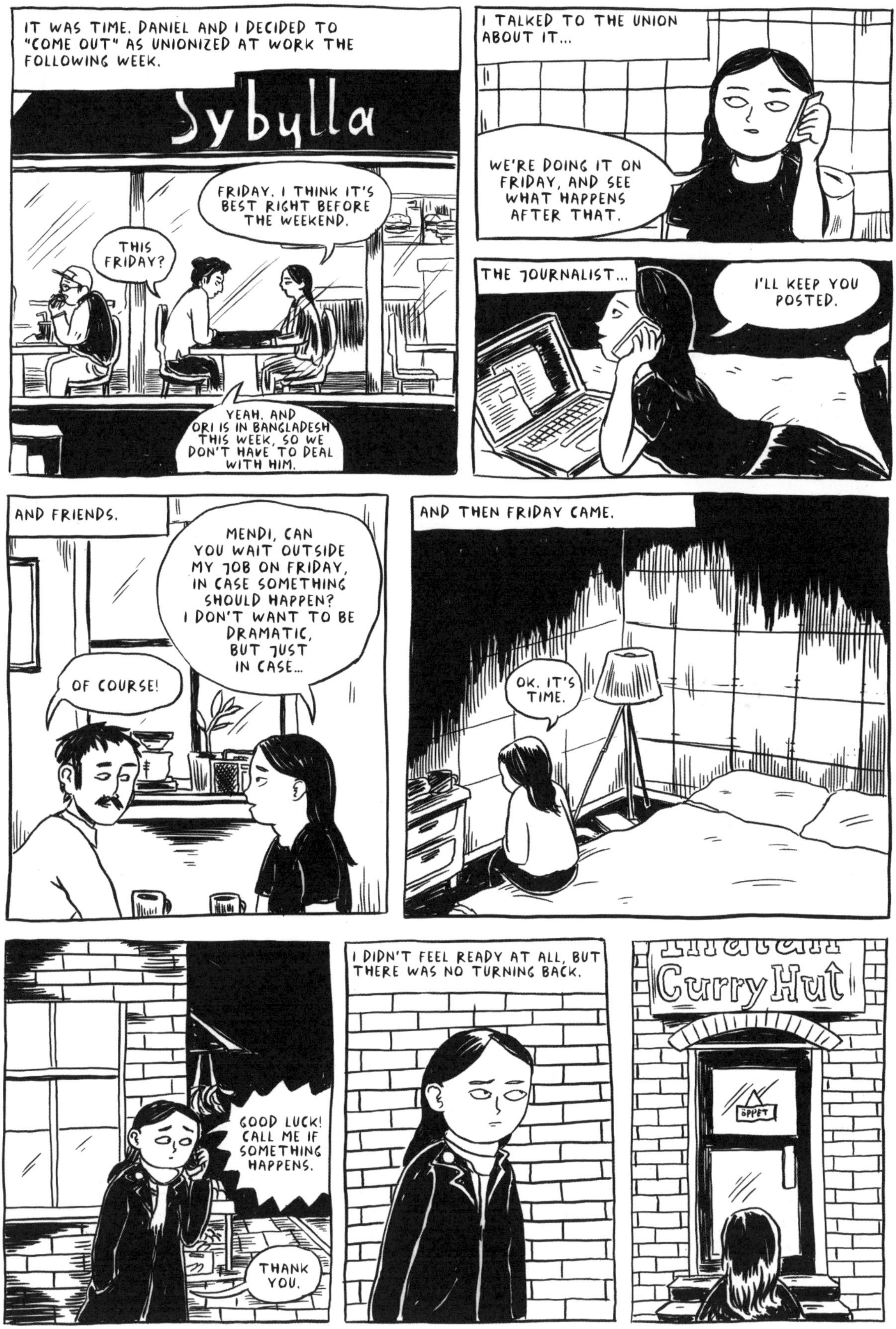
IT WAS TIME. DANIEL AND I DECIDED TO "COME OUT" AS UNIONIZED AT WORK THE FOLLOWING WEEK.
Sybulla
FRIDAY. I THINK IT'S BEST RIGHT BEFORE THE WEEKEND.
THIS FRIDAY?
YEAH. AND ORI IS IN BANGLADESH THIS WEEK, SO WE DON'T HAVE TO DEAL WITH HIM.
I TALKED TO THE UNION ABOUT IT...
WE'RE DOING IT ON FRIDAY, AND SEE WHAT HAPPENS AFTER THAT.
THE JOURNALIST...
I'LL KEEP YOU POSTED.
AND FRIENDS.
MENDI, CAN YOU WAIT OUTSIDE MY JOB ON FRIDAY, IN CASE SOMETHING SHOULD HAPPEN? I DON'T WANT TO BE DRAMATIC, BUT JUST IN CASE...
OF COURSE!
AND THEN FRIDAY CAME.
OK. IT'S TIME.
GOOD LUCK! CALL ME IF SOMETHING HAPPENS.
THANK YOU.
I DIDN'T FEEL READY AT ALL, BUT THERE WAS NO TURNING BACK.
Curry Hut
ÖPPET

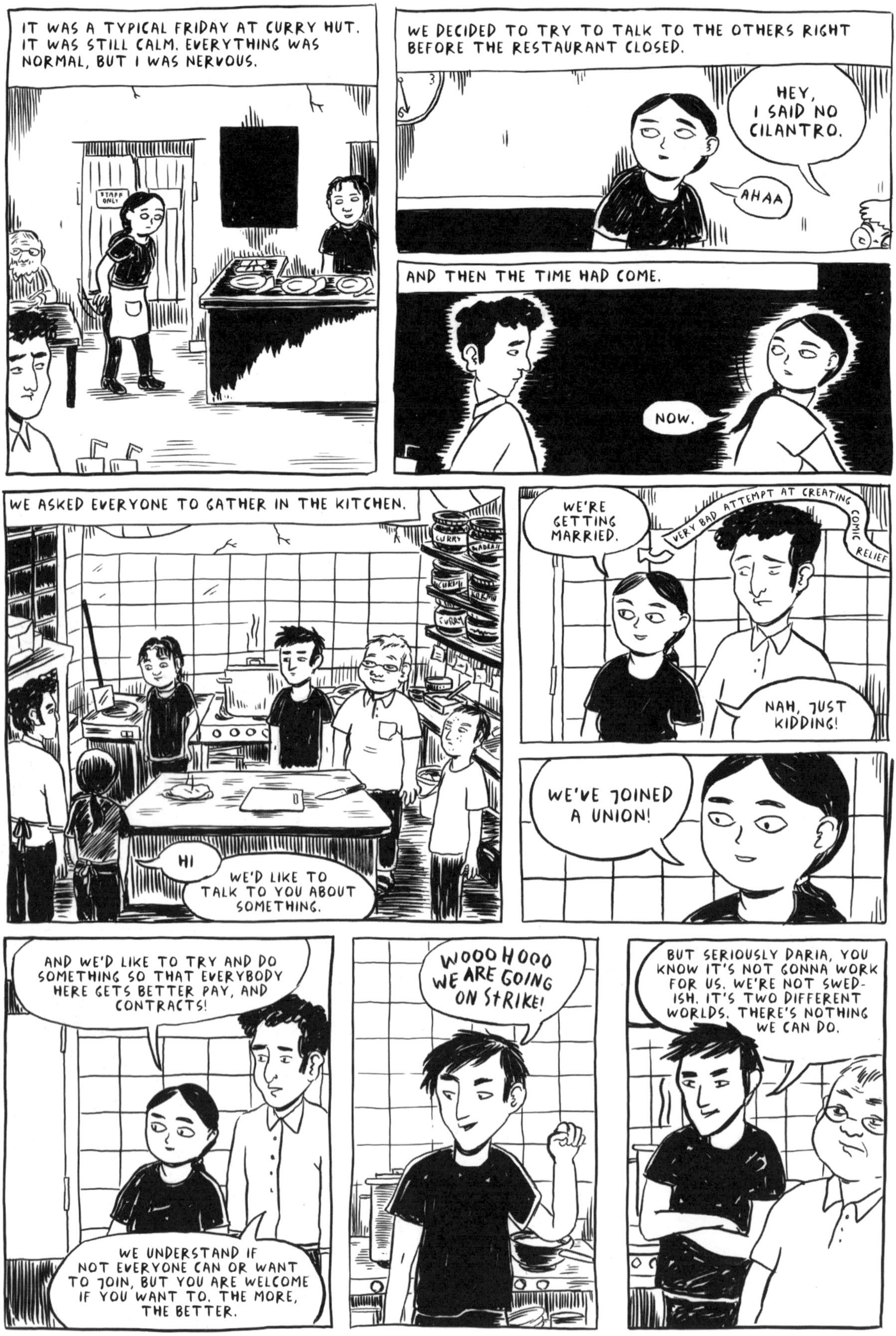
IT WAS A TYPICAL FRIDAY AT CURRY HUT. IT WAS STILL CALM. EVERYTHING WAS NORMAL, BUT I WAS NERVOUS.
STAFF ONLY
WE DECIDED TO TRY TO TALK TO THE OTHERS RIGHT BEFORE THE RESTAURANT CLOSED.
HEY, I SAID NO CILANTRO.
AHAA
AND THEN THE TIME HAD COME.
NOW.
WE ASKED EVERYONE TO GATHER IN THE KITCHEN.
CURRY
MADRAS
CURRY
KORMA
CURRY
HI
WE'D LIKE TO TALK TO YOU ABOUT SOMETHING.
WE'RE GETTING MARRIED.
VERY BAD ATTEMPT AT CREATING COMIC RELIEF
NAH, JUST KIDDING!
WE'VE JOINED A UNION!
AND WE'D LIKE TO TRY AND DO SOMETHING SO THAT EVERYBODY HERE GETS BETTER PAY, AND CONTRACTS!
WE UNDERSTAND IF NOT EVERYONE CAN OR WANT TO JOIN, BUT YOU ARE WELCOME IF YOU WANT TO. THE MORE, THE BETTER.
WOOO HOOO WE ARE GOING ON STRIKE!
BUT SERIOUSLY DARIA, YOU KNOW IT'S NOT GONNA WORK FOR US. WE'RE NOT SWEDISH. IT'S TWO DIFFERENT WORLDS. THERE'S NOTHING WE CAN DO.

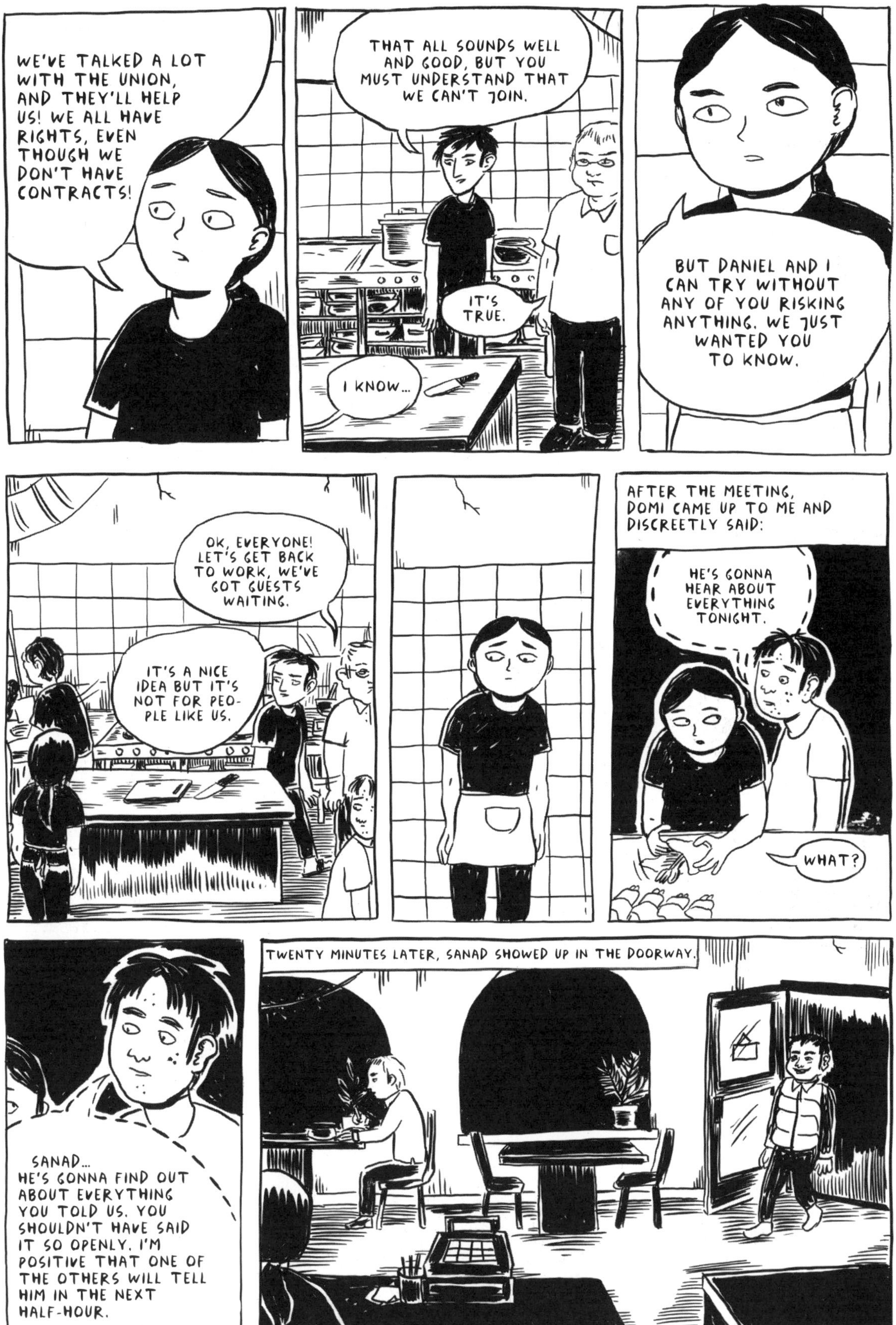

WE'VE TALKED A LOT WITH THE UNION, AND THEY'LL HELP US! WE ALL HAVE RIGHTS, EVEN THOUGH WE DON'T HAVE CONTRACTS!
THAT ALL SOUNDS WELL AND GOOD, BUT YOU MUST UNDERSTAND THAT WE CAN'T JOIN.
IT'S TRUE.
I KNOW...
BUT DANIEL AND I CAN TRY WITHOUT ANY OF YOU RISKING ANYTHING. WE JUST WANTED YOU TO KNOW.
OK, EVERYONE! LET'S GET BACK TO WORK, WE'VE GOT GUESTS WAITING.
IT'S A NICE IDEA BUT IT'S NOT FOR PEO-PLE LIKE US.
AFTER THE MEETING, DOMI CAME UP TO ME AND DISCREETLY SAID:
HE'S GONNA HEAR ABOUT EVERYTHING TONIGHT.
WHAT?
SANAD... HE'S GONNA FIND OUT ABOUT EVERYTHING YOU TOLD US. YOU SHOULDN'T HAVE SAID IT SO OPENLY. I'M POSITIVE THAT ONE OF THE OTHERS WILL TELL HIM IN THE NEXT HALF-HOUR.
TWENTY MINUTES LATER, SANAD SHOWED UP IN THE DOORWAY.

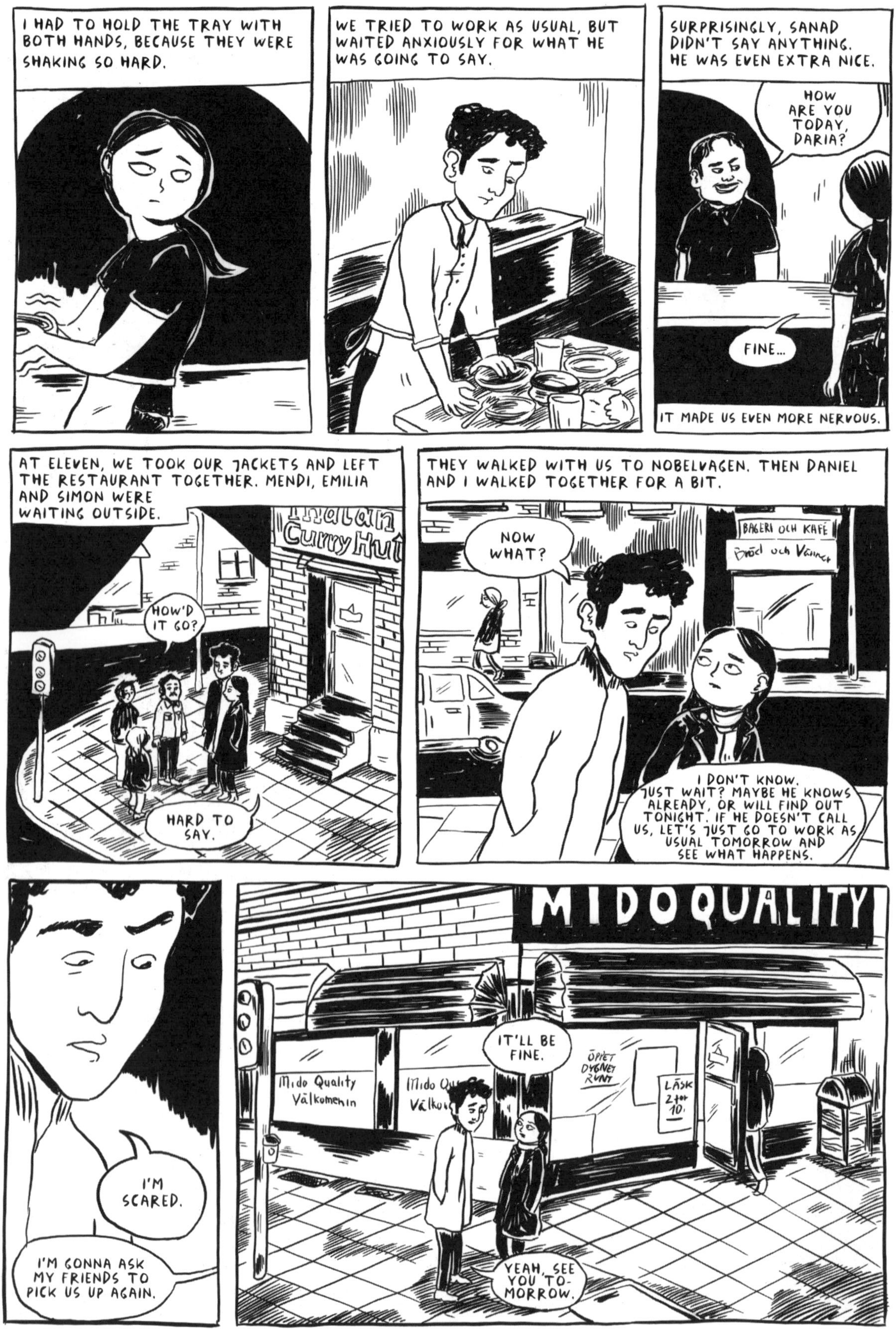

I HAD TO HOLD THE TRAY WITH BOTH HANDS, BECAUSE THEY WERE SHAKING SO HARD.
WE TRIED TO WORK AS USUAL, BUT WAITED ANXIOUSLY FOR WHAT HE WAS GOING TO SAY.
SURPRISINGLY, SANAD DIDN'T SAY ANYTHING. HE WAS EVEN EXTRA NICE.
HOW ARE YOU TODAY, DARIA?
FINE...
IT MADE US EVEN MORE NERVOUS.
AT ELEVEN, WE TOOK OUR JACKETS AND LEFT THE RESTAURANT TOGETHER. MENDI, EMILIA AND SIMON WERE WAITING OUTSIDE.
Curry Hut
HOW'D IT GO?
HARD TO SAY.
THEY WALKED WITH US TO NOBELVAGEN. THEN DANIEL AND I WALKED TOGETHER FOR A BIT.
BAGERI OCH KAFÉ
Bröd och Vänner
NOW WHAT?
I DON'T KNOW. JUST WAIT? MAYBE HE KNOWS ALREADY, OR WILL FIND OUT TONIGHT. IF HE DOESN'T CALL US, LET'S JUST GO TO WORK AS USUAL TOMORROW AND SEE WHAT HAPPENS.
I'M SCARED.
I'M GONNA ASK MY FRIENDS TO PICK US UP AGAIN.
MIDO QUALITY
Mido Quality Välkomen in
ÖPPET DYGNET RUNT
LÄSK 2 för 10:
IT'LL BE FINE.
YEAH, SEE YOU TO-MORROW.

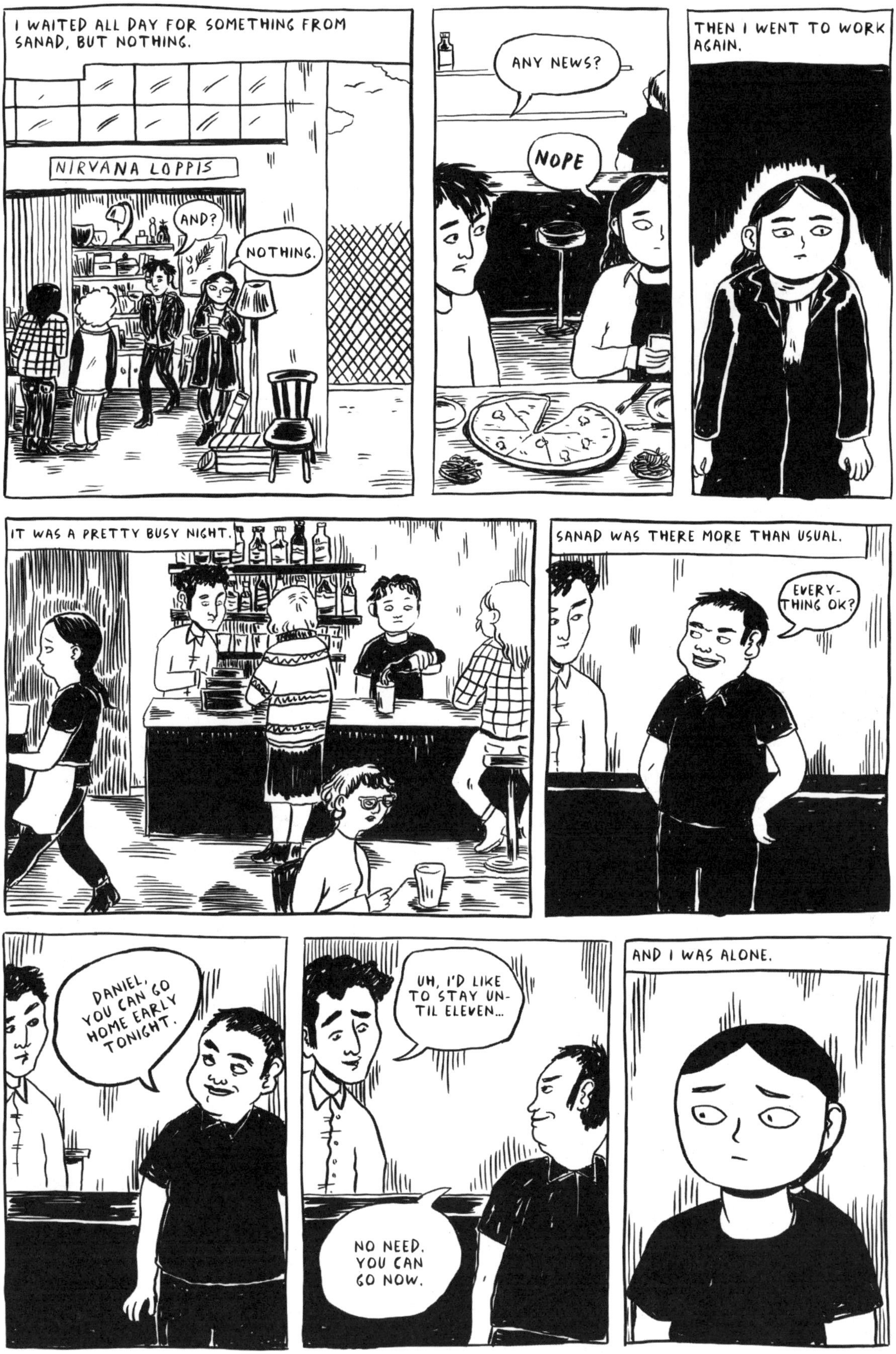
I WAITED ALL DAY FOR SOMETHING FROM SANAD, BUT NOTHING.
NIRVANA LOPPIS
AND?
NOTHING.
ANY NEWS?
NOPE
THEN I WENT TO WORK AGAIN.
IT WAS A PRETTY BUSY NIGHT.
SANAD WAS THERE MORE THAN USUAL.
EVERY-THING OK?
DANIEL, YOU CAN GO HOME EARLY TONIGHT.
UH, I'D LIKE TO STAY UN-TIL ELEVEN...
NO NEED. YOU CAN GO NOW.
AND I WAS ALONE.

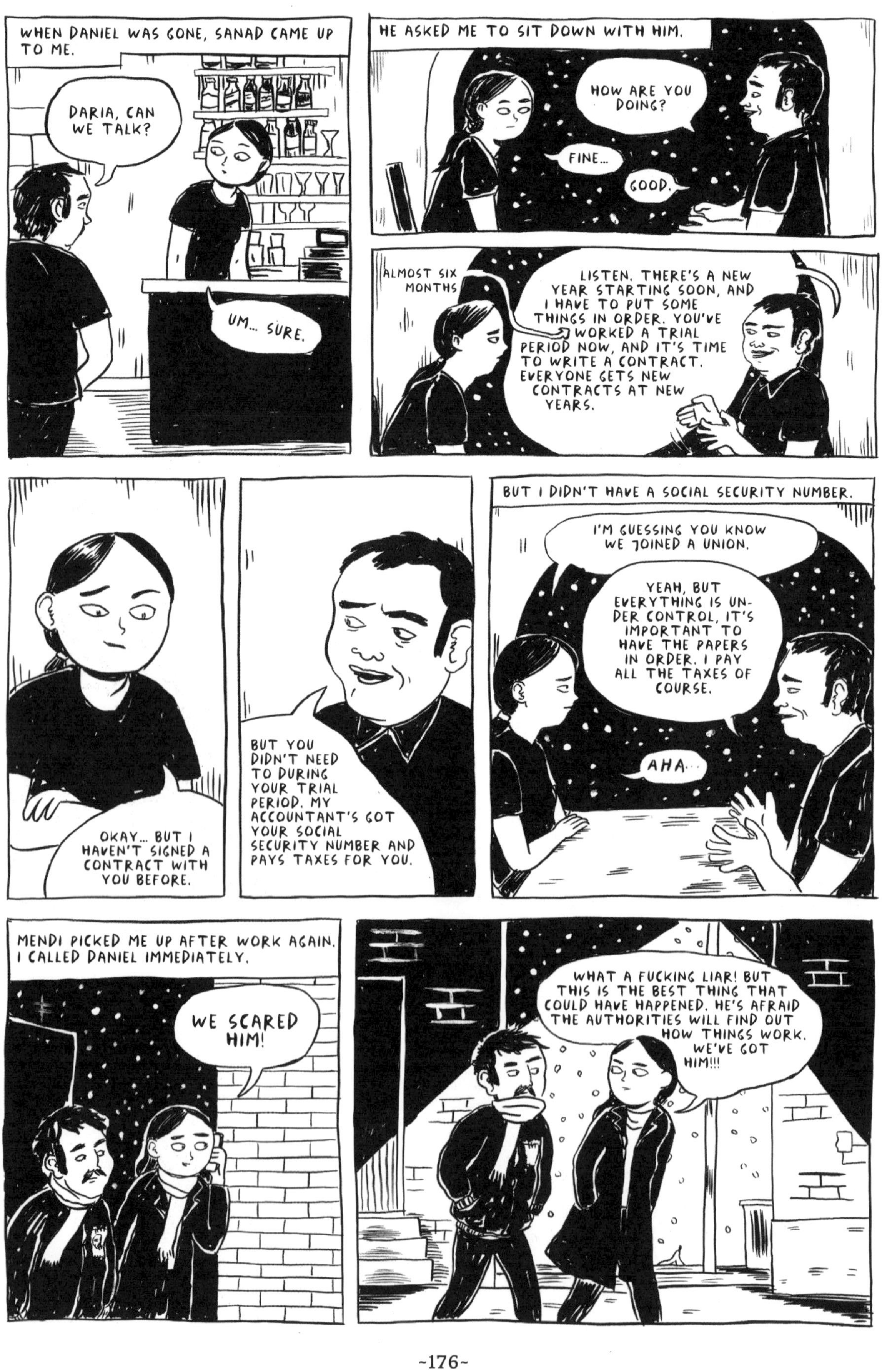

WHEN DANIEL WAS GONE, SANAD CAME UP TO ME.
DARIA, CAN WE TALK?
UM... SURE.
HE ASKED ME TO SIT DOWN WITH HIM.
HOW ARE YOU DOING?
FINE...
GOOD.
LISTEN. THERE'S A NEW YEAR STARTING SOON, AND I HAVE TO PUT SOME THINGS IN ORDER. YOU'VE WORKED A TRIAL PERIOD NOW, AND IT'S TIME TO WRITE A CONTRACT. EVERYONE GETS NEW CONTRACTS AT NEW YEARS.
ALMOST SIX MONTHS
OKAY... BUT I HAVEN'T SIGNED A CONTRACT WITH YOU BEFORE.
BUT YOU DIDN'T NEED TO DURING YOUR TRIAL PERIOD. MY ACCOUNTANT'S GOT YOUR SOCIAL SECURITY NUMBER AND PAYS TAXES FOR YOU.
BUT I DIDN'T HAVE A SOCIAL SECURITY NUMBER.
I'M GUESSING YOU KNOW WE JOINED A UNION.
YEAH, BUT EVERYTHING IS UNDER CONTROL, IT'S IMPORTANT TO HAVE THE PAPERS IN ORDER. I PAY ALL THE TAXES OF COURSE.
AHA...
MENDI PICKED ME UP AFTER WORK AGAIN. I CALLED DANIEL IMMEDIATELY.
WE SCARED HIM!
WHAT A FUCKING LIAR! BUT THIS IS THE BEST THING THAT COULD HAVE HAPPENED. HE'S AFRAID THE AUTHORITIES WILL FIND OUT HOW THINGS WORK. WE'VE GOT HIM!!!

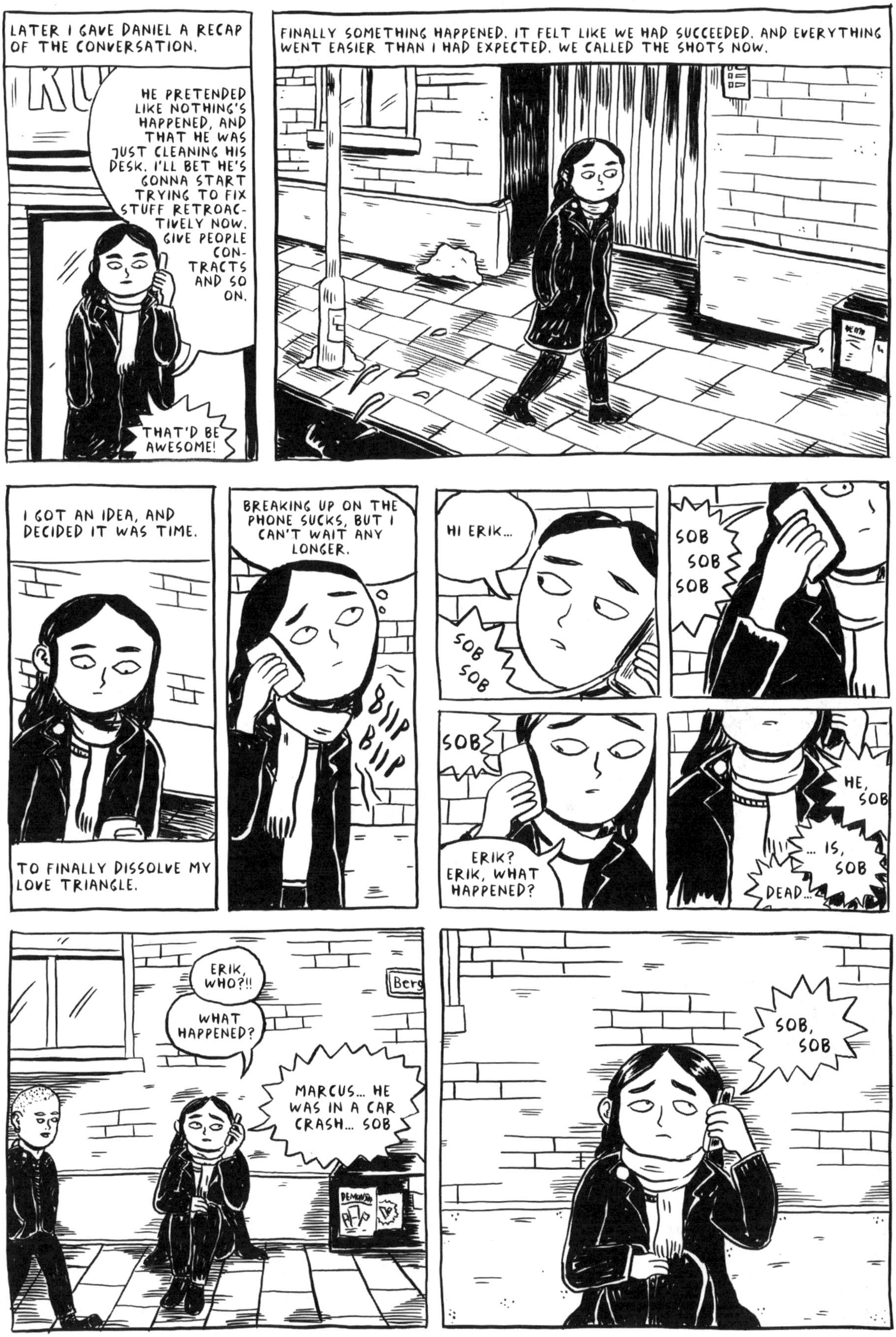
LATER I GAVE DANIEL A RECAP OF THE CONVERSATION.
HE PRETENDED LIKE NOTHING'S HAPPENED, AND THAT HE WAS JUST CLEANING HIS DESK. I'LL BET HE'S GONNA START TRYING TO FIX STUFF RETROACTIVELY NOW. GIVE PEOPLE CONTRACTS AND SO ON.
THAT'D BE AWESOME!
FINALLY SOMETHING HAPPENED. IT FELT LIKE WE HAD SUCCEEDED. AND EVERYTHING WENT EASIER THAN I HAD EXPECTED. WE CALLED THE SHOTS NOW.
I GOT AN IDEA, AND DECIDED IT WAS TIME.
TO FINALLY DISSOLVE MY LOVE TRIANGLE.
BREAKING UP ON THE PHONE SUCKS, BUT I CAN'T WAIT ANY LONGER.
BIIP BIIP
HI ERIK...
SOB SOB
SOB SOB SOB
SOB
ERIK? ERIK, WHAT HAPPENED?
HE, SOB
... IS, SOB
DEAD...
Berg
ERIK, WHO?!!
WHAT HAPPENED?
MARCUS... HE WAS IN A CAR CRASH... SOB
SOB, SOB

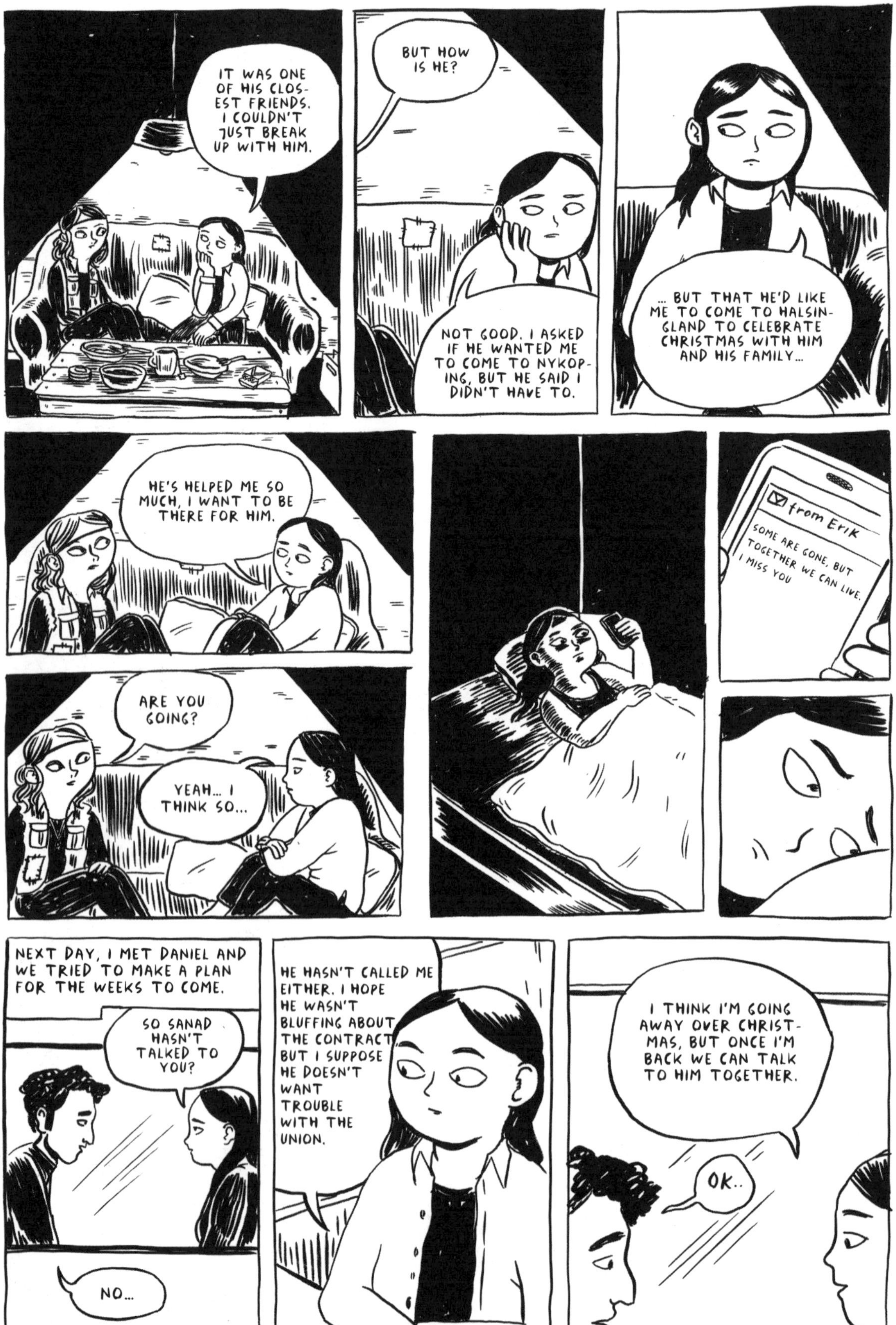
IT WAS ONE OF HIS CLOSEST FRIENDS. I COULDN'T JUST BREAK UP WITH HIM.
BUT HOW IS HE?
NOT GOOD. I ASKED IF HE WANTED ME TO COME TO NYKOPING, BUT HE SAID I DIDN'T HAVE TO.
... BUT THAT HE'D LIKE ME TO COME TO HALSINGLAND TO CELEBRATE CHRISTMAS WITH HIM AND HIS FAMILY...
HE'S HELPED ME SO MUCH, I WANT TO BE THERE FOR HIM.
ARE YOU GOING?
YEAH... I THINK SO...
from Erik
SOME ARE GONE, BUT TOGETHER WE CAN LIVE. I MISS YOU
NEXT DAY, I MET DANIEL AND WE TRIED TO MAKE A PLAN FOR THE WEEKS TO COME.
SO SANAD HASN'T TALKED TO YOU?
NO...
HE HASN'T CALLED ME EITHER. I HOPE HE WASN'T BLUFFING ABOUT THE CONTRACT BUT I SUPPOSE HE DOESN'T WANT TROUBLE WITH THE UNION.
I THINK I'M GOING AWAY OVER CHRISTMAS, BUT ONCE I'M BACK WE CAN TALK TO HIM TOGETHER.
OK..

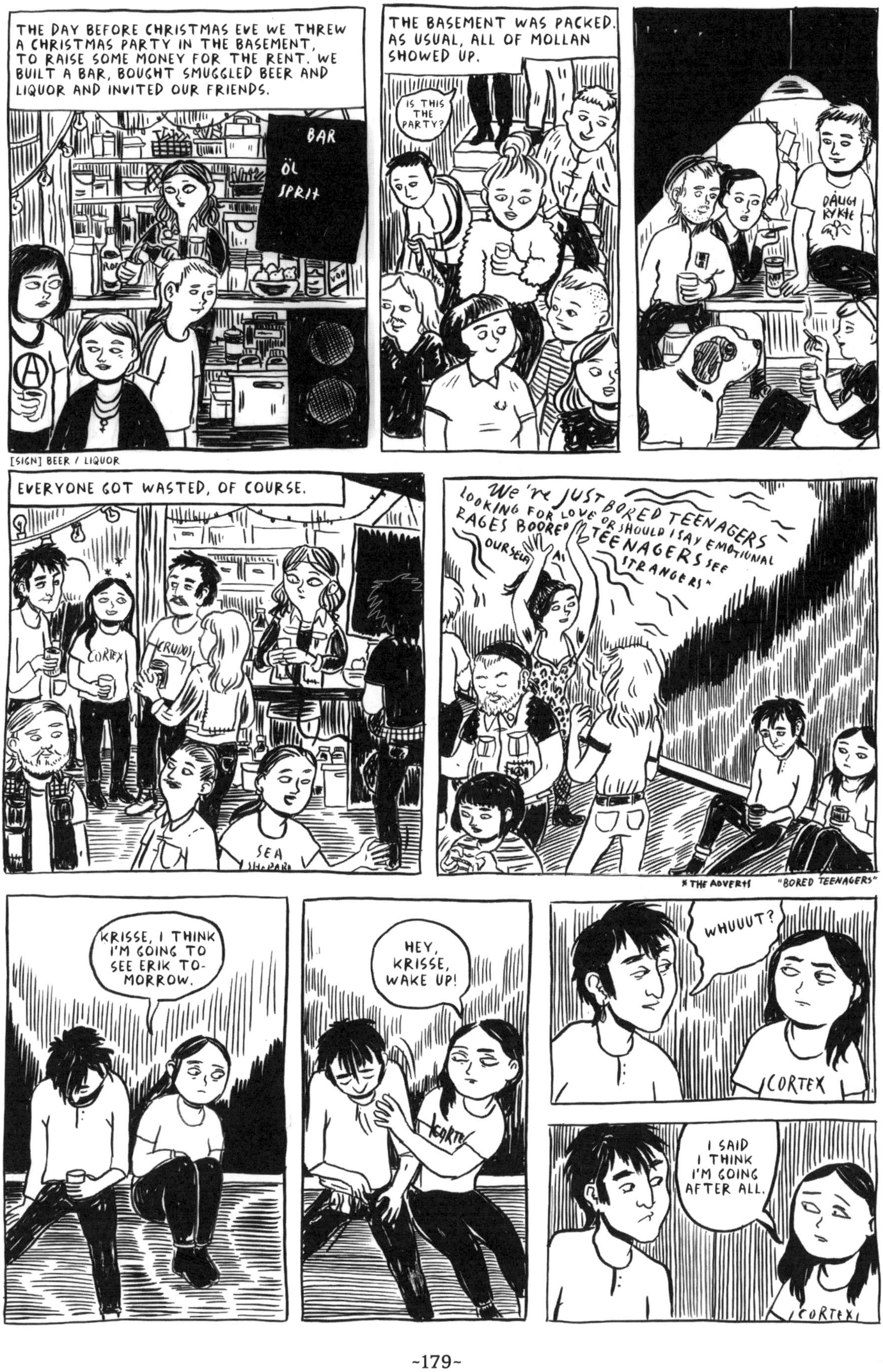
THE DAY BEFORE CHRISTMAS EVE WE THREW A CHRISTMAS PARTY IN THE BASEMENT, TO RAISE SOME MONEY FOR THE RENT. WE BUILT A BAR, BOUGHT SMUGGLED BEER AND LIQUOR AND INVITED OUR FRIENDS.
BAR
ÖL
SPRIT
[SIGN] BEER / LIQUOR
THE BASEMENT WAS PACKED. AS USUAL, ALL OF MOLLAN SHOWED UP.
IS THIS THE PARTY?
DÅLIGT KYNNE
EVERYONE GOT WASTED, OF COURSE.
CORTEX
CRUDOS
SEA SHEPARD
We're JUST BORED TEENAGERS
LOOKING FOR LOVE OR SHOULD I SAY EMOTIONAL
RAGES BOORED TEENAGERS SEE
OURSELF AS STRANGERS"
* THE ADVERTS "BORED TEENAGERS"
KRISSE, I THINK I'M GOING TO SEE ERIK TO-MORROW.
HEY, KRISSE, WAKE UP!
WHUUUT?
CORTEX
I SAID I THINK I'M GOING AFTER ALL.
CORTEX

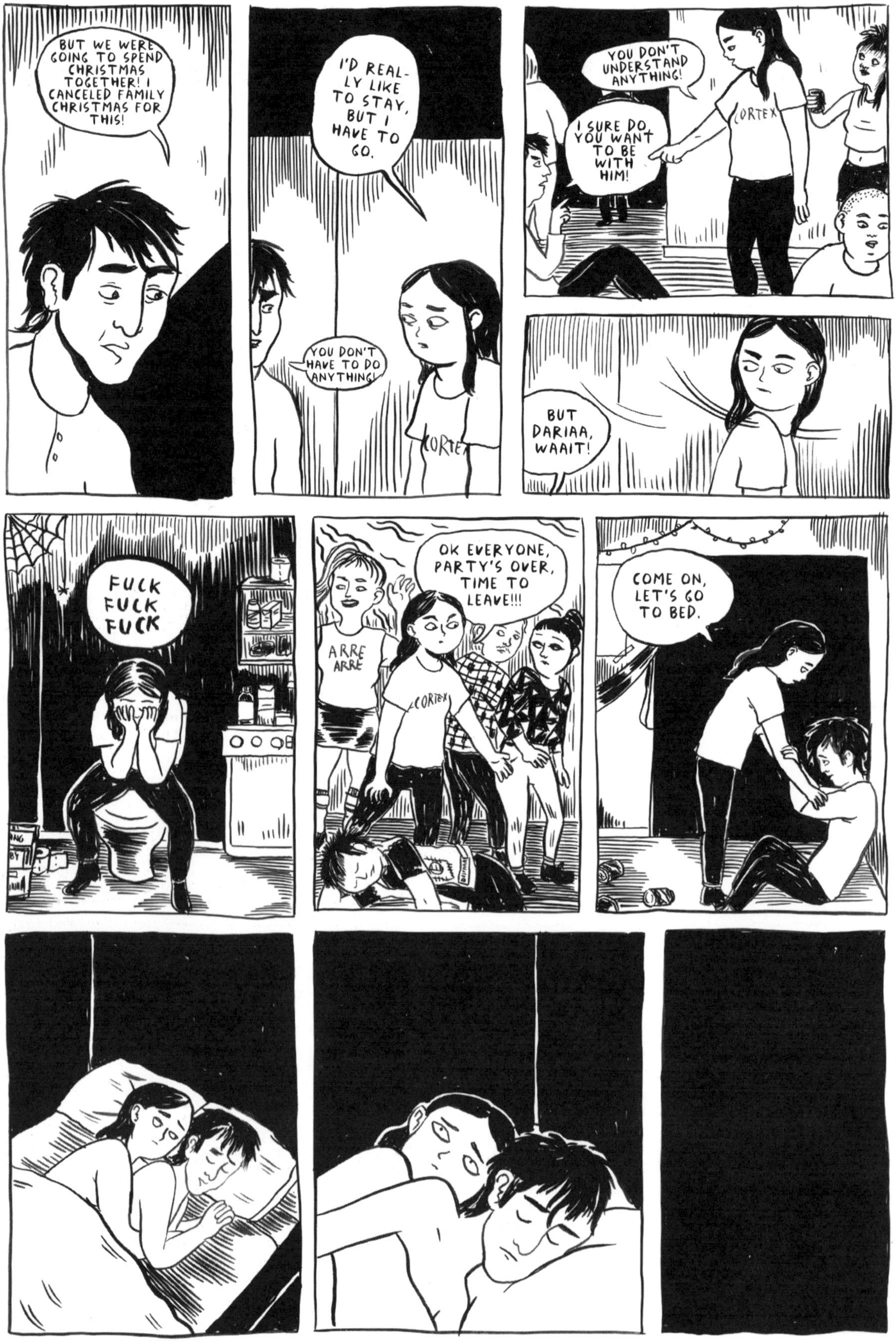
BUT WE WERE GOING TO SPEND CHRISTMAS TOGETHER! I CANCELED FAMILY CHRISTMAS FOR THIS!
I'D REALLY LIKE TO STAY, BUT I HAVE TO GO.
YOU DON'T HAVE TO DO ANYTHING!
YOU DON'T UNDERSTAND ANYTHING!
I SURE DO. YOU WANT TO BE WITH HIM!
CORTEX
BUT DARIAA, WAAIT!
FUCK FUCK FUCK
OK EVERYONE, PARTY'S OVER, TIME TO LEAVE!!!
ARRE ARRE
CORTEX
COME ON, LET'S GO TO BED.

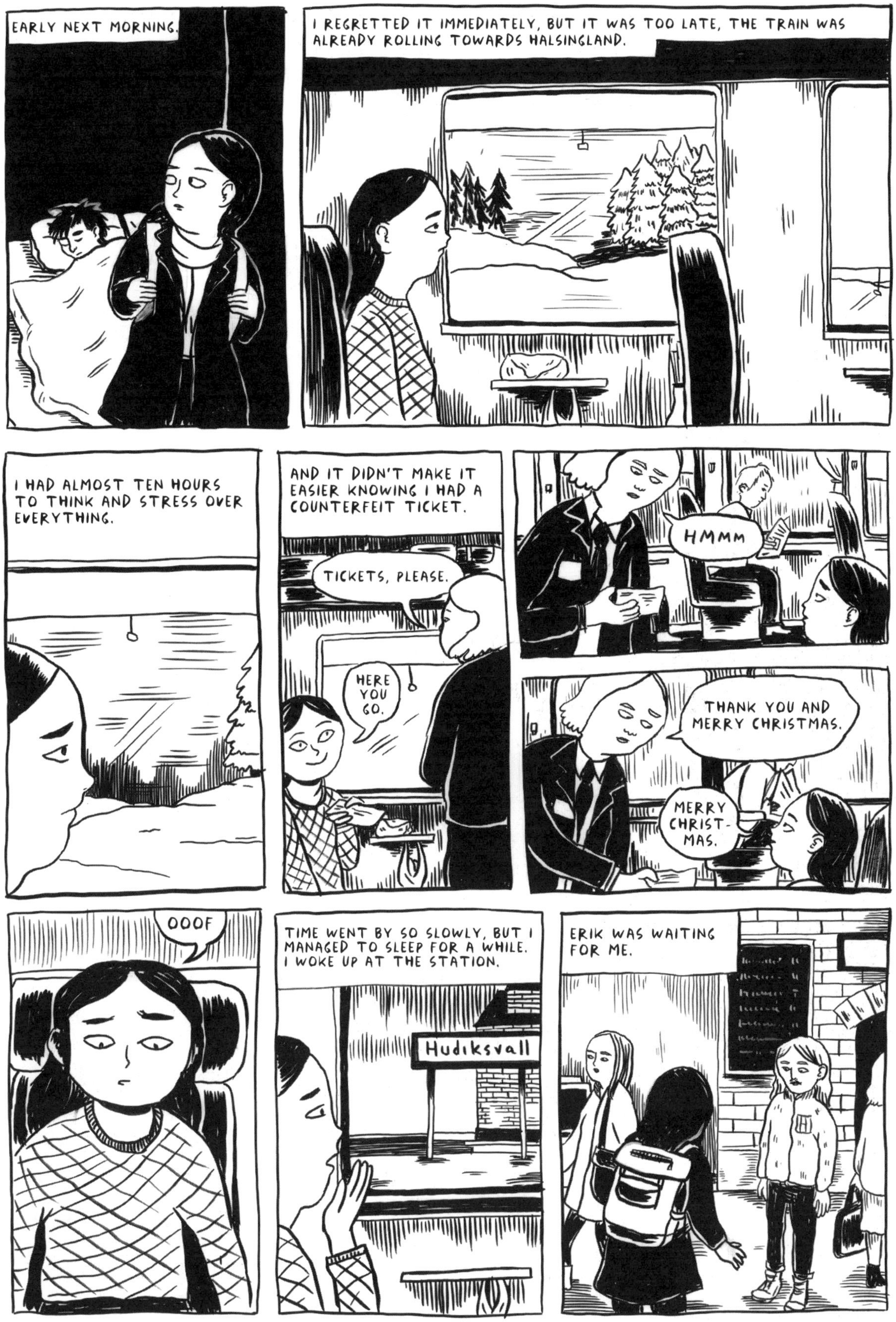
EARLY NEXT MORNING.
I REGRETTED IT IMMEDIATELY, BUT IT WAS TOO LATE, THE TRAIN WAS ALREADY ROLLING TOWARDS HALSINGLAND.
I HAD ALMOST TEN HOURS TO THINK AND STRESS OVER EVERYTHING.
AND IT DIDN'T MAKE IT EASIER KNOWING I HAD A COUNTERFEIT TICKET.
TICKETS, PLEASE.
HERE YOU GO.
HMMM
THANK YOU AND MERRY CHRISTMAS.
MERRY CHRIST-MAS.
OOOF
TIME WENT BY SO SLOWLY, BUT I MANAGED TO SLEEP FOR A WHILE. I WOKE UP AT THE STATION.
Hudiksvall
ERIK WAS WAITING FOR ME.

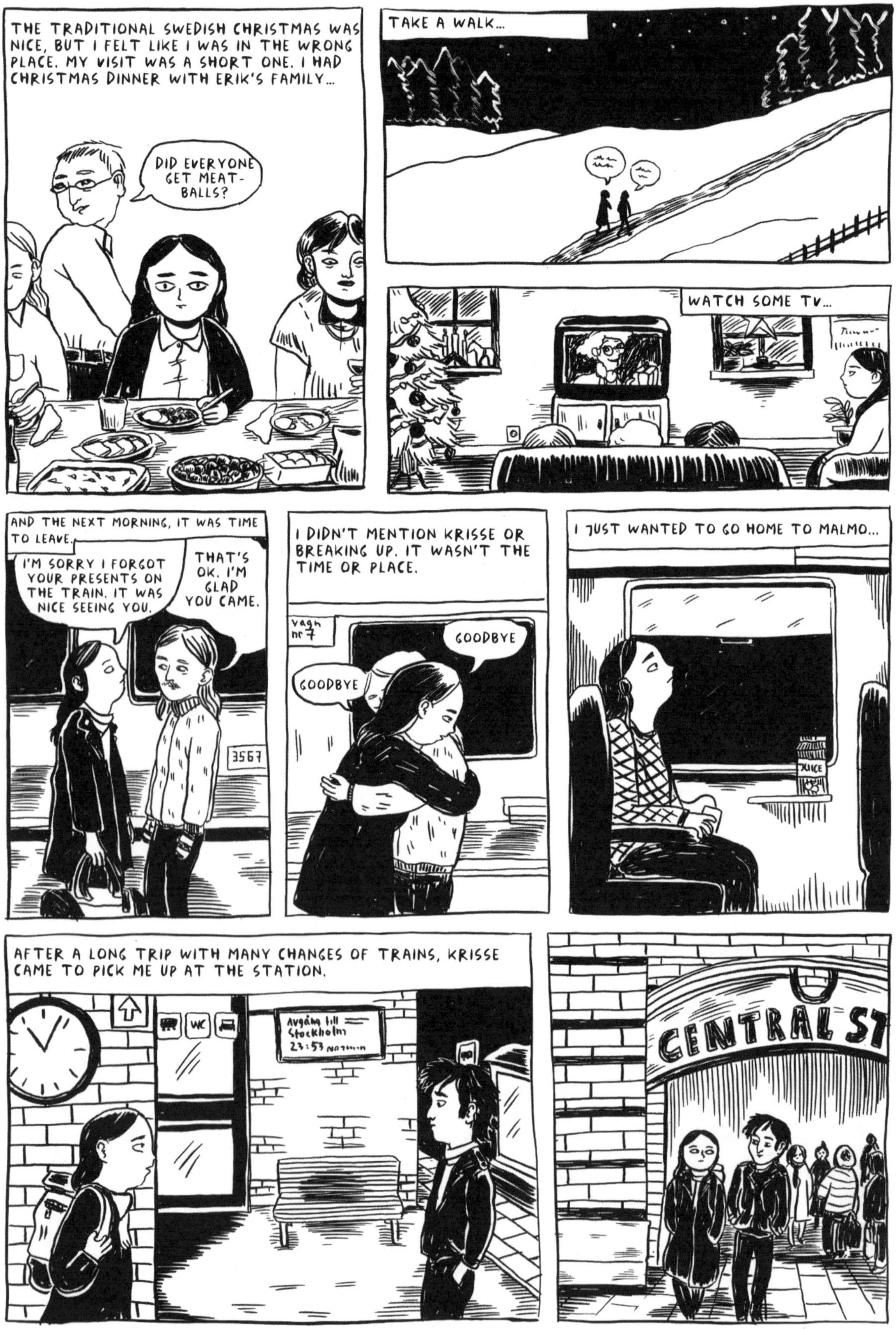
THE TRADITIONAL SWEDISH CHRISTMAS WAS NICE, BUT I FELT LIKE I WAS IN THE WRONG PLACE. MY VISIT WAS A SHORT ONE. I HAD CHRISTMAS DINNER WITH ERIK'S FAMILY...
DID EVERYONE GET MEAT-BALLS?
TAKE A WALK...
WATCH SOME TV...
AND THE NEXT MORNING, IT WAS TIME TO LEAVE.
I'M SORRY I FORGOT YOUR PRESENTS ON THE TRAIN. IT WAS NICE SEEING YOU.
THAT'S OK. I'M GLAD YOU CAME.
3567
I DIDN'T MENTION KRISSE OR BREAKING UP. IT WASN'T THE TIME OR PLACE.
vagn nr 7
GOODBYE
GOODBYE
I JUST WANTED TO GO HOME TO MALMO...
JUICE
AFTER A LONG TRIP WITH MANY CHANGES OF TRAINS, KRISSE CAME TO PICK ME UP AT THE STATION.
WC
Avgång till Stockholm 23:53
CENTRAL ST

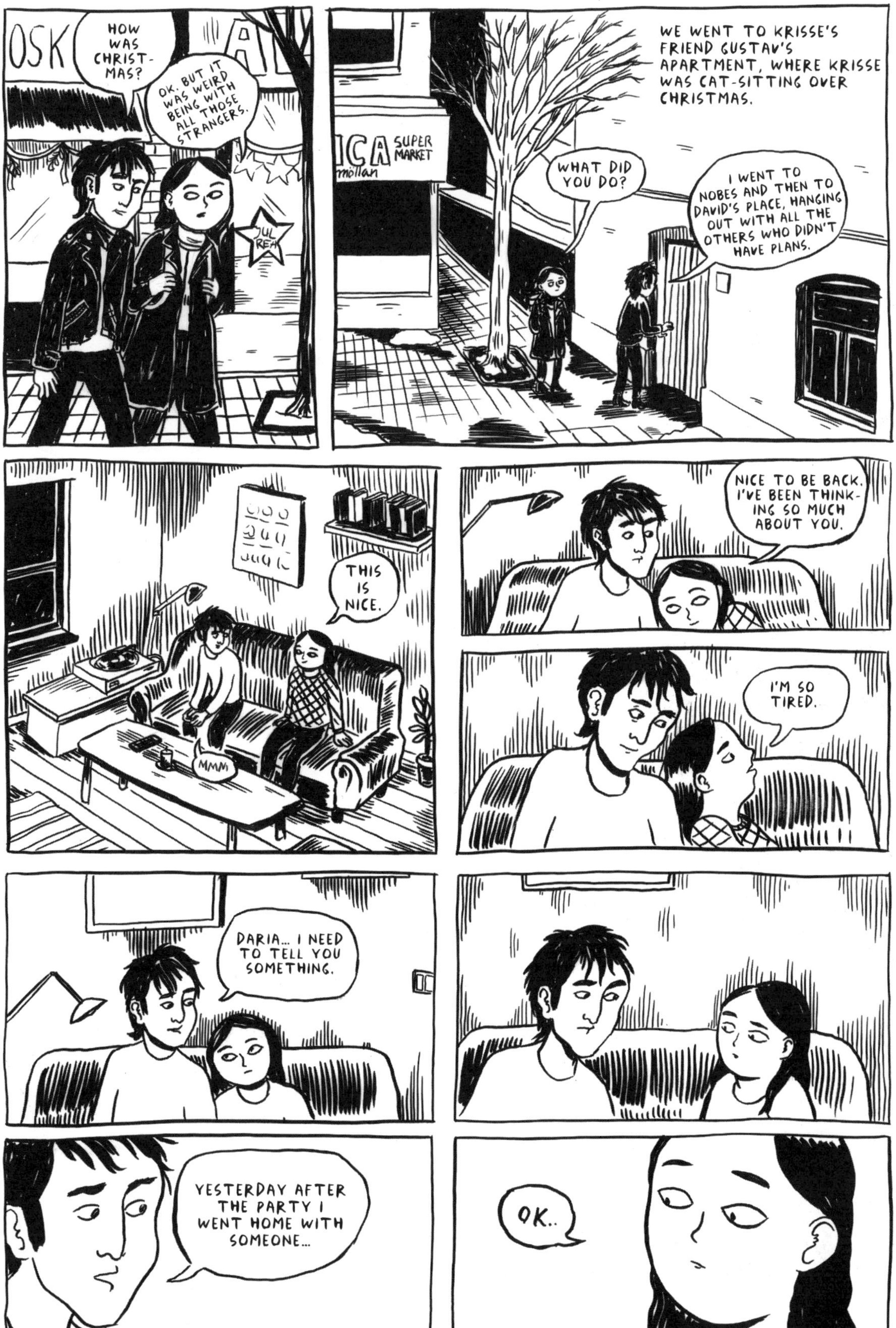
OSK
HOW WAS CHRIST-MAS?
OK, BUT IT WAS WEIRD BEING WITH ALL THOSE STRANGERS.
WE WENT TO KRISSE'S FRIEND GUSTAV'S APARTMENT, WHERE KRISSE WAS CAT-SITTING OVER CHRISTMAS.
ICA SUPER MARKET
WHAT DID YOU DO?
I WENT TO NOBES AND THEN TO DAVID'S PLACE, HANGING OUT WITH ALL THE OTHERS WHO DIDN'T HAVE PLANS.
THIS IS NICE.
MMM
NICE TO BE BACK. I'VE BEEN THINKING SO MUCH ABOUT YOU.
I'M SO TIRED.
DARIA... I NEED TO TELL YOU SOMETHING.
YESTERDAY AFTER THE PARTY I WENT HOME WITH SOMEONE...
OK..

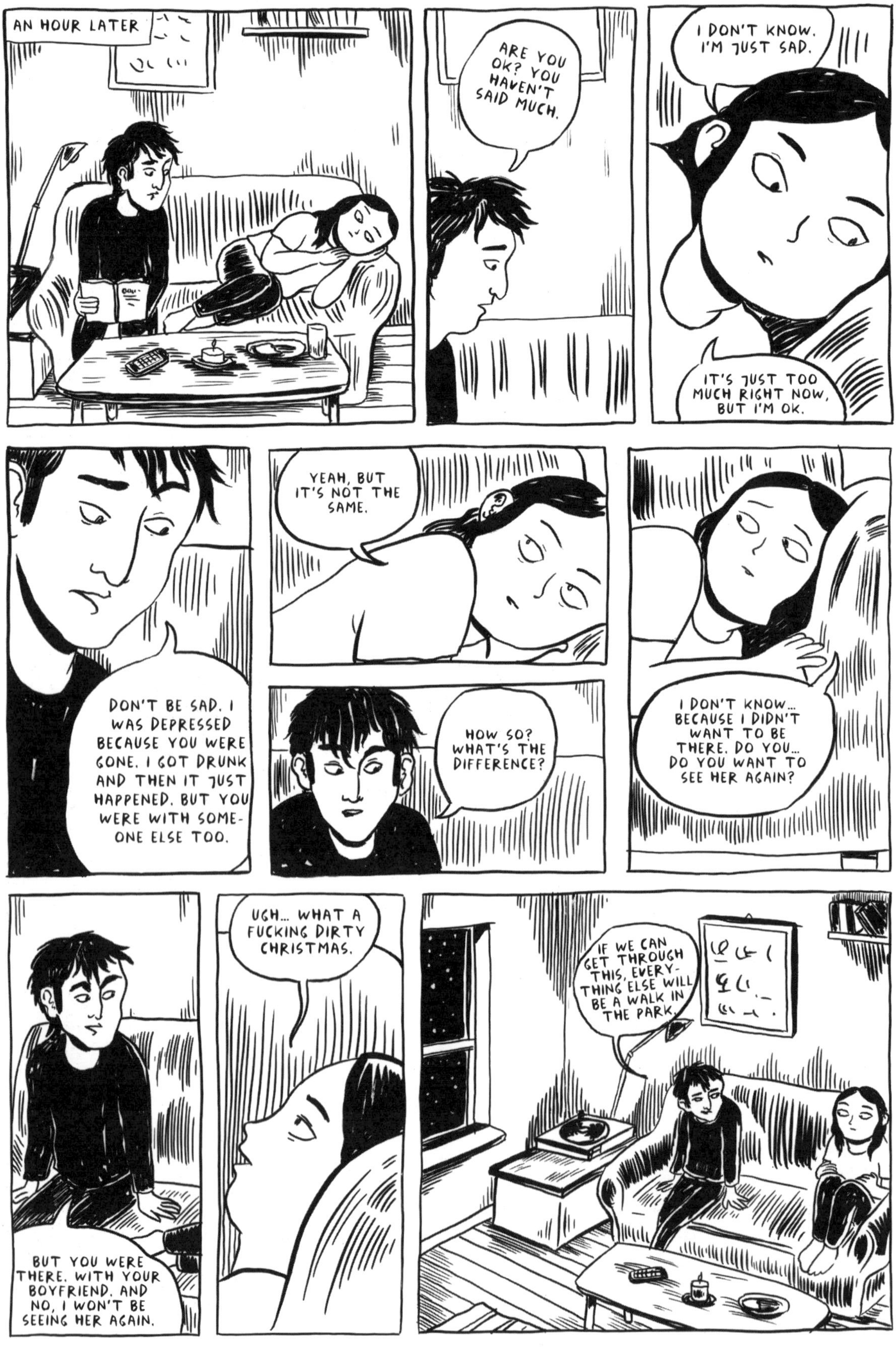
AN HOUR LATER
ARE YOU OK? YOU HAVEN'T SAID MUCH.
I DON'T KNOW. I'M JUST SAD.
IT'S JUST TOO MUCH RIGHT NOW, BUT I'M OK.
DON'T BE SAD. I WAS DEPRESSED BECAUSE YOU WERE GONE. I GOT DRUNK AND THEN IT JUST HAPPENED. BUT YOU WERE WITH SOME-ONE ELSE TOO.
YEAH, BUT IT'S NOT THE SAME.
HOW SO? WHAT'S THE DIFFERENCE?
I DON'T KNOW... BECAUSE I DIDN'T WANT TO BE THERE. DO YOU... DO YOU WANT TO SEE HER AGAIN?
BUT YOU WERE THERE. WITH YOUR BOYFRIEND. AND NO, I WON'T BE SEEING HER AGAIN.
UGH... WHAT A FUCKING DIRTY CHRISTMAS.
IF WE CAN GET THROUGH THIS, EVERY-THING ELSE WILL BE A WALK IN THE PARK.

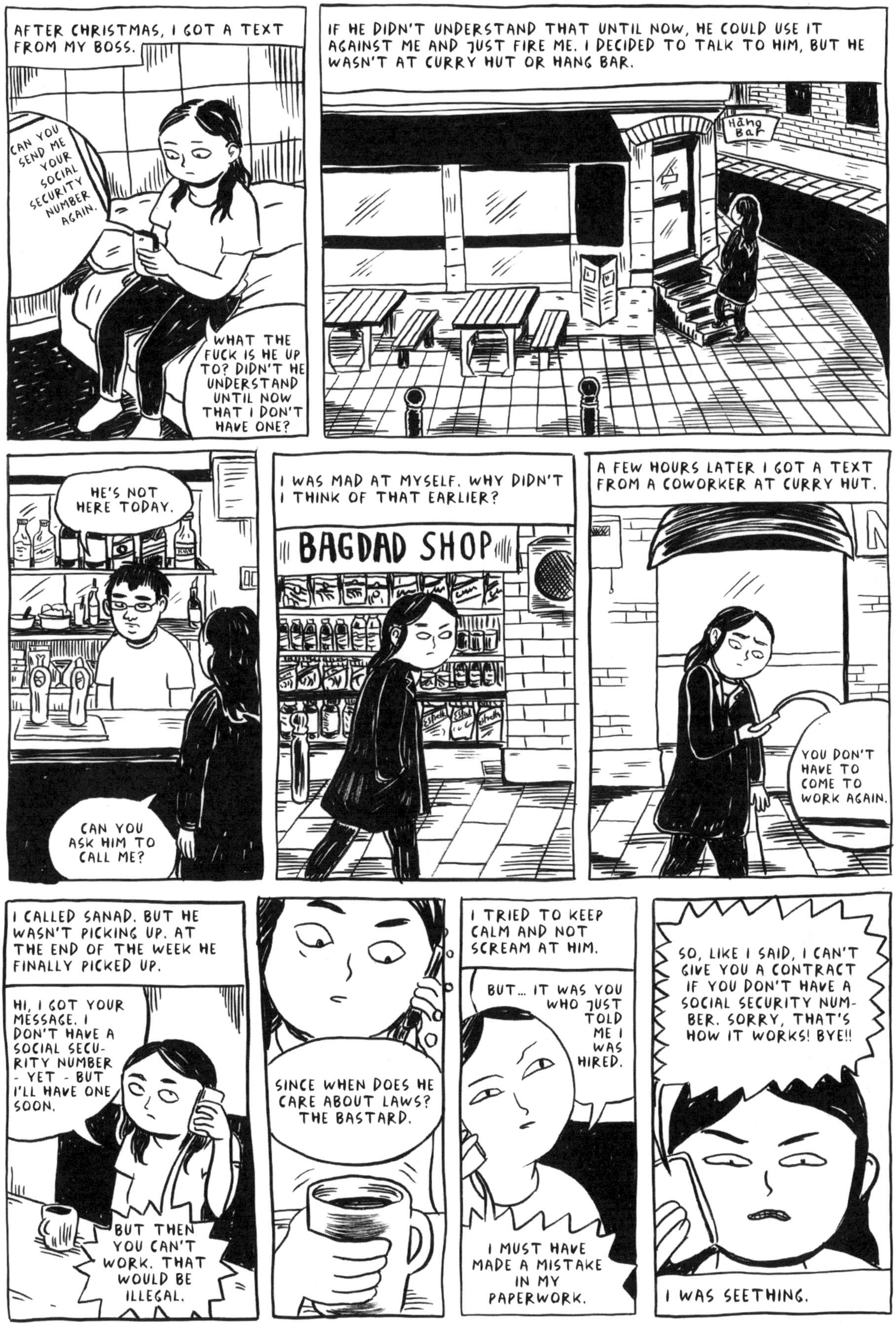
AFTER CHRISTMAS, I GOT A TEXT FROM MY BOSS.
CAN YOU SEND ME YOUR SOCIAL SECURITY NUMBER AGAIN.
WHAT THE FUCK IS HE UP TO? DIDN'T HE UNDERSTAND UNTIL NOW THAT I DON'T HAVE ONE?
IF HE DIDN'T UNDERSTAND THAT UNTIL NOW, HE COULD USE IT AGAINST ME AND JUST FIRE ME. I DECIDED TO TALK TO HIM, BUT HE WASN'T AT CURRY HUT OR HANG BAR.
Hăng Bar
HE'S NOT HERE TODAY.
CAN YOU ASK HIM TO CALL ME?
I WAS MAD AT MYSELF. WHY DIDN'T I THINK OF THAT EARLIER?
BAGDAD SHOP
A FEW HOURS LATER I GOT A TEXT FROM A COWORKER AT CURRY HUT.
YOU DON'T HAVE TO COME TO WORK AGAIN.
I CALLED SANAD. BUT HE WASN'T PICKING UP. AT THE END OF THE WEEK HE FINALLY PICKED UP.
HI, I GOT YOUR MESSAGE. I DON'T HAVE A SOCIAL SECURITY NUMBER - YET - BUT I'LL HAVE ONE SOON.
BUT THEN YOU CAN'T WORK. THAT WOULD BE ILLEGAL.
SINCE WHEN DOES HE CARE ABOUT LAWS? THE BASTARD.
I TRIED TO KEEP CALM AND NOT SCREAM AT HIM.
BUT... IT WAS YOU WHO JUST TOLD ME I WAS HIRED.
I MUST HAVE MADE A MISTAKE IN MY PAPERWORK.
SO, LIKE I SAID, I CAN'T GIVE YOU A CONTRACT IF YOU DON'T HAVE A SOCIAL SECURITY NUMBER. SORRY, THAT'S HOW IT WORKS! BYE!!
I WAS SEETHING.

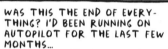

FUCK!

KLIK

I CALLED DANIEL TO TELL HIM EVERYTHING, BUT HE DIDN'T HAVE ANY GOOD NEWS FOR ME EITHER.

DARIA... I'M SO SORRY, BUT I'VE BEEN THINKING ABOUT EVERYTHING AND I HAVE TO BAIL. I CAN'T DO THIS, IT'S STRESSING ME OUT. I CAN'T SLEEP OR ANYTHING. I'VE STARTED LOOKING FOR A NEW JOB. I'M SORRY...

SO WE HAVE TO THINK OF A NEW PLAN.

DANIEL WAS MY LAST HOPE, AND NOW HE WAS GONE TOO.

I SAT THERE IN MY LITTLE ROOM, STARING INTO THE WALL.

WAS THIS THE END OF EVERYTHING? I'D BEEN RUNNING ON AUTOPILOT FOR THE LAST FEW MONTHS...

... WITHOUT EVEN THINKING ABOUT WHAT TO DO IF EVERYTHING FAILED.

FAILURE DIDN'T EVEN SEEM LIKE AN OPTION. I HAD TO DO SOMETHING. I DIDN'T WANT TO GIVE UP JUST YET.

I READ EVERYTHING I COULD FIND ON SKATTEVERKET'S, THE MIGRATION AGENCY'S AND THE UNION'S WEBSITES.

I WENT TO THE SKATTEVERKET OFFICE

YOUR EMPLOYER HAS TO FILL IN THIS FORM. THEN YOU SEND IT TO US AND WE'LL GIVE YOU A SOCIAL SECURITY NUMBER WITHIN A WEEK.

IT WAS WORTH A TRY.

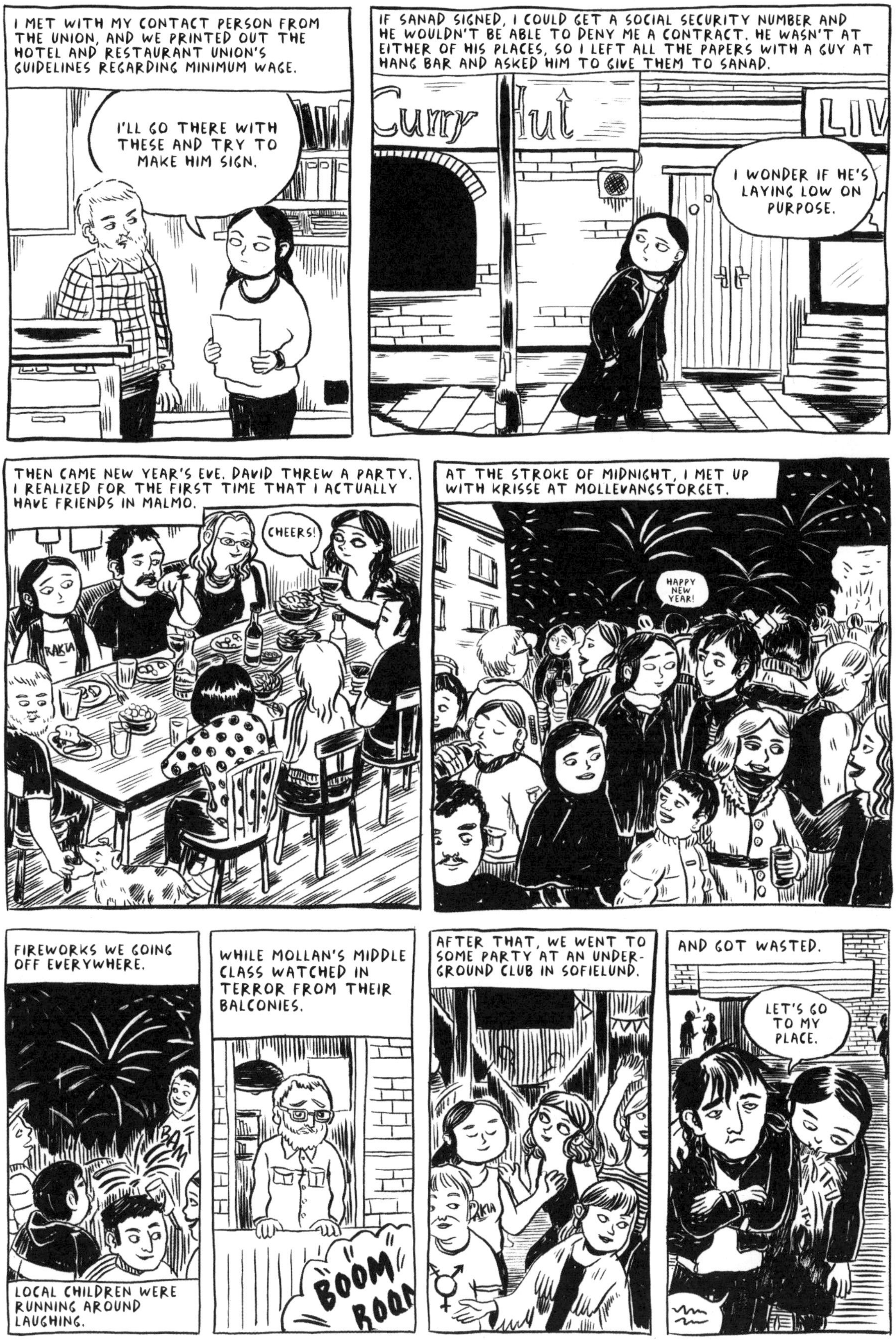
I MET WITH MY CONTACT PERSON FROM THE UNION, AND WE PRINTED OUT THE HOTEL AND RESTAURANT UNION'S GUIDELINES REGARDING MINIMUM WAGE.
I'LL GO THERE WITH THESE AND TRY TO MAKE HIM SIGN.
IF SANAD SIGNED, I COULD GET A SOCIAL SECURITY NUMBER AND HE WOULDN'T BE ABLE TO DENY ME A CONTRACT. HE WASN'T AT EITHER OF HIS PLACES, SO I LEFT ALL THE PAPERS WITH A GUY AT HANG BAR AND ASKED HIM TO GIVE THEM TO SANAD.
Curry Hut
LIV
I WONDER IF HE'S LAYING LOW ON PURPOSE.
THEN CAME NEW YEAR'S EVE. DAVID THREW A PARTY. I REALIZED FOR THE FIRST TIME THAT I ACTUALLY HAVE FRIENDS IN MALMO.
CHEERS!
RAKIA
AT THE STROKE OF MIDNIGHT, I MET UP WITH KRISSE AT MOLLEVANGSTORGET.
HAPPY NEW YEAR!
FIREWORKS WE GOING OFF EVERYWHERE.
BAM
LOCAL CHILDREN WERE RUNNING AROUND LAUGHING.
WHILE MOLLAN'S MIDDLE CLASS WATCHED IN TERROR FROM THEIR BALCONIES.
BOOM
ROOM
AFTER THAT, WE WENT TO SOME PARTY AT AN UNDER-GROUND CLUB IN SOFIELUND.
RAKIA
AND GOT WASTED.
LET'S GO TO MY PLACE.

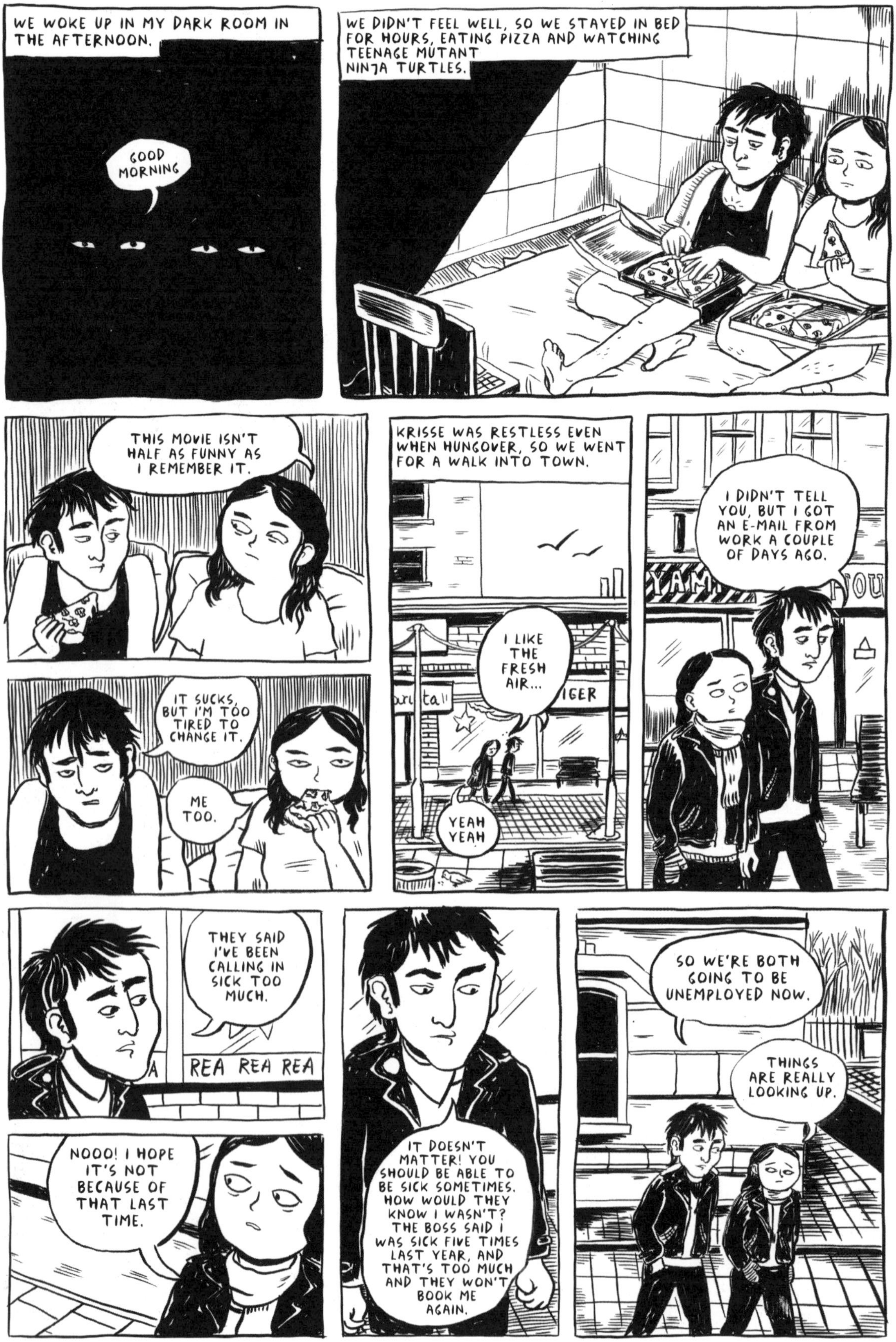
WE WOKE UP IN MY DARK ROOM IN THE AFTERNOON.
GOOD MORNING
WE DIDN'T FEEL WELL, SO WE STAYED IN BED FOR HOURS, EATING PIZZA AND WATCHING TEENAGE MUTANT NINJA TURTLES.
THIS MOVIE ISN'T HALF AS FUNNY AS I REMEMBER IT.
IT SUCKS, BUT I'M TOO TIRED TO CHANGE IT.
ME TOO.
KRISSE WAS RESTLESS EVEN WHEN HUNGOVER, SO WE WENT FOR A WALK INTO TOWN.
I LIKE THE FRESH AIR...
YEAH YEAH
I DIDN'T TELL YOU, BUT I GOT AN E-MAIL FROM WORK A COUPLE OF DAYS AGO.
THEY SAID I'VE BEEN CALLING IN SICK TOO MUCH.
REA REA REA
NOOO! I HOPE IT'S NOT BECAUSE OF THAT LAST TIME.
IT DOESN'T MATTER! YOU SHOULD BE ABLE TO BE SICK SOMETIMES. HOW WOULD THEY KNOW I WASN'T? THE BOSS SAID I WAS SICK FIVE TIMES LAST YEAR, AND THAT'S TOO MUCH AND THEY WON'T BOOK ME AGAIN.
SO WE'RE BOTH GOING TO BE UNEMPLOYED NOW.
THINGS ARE REALLY LOOKING UP.

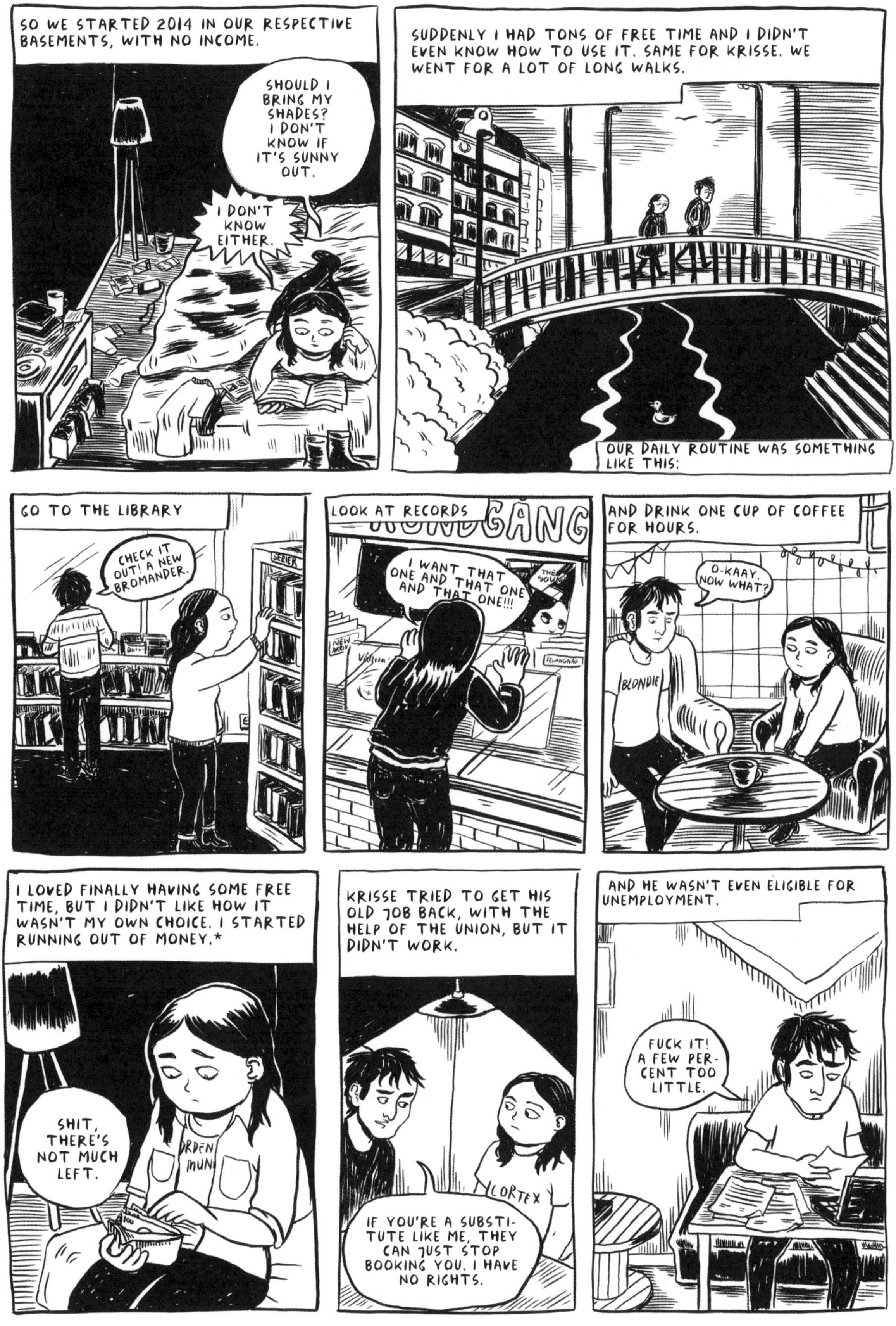

SO WE STARTED 2014 IN OUR RESPECTIVE BASEMENTS, WITH NO INCOME.
SHOULD I BRING MY SHADES? I DON'T KNOW IF IT'S SUNNY OUT.
I DON'T KNOW EITHER.
SUDDENLY I HAD TONS OF FREE TIME AND I DIDN'T EVEN KNOW HOW TO USE IT. SAME FOR KRISSE. WE WENT FOR A LOT OF LONG WALKS.
OUR DAILY ROUTINE WAS SOMETHING LIKE THIS:
GO TO THE LIBRARY
SERIER
CHECK IT OUT! A NEW BROMANDER.
LOOK AT RECORDS
I WANT THAT ONE AND THAT ONE AND THAT ONE!!!
AND DRINK ONE CUP OF COFFEE FOR HOURS.
O-KAAY. NOW WHAT?
BLONDIE
I LOVED FINALLY HAVING SOME FREE TIME, BUT I DIDN'T LIKE HOW IT WASN'T MY OWN CHOICE. I STARTED RUNNING OUT OF MONEY.*
SHIT, THERE'S NOT MUCH LEFT.
KRISSE TRIED TO GET HIS OLD JOB BACK, WITH THE HELP OF THE UNION, BUT IT DIDN'T WORK.
CORTEX
IF YOU'RE A SUBSTITUTE LIKE ME, THEY CAN JUST STOP BOOKING YOU. I HAVE NO RIGHTS.
AND HE WASN'T EVEN ELIGIBLE FOR UNEMPLOYMENT.
FUCK IT! A FEW PERCENT TOO LITTLE.

* NOT ELIGIBLE FOR STUDENT LOANS OR WELFARE

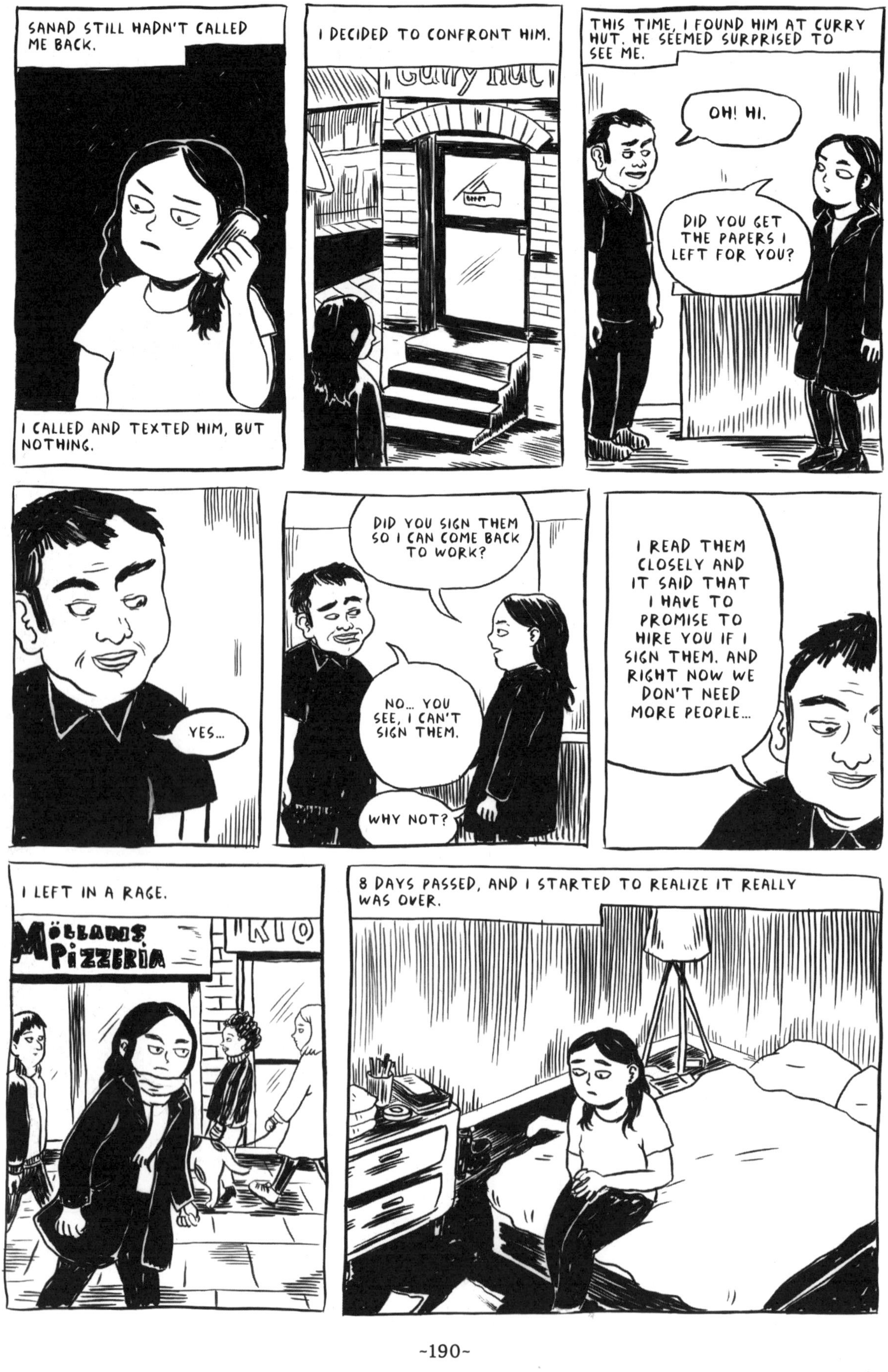
SANAD STILL HADN'T CALLED ME BACK.
I CALLED AND TEXTED HIM, BUT NOTHING.
I DECIDED TO CONFRONT HIM.
Curry Hut
THIS TIME, I FOUND HIM AT CURRY HUT. HE SEEMED SURPRISED TO SEE ME.
OH! HI.
DID YOU GET THE PAPERS I LEFT FOR YOU?
YES...
DID YOU SIGN THEM SO I CAN COME BACK TO WORK?
NO... YOU SEE, I CAN'T SIGN THEM.
WHY NOT?
I READ THEM CLOSELY AND IT SAID THAT I HAVE TO PROMISE TO HIRE YOU IF I SIGN THEM. AND RIGHT NOW WE DON'T NEED MORE PEOPLE...
I LEFT IN A RAGE.
PIZZERIA
8 DAYS PASSED, AND I STARTED TO REALIZE IT REALLY WAS OVER.

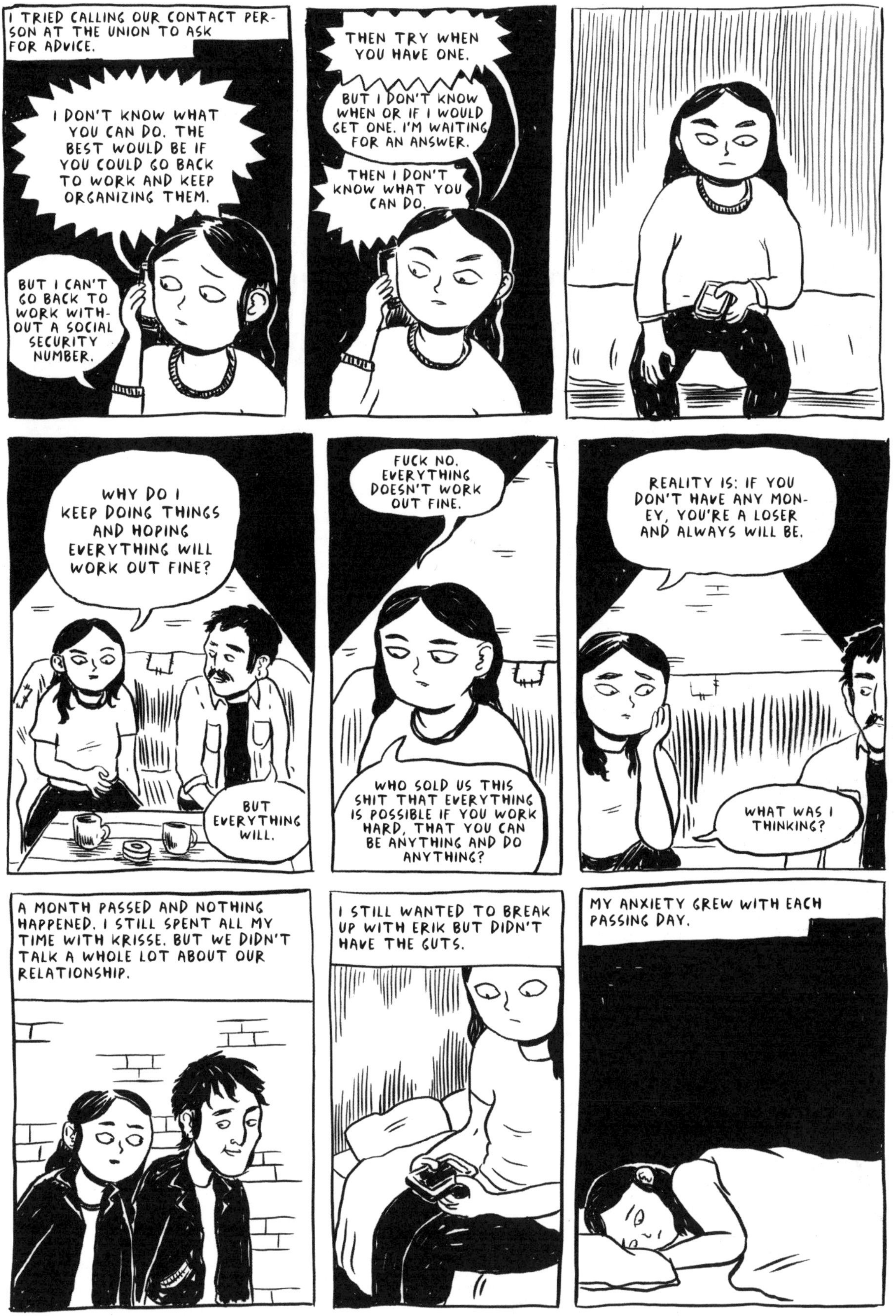
I TRIED CALLING OUR CONTACT PERSON AT THE UNION TO ASK FOR ADVICE.
I DON'T KNOW WHAT YOU CAN DO. THE BEST WOULD BE IF YOU COULD GO BACK TO WORK AND KEEP ORGANIZING THEM.
BUT I CAN'T GO BACK TO WORK WITHOUT A SOCIAL SECURITY NUMBER.
THEN TRY WHEN YOU HAVE ONE.
BUT I DON'T KNOW WHEN OR IF I WOULD GET ONE. I'M WAITING FOR AN ANSWER.
THEN I DON'T KNOW WHAT YOU CAN DO.
WHY DO I KEEP DOING THINGS AND HOPING EVERYTHING WILL WORK OUT FINE?
BUT EVERYTHING WILL.
FUCK NO. EVERYTHING DOESN'T WORK OUT FINE.
WHO SOLD US THIS SHIT THAT EVERYTHING IS POSSIBLE IF YOU WORK HARD, THAT YOU CAN BE ANYTHING AND DO ANYTHING?
REALITY IS: IF YOU DON'T HAVE ANY MONEY, YOU'RE A LOSER AND ALWAYS WILL BE.
WHAT WAS I THINKING?
A MONTH PASSED AND NOTHING HAPPENED. I STILL SPENT ALL MY TIME WITH KRISSE. BUT WE DIDN'T TALK A WHOLE LOT ABOUT OUR RELATIONSHIP.
I STILL WANTED TO BREAK UP WITH ERIK BUT DIDN'T HAVE THE GUTS.
MY ANXIETY GREW WITH EACH PASSING DAY.

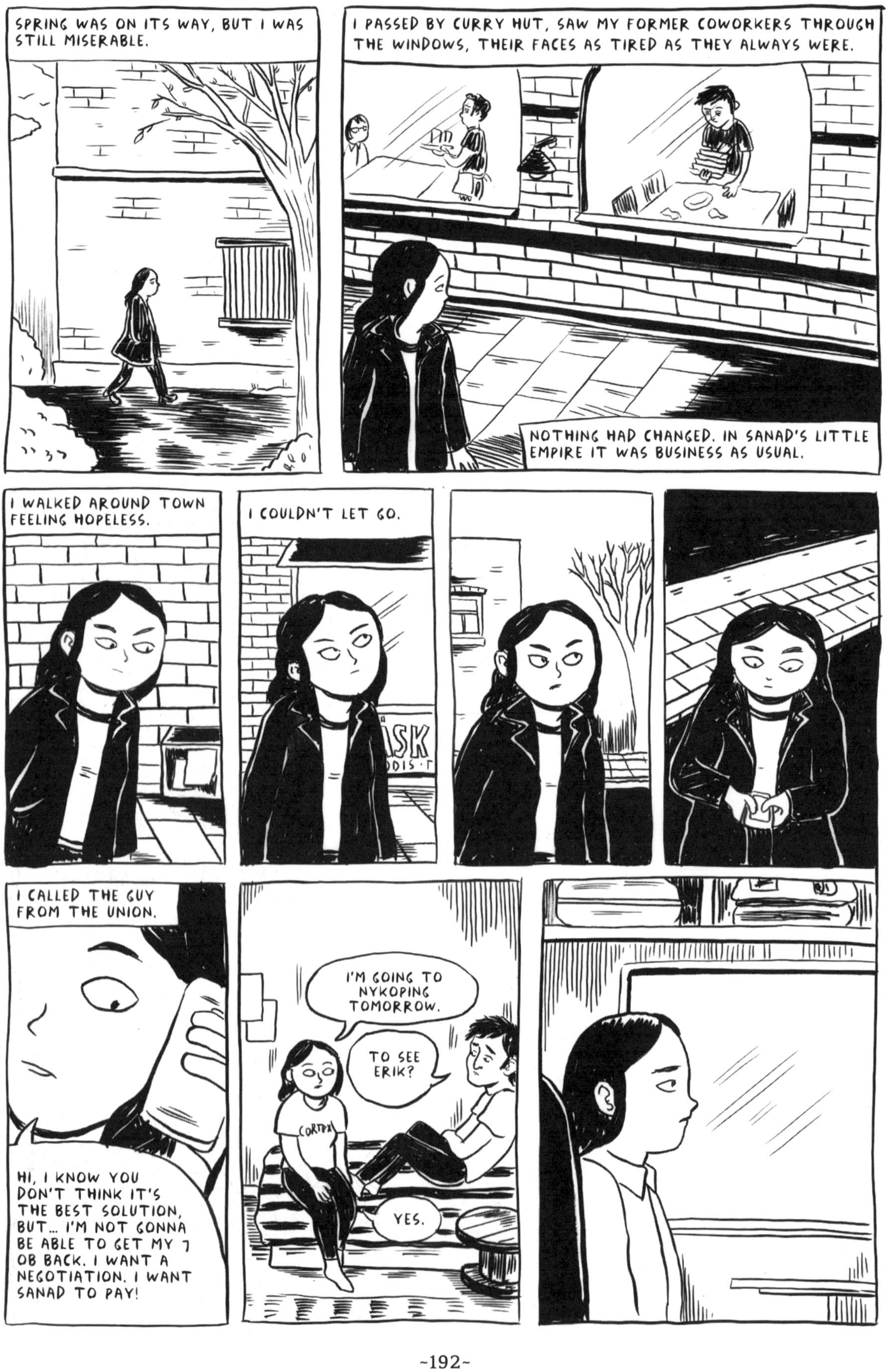
SPRING WAS ON ITS WAY, BUT I WAS STILL MISERABLE.
I PASSED BY CURRY HUT, SAW MY FORMER COWORKERS THROUGH THE WINDOWS, THEIR FACES AS TIRED AS THEY ALWAYS WERE.
NOTHING HAD CHANGED. IN SANAD'S LITTLE EMPIRE IT WAS BUSINESS AS USUAL.
I WALKED AROUND TOWN FEELING HOPELESS.
I COULDN'T LET GO.
I CALLED THE GUY FROM THE UNION.
HI, I KNOW YOU DON'T THINK IT'S THE BEST SOLUTION, BUT... I'M NOT GONNA BE ABLE TO GET MY JOB BACK. I WANT A NEGOTIATION. I WANT SANAD TO PAY!
I'M GOING TO NYKOPING TOMORROW.
TO SEE ERIK?
YES.

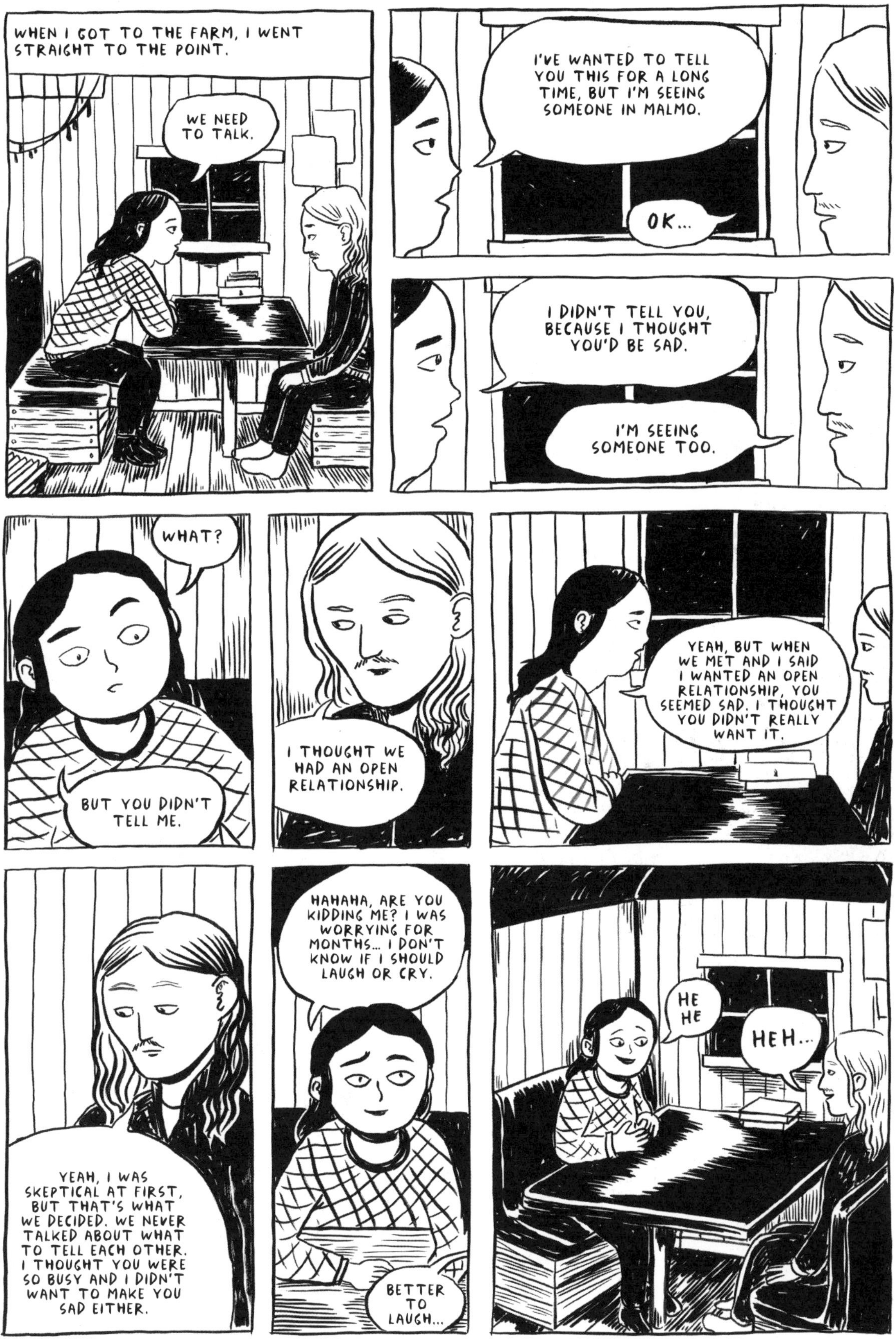

WHEN I GOT TO THE FARM, I WENT STRAIGHT TO THE POINT.
WE NEED TO TALK.
I'VE WANTED TO TELL YOU THIS FOR A LONG TIME, BUT I'M SEEING SOMEONE IN MALMO.
OK...
I DIDN'T TELL YOU, BECAUSE I THOUGHT YOU'D BE SAD.
I'M SEEING SOMEONE TOO.
WHAT?
BUT YOU DIDN'T TELL ME.
I THOUGHT WE HAD AN OPEN RELATIONSHIP.
YEAH, BUT WHEN WE MET AND I SAID I WANTED AN OPEN RELATIONSHIP, YOU SEEMED SAD. I THOUGHT YOU DIDN'T REALLY WANT IT.
YEAH, I WAS SKEPTICAL AT FIRST, BUT THAT'S WHAT WE DECIDED. WE NEVER TALKED ABOUT WHAT TO TELL EACH OTHER. I THOUGHT YOU WERE SO BUSY AND I DIDN'T WANT TO MAKE YOU SAD EITHER.
HAHAHA, ARE YOU KIDDING ME? I WAS WORRYING FOR MONTHS... I DON'T KNOW IF I SHOULD LAUGH OR CRY.
BETTER TO LAUGH...
HE HE
HEH...

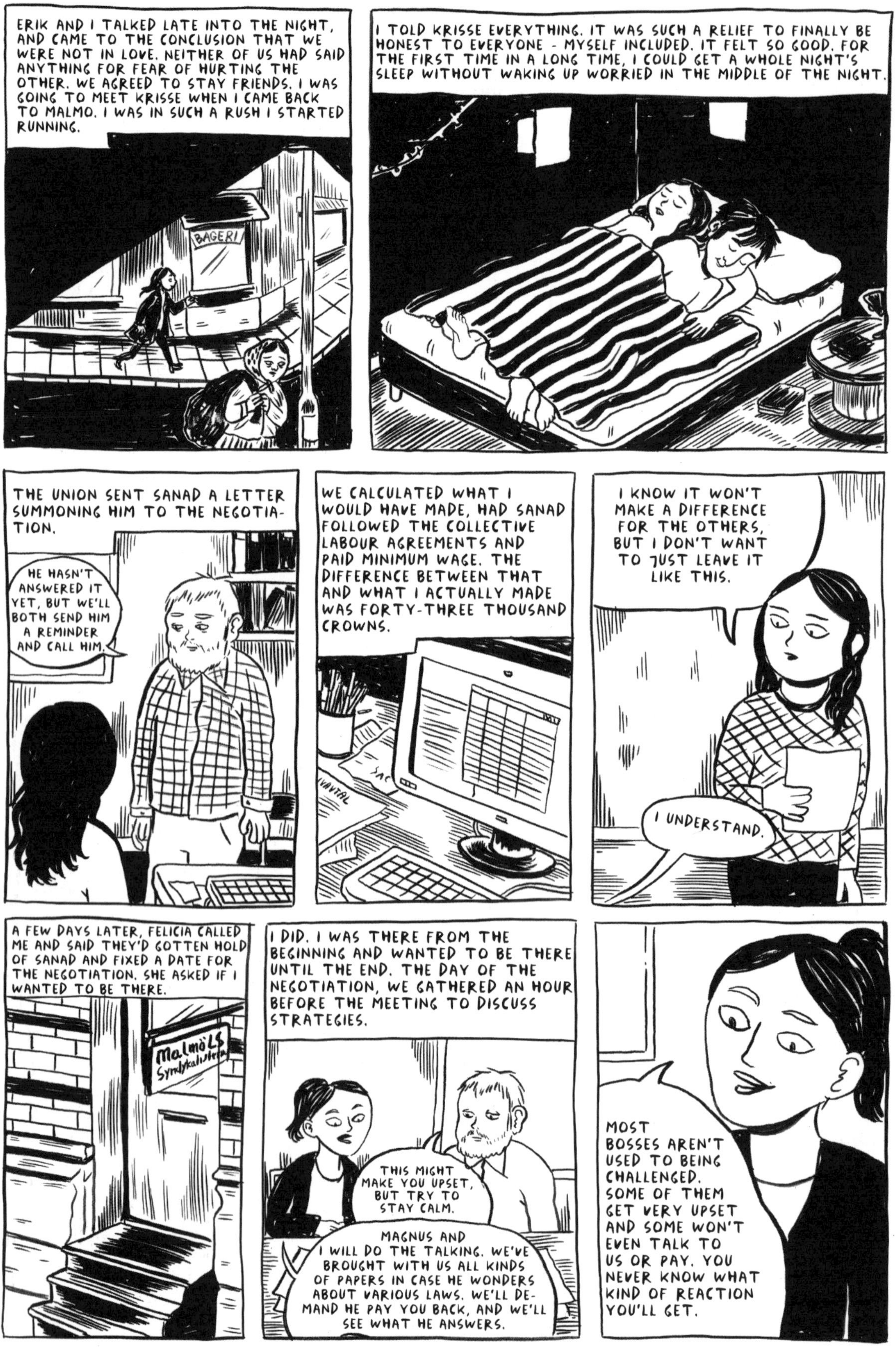

ERIK AND I TALKED LATE INTO THE NIGHT, AND CAME TO THE CONCLUSION THAT WE WERE NOT IN LOVE. NEITHER OF US HAD SAID ANYTHING FOR FEAR OF HURTING THE OTHER. WE AGREED TO STAY FRIENDS. I WAS GOING TO MEET KRISSE WHEN I CAME BACK TO MALMO. I WAS IN SUCH A RUSH I STARTED RUNNING.
BAGERI
I TOLD KRISSE EVERYTHING. IT WAS SUCH A RELIEF TO FINALLY BE HONEST TO EVERYONE - MYSELF INCLUDED. IT FELT SO GOOD. FOR THE FIRST TIME IN A LONG TIME, I COULD GET A WHOLE NIGHT'S SLEEP WITHOUT WAKING UP WORRIED IN THE MIDDLE OF THE NIGHT.
THE UNION SENT SANAD A LETTER SUMMONING HIM TO THE NEGOTIATION.
HE HASN'T ANSWERED IT YET, BUT WE'LL BOTH SEND HIM A REMINDER AND CALL HIM.
WE CALCULATED WHAT I WOULD HAVE MADE, HAD SANAD FOLLOWED THE COLLECTIVE LABOUR AGREEMENTS AND PAID MINIMUM WAGE. THE DIFFERENCE BETWEEN THAT AND WHAT I ACTUALLY MADE WAS FORTY-THREE THOUSAND CROWNS.
I KNOW IT WON'T MAKE A DIFFERENCE FOR THE OTHERS, BUT I DON'T WANT TO JUST LEAVE IT LIKE THIS.
I UNDERSTAND.
A FEW DAYS LATER, FELICIA CALLED ME AND SAID THEY'D GOTTEN HOLD OF SANAD AND FIXED A DATE FOR THE NEGOTIATION. SHE ASKED IF I WANTED TO BE THERE.
Malmö LS
I DID. I WAS THERE FROM THE BEGINNING AND WANTED TO BE THERE UNTIL THE END. THE DAY OF THE NEGOTIATION, WE GATHERED AN HOUR BEFORE THE MEETING TO DISCUSS STRATEGIES.
THIS MIGHT MAKE YOU UPSET, BUT TRY TO STAY CALM.
MAGNUS AND I WILL DO THE TALKING. WE'VE BROUGHT WITH US ALL KINDS OF PAPERS IN CASE HE WONDERS ABOUT VARIOUS LAWS. WE'LL DEMAND HE PAY YOU BACK, AND WE'LL SEE WHAT HE ANSWERS.
MOST BOSSES AREN'T USED TO BEING CHALLENGED. SOME OF THEM GET VERY UPSET AND SOME WON'T EVEN TALK TO US OR PAY. YOU NEVER KNOW WHAT KIND OF REACTION YOU'LL GET.

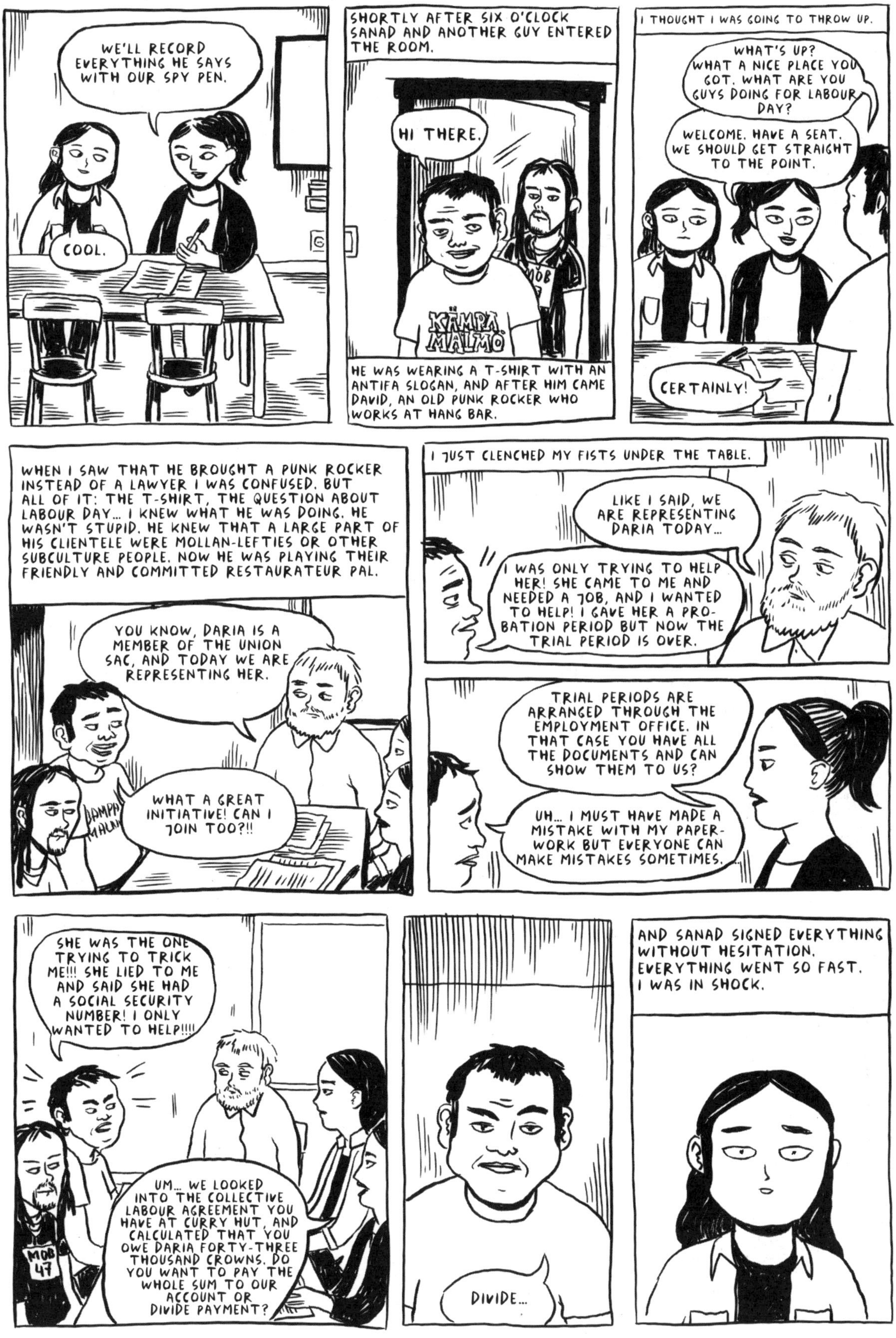
WE'LL RECORD EVERYTHING HE SAYS WITH OUR SPY PEN.
COOL.
SHORTLY AFTER SIX O'CLOCK SANAD AND ANOTHER GUY ENTERED THE ROOM.
HI THERE.
KÄMPA MALMÖ
MOB
HE WAS WEARING A T-SHIRT WITH AN ANTIFA SLOGAN, AND AFTER HIM CAME DAVID, AN OLD PUNK ROCKER WHO WORKS AT HANG BAR.
I THOUGHT I WAS GOING TO THROW UP.
WHAT'S UP? WHAT A NICE PLACE YOU GOT. WHAT ARE YOU GUYS DOING FOR LABOUR DAY?
WELCOME. HAVE A SEAT. WE SHOULD GET STRAIGHT TO THE POINT.
CERTAINLY!
WHEN I SAW THAT HE BROUGHT A PUNK ROCKER INSTEAD OF A LAWYER I WAS CONFUSED. BUT ALL OF IT: THE T-SHIRT, THE QUESTION ABOUT LABOUR DAY... I KNEW WHAT HE WAS DOING. HE WASN'T STUPID. HE KNEW THAT A LARGE PART OF HIS CLIENTELE WERE MOLLAN-LEFTIES OR OTHER SUBCULTURE PEOPLE. NOW HE WAS PLAYING THEIR FRIENDLY AND COMMITTED RESTAURATEUR PAL.
YOU KNOW, DARIA IS A MEMBER OF THE UNION SAC, AND TODAY WE ARE REPRESENTING HER.
WHAT A GREAT INITIATIVE! CAN I JOIN TOO?!!
I JUST CLENCHED MY FISTS UNDER THE TABLE.
LIKE I SAID, WE ARE REPRESENTING DARIA TODAY...
I WAS ONLY TRYING TO HELP HER! SHE CAME TO ME AND NEEDED A JOB, AND I WANTED TO HELP! I GAVE HER A PROBATION PERIOD BUT NOW THE TRIAL PERIOD IS OVER.
TRIAL PERIODS ARE ARRANGED THROUGH THE EMPLOYMENT OFFICE. IN THAT CASE YOU HAVE ALL THE DOCUMENTS AND CAN SHOW THEM TO US?
UH... I MUST HAVE MADE A MISTAKE WITH MY PAPERWORK BUT EVERYONE CAN MAKE MISTAKES SOMETIMES.
SHE WAS THE ONE TRYING TO TRICK ME!!! SHE LIED TO ME AND SAID SHE HAD A SOCIAL SECURITY NUMBER! I ONLY WANTED TO HELP!!!!
MOB 47
UM... WE LOOKED INTO THE COLLECTIVE LABOUR AGREEMENT YOU HAVE AT CURRY HUT, AND CALCULATED THAT YOU OWE DARIA FORTY-THREE THOUSAND CROWNS. DO YOU WANT TO PAY THE WHOLE SUM TO OUR ACCOUNT OR DIVIDE PAYMENT?
DIVIDE...
AND SANAD SIGNED EVERYTHING WITHOUT HESITATION. EVERYTHING WENT SO FAST. I WAS IN SHOCK.

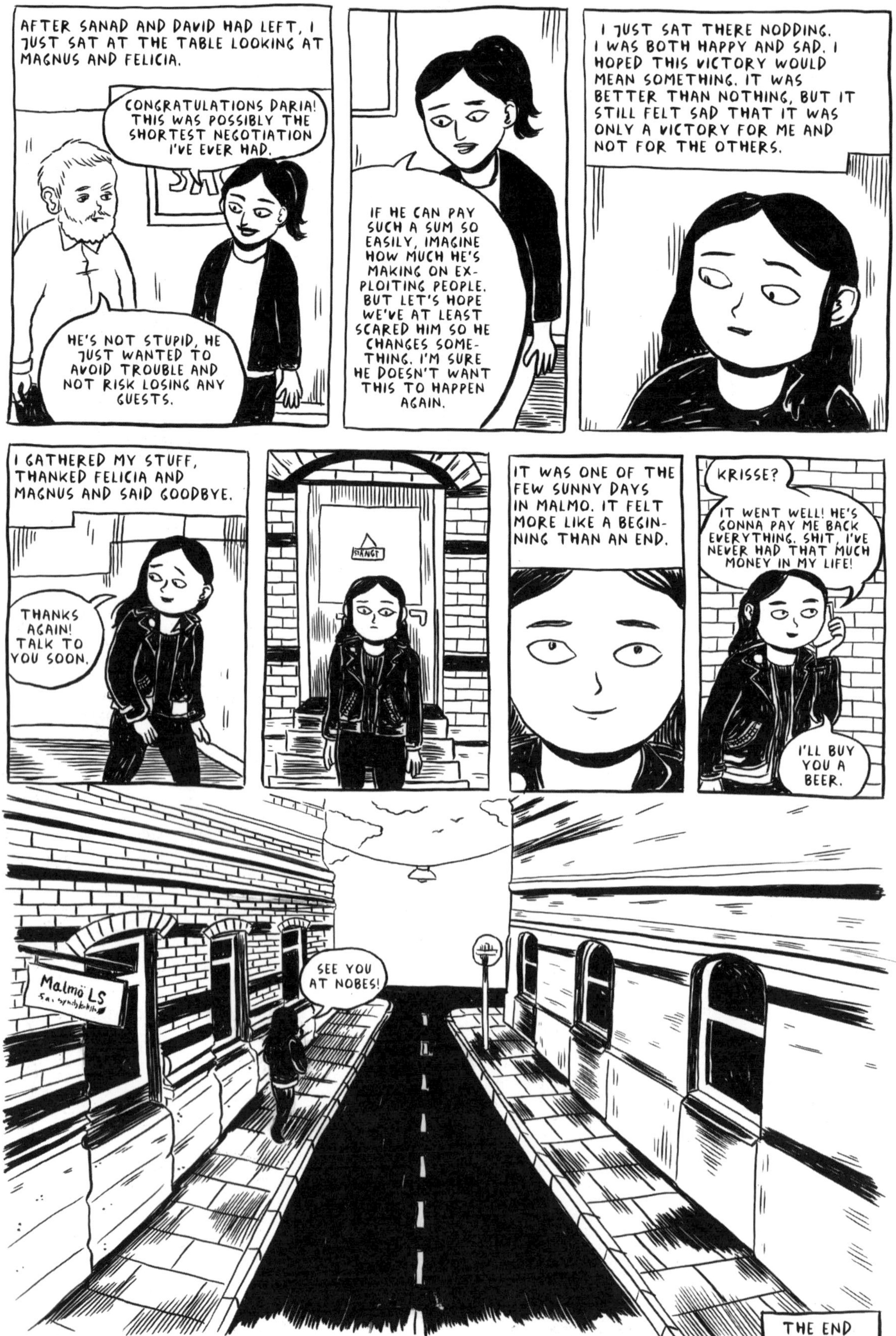
AFTER SANAD AND DAVID HAD LEFT, I JUST SAT AT THE TABLE LOOKING AT MAGNUS AND FELICIA.
CONGRATULATIONS DARIA! THIS WAS POSSIBLY THE SHORTEST NEGOTIATION I'VE EVER HAD.
HE'S NOT STUPID, HE JUST WANTED TO AVOID TROUBLE AND NOT RISK LOSING ANY GUESTS.
IF HE CAN PAY SUCH A SUM SO EASILY, IMAGINE HOW MUCH HE'S MAKING ON EXPLOITING PEOPLE. BUT LET'S HOPE WE'VE AT LEAST SCARED HIM SO HE CHANGES SOMETHING. I'M SURE HE DOESN'T WANT THIS TO HAPPEN AGAIN.
I JUST SAT THERE NODDING. I WAS BOTH HAPPY AND SAD. I HOPED THIS VICTORY WOULD MEAN SOMETHING. IT WAS BETTER THAN NOTHING, BUT IT STILL FELT SAD THAT IT WAS ONLY A VICTORY FOR ME AND NOT FOR THE OTHERS.
I GATHERED MY STUFF, THANKED FELICIA AND MAGNUS AND SAID GOODBYE.
THANKS AGAIN! TALK TO YOU SOON.
STÄNGT
IT WAS ONE OF THE FEW SUNNY DAYS IN MALMO. IT FELT MORE LIKE A BEGINNING THAN AN END.
KRISSE?
IT WENT WELL! HE'S GONNA PAY ME BACK EVERYTHING. SHIT, I'VE NEVER HAD THAT MUCH MONEY IN MY LIFE!
I'LL BUY YOU A BEER.
Malmö LS
SEE YOU AT NOBES!
THE END

EPILOGUE

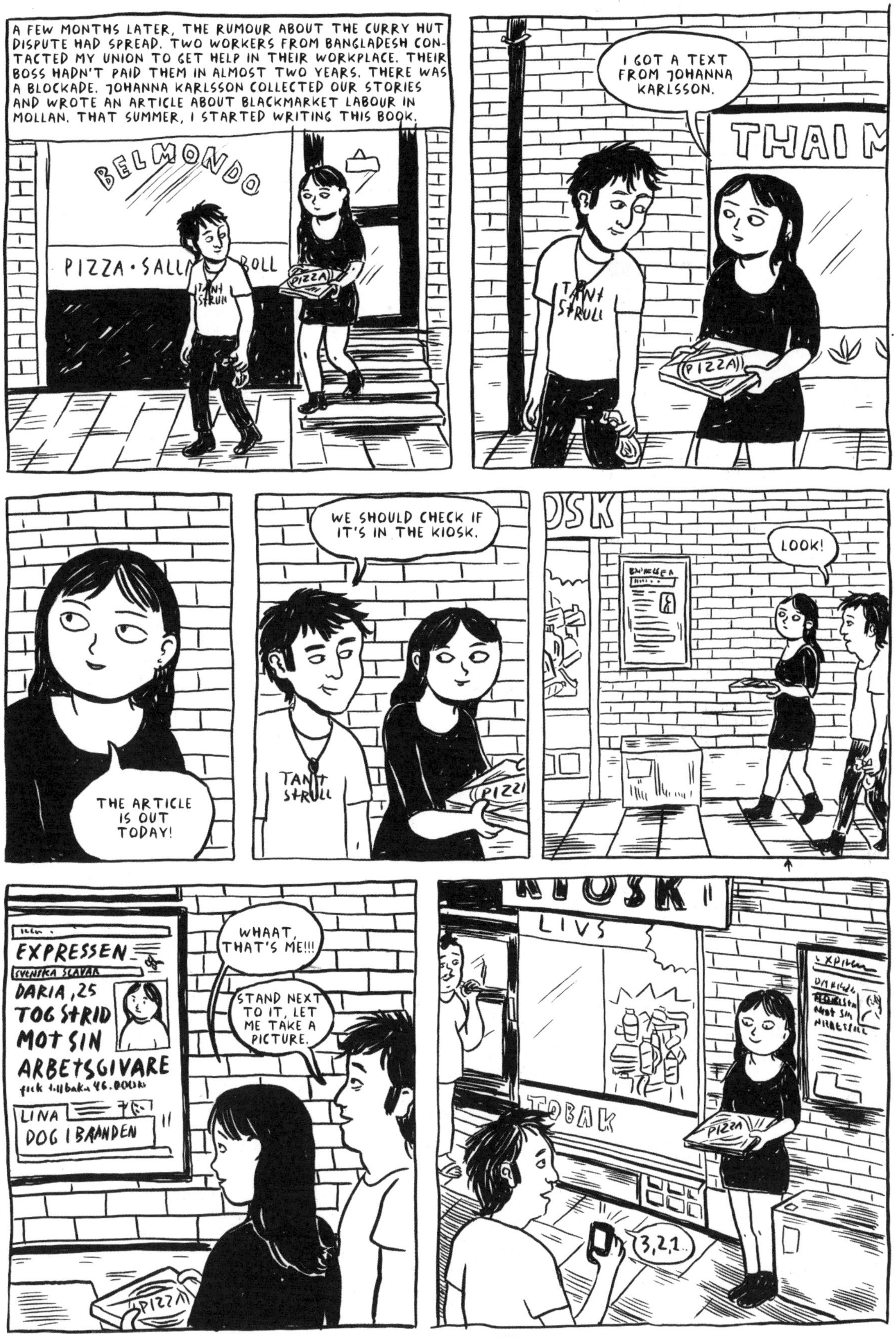
A FEW MONTHS LATER, THE RUMOUR ABOUT THE CURRY HUT DISPUTE HAD SPREAD. TWO WORKERS FROM BANGLADESH CONTACTED MY UNION TO GET HELP IN THEIR WORKPLACE. THEIR BOSS HADN'T PAID THEM IN ALMOST TWO YEARS. THERE WAS A BLOCKADE. JOHANNA KARLSSON COLLECTED OUR STORIES AND WROTE AN ARTICLE ABOUT BLACKMARKET LABOUR IN MOLLAN. THAT SUMMER, I STARTED WRITING THIS BOOK.
BELMONDO
PIZZA • SALL
BOLL
TANT STRULL
PIZZA
I GOT A TEXT FROM JOHANNA KARLSSON.
THAI M
TANT STRULL
PIZZA
THE ARTICLE IS OUT TODAY!
WE SHOULD CHECK IF IT'S IN THE KIOSK.
TANT STRULL
PIZZ
OSK
LOOK!
EXPRESSEN
SVENSKA SLAVAR
DARIA, 25 TOG STRID MOT SIN ARBETSGIVARE
LINA DOG I BRANDEN
WHAAT, THAT'S ME!!!
STAND NEXT TO IT, LET ME TAKE A PICTURE.
PIZZA
KIOSK
LIVS
TOBAK
PIZZA
3,2,1...

[POSTER:] EXPRESS: SWEDISH SLAVES / DARIA, 25, TOOK ON HER EMPLOYER / GOT BACK 46,000 KR

LINA DIED IN THE FIRE

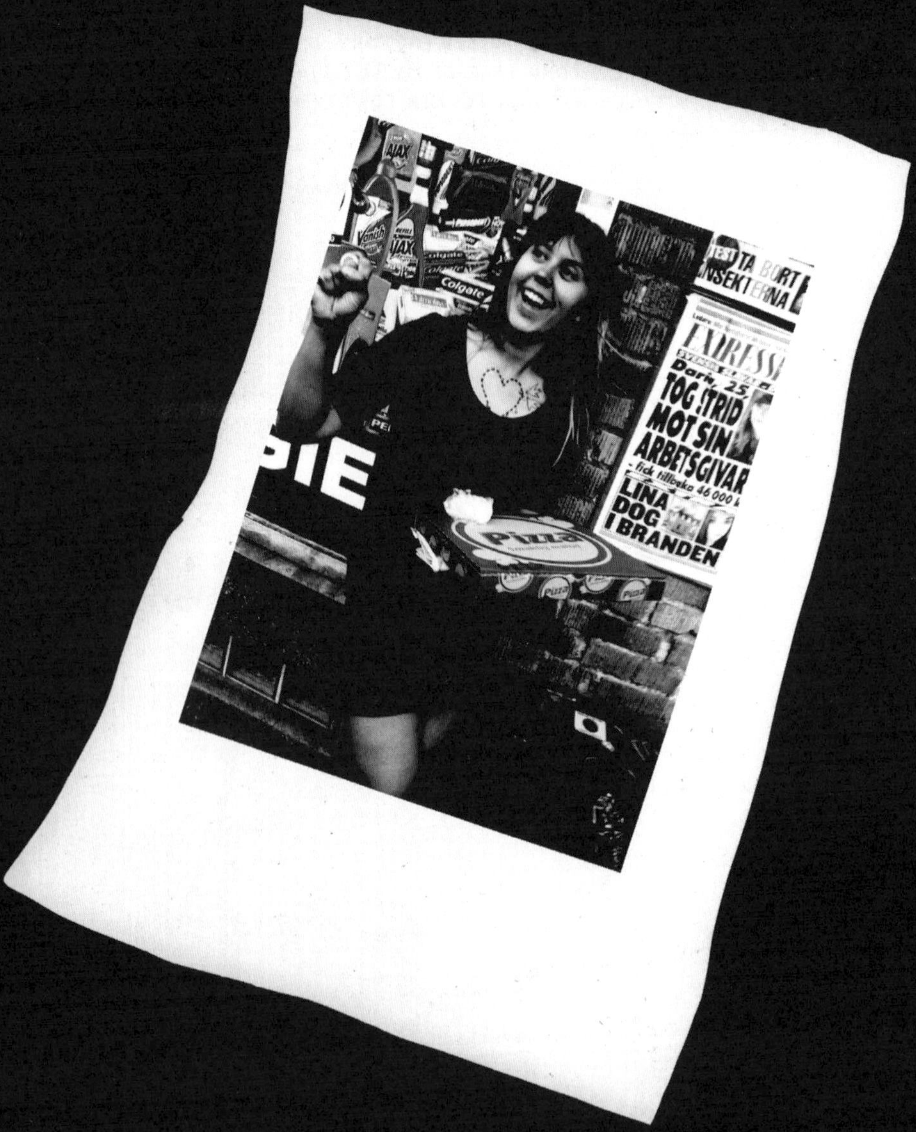
AJAX
Vanish
Colgate
PIE
Pizza
TA BORT
INSEKTERNA
TOG STRID
MOT SIN
LINA
DOG
I BRANDEN

DURING THE SUMMER, THE BASEMENT I WAS LIVING IN WAS FLOODED AND WE HAD TO MOVE OUT. I MOVED TO AN OLD FACTORY IN KIRSEBERG AND WAS READY TO START THE SECOND YEAR OF MY SCHOOL. AFTER THE CONFLICT, I HADN'T BEEN IN TOUCH WITH MY FORMER COWORKERS. I OFTEN WONDERED HOW THEY WERE DOING.

ONE DAY I MET ONE OF THEM AT MOLLEVANGSTORGET. HE HAD QUIT CURRY HUT AND WAS NOW WORKING AT AN ITALIAN RESTAURANT THAT TREATED HIM MUCH BETTER. ONE THING HE SAID REALLY MADE ME HAPPY. HE SAID THAT EVERYONE AT CURRY HUT THOUGHT THAT WHAT I HAD DONE WAS GOOD, AND THAT HE REGRETTED NOT JOINING ME. THAT WAS NICE TO HEAR.

TWO YEARS LATER, SANAD OPENED A NEW RESTAURANT IN FOLKETS PARK, BUT BUSINESS WASN'T GOOD. AFTER LESS THAN A YEAR HE CLOSED IT. A MONTH AGO I FOUND OUT THAT HANG BAR IS CLOSING TOO. THEY DIDN'T GET THEIR LEASE RENEWED.

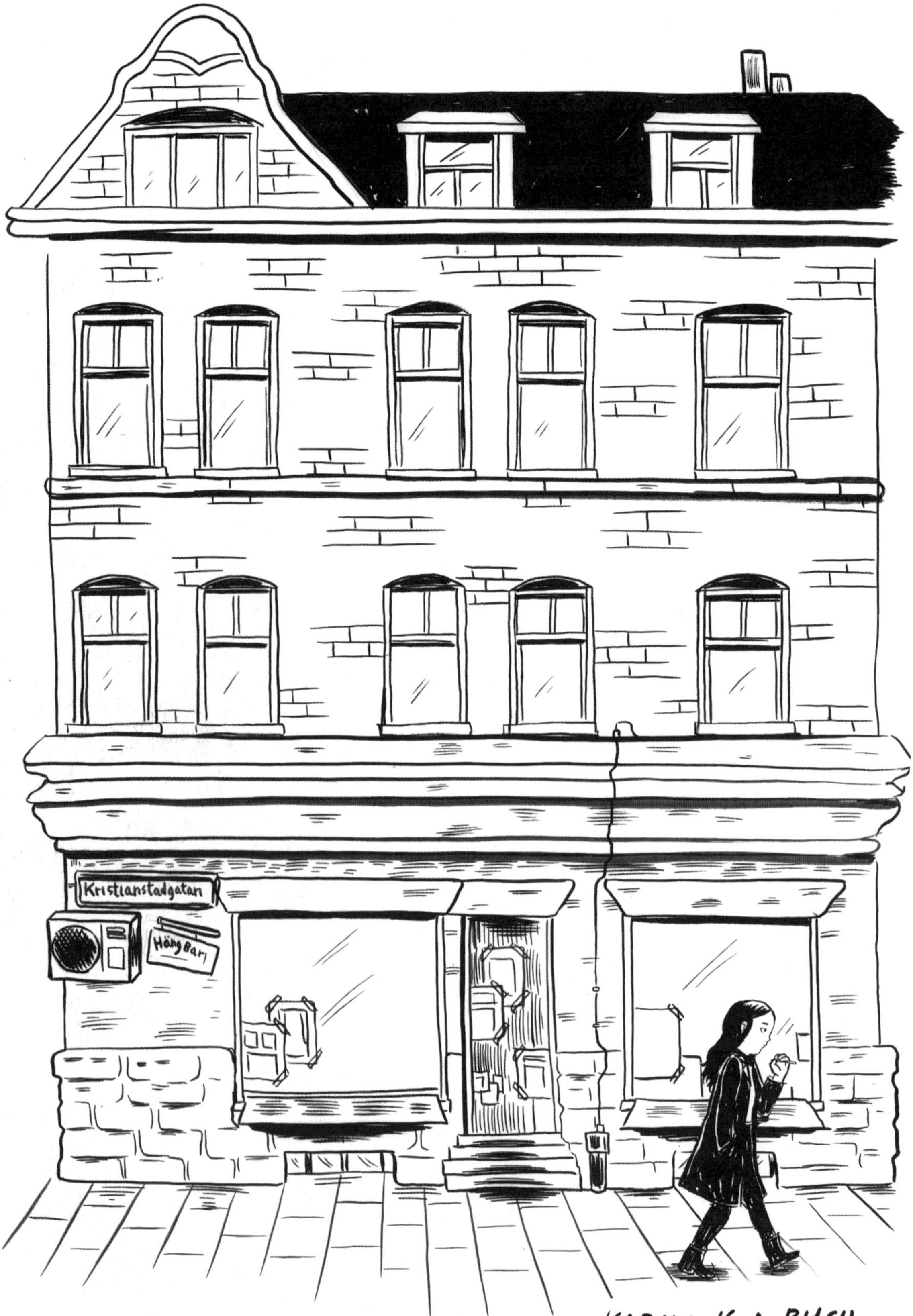
Kristianstadgatan
Häng Bar

KARMA IS A BITCH